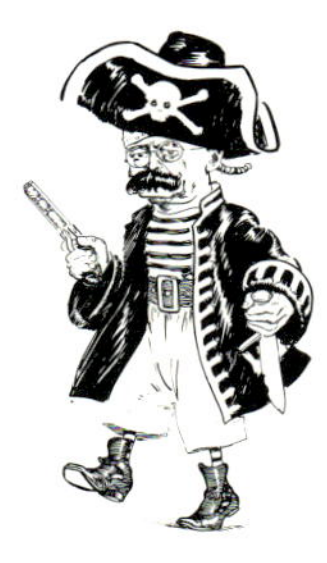

THE IMAGE OF AMERICA
IN CARICATURE & CARTOON

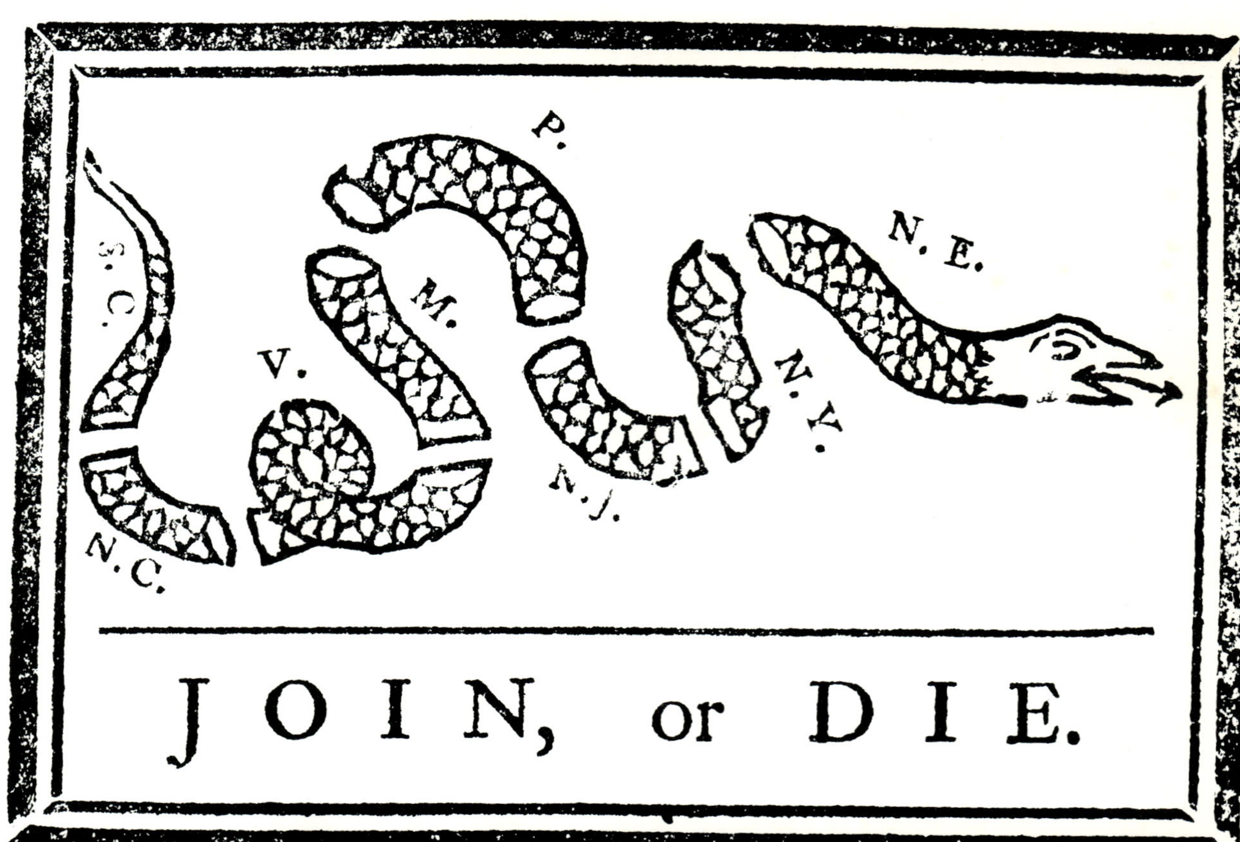

S. C.
N. C.
V.
M.
P.
N.J.
N.Y.
N. E.
JOIN, or DIE.

THE IMAGE OF AMERICA
IN CARICATURE & CARTOON

Accompanying Exhibition Presented at:

Amon Carter Museum, Fort Worth

Fort Wayne Public Library, Fort Wayne

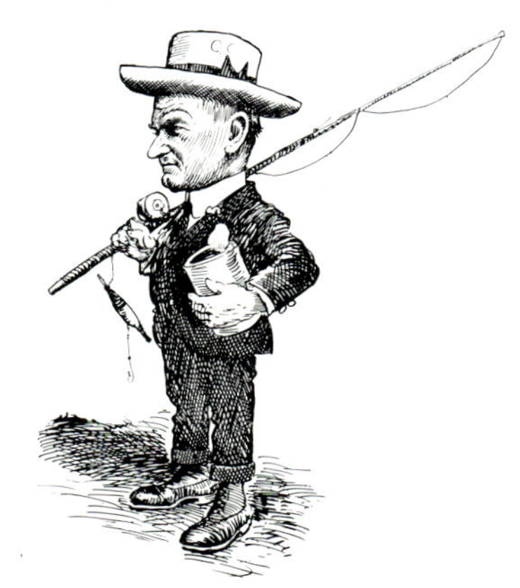

AMON CARTER MUSEUM OF WESTERN ART, *Fort Worth,*

In cooperation with the Swann Foundation, *New York City,*

and the Lincoln National Corporation, *Fort Wayne*

THE AMON CARTER MUSEUM was established in 1961 under the will of the late Amon G. Carter for the study and documentation of westering North America. The program of the Museum, expressed in publications, exhibitions, and permanent collections, reflects many aspects of American culture, both historic and contemporary.

The Museum has been assisted by the National Endowment for the Arts, a federal agency, and the Lincoln National Corporation in publication of this catalogue and the accompanying exhibition.

© 1975 Amon Carter Museum of Western Art
All rights reserved in all countries. No part of this book may be reproduced or translated in any form, including microfilming, without written permission from the publisher.
International Standard Book Number 0-88360-022-6
Library of Congress Card Catalog Number 75-22592
Lithographed in U.S.A.

Type set by G & S Typesetters, Austin
Printed by Brodnax Printing Company, Dallas
Bound by Universal Bookbindery, San Antonio
Design by William D. Wittliff, Austin

TO ERWIN SWANN

Whose enthusiasm and encouragement kept the idea alive; whose generosity and cooperation made it possible; whose friendship and counsel are now sadly missing as this project, near and dear to his heart, is completed.

It is our hope that *The Image of America* helps fulfill the purpose of the Swann Foundation in its sponsorship of scholarly exhibitions and catalogues.

INTRODUCTION

THIS EXHIBITION is eloquent testimony to the continuing vigor of American popular government. The energy, ingenuity, wit, and perceptiveness with which these artists observed the American scene are proof of the traditionally high level of interest Americans take in their political life. The long survival of the art of political cartooning speaks well, too, for the good sense, skeptical outlook, and jovial attitude of the artists' audience. America is a country which has not feared self-criticism. This is a healthy trait that merits celebration and one that should not be overlooked as we reflect on what has made our two centuries of history so successful.

Art critics who study high culture sometimes call a bad painting a "mere cartoon"; they have largely ignored American political cartoons. Historians think of cartoons only when book publishers demand illustrations to enliven their text. The art critic is puzzled by political history, and the historian deals with words and statistics rather than pictures.

Nevertheless, political cartoons remain an extremely popular art form, and to view American history through this medium is to see the American experience as the people saw it—in popular images, widely distributed and within the reach of most pocketbooks. This is an art exhibit appropriate for a democracy.

To view American history through political cartoons is also to see the controversy, criticism, and downright acrimony which at times marked that history. The Lincoln National Corporation is named for the President who steered this country through its greatest period of controversy by far. The Lincoln supports this exhibit because we are confident that America, like Abraham Lincoln's durable reputation, has the strength to benefit from criticism and the vitality to survive controversy.

THOMAS A. WATSON, President
Lincoln National Corporation
Fort Wayne, Indiana

ACKNOWLEDGMENTS

BY REASON of the ephemeral nature of cartoons and because the vast holdings of many institutions have defied cataloguing, the presentation of this exhibition required more than three years of research and organization. The Museum began by mailing a detailed questionnaire to more than 2,000 institutions and individuals throughout the country, then followed as many as possible with correspondence and personal visits. Such a graphic distillation of the more than 200 years of American history would not have been possible without the determined work of many people. Mildred Constantine of New York City worked closely with the Museum throughout the project, advising on picture selection and assisting in research. Amon Carter Museum Trustee John Entenza and former Trustee William H. Goetzmann offered invaluable criticism along the route.

The exhibition has been assembled from the seventy-seven participating institutions with the indispensable aid of curators and librarians across the nation. Notable among them are Wendy Shadwell of The New-York Historical Society, Dr. Alan Fern of the Library of Congress, Alison Dodd of the Swann Collection (which will soon be housed at the Library of Congress), Mrs. Paul Rhymer, former print curator, and Julia Westerberg, curator, of The Chicago Historical Society, Stefanie Munsing of the Library Company of Philadelphia, Dr. William Cagle of The Lilly Library, Indiana University, Kathleen Gee of The Iconography Collection, Hu-

manities Research Center, University of Texas at Austin, and Dr. James Whitehead of the Franklin D. Roosevelt Presidential Library.

Working cartoonists have been most generous in their support. Draper Hill of *The Commercial Appeal* loaned from his personal collection as well as his personal drawings. Bill Mauldin of the Chicago *Sun-Times*, Pat Oliphant of the Washington *Star*, and Brad Holland, Richard Hess, John Cayea, Ralph Steadman, André François, and William Gropper, whose works have appeared in numerous magazines and newspapers, including the New York *Times*, have also loaned their personal drawings.

Dr. Frank T. Reuter of Texas Christian University and Dr. Mark Neely, Jr., of the Lincoln National Life Foundation read the manuscript. Jozanne Rabyor, Kay Krochman, and Karen Dewees of the Museum staff aided in the research and caption writing. Many others aided with the preparation of the exhibition and catalog. Their individual institutions are noted in the credit lines accompanying the illustrations.

A few explanations will aid in interpretation of the catalogued material. If the title of the picture is unknown, we have supplied a title in brackets. If we are uncertain as to artist or title, a question mark appears in parenthesis after the entry. If we do not know the artist, the picture is listed as anonymous. In measuring, height precedes width.

RON TYLER

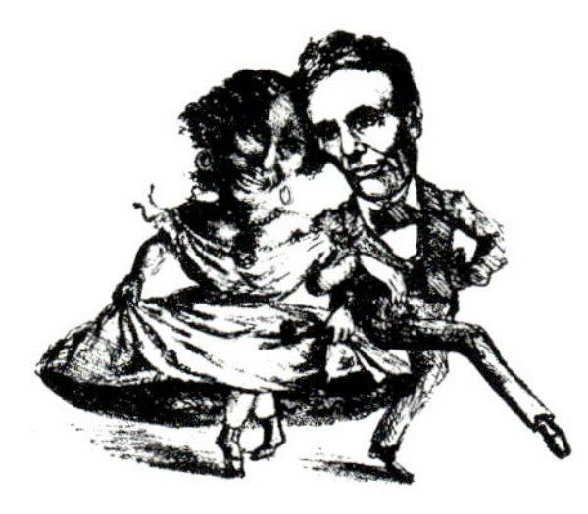

THE IMAGE OF AMERICA
IN CARICATURE & CARTOON

THE IMAGE OF AMERICA

CARICATURE AND CARTOON were long-practiced and sophisticated methods of expression by the time the Americans rebelled in 1776. Caricature had originated during the Renaissance as the individual gradually gained stature and respect. A distortion of personal features, type, or action, it was a reaction to the orderliness and decorum of the early sixteenth century that derived its name from the Italian verb *caricare* (to change, burden, or overload) and is similar to the word *caraterre* (character). Cartoons, originally defined only as full-size patterns for a painting, tapestry, or mosaic and related to the Italian *cartone* (pasteboard), gradually acquired a new meaning as caricatures were combined to create a new style. Directing his barbs toward groups and types rather than individuals, William Hogarth employed cartoons in what became the classic style in his series entitled "Marriage à la Mode." This is not to say that comic and grotesque drawings of the human figure did not appear until the Renaissance, for such visual exaggeration is probably as old as drawing. Ancient Egyptians and Greeks created mythical figures by combining certain aspects of humans and animals, by distortion, by humorous and allegorical creations. Albrecht Dürer and Leonardo da Vinci exaggerated and experimented with facial characteristics; other artists followed, infusing humor and satire to develop cartoons in the modern sense by the mid-seventeenth century.

Few Americans had produced cartoons by 1776. Some pictures like Benjamin Franklin's *Join or Die* (fig. 1) had appeared in colonial newspapers, badly reproduced because of the inferior nature of printing equipment shipped to America only after British printers had discarded it. (One of the more peculiar circumstances about American printing is that it began so late—Mexican printers had been at work more than a century when the first wood engraving appeared in what became the United States in 1670.) Undoubtedly there were qualified engravers in America, because when the first intaglio-engraved paper money published in the colonies appeared in 1690, it was quickly counterfeited by unknown craftsmen possessing abilities to rival those of the official engravers.

The earliest American cartoons appeared as illustrations in the colonial newspapers—*Join or Die* (fig. 1), *The Federal Edifice* (fig. 15). Only later were prints issued in the British tradition and sold separately in bookstores, or printed at the order of and distributed by political parties. Most of the early American cartoons were copied after British models, such as *The Deplorable State of America, or Sc---h Government* (fig. 2), which was copied by John Singleton Copley and Wilkinson of Philadelphia. The best known engraver of early America, Paul Revere, also copied British prints. His *Cabinet Junto* (fig. 7) was most likely inspired by the London cartoon of a similar title and composition, showing the same figures grouped around a table discussing the end of American liberties. Revere also copied *The Able Doctor, or America Swallowing the Bitter Draught* from *London Magazine* of April, 1774 (fig. 5).

Almost simultaneously with the cartoons certain constant American themes developed. To organize an exhibition of cartoons around American history and culture is almost to presuppose a conflict theme, for cartoons most eloquently portray conflict and confrontation. The colonists objected to English domination—to the Stamp Act, the Intolerable Acts, the economic dependence. American political parties continued the strife almost immediately. Today conflict has permeated the whole of society, as diverse citizens define their relationship to each other and to the government. It is also true that during periods of less conflict and strife, there are fewer and less powerful cartoons, such as during the Era of Good Feelings and during World War II, when the nation was virtually unanimous in support of the war.

Americans have historically feared power, whether from within or without, providing another theme for cartoonists. The basic reason for a weak national government (the Articles of Confederation) with no executive was fear of a powerful centralized government or a dictatorship, and any strong president or nominee risked being portrayed as a dictator: Andrew Jackson as Richard III (fig. 31), Martin Van Buren as his heir (fig. 37), Grant in Andrew Johnson's shadow (fig. 72), and Senator Huey P. Long of Louisiana, who might have been a presidential contender had he not been assassinated, in company with Hitler, Stalin, and Mussolini (fig. 159). Because they feared power from the outside, the founding fathers encouraged no "entangling alliances" with foreign countries, and the Federalists lived in dread of the French threat throughout Jefferson's administration (fig. 21). Later politicians tucked the cloak of isolationism around the United States to ward off the foreign threat. The Monroe Doctrine is the most important isolationist statement (fig. 106), but the isolationist leanings of the 1930s were actually drafted into law in the form of neutrality acts, and Congress almost passed a bill requiring that there be a national referendum before Congress could declare war.

Significant visual themes, soon to become recognized American icons, also emerged in the cartoons. The United States initially was portrayed by European artists as an innocent Indian or as virginal Columbia. It was also shown as an eagle, the official bird, and later, as Uncle Sam, a character probably first used in the early 1830s by H. R. Robinson, the prolific Whig lithographer, in a print showing an almost unrecognizable Uncle Sam. But he quickly developed into the character that we know today (fig. 74 might be a step in the development; fig. 87 is the fully developed character). The eagle recurs to show the state of the nation in the Civil War (fig. 55) and the Vietnam War (fig. 263). Presidential aspirant Martin Van Buren appeared in a cartoon for the 1848 contest on a bison (fig. 39), one of the best-known animals found in America. After the Statue of Liberty was placed in New York harbor it became a well-known symbol. Most frequently this emblem of American welcome to the world has been used to point out shortcomings in American society: Thomas Worth's racial image (fig. 79), Leslie Illingworth's reference to McCarthyism (fig. 192), Mark Podwall's and R. O. Blechman's comments on visual and urban pollution (figs. 261, 262).

Literary and historical figures are often adapted by cartoonists to make a contemporary point. Adalbert Volck employed the Don Quixote and Sancho Panza image to point out the relationship between Lincoln and Butler (fig. 58), Saul Steinberg used it to comment on Uncle Sam's reputation as the world's Santa Claus (fig. 205). Gregory Duncan compared Roosevelt's New Deal policy toward business to the Dutchess of *Alice in Wonderland* trying to cure the baby of the illness that the cook had brought on (fig. 161). Successfully recalling the image of Louis XIV to comment on the royal trappings of the Nixon administration, Edward Sorel published *Milhous I* on the cover of *The Rolling Stone* (fig. 244).

Through caricature and cartoon this exhibition covers more than 200 years of American history, beginning in 1754 with Benjamin Franklin's *Join or Die* and concluding in 1974 with John Cayea's *American Eagle*. These pictures illustrate or interpret literally hundreds of opinions, facts, and events of our history, and are the actual images that persons contemporary with each event or personality might have seen. Because of the nature of cartoon and caricature, they tend toward the critical, but this does not lessen the truth or history they contain. This exhibition is a contemporary record of our society through more than two centuries.

I

1754–1787

Aᴅᴇᴄᴇᴘᴛɪᴠᴇ ᴄᴇʀᴛᴀɪɴᴛʏ permeates the history of the United States: although the original thirteen colonies made up of "different schemes, notions, customs, and manners" overcame their differences to win independence from the greatest imperial power of the day, seldom is the frailty of the Congress, the Army, and the nation itself recognized today, 200 years after the fact.[1] Founded in the immutable truths of the Enlightenment and led by luminaries like Washington, Jefferson, and Adams, the nation seemed destined for immediate success. Nor is this a phantom of hindsight, for the founders themselves expressed irrepressible confidence in the soundness of their venture. "The foundation of our empire was not laid in the gloomy age of ignorance and superstition," wrote George Washington, "but at an *epocha* when the rights of mankind were better understood and more clearly defined, than at any former period, the researches of the human mind after social happiness have been carried to a greater extent, the treasures of knowledge . . . are laid open for our use, and their collected wisdom may be happily applied in the establishment of our forms of government."[2] "The . . . accomplishment . . . was perhaps a singular example in the history of mankind," concluded John Adams. "Thirteen clocks were made to strike together—a perfection of mechanism which no artist had ever before effected."[3]

Such statements completely obscure the experimental nature of America. Created during an era in which both kings and philosophers wanted a better society but were incapable of bringing it to a Europe weighed down by tradition, fastened in rigid class, and divided by war, America was an experiment in at least two senses. First, it was the pragmatic attempt of thirteen self-contained colonies to create a workable government and "the world does not afford a precedent to go by," commented Elbridge Gerry.[4] Second, it was an experiment implemented according to the principles of the enlightened philosophers of Europe by their American disciples. The ruling monarchs of Europe could not condone such an experiment themselves, for the very nature of the divine right rule prevented kings from resigning their thrones for so little a matter as the happiness of the individual. America was their test case, where reason, nature, order, and humanitarianism would be enthroned and maintained by the popular will. "This country opens to the philosophic view an extensive, rich and unexplored field," Charles Thomson, the Secretary of Congress, wrote Jefferson in 1782.[5]

One could not have predicted the American Revolution without a careful knowledge of these philosophical concepts and of the Americans themselves. To Andrew Burnaby, an Englishman who visited the colonies in 1760, "fire and water are not more heterogeneous than the different colonies in North America. Nothing can exceed the jealousy and emulation, which they possess in regard to each other." But Benjamin Franklin, speaking from his unparalleled knowledge of the colonies, disagreed: "tyranny and oppression," specific violations of the enlightened concepts the colonists held dear, could alter the situation.[6]

As the Revolutionary conflict developed, the usually business-minded Americans carefully prepared their philosophical justification. The hated Stamp Act was termed "taxation without representation," despite the Parliament's contention that it represented all the empire. At Patrick Henry's urg-

4

ing the Virginia Assembly passed a resolution claiming that all laws applying to Englishmen in America had to be "derived from their own consent." Massachusetts was more violent. The proposed distributor of stamps was hanged in effigy from the "Liberty tree," his house ransacked, and he was forced to resign his office. English cartoonists depicted Liberty lamenting, "Tis all over with me" as Britain forced the Stamp Act on her (fig. 2). When the Stamp Act was finally repealed the new Rockingham ministry ordered printed a cartoon entitled *The Repeal*, depicting former Prime Minister Grenville taking his dead brainchild to the "Family Vault," which proved to be one of the most popular cartoons of the Revolutionary period and sold more than 16,000 copies (fig. 3). Both *The Deplorable State of America, or Sc---h Government* and *The Repeal* were copied by American engravers in a slightly altered form.

The traditional ties between mother country and colonies that Benjamin Franklin pointed out in testifying against the Stamp Act before Parliament did not prevent the ultimate breach. Colonists declared the March, 1770, incident in Boston a "massacre." The Tea Act of 1773 led to the famous "Boston Tea Party" in December, again inspiring the cartoonists to comment on the royal treatment of the colonies. In *The Able Doctor* America is restrained by rather lewd characters while Lord North pours "the Bitter Draught" down her throat (fig. 5). Colonists also claimed the Coercive Acts of 1774 which the Boston Port Bill represents were beyond the power of Parliament. This popular cartoon, originally published in London, was copied in both Ireland and America (by Revere). When Commissioner of Customs John Malcomb tried to enforce the new laws, Bostonians tarred and feathered him, an incident that led publisher Carington Bowles to issue his print (fig. 6) of *A New Method of Macarony Making* (Macarony referring to a dandy or fop).

Thomas Paine, a new arrival to the colonies, added enlightened logic and rhetoric to the Revolutionary cause after the British had let American blood at Lexington, Concord, and Bunker Hill. Is it logical for an island to rule a continent? he asked in his none-too-subtly-titled pamphlet *Common Sense*. King George III was a tyrant who did not deserve his position, and the only alternative remaining for Americans with "common sense" was independence. Even George Washington concluded after reading Paine's pamphlet that America was the victim of King George and that "we are determined to shake off all connections with a state so unjust and unnatural."[7]

Parliament helped the nation-makers overcome their hesitation in February, 1775, by declaring them in open rebellion. Delegates to the Second Continental Congress meeting in Philadelphia, now facing execution as rebels, agreed to "mutually pledge to each other our lives, our fortunes and our sacred honor" and began the grand experiment while General George Washington and his tiny Continental Army held 35,000 Redcoats in New York at bay. Although Thomas Paine characterized the following days as "the times that try men's souls," others saw them as the dawn of a new era. The American Revolution was "the beginning of a new social order for the entire world," exulted the Marquis de Lafayette. A change had occurred "in the minds and hearts of the people," John Adams later wrote, "a change in religious sentiments of their duties and obligation," a "radical change in the principles, opinions, sentiments, and affections of the people. . . ."[8]

The Revolution itself was a rather languid affair that began with Lexington and Concord in April, 1775, proceeded through Washington's Valley Forge winter, General Horatio Gates' surprising victory over the Redcoats at Saratoga, and Washington's brilliant capture of Lord Cornwallis at Yorktown (fig. 10). Meanwhile, Gates' victory had encouraged the French to enter the fray in support of the Americans, and John Paul Jones led the rebel privateering effort at sea (fig. 9). Aboard the *Ranger*, he slipped through the British blockade in November, 1777, and captured two prizes in April, 1778.

He then landed at Whitehaven, England, spiked the cannons of the fort, and set fire to another ship. The American sailors were particularly vexing to British trade, and were rendered even more troublesome when Holland permitted them to refit in Dutch harbors.

The British probably could have quelled the resistance but for the lackadaisical attitude and bungling conduct of their commanders in America. Feeling that they could defeat the Americans by holding the provincial cities of New York, Philadelphia, and Boston, the British generals did not pursue Washington's army at times when they could have routed him. The vulnerability of America is seen in the cartoons that picture the colonies as the weak and feminine Columbia or a naïve Indian. The British colossus is seen as a feeble old man (fig. 8) or a huge dog held at bay by the European allies while America escapes (fig. 9). The image of America suddenly changed with the surprising victory at Yorktown. Then the huge American rattlesnake was shown engulfing the small British armies (fig. 11). "The Serpent in the Congress reigns, as well as in the French," commented the cartoonist.

Although the Americans were creating a new government, "as in the beginning of the world," said Paine, they "had no occasion to roam for information into the obscure fields of antiquity, nor hazard ourselves upon conjecture." Insight from Jefferson, Franklin, and other Congressional thinkers allowed them to see "government begin, as if we had lived in the beginning of time." Jefferson took the concept of a *tabula rasa* (blank tablet), property rights, the right to happiness, and personal freedom from the English philosopher John Locke. He wrote in the Declaration of Independence that "all men are created equal," meaning that everyone (specifically Englishmen and Americans) stands equal before the law and that "talent and virtue" should be the criteria of superiority rather than class and wealth. Thus natural order would prevail. It was a radical philosophical change, but, as Jefferson pointed out, "the creation change, but, as Jefferson pointed out, "the creation of a proper political system was the whole object of the revolution, for should a bad government be instituted for us in the future, it would have been as well to have accepted at first the bad one offered to us from beyond the water."[9]

America was indeed a *tabula rasa* for immigrants who fled the rigid social structure, the overcrowding, and the disease of Europe to begin life over as a member of a classless frontier society where there was more land than could be occupied. "A European, when he first arrives, seems limited in his intentions, as well as in his views," wrote Hector St. John de Crèvecoeur in his *Letters From an American Farmer*, "but he very suddenly alters his scale. . . . He no sooner breathes our air than he forms new schemes, and embarks in designs he never would have thought of in his own country. . . . He begins to feel the effects of a sort of resurrection; hitherto he had not lived, but simply vegetated; he now feels himself a man, because he is treated as such. . . . The American is a new man, who acts upon new principles; he must therefore entertain new ideas, and form new opinions."[10] The Revolution itself helped the new man along in his development, because Americans then abolished primogeniture and entail, separated church and state, and expanded educational opportunities. Many loyalists returned to England, thereby removing a conservative and wealthy element and modifying the social structure even more.

European philosophers had anticipated this "new man" just as they had earlier looked for the noble savage, but they were hesitant to accept him as proof of the successful American experiment until time had proven his durability. There were drawbacks, as contemporaries claimed. America was said to be full of swamps and impenetrable forests, "with humid and noxious vapors" in the atmosphere that were "unable to purify themselves or to profit by the influence of the sun, which darts in vain his most enlivening rays upon this frigid mass." Such an environment would naturally affect even the healthiest man, boasted De Paw: "the least vigorous European is more than a match for the strongest American." Nor had the political system helped: "You have kept all the bad English laws, and all of England's bad customs," Du Pont de Nemours wrote Jefferson. "One of the worst is the establishment of popular elections."[11] Others felt that America possessed more land than could be controlled. How could a decentralized government administer such a vast territory? How would it defend the frontier? What about communication? Transportation? No less a figure than Samuel Johnson predicted that "a nation scattered in the boundless regions of America resembles rays diverging from a focus. All the rays remain but the heat is gone."[12]

Americans readily admitted that the vastness would have to be overcome. As early as 1754 Benjamin Franklin had called the colonies together at Albany and warned that they would have to unify for the common defense or be gradually beaten by the French and the Indians. Nathaniel Hawthorne wrote despairingly to his friend Longfellow years later that "we have so much country that we really have no country at all." Even Patrick Henry feared that governing the whole continent was "a work too great for human wisdom."[13] In unity, however, they saw the solution. Franklin's *Join or Die* snake cartoon (fig. 1) remains one of the lasting images in American history. Christopher Gadsden agreed with Franklin's urging the Stamp Act Congress toward unity in 1765, saying that "there ought to be no New England man, no New Yorker, known on the Continent; but all Americans."[14]

In reality the large land mass worked to America's advantage, so much so that President Jefferson felt compelled to add to it at the first opportunity over his own and other doubts about his constitutional authority to do so. Distant boundaries kept possible enemies farther away. Unoccupied lands meant space for what would become the greatest movement of peoples in the history of the world. Immigrants carved out ethnic communities in the cities; they built utopian villages like Bishop Hill and New Harmony in the wilderness. They helped carry the American flag from the Appalachian Mountains to the Pacific Coast in less than fifty years, and they helped the United States become the leading industrial power in the world by 1885 and the greatest power in the world by 1946.

Jefferson defended the new United States against the charge of Abbé Raynal, who wondered why America had not produced a "single good poet, or able mathematician, or a man of genius in any one of the arts or the sciences." Washington and Franklin should be geniuses enough to satisfy the Abbé, Jefferson argued, but America's real contribution was on a higher level: America had "given hopeful proofs of genius of the nobler kinds, which arouse the best feelings of man, which call him to action, which substantiate his freedom, and conduct him to happiness."[15] John Adams in noting the youth of the country answered the question more directly: "I must study politics and war that my sons may have liberty to study mathematics . . . philosophy . . . and agriculture . . . in order to give their children . . . painting, poetry, music."[16]

In asking such a question Raynal ignored the great, democratic contribution America had made to learning. American literature, unlike European writings, was not produced for the intelligentsia. It was directed, instead, toward the common man, the new man, who could read because of the American belief in mass education. Europeans disregarded this literature—*Poor Richard's Almanac*, Parson Weems' fable—as unworthy of consideration, but it revealed the mind of the American. Much of American society was classed with this "subliterature" and ignored by European visitors and haughty native writers. This new man unfolded his secrets not in the halls of learning or the salons, but in rude, embarrassing, sometimes crudely done, vulgar expressions accurately representing his part of American society and culture. Even when the cartoons in this exhibition are considered, they are not often seen as serious attempts at art, but rather as political and social satire. This is hardly unusual, considering that caricatures were originally a "counter-art" intended to be outside the normal modes of aesthetic expression, but with the same qualities that characterized the new man—extroversion, utopianism, naïveté. It was virtually impossible for this art to be sophisticated. In this the Americans were again only copying the English tastes, for they were forthright in their expressions as well. *The General P--s, or Peace* (fig. 14) is an excellent example of the vulgar expressions of the day, while *The Federal Edifice* (fig. 15) conveys the message intended, but is not as well drawn as the British cartooning of the day.

Even after the Articles of Confederation had been proved unsound and replaced by the Constitution, after the United States had solved its colonial problem by the unique method of taking new territory into the nation as states, and after the solution of the undeclared naval war with France, skeptical Europeans were not ready to admit the twenty-five year old experiment a success. Americans were less hesitant. Full of confidence generated in the conquest of the noblest of all enemies, nature, they reflected upon their past. "Never did a government commence under auspices so favorable, not ever was success so complete," wrote James Monroe in his first inaugural address. "They *realized* the theories of the wisest writers," said John Adams.[17]

"A thousand years hence, perhaps in less, America may be what Europe is now," predicted Thomas Paine. "The innocence of her character . . . may sound like a romance, and her inimitable virtue as if it had never been. . . . The ruin of that liberty which thousands bled for or struggled to obtain may just furnish materials for a village tale. . . . When the empire of America shall fall, the subject for contemplative sorrow will be infinitely greater than crumbling brass and marble can inspire. It will not then be said, here stood a temple of vast antiquity, here rose a Babel of invisible height, or there a palace of sumptuous extravagance, but here, ah painful thought, the noblest work of human wisdom, the grand scheme of human glory, the fair cause of freedom, rose and fell."[18]

II

1788–1851

THE EVENT that proved to a distrustful Europe the success of the United States was the War of 1812. Knowledgeable observers had predicted disaster for the country even after ratification of the new Constitution. "The future grandeur of America and its being a rising empire . . . is one of the idlest and most visionary notions that ever was conceived, even by writers of romance," claimed the economist and cleric Dean Josiah Tucker. Alexis de Tocqueville, the Frenchman who traveled across the United States interviewing President and slave alike thirty years later agreed: "I shall refuse to believe in the duration of a government which is called upon to hold together forty different peoples, disseminated over a territory equal to one half of Europe."[1]

Perhaps American cartoonists subconsciously reserved judgment, for they had not yet developed a composite character to represent the new country as John Bull embodied Britain. European artists had presented the United States as the virginal Columbia or as an American Indian lurking in the background as Europe occupies center stage. But American artists stuck to well-known figures such as Washington and Jefferson, or copied from the Europeans. American cartoonists also pictured their exaggerated characters grappling not with specific issues but with the fate of the country itself, perhaps an unconscious reference to the precarious existence of the country, for the political partisans of 1796 and 1800 actually felt that the fate of the country hinged on their victory. The ever-present theme of conflict is easily seen as President Washington at the reins of a Federal cabriolet tries to stop an invasion of French Republican "cannibals" (fig. 16). Jefferson and his Gallic friends are trying to halt Washington, while the Federalist artist has predicted on the left side of the print the fate of the country if the cannibals are allowed to land. One of the most divisive conflicts of the day was what attitude America would take toward the raging French Revolution. Realizing the weakness of the new country, Washington opted for neutrality. But Jefferson, who had spent years in Paris as the American envoy and had grown to love the French and their culture, favored closer ties with the emerging Republic. Thus a Federalist cartoon for the 1800 presidential election shows candidate Jefferson bowed before the altar of French despotism where the works of Paine, Rousseau, and Voltaire are already burning (fig. 21). The American Eagle has just snatched the Constitution from a similar fate, which might be interpreted as the essence of American survival.

Another conflict that led to innumerable cartoons was the emergence of political parties. Political strife was particularly bitter during the Jeffersonian years in office. The embargo, which prevented Americans from trading freely with merchants from other nations, severely hampered the nation's prosperity without achieving its diplomatic goals (fig. 22). Many federalists also resented Jefferon's so-called favoritism toward France, a favoritism which was punished several times as Jefferson extended the hand of friendship to Napoleon, who tried to use the United States in his almost global conflict with Britain.

The War of 1812 was, however, one of the turning points of American history. The war had proceeded badly. The Americans were bedeviled at sea (fig. 23), frustrated in their attempt to invade Canada, and even suffered the invasion and burning of Washington, D. C. (fig. 27). The only bright spot was General Andrew Jackson's defeat of crack British troops at the Battle of New Orleans—after the peace treaty had been signed at Ghent. But the war accomplished two things: Americans matured politically when they overcame sectionalism sufficiently to prosecute the war, and by negotiating as equals at Ghent they shed the cloak of British diplomacy that had obscured their independence since 1776. It also "renewed and reinstated" the feeling of the Revolution, said Albert Gallatin, a member of the peace commission. "The people have now more general objects of attachment with which their pride and political opinions are connected. They are more American; they feel and act more like a nation."[2]

Despite the indignities of the war, Americans, remembering the New Orleans victory over troops fresh from the Napoleonic campaign and the favorable portions of the settlement at Ghent, gained confidence. But they were still an inscrutable people. Both Charles Dickens and Mrs. Anthony Trollope reached erroneous conclusions—that they were "not a humorous people, and their temperament always impressed me as being of a dull and gloomy character"—but when Mrs. Trollope discovered the political and comic character Jack Downing, invented by Seba Smith and used in both writings and cartoons, she recognized another facet of the American character and admitted that she had been wrong. With this developing sense of nation a new kind of humor, not as biting or as sophisticated (if that term can be used) as that of the contemporary British cartoons, appeared in American cartoons and subliterature. The leading political artist of the day was David Claypool Johnston, of Boston, dubbed the "American Cruikshank" by contemporary critics. Johnston's humor developed, perhaps, more rapidly than his victims' sportsmanship, for in one well-publicized encounter he was physically attacked by a rival journalist who wanted to stop distribution of a particularly offensive cartoon. The attack backfired when Johnston threw the attacker out of his office and issued a print depicting the event.

The humor that appeared in the subliterature was less political than vulgar. Often centered around mythical characters like Jack Downing and Mike Fink, with fictional or semi-fictional stories about historical heroes like Davy Crockett, the sub-literature was as grossly exaggerated as the most far-fetched caricatures. The woodcuts that appeared in *Davy Crockett's Almanac* marked a change in that they were intended to personify the personality of Crockett rather than an incident, really the first time that American cartoonists had become interested in personality per se. Crockett supposedly killed four wolves by the time he was four, hugged a bear to death, and killed a rattlesnake with his teeth. He actually did become the "coonskin congressman" from Tennessee and fight in the Battle of the Alamo, so his readers might have had some difficulty separating fact from fiction. These unsophisticated stories were humorous primarily because of their heroic, mythic qualities as well as for the crude woodcuts (fig. 36). The fact that they also included some truth or were based on real characters gave them their credibility.

Now confident of their abilities and with the British no longer in possession of the Old Northwest forts, Americans began the unimpeded conquest of the continent. Louisiana Territory stretched almost as far as the imagination with a western boundary yet to be determined. Few details were known about it except for the monumental Lewis and Clark report, but enthusiasm was so great that settlers preceded even the explorers, fear of the unknown subservient to the desire for a new land (fig. 19). Not even Colonel Stephen H. Long's pessimistic 1819 report of a Great American Desert slowed the pioneers. "What of the 'Great American Desert,' which occupied so much space on the map a generation ago?" Josiah Strong, a popular Congregationalist minister, later asked rhetorically. "It is *nomadic* and elusive; it recedes before advancing civilization like the Indian and buffalo . . . . [It] seems to have become a fugitive and vagabond on the face of the earth. It was located for a time by the map-makers in Utah, but being persecuted there, it fled to Arizona and Nevada."[3]

Social equality provided the dynamics the country needed to settle an almost limitless amount of land. Benjamin Franklin had first noticed the trait when he returned from Europe. Few Americans are "so miserable as the poor of Europe" or as rich as the European upper class, he had said, but consist of "a general happy mediocrity." Speaking from his experience, Tocqueville was firmer: American men were "on a greater equality in point of fortune and intellect . . . more equal in their strength, than in any other country in the world," he concluded.[4] The same independence that Baron von Steuben noticed during the Revolutionary War—he had to explain the "why" to a soldier before he would carry out an order—now led them to migrate westward. Andrew Jackson, the victor at New Orleans, was their hero, and it was Jackson who forced the Easterners to realize that the western lands were an increasingly important part of the country, and that the western man was the new American image.

"Far from desponding of the great political experiment in the lands of the American people," President Madison yielded the presidency to James Monroe, who witnessed the enthronement of the common man.[5] It did not come at once, because of the safeguards the founding fathers had written into the Constitution. Although Andrew Jackson led the 1824 election in popular votes, no one had a majority in the Electoral College, and the House of Representatives chose John Quincy Adams, son of the second President, to be the sixth President. "The Era of Good Feelings," the accolade accorded the years from 1815 to 1824, came to a hectic close marked by the assumption of power by a new social class and by the renewal of bitter political cartoons (fig. 30).

Some of the most sardonic political cartoons and caricatures of our history punctuate the decade following 1827, the years roughly corresponding to Andrew Jackson's terms in office. Issue-related cartoons intended to influence the election of 1828 began to appear in 1827. That summer Jackson had

10

renewed the charges of a "corrupt bargain," in which Henry Clay supposedly supported Adams in the 1824 House election in return for a Cabinet appointment. Johnston, the Boston caricaturist, patterned an acrimonious caricature of Jackson as a military despot after a similar picture of Napoleon, recalling Jackson's brutal treatment of Indians in Spanish Florida in 1819 and his victory over the British at New Orleans (fig. 31). "I cannot believe that killing 2500 Englishmen at New Orleans qualifies [him] for the various difficult and complicated duties of the Chief Magistracy," scowled Clay.[6] Clay soon became an influential member of the new Whig Party, which took its name from the loyal opposition in the English Parliament that had as its unifying factor dislike of arbitrary power. But even Clay would not have pictured Jackson with a face composed of bodies of dead Indians, an epaulet made of six hanging men, a collar made of two pieces of artillery, a military tent for a hat, and a cannon belching smoke as a pompon, as did Johnston.

Two reasons probably explain the explosion of cartoons during the Jacksonian era. One was the widespread use of lithography, a method of printing perfected in Germany in the 1790s but not allowed to spread to other countries until the turmoil of the Napoleonic wars had ceased and international commerce was restored. True, a New York craftsman had experimented with imported stones and ink in 1808, but the European process proved far superior to the crude work he produced. The first now-known American lithograph was finally produced in Philadelphia in 1819, and the simple process spread as rapidly as the fine stones could be imported from Bavaria. The first lithographic cartoon in America showed Jackson (on the alligator) and Adams (on the tortoise) contesting the 1828 election (fig. 32). Craftsmen who had spent long hours etching a metal plate welcomed the simpler method, which could produce as detailed a picture in finer tones more quickly. The second reason was the controversy surrounding Jackson

and his policies. Artists had developed the capability of producing fine cartoons during the Era of Good Feelings, when they were without inspiration for their acerbity, but "Old Hickory" provided controversial politics as well as a scandalous social climate for sedate Washington.

Some of the finer prints were hand-colored, making them more attractive to a public that already sought the lurid details of a political squabble or an international encounter. The cartoons were distributed through bookstores or by peddlers who picked up their prints each day and left a deposit. They walked the streets or set up small stands hawking them to the public, then paid for the prints they had sold, returned the others, and reclaimed the day's deposit. Compared to modern standards distribution was limited, but firms like Nathaniel Currier (later with James Ives) managed to sell thousands of prints. Existing records indicate that a popular picture was often reprinted months later to meet the continuing demand. Some cartoons might have been issued during more than one campaign, because some of the same issues and candidates were current throughout the Jackson years.

Jackson's portrait as Richard III is clearly one of Johnston's best, incorporating the events of Jackson's career with an artistic technique not fully developed until the twentieth century, and made more trenchant by the quotation from *Richard III*: "Methought the souls of all that I had murder'd came to my tent." Lithographs also made possible new and bolder designs by better artists. The pseudonym "Hassan Straightshanks" conceals the identity of one of the ablest cartoonists of the nineteenth century, particularly in terms of concept and design. His interpretation of Jacksonian government as a refuse wagon pulled by an ass (with Jackson's head) and led by Martin Van Buren is typical of the era. But the wagon driver is not. A combination of kitchen implements—a pot, tongs, a bellows, coffee pots, among others, the driver is unusual in nineteenth century lithography (fig. 33). Perhaps it is a complex reference to Jackson's Kitchen Cabinet, an unofficial group of advisors who counseled the President instead of his official Cabinet.

One of the most popular subjects for early cartoonists was the Bank of the United States, established by Alexander Hamilton in 1791 (rechartered in 1816 for twenty years) to regulate the nation's economy much as the Federal Reserve System does today. The Bank proved unpopular with regional financiers because it limited circulation of notes from smaller state banks. Farmers traditionally resented the small group of moneyed men whom they thought regulated their prices, and New York City bankers were jealous of the economic power centered in Philadelphia. Jackson hoped to make political gain of these sectional concerns and therefore opposed the bank's 1836 charter renewal. In an effort to secure the bank's recharter, Bank President Nicholas Biddle attempted to bring political pressure on Jackson in 1832, an election year. But Biddle had miscalculated Jackson's resolve and popular support. Congress passed the renewal, but Jackson successfully vetoed it (fig. 34). Meanwhile, cartoonists had a field day portraying President Jackson and the "Many-headed Monster," *The Modern Balaam and his Ass* (fig. 35), and other humorous or cynical interpretations of the gargantuan struggle that left the United States without any clear financial policy or direction, and led directly to the Panic of 1837.

Although Jackson did not run for reelection in 1836, he continued to dominate the Democratic Party and American politics until his death in 1845 and his protégé, Martin Van Buren, followed him into office. The tremendous popular support accumulated by War of 1812 hero General William H. Harrison pulled Van Buren from his "executive throne" in 1840, as pictured by lithographer Henry R. Robinson (fig. 37). Another Jackson candidate won office in 1844 on a platform of annexation of Texas and Oregon. Called "Little Hickory" because of his allegiance to Jackson, James K. Polk was the first "dark horse" candidate to be elected President.

The most important campaign issue was expansion, with annexation of Texas accompanied by the threat of war with Mexico and annexation of Oregon Territory with its possibility of conflict with Great Britain. Printer James Baillie produced a cartoon showing Dame Texas in all her hideousness, waiting to see which Democratic presidential aspirant, Van Buren or Polk, would welcome her (fig. 38). She need not have worried, for the incumbent President, John Tyler, also campaigned on an independent ticket for "Tyler and Texas." Whig candidate Henry Clay was less enthusiastic.

The bitterness involved in the Texas issue was not clear until Generals Zachary Taylor and Winfield Scott invaded and conquered Mexico, and the Southwest had been added to the national domain at the expense of enduring Mexican suspicion. A sectional effort at best, the Mexican war created division and even resistance in some quarters, while establishing one of the firmest traditions in American political history: military heroes make good presidential candidates (fig. 40). George Washington, Andrew Jackson, and William H. Harrison had preceded Taylor in the office. Democratic cartoonists created one of the most memorable pictures of the nineteenth century when they depicted General Taylor atop a pyramid of skulls, "the one qualification for a Whig President."

One bright spot in the conflict was the acquisition of California, one of the most fortunate incidents in our history, for gold was discovered in enormous quantities just a few months after the war ended. With the press full of fantastic rumors of wealth and citizens heading for California by the thousands, lithographers produced outrageous prints that depicted the mania that had commandeered the country in 1849 (fig. 41). California was America's (fig. 42). No other country could participate in the bonanza, but even Europe noticed the discovery of gold, as Honoré Daumier, the great French caricaturist, issued a cartoon showing two Frenchmen absorbed in talk of the gold rush (fig. 43).

Shortly after effects of California's wealth

reached the East Coast, Senator Henry Clay spoke on the floor of Congress in defense of a bill destined to be known as the Compromise of 1850, one of the most heralded but most disastrous agreements in our country's history. With increased population and wealth, California had requested statehood. Would it enter slave or free? The question was fraught with potential political consequences since the South had managed to hold a balance between slave states and free states in the Senate. Should California be admitted as a free state, the balance would swing in favor of the North, probably forever. Hoping to settle the differences between North and South enough to allow California to enter, Senator Clay offered his Great Compromise. In return for the admission of California, New Mexico territory would be organized without mention of slavery, and a Fugitive Slave Act would be passed requiring Northerners to help capture runaway slaves. The bill passed, momentarily halting the country's rush to self-destruct.

But slavery was an issue that would not compromise. Sidney Smith, of the *Edinburgh Review* spoke with perhaps more insight than most Americans when he predicted that "it is scarcely possible to conceive that such an empire should very long remain undivided or that dwellers on the Columbia should have common interest with the navigators of the Hudson and the Delaware."[7] Clay's effort did little to avert the onrushing disaster and many Europeans wondered if they might have prematurely declared the experiment a success.

III

1852–1875

THE ONE GREAT and abiding issue that would not recede, would not be side-stepped, would not resolve itself, and that made the Civil War inevitable, was slavery (fig. 46). Historians for decades have argued that the differences between North and South were many and complex, that they had developed over centuries of separate existence, that they and not slavery combined to guide the squabbling sections down the narrowing path to fratricidal conflict. But the inescapable fact, proclaimed at the time by abolitionists and moral men across the nation, was that slavery would not endure in spite of its profitability and rapid expansion.[1] These "Free-Soilers" promised to lead the death-defying crusade until the words that Thomas Jefferson had enshrined in the Declaration of Independence three quarters of a century before applied to men of all color—that all men are created equal before the law.

Once slavery is seen in its proper context, the issues leading to the Civil War simplify considerably. New York Senator William H. Seward insisted that the conflict was "irrepressible" as long as "a slaveholding nation" existed in the South.[2] Some early writers agreed but were overcome by stacks of economic and philosophical data gathered by later historians that pointed to irreconcilable regional differences as the cause of the war. Writing after the war, historian James Ford Rhodes noted the "risk in referring any historic event to a single cause," but concluded that "it may safely be asserted that there was a single cause [for the Civil War], slavery."[3] Rhodes' "single cause" was discredited years later by the work of revisionist authors like Charles and Mary Beard, who explained the conflict as economic in origin. The truth is, however, that slavery was the only irreconcilable difference between North and South, and it alone fastened conflict on the country.

There were, of course, significant regional differences between North and South. The South was an agrarian community, the North an industrial one; the North knitted together by miles of railroad, the South a scattering of farms and plantations. One was a society of class, the other a society of merchants and industrialists; one spawned shipbuilders and sailors, the other horsemen and leaders. The North harked to the puritanical voice of Henry Ward Beecher, the South to Methodism and Episcopalianism. But as concrete as these facts are they could hardly have caused the war, or the two sections would still be locked in mortal combat, for the South remains a basically agrarian region, the North an industrial one. The South maintained its class structure through the war, the North became even more democratized. And, although there was great psychological difference between slavery and freedom, the condition of the Negro changed little after the war, some blacks even commenting that they had lived better under slavery. Economic and civil rights for the black man did not come simply with the military victory of North over South, or even after rancorous Reconstruction that probably created more hatred than the war.

The cartoons of the 1850s and 1860s clearly emphasize the importance of slavery (fig. 46). Artists dwelt on racism, crusading characters, and war-delaying political compromises that pleased neither side. Were these cartoonists all abolitionists? Were they more sensitive to moral truth than most of their contemporaries? Or did slavery and abolition simply lend themselves to easier depiction in caricature and cartoon?

Perhaps many of the cartoonists were abolitionists; at least they were Northerners. Most of the lithographers worked in Northern cities like New York, Boston, and Philadelphia. But important regional centers had developed by 1860 and fine etchings and lithographs were produced in Cincinnati, Richmond, and Baltimore, and by no means were all the cartoonists pro-Negro. Although most of the artists were born in the North, several—Thomas Nast and Adalbert Volck—were German-born. It is also true that slavery, being a controversial issue with complex implications, obviously was an easier subject to treat than, say, agrarianism vs. industrialism, although later artists sharpened their techniques on the farm vs. the city theme without sacrificing poignancy.

With the Compromise of 1850 still fresh in mind, both the Whigs and the Democrats adopted platforms for the 1852 election supporting its clauses, even the controversial Fugitive Slave Bill (fig. 47). When Illinois Senator Stephen A. Douglas, the "Little Giant," introduced legislation organizing Kansas and Nebraska territories, the immediate question became whether slavery would be permitted in the territories (fig. 49). Douglas hoped to solve the problem (and thrust himself into contention for the 1856 presidency) by allowing the voters in the territory to decide the question for themselves. Known as "popular sovereignty," this doctrine was accepted in 1854 by Congress, but led to violence in "bloody" Kansas (fig. 48). Advocates of both sides streamed into the territory, anxious to have a majority so they could dictate the terms of the new state constitution. Neither side worried when violence furthered their cause; abolitionists felt morally justified, slaveholders needed another state for balance in the Senate. Propagandists spread literature and prints across the nation, including one by J. L. Magee showing the Democrats "Forcing Slavery Down the Throat of a Freesoiler" (fig. 48). So worried about the slavery issue in Kansas were the Democrats that Franklin Pierce and Douglas, who had committed themselves irrevocably on the issue, lost the nomination to James Buchanan (who had been out of the country as American minister in England) and John C. Breckenridge.

Slavery also dominated Douglas' race for reelection to the Senate when Abraham Lincoln, a little-known former member of Congress who regarded slavery as "a moral, a social, and a political wrong," challenged him.[4] Douglas responded with his "Freeport Doctrine," arguing (contrary to the Dred Scott decision) that a state or territory could legally exclude slavery, a position that cost him Southern support and ultimately perhaps the presidency (fig. 52).

But even Lincoln, the "Great Emancipator," was not as radical as the abolitionists (fig. 50). While contending that slavery was morally wrong, he admitted in his debates with Douglas that "I have no purpose to introduce political and social equality between the white and black races."[5] His 1860 platform was a carefully drawn document reaffirming the principles of the Declaration of Independence, the Wilmot Proviso (stating that slavery would be prohibited from the territories), and the right of each state to control its domestic institutions, rather than a strident manifesto calling for abolition. A moderate on the issue of slavery, he swept the North, winning a clear majority in the electoral college (without a single Southern vote), substantial enough to have defeated his three opponents even if they had unified against him.

True to their word Southern states began seceding (fig. 54). Without waiting for the newly-elected President to speak, South Carolina passed an ordinance on December 20, 1860, declaring that "the union now subsisting between South Carolina and the other States, under the name of the 'United States of America,' is hereby dissolved." Some, even Southerners, thought South Carolina's action precipitate: an Arkansas editor castigated South Carolina for having "whirled herself" out of the Union "without even passing the compliments of the season" with her sister slaveholding States.[6] But the six other lower South states immediately followed course, with four of the upper South states joining later (fig. 55).

European observers who had watched the United States for the past half-century felt certain that the great democracy had finally ended. They had often pointed out that the raw materials of the South fed the industrial might of the North and predicted that neither could survive without the other. Britain, the mother country—sympathetic as any offended mother might be—hesitated, not knowing whether to support the South, with whom she agreed socially, or the North, with whom she agreed morally. The South won a diplomatic victory when Britain declared neutrality in regard to the Northern blockade of Southern ports, thereby recognizing the South as a belligerent power, but all observers could agree with the cartoonist Woolf that the national bird had been "murdered" (fig. 55). The French comment might have been more appropriately the European opinion: "I do not understand anything about it all" (fig. 56).

The war began slowly, with the South hoping to strike a blow that would convince Northerners of its ability and will, then reach a quick settlement that would recognize its independence. Lincoln initially rested his case on the sanctity of the Union, a course with impressive historical support among the founding fathers as well as great popular appeal, but Northerners inspired by Harriet Beecher Stowe's *Uncle Tom's Cabin* were not as willing to fight for an idea as they were a cause. Lincoln's modest goal of luring the South back into the Union by remaining silent on the question of slavery and loyal to the principles of the Constitution had failed. After several bloody matches at Bull Run, Shiloh, Antietam, and Fredericksburg, the President finally concluded that the major issue of the war could not be avoided. He issued the Emancipation Proclamation on January 1, 1863 (fig. 57). While true that the document applied only to those slaves in states that had seceded (and not those in border states like Maryland that remained in the Union), it is not true, as is often stated, that it therefore did not free a single slave. The rationale that all masters in Confederate states disregarded Lincoln's proclamation is not based on documentation. Loyal Unionists living in the South, such as Sam Houston, who gave up the Texas governorship rather than swear allegiance to the Confederacy, freed their slaves as soon as they learned of the Proclamation.[7] Lincoln, the final architect of abolition, was now even more hated by Southerners. David H. Strother of Richmond, an illustrator for the short-lived magazine called *Southern Punch*, probably represented the majority Southern view of Lincoln when he drew him as a monkey presenting the Emancipation Proclamation to the overjoyed but obviously naïve Negro.

Strother was joined in his intense dislike of Lincoln by another Southern artist, Baltimore dentist Adalbert Volck, who pictured the President and General Benjamin F. Butler, a particularly despised Northern officer whom many Southerners had depended on to join their cause (fig. 58). For no reason other than that Lincoln and Butler were equally disliked, Volck pictured them together as Don Quixote and Sancho Panza. Thomas Nast, a pro-Union cartoonist for *Harper's Weekly*, also included Lincoln and Butler in a cartoon. Nast depicted Butler as if he were a valued Northern leader whom Lincoln planned to cut into several pieces so he could send him to different places simultaneously (fig. 59). Butler's presence in the cartoons of the era is a graphic lesson in how history virtually forgets a personality that occupied only a supporting role throughout his career (fig. 66). Although Butler had presidential aspirations following the Civil War and actually ran on the Greenback Party ticket in 1884, the most influential position he held was member of Congress, and his reputation rested primarily on his dictatorial rule of New Orleans during the early years of the war.

The final victory of the overwhelming Union forces by no means settled the issues that had precipitated the war. More than 600,000 men lay dead, slavery had been eliminated; nevertheless, Negroes did not automatically receive equal treatment or even equality under the law. And any national hope of seeking solutions under Lincoln's leadership was obliterated by the assassin's bullet in 1865 (fig. 62). Andrew Johnson of Tennessee took office to face one of the most troubling problems of the Republic, the readmission of the Confederate states to the Union. What would be the terms? Would the Southerners be granted full citizenship? Were they to be punished? Although the nation faced difficult problems, it had survived its greatest crisis. Skeptical Europeans who had predicted the decline of "the last best hope of earth," as Lincoln had put it, were wrong. And they were once again reminded of their dislike for the hybrid that had developed in North America and of how it might now flex its new-found muscles internationally (fig. 74).

Lincoln's plan to normalize the country was lenient. Arguing that the Confederate states had never left the Union, he offered amnesty to all Southerners who would swear allegiance to the government and planned to recognize state governments when ten percent of the 1860 electorate had taken the oath. Certain radical Republicans in Congress, however, viewed the South as a defeated enemy and demanded punishment. The Wade-Davis Bill, submitted to Congress before the war ended, would have restructured Lincoln's plan by requiring that a majority of the electorate in each state take the oath before the state would be readmitted. Lincoln pocket-vetoed the bill, and Johnson made it clear upon his assumption of power that he favored Lincoln's terms.

The Radicals immediately realized that if their plan were to be instituted it would be in spite of Johnson. Under the leadership of Thaddeus Stevens of Pennsylvania, the Radicals outlined a reconstruction program designed to chastise the South and, if necessary, rid themselves of an uncooperative President. Stevens claimed that the Southern states were "conquered provinces." Senator Charles Sumner of Massachusetts considered them to have committed "suicide." In either case the states would have given up their membership in the Union, and to be readmitted they would come under the authority of Congress, just as the territories do. Then Congress drafted the thirteenth and fourteenth amendments abolishing slavery and granting all citizens due process of law before any of their rights could be abridged, two moderate measures that Lincoln himself had favored.

Johnson's cause was not helped when New Orleans erupted in a racial riot in July, 1866 (fig. 64). Thousands of freedmen expecting radically different treatment headed for the Crescent City, only to find that little had changed, that the government was in the hands of the Democratic party in accordance with Lincoln's and Johnson's plans. The

Radicals tried to take over the government by re-convening the "loyalist" convention of 1864, but they were attacked by police and a white mob. Thirty-seven Negroes and three white sympathizers were killed. The riot stirred great indignation in the North, and Congress blamed Johnson. When the 1866 congressional elections placed more Radicals in office, they moved to tighten their grip on Johnson and the government. Virtually removing the President's power over the army by the Command of the Army Act requiring him to issue orders through the General of the Army, U. S. Grant, the Radicals then passed the Tenure of Office Act, stating that officials appointed by and with the advice of the Senate could be removed only by the same procedure, thus fixing Johnson with a host of officials hostile to his goals.

Congress proceeded to outline the manner in which former Confederate states could return to the Union (fig. 65). The First Reconstruction Act passed over President Johnson's veto in 1867 divided the South into five military districts and established martial law. For civil authority to return, the states would have to present a new constitution for Congressional approval, adopt universal manhood suffrage, and ratify the fourteenth amendment. If Southerners refused to act, Congress required the military commanders in each district to initiate the measures.

Johnson, doubting the constitutionality of the Tenure of Office Act, determined to test it by dismissing Secretary of War Edwin Stanton. The House of Representatives then impeached Johnson, charging that he had violated the Tenure of Office Act, the Command of the Army Act, and had disgraced and ridiculed the Congress (fig. 66). In a six-week trial before the Senate, Johnson was acquitted, but he could no longer block Radical legislation. They finally defeated him as war-hero Grant swept into office in 1868 (fig. 67).

Congressional Reconstruction of the South has been one of the most controversial issues of our nation's past. The traditional view holds that by disenfranchising all the Southerners who had supported the Confederacy Congress allowed outsiders and turncoats ("carpetbaggers" and "scalawags") to take legal advantage of honest former Confederates who wanted nothing more than to return peacefully to the Union. The official law enforcement agencies were often corrupt and military commanders concerned themselves as much with illegal activity by the Southerners (in the Ku Klux Klan and similar organizations) as by the intruders. "Our principal danger was from lawless bands of marauders . . .," said one observer. "Our country was full of highwaymen . . . the off-scourings of the two armies and of the suddenly freed negro population." As late as 1879 a journalist reported that the migrants from the Old South to Texas had "no progress in them, no love for adventure, no ambition." And a Northern visitor to New Orleans in 1873 was shocked when he saw "these faces, these faces. One sees them everywhere; on the street, at the theater, in the salon, in the cars; and pauses for a moment struck with the expression of entire despair." Mobile was "dilapidated and hopeless." Norfolk was "asleep by her magnificent harbor." Savannah was "at a standstill."[8]

The contrary view contends that Reconstruction had its faults, as would any military occupation, but that the end—in this case equal rights for blacks—justified the means since Southerners would not voluntarily cooperate. Some revisionist writers even suggest that the basic problem with Reconstruction was that it did not go far enough, that the Southern states were readmitted to the Union before transformation was complete. This point of view further alleges that proper reconstruction would have rendered most of the civil rights problems of the 1960s avoidable.

Even adequate reconstruction would have left the prejudices of the Northern states intact, prejudices which only fully emerged in the 1970s. Historical hindsight has permitted us to criticize both views, and to observe that perhaps the Northern states were no more ready for total equality than were the Southern states. When those rights did materialize more than 100 years after the bitter war, however, the legal foundation was the constitutional amendments written and passed after the Civil War.

As soon as the Confederate states were readmitted to the Union with full political rights, the military districts were abolished and home rule returned. With the presidential election of 1876 politics returned to a "business as usual" status, and the Democratic Party again contended for national offices. It was by coincidence that the most dangerous threat to the experiment begun in 1776 was finally over on the 100th birthday of the experiment, overcome by a tenacious President who refused to acquiesce when almost half the country attempted to secede.

IV

1876–1900

ONCE SURVIVAL of the grand experiment had been clearly established, the years from 1876 until 1900 seem marked by a resolution to solve the country's fundamental problems. The memories of this era, however, appear to be of the worst failures of society. These were years when reformers and problem-solvers crusaded for black rights, for prohibition, for governmental and political reforms, for humanitarian reforms, and for business regulation. But most of all, these were years of industrialization and urbanization, years during which the foundations of modern American society were laid.

Americans abroad in 1876 were seldom so sophisticated or talented as the first ambassadors who visited France and England, but all had to be taken more seriously for they represented an increasingly powerful force in world affairs. From the brilliance of Jefferson and the creativity and wit of Franklin the American image had evolved into the democracy of Jackson and the stoic martyrdom of Lincoln. The post-Civil War American spirit, however, was personified in a G. Bridgman caricature—the businessman (fig. 74). Dressed in the best Yankee tradition, the new "national type" swashbuckled onto the world's economic stage with a bag of "greenbacks" under his arm, a Cuban cigar clenched in his teeth, and a ravenous home market to supply. By 1885 the United States had become the leading industrial nation in the world.

Undreamed of technological advances made possible the new age of industrialism. Farm boys from the Midwest and recently arrived immigrants alike were whisked to their urban destinations by the railroad, which soon linked coast to coast via five transcontinental lines. Inland waterways served as arteries for steamboat traffic, and new pipelines brought oil to the developing markets. Businessmen soon made important contacts via the telegraph and newly-developed telephone as each phase of industry leapt forward to keep up with the pacesetters.

Quick-minded, shrewd businessmen, inspired as much by the quest for power and money as by the possession of them, found numberless opportunities in the developing economy. They designed new methods of distribution, discovered new resources or new ways of using old ones, and invented solutions to problems that only they could foresee. Thomas A. Edison pointed out the difference between invention (purposeful creation) and discovery (more or less an accident), then chose to enter the "invention business": America did not have time to wait for discovery. John D. Rockefeller, according to one of his contemporaries, not only had foresight, he "could see around the corner"[1] (fig. 140). Prompted by a government that espoused capitalism itself and allowed the entrepreneur to keep the profits, they built undreamed of fortunes. Rockefeller refined the increasing oil flow until he controlled ninety percent of the country's refineries. He was the first man to accumulate more than a billion dollars' worth of personal wealth. Andrew Carnegie, a Scottish immigrant working on the railroad, wisely predicted the many possibilities for steel and earned millions more dollars than he could spend when he sold his Carnegie Steel Company to the company that eventually became United States Steel. Charles Goodnight, thinking of himself as a "solitary adventurer . . . in a great land as fresh and new as a spring morning," turned worthless longhorn beef into millions of dollars by driving the animals overland to starved markets. These entrepreneurs knew that "there's gold from the grass roots down," as a guide in the Dakota gold country of the 1870s said, but they quickly learned that "there's more gold from the grass roots up."[2]

America's industrial titans shared another mania —philanthropy. At age sixty, the religious Rockefeller began to disperse his fortune, believing that God had intended it for the good of mankind. Establishing the world-famous Rockefeller Foundation, he gave away more than $530 millions before his death. Carnegie shared his philosophy as well as his wealth with the world. Believing that "the problem of our age is the proper administration of wealth," he donated church organs, library buildings, and money for an endowment for peace. Of his estimated fortune of $400 millions, more than $350 millions went to public benefactions. "The man who dies rich dies disgraced," he announced.

Neither Rockefeller nor Carnegie earned their money with a new discovery or invention. Their contribution was organization—organization in an oil industry consisting of hundreds of small refineries, producers, and consumers with no industry-wide cooperation; in a steel industry unaware of the potential for new bridges, steamships, and a thousand other necessities. America provided few manufactured goods that were not already available in other countries. The great genius of America—and the great democratizing agent— was distribution which made manufactured goods available to all Americans at a low price. The emerging urban centers demanded—and consumed— goods at an impressive rate. "Palaces of consumption," chain stores, mail order houses, and department stores like R. H. Macy's and Lord & Taylor in New York City, John Wanamaker's in Philadelphia, and Field, Leiter & Company (later Marshall Field & Company) in Chicago, met the demand with clothing, drugs, hardware, jewels, hats, furniture, and shoes (fig. 75). These huge emporiums drove many small businessmen into bankruptcy or into another line of work by centralizing distribution of related items, lowering overhead, and selling at a fixed, lower-than-usual price that put an end to price haggling. The American public got more and better goods than the citizens of any other industrialized country in the world.

Few countries could have supplied the workers to support this expansive economy, but America was the recipient of hundreds of thousands of immigrants who, still speaking their own tongues, moved directly into the work force (fig. 76). Immigration reached a nineteenth century peak in 1882 when almost 800,000 foreigners arrived, then leveled off to approximately 400,000 per year; 1,285,000 arrived in 1907. In all some 20 millions came to the United States from 1865 to 1914, most settling in eastern cities and living in their own ethnic communities isolated from the English language until their children enrolled in public school.

Industrialization and urbanization was possible because of another American miracle: farm productivity. Although young people left farm communities in growing numbers, production did not suffer. Improvements in the plow facilitated planting, while McCormick's reaper speeded up the harvest. Other mechanical devices aided virtually every facet of farming. By 1900 there were more acres under cultivation and more animals grazing the land than ever before in the history of the country; the United States led the world in agricultural production while employing the smallest percentage of its population on the farm.

As the number of immigrants grew and American labor began its fledgling efforts at organization, an understandable animosity developed between the two. Anxious to improve conditions in what they publicized as a "slave market," workers resented foreigners who migrated to this country and took jobs at a lower wage. Thousands of Chinese workers, brought in to work on the railroad and in the gold mines in California, stirred resentment among white workers there, while the East Coast, used to immigrants from northern Europe, pictured itself as inundated by a stream of South and East European immigrants, the "new" immigration. These people spoke different languages, were Catholic, and had darker skins, factors that placed them under immediate suspicion when contrasted with the "old" immigration that had been going on for decades (fig. 77). The "sandlot riots" in San Francisco in July, 1877, resulted in a new treaty with China that permitted the United States to "regulate, limit or suspend" Chinese immigration, but not to prohibit it, and anti-foreign pressure produced the Contract Labor Act of 1885 which forbade the importation of laborers already contracted for a job (fig. 78).

Few people realized or cared about the conditions the immigrants found when they arrived, but the experience was traumatic from the moment of departure on over-crowded ships to arrival at Ellis Island, "the isle of tears," to settlement in a fast-growing urban slum. Thomas Worth, a cartoonist for Currier & Ives, mixed racism with his comment on immigration as he pictured a "frightening" Statue of Liberty waiting to abuse the immigrants who came under her care (fig. 79). New York Port quickly became famous for corruption, both in the treatment of immigrants and for the criminal way in which the jobs were parceled out to political hacks. More than one politician made his reputation while lining his pockets at the expense of the poor immigrants, and at least one national figure, Roscoe Conkling, ended his career in a huff because New York Port patronage had gone to a political rival.

As the Industrial Revolution came of age, pools, trusts, and holding companies concentrated unprecedented economic power in the hands of a few, raising fundamental questions about the role of government in a capitalistic society. Business operated according to unwritten codes, asking for a *laissez faire* policy yet soliciting support such as land grants for railroads as encouragement to lay more track. One economic expert saw the "progress of the country" as being "independent of legislation." Nor would any good businessman want regulation in the manner of William M. ("Boss") Tweed, the head of Tammany Hall (fig. 80). To get a New York City contract a supplier had to agree to a "kickback" return of a certain percentage of the total contract to Tweed and his henchmen. The city paid more than $11 millions for a courthouse worth not more than $3 millions and more than $2 millions for stationery alone during Tweed's reign. "'Things regulate themselves,'" claimed Harvard Professor Francis Bowen in explaining the philosophy of *laissez faire*, which "means, of course, that God regulates them by his general laws."[3] Business operated so independently of government that H. H. Rogers, one of Rockefeller's associates, told a New York State legislative committee in 1879 that there was a "question" in his mind as to "whether it is a proper thing for me, even if there is not harm done by it, to divulge my business secrets."[4]

Despite the dogged opposition of businessmen, Congress passed several landmark laws to correct the most serious abuses. The Interstate Commerce Act of 1887 and the Sherman Antitrust Act of 1890 established the precedent of government regulation of business and laid the foundation for future legislation, while correcting unfair practices such as the long and short "haul," (railroads charging more for a short trip than a long one because of lack of competition) and "restraint of trade" by trusts controlling one or more industries.

The theories of Charles Darwin (first published in his book, *The Origin of Species*, in 1859) apparently offered an alternative to the Biblical version of the creation—evolution. Darwin upset Christian fundamentalists by implying that humans lived by the same principles, a theory which they saw as animalistic and degrading to a creature made in God's image (fig. 82). Most preachers condemned this attack on their theology, but Henry Ward Beecher, brother of Harriet Beecher Stowe and preacher for a 2,500 member congregation in Brooklyn, espoused it, claiming that evolution and Christianity were truths that could exist side by side. He hoped to win respect for an enlightened Christianity that would admit the findings of science, but he unfortunately discredited his cause when a member of his congregation sued him for adultery (fig. 82).

1876 was America's centennial year, a time of back-slapping and reaffirmation of the country's traditional values. It was also a time during which values that many Americans held dear were under attack (fig. 83). "Demon Rum," a personal blight to many, was assaulted by the Woman's Christian Temperance Union, the Anti-Saloon League, and religious groups. It was also a political issue that helped doom Senator James G. Blaine's presidential hopes when he neglected to disagree with a preacher who denounced "rum, Romanism, and rebellion" in his presence. An enterprising reporter promptly publicized the remark for all immigrants and Southerners (many of whom loved rum and were Catholics and former Rebels) to see.

A more tangible attack on traditional values was the small but vocal crusade for woman's rights that began after the war, continued into the 1872 presidential contest when Victoria Woodhull announced her candidacy, and found its greatest expression in the cities, where women assumed new roles as clerks, secretaries, and shopkeepers (fig. 72). A host of myths had to be debunked before women would be admitted to schools, jobs, and certain societies, but there was no denying Southern women who had managed plantations and farms while their husbands were away at war, or Northern women who organized charities, including the forerunner of the Red Cross, during the Civil War (fig. 70). Conservatives feared that "enforced familiarity" in the classroom would lead to losing "the delicate bloom of womanhood," resulting in "race suicide" when the process reached its natural end. Mark Twain, on the other hand, welcomed the "new woman" (fig. 84). "I dearly want the women to be raised to the political altitude of the negro, the imported savage, and the pardoned thief, and allowed to vote," he wrote in 1873, "it will be the last time . . . to give over trying to save the country by human means."[5] The "weaker vessel" was finally admitted to colleges and universities after the Civil War, most institutions following suit by the 1870s, but equality under the law, guaranteed by the fourteenth amendment, was not seriously offered until a century later.

"The Gilded Age," to use Mark Twain's famous phrase, reached its apex during the "gay nineties," a heady era that followed a resurgence of the economy and the election of a Republican president in 1896. America became embarrassingly aware of itself and the criticisms of sophisticated Europeans. Walt Whitman bemoaned the fact that "America has yet morally and artistically originated nothing," and the Irish poet Mary Colum called it "intellectually America's most colonial period." American humor was to real literature what Negro minstrel shows were to drama, said the *Nation*, the intellectual conscience of the country in 1883. American letters could not yet claim another Jefferson, but Henry James and Twain created some of the greatest prose of any American, and artists like William M. Harnett, Thomas Eakins, and Winslow Homer produced superb canvases.

The 1890s fed instead on the practical genius of America. Louis D. Brandeis pointed out that American creativeness was directed more toward a "scientific management" of business, and Americans took pride in the inventions of Thomas A. Edison (first practical incandescent light, first phonograph, first motion picture projector).[6] Presidential hopeful William Jennings Bryan returned from a trip to Europe to declare himself "more widely informed, but more intensely American," and a young Henry Cabot Lodge predicted that "Americans may reasonably look forward to a time when they will have produced a civilization grander than any the world has known."[7]

As opposite as they might seem, industrial advances also aided the artist. With the aid of huge steam presses, publishers like Louis Prang of Boston were able to adapt the lithographic method to mechanical printing and produce multi-colored reproductions of original paintings as well as famous "old masters," which he called "chromos." The technique was quickly employed by several cartoon magazines like *Judge* and *Puck*, patterned after the English humor magazine *Punch*. With a circulation of around 90,000 by the mid-1890s, *Puck* made colored chromolithographic cartoons easily available and immensely popular (figs. 75, 76, 81, 82). Because most chromos were copies of original art and because of the wide-spread intellectual disillusionment with the Gilded Age, this era is often dubbed the "chromo civilization." But recent re-evaluation of the artistic and intellectual attainment of these years and of the chromo has turned the epithet into a compliment.

The Spanish-American War that ended a century of unparalleled progress marked America's entrance into world affairs as a respected participant (fig. 88). A people who had just rooted inhuman slavery from its own bosom at a tremendous expense now looked at other nations' problems with a puritanical eye and zealous heart. Americans only mourned the subjugation of the home of ancient liberties, Greece, by Turkey, but took a more active interest in Spain's domination of Cuba, located just ninety miles off the coast of Florida and close enough to affect (fig. 87). Outright meddling in the Spanish colonial affairs plus militant "yellow journalism" in New York City produced a demand for war on behalf of the Cuban colonials that President William McKinley was not prepared to resist. Although the weak Spanish government agreed to the humanitarian demands that the Americans made, the United States proceeded with a war that lasted only a few months and resulted in the enlargement of America's colonial empire (fig. 89).

America entered the twentieth century ebullient and hopeful of even greater things. The tragic assassination of McKinley left the government in the hands of "that damn cowboy," Theodore Roosevelt, whose enthusiasm encouraged the national euphoria and provided the nation a sense of philosophical progress that it had felt before only when it flexed its industrial and military muscles. The image of America included Progress, which most Americans thought an exclusive gift of democracy.

V

1901–1929

THEODORE ROOSEVELT is a familiar figure— the flashing teeth, the steel-rimmed glasses, the close-cropped hair and busy mustache, the striving, the sportsmanship (fig. 90). Roosevelt was so well-liked, so controversial that he often appears in caricature today. He was caricatured then too: a barrel-chested, falsetto-voiced demigod could not help but make an impression. And when he came with other features so easily recognizable and drawn, he, like Abraham Lincoln and Franklin D. Roosevelt, was a natural, a stereotype, a cartoonist's favorite. He is the remarkable combination of Harvard and the Old West, the military and shrewd politics. He has come to stand for personal energy, vigor, and jingoism. It was Theodore Roosevelt who ushered the United States into the twentieth century.

This inexhaustible man provided excellent leadership for a government languishing under vapid

Republicanism (fig. 91). Torpid William McKinley hardly exuded his own personality; he lent none to the government. Turn-of-the-century reformers struggled with monopolies and trusts of unprecedented size and power (figs. 97, 102). Muckrakers—a term Roosevelt coined—found rapidly developing slums and starving children in the midst of the greatest urban centers. Antiquated laws simply did not provide the legal means necessary to eradicate these problems. This new "Progressive" movement needed a leader, someone to direct its energies, to make it palatable to the established authorities on Wall Street, on Capitol Hill. Roosevelt was that man. "We know that self-government is difficult," he conceded in his 1905 inaugural address, "but we have faith that we shall not prove false to the memories of the men of the mighty past."[1]

Many Americans look back on these magniloquent years and suggest that they were a period of national mindlessness during which the people abandoned their basic values in the face of world pressure. Roosevelt's maverick campaign in 1912 was only one of the unlikely happenings during the almost three decades from 1901 to 1929. Soon American doughboys would march across Europe to snatch victory from the hands of the Kaiser in what had seemed a purely European war. Jazz and prohibition swept the cities, the Republican Party certified its moral bankruptcy in the Teapot Dome oil scandal, materialism was evidently the national philosophy (fig. 128). Calvin Coolidge took office as President and high priest of consumption declaring that "The business of the United States is business."[2] "It was an easy, quick, adventurous age, good to be young in," said Malcolm Cowley, writer and critic, "and yet on coming out of it one felt a sense of relief, as on coming out of a room too full of talk and people into the sunlight of the winter streets."[3] Yet these years are not disharmonious with the rest of our history. The nation reveled in its reckless and self-confident character. Too peripheral to be noticed before, Americans had now earned the right to be heard. America was just being itself.

Cartoonists provided images for the awakening. Coming on the heels of such a lackluster President as McKinley, Roosevelt captured the hero-fancy of Americans. Frank Nankivell showed him as pirate (fig. 90). Otho Cushing pictured him as Ulysses in *The Teddessy*, withstanding the lure of sirens Carnegie, Rockefeller, and J. P. Morgan from his reform position (fig. 92) tied to the mast. Perhaps the most poignant cartoon of Teddy's determination is John Clubb's depiction of him on Sagamore Hill, his home, ready to fly off to war in 1916 (fig. 111). (Roosevelt called on President Woodrow Wilson when the United States entered World War I and offered his services; Wilson declined.) J. S. Pughe (fig. 94), T. E. Powers (fig. 106), and C. K. Berryman (fig. 107) offered a lanky, beared Uncle Sam who stumbled like the adolescent that he was, but spoke with increased authority. The nation could relax with Sam and Teddy at the helm.

Offering the country a "Square Deal," Roosevelt carefully outlined antitrust legislation, government reforms, pure food and drug legislation, and conservation measures (fig. 96). Abroad he flexed the country's new-found muscles, counseling his adversaries that the maturing world power wielded a big stick in spite of its soft voice (fig. 94). He initiated construction on the badly-needed Panama Canal, added the Roosevelt Corollary to the Monroe Doctrine (admitting that the United States probably would have to become the international policeman for Latin America), and maintained the balance of power between the Asian powers of Russia and Japan, winning a Nobel Prize by mediating the dispute.

Roosevelt's aggressiveness is reflected in foreign policy. An ardent supporter of Admiral Alfred T. Mahan, he oversaw the building of a Navy and a show of force in the Pacific as Japan spread its empire. Roosevelt authorized the "Great White Fleet" to make a courtesy call on Japan, even though Congress had not appropriated money for the trip (fig. 94). Reasoning that the demonstration was necessary and that Congress would not allow the fleet to remain on the far side of the Pacific, he ordered the voyage, then left it to Congress to get the fleet back home. The "American scarecrow" might have appeared clumsy to the adroit Japanese, but the point was made: American force—the big stick—was present in the Pacific. Roosevelt invoked the Monroe Doctrine to keep Germany from interfering in Latin America, and his friend Henry Cabot Lodge initiated congressional action to keep Japan from speculating in land on the west coast of Mexico (fig. 106).

Stepping aside to allow his hand-picked successor William Howard Taft (fig. 98) to take office in 1908, Roosevelt turned to personal matters: he went big game hunting and bestowed his trophies on the Smithsonian Institution; he visited scenic spots in the West, thereby calling attention to our national resources; and he otherwise played the senior statesman. But four years on the sidelines left him restless and unsure of Taft. Roosevelt had satisfied himself by regulating monopolies with the countervailing power of government, but Taft had taken more direct action. His attorney general had initiated more antitrust suits during four years than Roosevelt's had in almost two full terms. Displaying the energy and enthusiasm that had become his trademark, Roosevelt again sought the presidency, this time on the Bull Moose (Progressive) Party ticket in 1912. He announced to a curious convention of Eastern industrialists, Western liberals, and old-time Roosevelt followers that "we stand at Armageddon and battle for the Lord."[4]

The progressive cause gained momentum as Woodrow Wilson, the Princeton academician, was nominated by the Democrats (fig. 104). He promised the country the "New Freedom," putting monopoly control at the head of his domestic program. Unlike Roosevelt, Wilson wanted to control trusts by actually breaking them up. With the Republican vote split between Taft, the official party nominee, and Roosevelt, Wilson won easily.

The eyes of the world, meanwhile, were on Europe. "What shall we say of the Great War of Europe, ever threatening, ever impending, and which never came?" asked the director of the World Peace Foundation in 1913. "Humanly speaking, it is impossible." A leader in the American peace movement agreed that this would be the "age of treaties rather than the age of wars, the century of reason rather than the century of force," and a Maine editor claimed that "never since Christ was born in the Manger was the outlook for the universal brotherhood of man brighter than it is today."[5]

World War I began inconspicuously enough in the summer of 1914 with the assassination of the heir to the Austro-Hungarian throne. Traditional hostilities plus a series of entangling alliances had Europe at war by August 4. How could this happen in such an enlightened era, Secretary of Agriculture David Houston asked himself. "I had a feeling that the end of things had come. I stopped in my tracks, dazed and horror-stricken." Then bitterness: "We never appreciated so keenly as now the foresight exercised by our forefathers in emigrating from Europe," declared a Midwestern editor.[6] Following traditional isolationist policy, the United States declared itself neutral and hoped to avoid the conflict that a depraved Europe seemed determined to wage.

But the war was an unprecedented and bloody affair. Sixty thousand British troops perished on the Somme in one single day, over a million men on both sides died in the first five months of battle—and no one gained the advantage. German U-boats sank neutral ships, forcing Wilson to issue progressively adamant diplomatic notes and pacifist Secretary of State William Jennings Bryan to resign rather than send them (fig. 108). To Chicago cartoonist Luther Bradley, Wilson had discovered Roosevelt's big stick (fig. 109), while Louis Raemaekers personified the coming global confrontation in his caricature of Wilson and the Kaiser, the Kaiser astounded at the American's firmness: "Do You Mean to Make a Real War?" (fig. 110).

Many cartoonists supported the intervention; several members of the liberal *The Masses* staff even resigned rather than have the editor put antiwar captions under their drawings. But the artists also called attention to the calculated dementia of war. Robert Minor noted the belittling of the individual's intelligence (fig. 113), Dalrymple the injustice of men dying while others prosper (fig. 114), Boardman Robinson the threat of the October Revolution in Russia (fig. 115). Cartoonists objected to the two-faced attitudes of the United States in jailing men like Eugene V. Debs, a five-time presidential candidate on the Socialist Party ticket, for violation of the Espionage Act, while committing atrocities in the name of liberty in American-owned or dominated territories. Art Young and several other members of *The Masses* staff were even tried for obstructing the draft because of the subject matter in some of their cartoons.

The United States entered the fray in time to insure victory for the Allied powers, but not before sixty percent of the more than fifty-eight millions who participated in it were killed, wounded, captured, or reported missing. Such devastating statistics shocked Americans. Roosevelt's saber-rattling could lead to undreamed-of horror. Wilson's war to make the world "safe for democracy" cost too great a price (fig. 112). Progress that brought the automobile, electricity, mass-production, and the airplane also brought poison gas, machine-guns, tanks, and mobile artillery. "The plunge of civilization into this abyss of blood and horror . . . gives away the whole long age during which we have supposed the world to be, with whatever abatement, gradually bettering," wrote Henry James, a cynical and detached observer. "What the treacherous years were really making for and *meaning* is too tragic for any words." World War I, concluded James, is the "unspeakable giveaway of the whole fool's paradise of our past."[7]

The Unknown Soldier, an anonymous doughboy who was intended to personify the many who died serving the country, seemed instead to emphasize the impersonal quality of a conflict conducted on such a machine-like basis. The nature of patriotism had changed. "I can't explain it," claimed one of John Dos Passos' fictional soldiers, "but I'll never put a uniform on again." The whole world had changed for painter Maynard Dixon too: "people, morals, patriotism—all had a different meaning to me ever since."[8] Americans noted with increasing wonderment the statement attributed to Lloyd George at the Versailles peace conference: "Is it Upper or Lower Silesia that we are giving away?"[9] The Washington disarmament conference of 1921 began with great enthusiasm but finally fell victim to the suspicion and doubt of the age and achieved little in the way of lasting disarmament (fig. 118).

America was ready for peace, but not for world responsibility. The intellectuals turned nihilist, while the country at large drifted toward isolationism. The Senate rejected the League of Nations; mail from the organization's Geneva headquarters lay unopened on a State Department desk for months. Idaho Senator William Borah declared that even "if the Savior of man would revisit the earth and declare for a League of Nations, I would be opposed to it."[10] President Warren Harding's solution was "not heroics but healing; not nostrums but normalcy; not revolution but restoration"[11] (figs. 116, 117). The flapper ruled the day, and politicians were incapable of inspiring greater world consciousness in the nation even if they had favored it. Ever since its birth, the United States had possessed a fear of outsiders, whether represented as immigrants or in foreign affairs. The 1920s were no exception.

Seized with a fit of conscience at the end of the Spanish-American War because of the consequent colonialism, Americans had adopted far-reaching reforms, politically, economically, and socially during the ensuing three decades (fig. 119). With colonies or territories scattered throughout both the Atlantic and the Pacific, the United States suddenly succumbed to the charge of imperialism. Most

Americans shunned the accusation, believing America to be the only powerful anti-imperialistic country in the world. But the workings of over-wrought consciences had their effect. Muckrakers investigated corrupt machine politicians in the cities (fig. 103), urban slums kept by wealthy landlords in violation of city ordinances, and food manu-facturing and packaging. The cartoonists popu-larized the findings, with Winsor McKay illustrat-ing the technological revolution of the cities (fig. 125), and A. Redfield picturing William Randolph Hearst shouting the doomsday headlines from the back of his snorting nag in the Paul Revere manner (fig. 100).

Americans sought in religion an underpinning for traditional values. Amid the trials of urban liv-ing, pastors tried to adapt the latest scientific find-ings to Biblical principle, tried to show their parish-ioners that science and religion were in harmony. Charles Sheldon, author of the best-selling *In His Steps*, urged his readers to ask themselves what Christ would have done when confronted with a certain problem. This simplistic message was re-iterated thousands of times across the country as evangelists like Billy Sunday held crusades and camp meetings and set up Bible institutes on the college and university campuses (fig. 133). It suf-fered a publicity setback when William Jennings Bryan and Clarence Darrow debated the theory of evolution in the Tennessee Scopes Monkey Trial (figs. 131, 132), but renewed when advocates of An-drew Carnegie's "Gospel of Wealth" connected spirituality with correct business practice. The dean of the University of Chicago Divinity School explained to an inquiring reporter that one could make more money if he prayed about his business. A stockbroker pointed out that the book of Exodus contained tips on risk and liability, and a Chicago man revealed that his business philosophy came from Ezekiel. "It is better to trust in the Rock of Ages than to know the age of rocks," counseled William Jennings Bryan.[12]

Reformers turned their attention to their natural surroundings as a new wave of social scientists pointed out the importance of environment. Charles A. Beard reinterpreted American history according to the principles of economic determin-ism, shocking traditionalists with plausible gen-eralizations that the founding fathers behaved ac-cording to their economic class. Economists and sociologists published equally unsettling findings about the relationship between poverty, slums, and crime. "I have an important piece of news for you," a clubwoman told her members in 1904. "Dante is dead. He has been dead for several centuries, and I think it is time that we dropped the study of his in-ferno and turned attention to our own."[13]

No conservatives ran in the presidential election of 1912. Everyone called himself one kind of Progressive or another, emphasizing reform. The sixteenth amendment to the Constitution per-mitting Congress to levy direct, graduated taxes—an income tax—had been submitted to the states in 1909 and was approved in February, 1913. The seventeenth amendment calling for the direct elec-tion of United States Senators was submitted to the states in May and ratified in two weeks. Perhaps the nineteenth amendment granting full citizen-ship to all citizens regardless of sex was the most overdue. The woman's rights movement in the United States had been active since the mid-nine-teenth century, and had proceeded with various frustrations ever since (fig. 126). ("Call on God," was the now-famous dictum of a philanthropic Mrs. August Belmont to a despairing suffragette, "She will help you.") Successful efforts in other western countries helped the American movement until, in August, 1920, the amendment was ratified.

Religion and reform combined to produce a par-ticular aberration of this abnormal era. Carrie Na-tion had not chopped up saloons nor pastors called on their congregations to "take the pledge" for naught. After a long fight the Women's Christian Temperance Union, the Anti-Saloon League, and even the Ku Klux Klan succeeded in getting the eighteenth amendment (the prohibition amendment) adopted in 1917 (fig. 127). The new prohibition commissioner promised a revolution overnight: liquor would neither be manufactured "nor sold, nor given away, nor hauled in anything on the surface of the earth or under the earth or in the air," he boasted. But his was an impossible task. Not long after the law went into effect a former Assistant Attorney General in charge of prohibition prosecutions admitted that whiskey could be bought "at almost any hour of the day or night, either in rural districts, the smaller towns, or the cities"[14] (fig. 129). Prohibition is one of the clear examples of the dictatorship of the majority, as well as proof that the minority cannot be successfully controlled in a democratic country.

This widespread religious zeal and the isolationist attitude of the twenties combined to resist immigration. Immigration reached its peak in the years before World War I, and totaled more than 5,000,-000 from 1911 to 1920 (fig. 101). With the Bolshevik Revolution in Russia, "internationalism" took on a new anti-American meaning, and foreigners were immediately suspect (fig. 130). Attorney General A. Mitchell Palmer arrested more than 4,000 persons suspected of being Communists. Two anarchists arrested for murder in Massachusetts became a *cause célèbre*. Nicola Sacco and Bartolomeo Vanzetti were finally convicted on flimsy evidence (fig. 193). Liberals and radicals around the world carried on a spectacular propaganda campaign in their behalf, but the conviction was upheld. "I am suffering because I am a radical," said Vanzetti in his last statement, "I am suffering because I am Italian. . . ."[15] They were executed in 1927. The "Red Scare" reached its climax when a terrorist bomb exploded on Wall Street in New York City, killing thirty-eight people.

Dozens of suspected Communists were deported (fig. 130). Others were harassed and arrested without proven charges. The California State Legislature passed an Aliens Land Act which effectively barred Japanese from becoming citizens, the American Federation of Labor supported literacy tests to restrict the number of immigrants, and the anti-Semitic Ku Klux Klan membership reached more than 2,500,000 by 1923 (fig. 134). By 1924 Congress had settled on an immigration formula that was assured to maintain the "racial preponderance [of] the basic strain of our people," and the number of newcomers at Ellis Island declined.[16]

It is unfortunate that the political and social reforms did not extend to the business sector (fig. 97). Businessmen did not want a demonstrably inept government tampering with their money (fig. 102), as government handling of the railroads during the war illustrated (fig. 116). During the war home factories took over markets that foreign companies had supplied, and Americans themselves bought more; they were becoming a consumer society. Henry Ford's first "flivver" rolled off the assembly line in 1909, the fifteen millionth in 1927. President Harding seemed to set the economic pace after the war, stating that "What we want in American is less government in business and more business in government." The bromide seemed true, as government turned to the business community for leadership during war, and business experienced a tremendous boom after the war closed. DuPont and Dow chemicals took over supply of products that were no longer available from German-held North Africa. The economic expansion soon affected other industries as the building boom of the 1920s gave New York City a new skyline (fig. 149). Spurred by the current interpretation of Christian ideals, business seemed en route to perpetual boom. "The man who builds a factory builds a temple," theorized President Calvin Coolidge, "the man who works there worships there." Even Jesus reminded his earthly parents that he had to "be about my father's business" when they suggested that he pay more attention to their instructions. "Brains are wealth and wealth is the chief end of man," said Coolidge, capturing the philosophical creed of the twenties[17] (fig. 117).

The ultimate solution to all the nation's problems was for everyone to own stock in it, said Franklin

D. Roosevelt (fig. 144). "If every family owned even a $100 bond of the United States or a legitimate corporation, there would be no talk of bolshevism, and we would incidentally solve all national problems in a more democratic way." Indeed, the system seemed to be working. The Teapot Dome oil scandal only slowed the growth until it had been removed from the public conscience. In 1928 the United States invested as much in education as the rest of the world combined. The American labor movement (fig. 124) was notably calm compared to other industrial nations, and the muckrakers seemed to have found interests elsewhere. Even Lincoln Steffens, long a critic of capitalism, admitted that "Big Business in America is producing what the Socialists held up as their goal; food, shelter and clothing for all," and economist Stuart Chase suggested that "we lay a wreath on the Uplift Movement in America."[18]

Steffens continued to predict that the full glory of the new order would be exhibited during President Herbert Hoover's administration, and many other knowledgeable men agreed (fig. 143). Average wages were up, business increased each year, and many assumed that this would be the perpetual state of the economy. "Stock prices have reached what looks like a permanently high plateau," concluded Professor Irving Fisher of Yale.

But all was not well, either with the economy or the society. Organized crime was soon recognized as a real problem in the cities (figs. 129, 150); political corruption was so widespread that many citizens lost confidence in the government's ability to remedy the situation (fig. 103). Nor was the booming business community well. Although average wages were up, forty-two percent of all families still earned less than $1,500 per year in 1929. Business profits were up, but they went mostly to the big corporations, who had loaned some thirteen billions of dollars abroad so that foreigners might buy American products. Small businesses were going bankrupt at a startling rate. America had reached the point of manufacturing more than the people

could buy, but few realized it because municipal and state governments borrowed more than three billions of dollars to continue the purchases. When the borrowing halted, when products went begging for want of buyers, the stock market crashed. "Black Thursday" was October 24, 1929 (fig. 145). "Wall Street lays an egg," announced the chic show business paper, *Variety*.[19] Two weeks after that fateful day the average price on all stocks was down forty percent. United States Steel dropped from 262 to 22 in three years following Black Thursday. The boom was over. The national euphoria ended.

VI

1930–1945

"THIS NATION asks for action, and action now," declared the new President. "We must act, and act quickly . . . . We must move as a trained and loyal army willing to sacrifice for the good of a common discipline . . . ." The depression-chastened audience gathered on the windy and misty March day cheered hopefully as President Franklin D. Roosevelt took the leadership of a great but troubled nation. "In this dedication of a Nation we humbly ask the blessing of God. May He protect each and every one of us. May He guide me in the days to come."[1]

Former President Herbert Hoover had come into office in 1929 full of confidence that his would be an administration of national prosperity: two chickens in every pot, a car in every garage. He was victimized by the Crash of 1929, crushed by the ensuing Great Depression, and ushered unceremoniously out of office by the voters in 1932. "We are at the end of our rope," he had said at midnight of his last day in office. "There is nothing more we can do."[2]

Franklin Roosevelt had little more idea than

Hoover about what could be done to end the depression that had settled over the country. The statistics were grim. Twenty-five percent of the work force—twelve to fifteen million people—was unemployed (fig. 146). Thousands of stores and factories stood vacant, darkened, decaying. Countless vagabond children roamed the streets and highways, begging for food; twenty percent of New York City's school children suffered from malnutrition (fig. 148). Meanwhile, the suppliers had such surpluses of grain and dairy products that there was no market for the new produce. Farmers had turned to violence: milk trucks in several midwestern states had been stopped, the milk poured into the ditch in a desperate effort to create a new market for their produce. People no longer trusted the mouthings of government officials, nor respected even President Hoover's fruitless efforts to end chaos in the economic community. Testifying before a Congressional committee, the head of the American Federation of Labor predicted that "if the lawfully constituted leadership does not soon substitute action for words, a new leadership, perhaps unlawfully constituted, will arise and act."[3]

Hoping to develop a firm plan, Roosevelt solicited ideas from government and business leaders. A prominent attorney spoke for them all: "I have nothing to offer, either of fact or theory. There is no panacea."[4] The only thing Roosevelt's advisors did agree on was that delay meant further disaster. The budget was in shambles, banks were closing their doors. Without a well-planned approach, Roosevelt simply began (fig. 147). He declared a bank holiday and closed the banks for four days. Then he called Congress into special session, marking the beginning of the "hundred days," during which an almost record amount of legislation was passed. The Emergency Banking Act placed banks under Treasury Department licenses and took the United States off the gold standard. The Unemployment Relief Act created the Civilian Conservation Corps (CCC), the first of the many New

Deal "alphabet agencies." The Agricultural Adjustment Act (AAA) was intended to aid farmers, and the Tennessee Valley Authority (TVA) was established to construct dams and power plants in the Tennessee River Valley (fig. 198). Roosevelt also went on the radio with the first of his "fireside chats." Speaking in plain language that the common people could understand, he explained the banking crisis, then admonished, "Let us unite in banishing fear . . . . It is your problem no less than it is mine. Together we cannot fail."[5]

Roosevelt's personal touch turned the tide. He had spoken to every citizen who sat with his family in the living room. He had brought tears of emotion and pride to their eyes, had touched them as had no leader since his distant cousin Theodore Roosevelt. The President had not changed many of the circumstances, for the Depression required fundamental adjustments in the system, but he had involved the common man. Americans cared again, they felt confident again. We "got a man in there who is wise to Congress, wise to our so-called big men," said Will Rogers on behalf of the nation. "The whole country is with him, just so he does something. If he burned down the capitol we would cheer and say 'well, we at least got a fire started anyhow.'"[6]

Cartoonists did not miss the point. From powerful messages of social discontent and the impoverished worker, William Gropper changed his imagery to an abundantly endowed Roosevelt (as Mae West) inviting the Wall Street bankers to "come up and see me sometime" (fig. 152). James Thurber humorously depicted the state of business, and many laughed at their predicament for the first time (fig. 157). The message is still bad, but the drawing is amusing. The mood of the country and the cartoonists had changed.

Roosevelt's efforts toward recovery were only partially successful, but the new federal programs had surmounted the national emergency. Unemployment was still high, farmers still ridded themselves of surplus crops for a government stipend, and the National Recovery Administration (NRA) had proved itself incapable of bringing order out of the chaos of business before the Supreme Court declared it unconstitutional. The "pump-priming" monies spent on public programs were not enough to have any long-range effect on the economy (fig. 156). The situation undoubtedly reminded many people of the well-known Rube Goldberg's cartoons (fig. 173)—in an effort to provide work, raise prices, and feed starving people, the government instituted a program whereby crops were destroyed, unemployed workers were put on the public payroll, and government spending increased. "Do it the hard way," Goldberg advised, as many conservatives thought his convoluted cartoons better designed than Roosevelt's economic measures.

Yet the New Deal had made substantial contributions to the welfare of the country. The Tennessee Valley Authority constituted a successful new approach to flood control and power production (fig. 198). Legislation now guaranteed labor's right to collective bargaining, a minimum wage, and an insurance and retirement program (fig. 154). The cultural life of the country received a boost when the Works Progress Administration undertook the Federal Writers, Arts, and Theater projects (fig. 166). Talented writers, painters, and dancers, now able to exercise their talents in return for a living wage, looked to America as inspiration for creative works and established world-wide reputations reversing the trend that had depicted America as an industrial giant and a mental pygmy (fig. 167).

The AAA and the NRA had served well, but they had not broken the back of the Depression, and the Supreme Court had declared them unconstitutional. Meanwhile, criticism mounted (fig. 163). Father Charles Coughlin, the outspoken radio priest from Detroit, demanded in his weekly broadcasts that the government inflate the currency to put more money in circulation. Dr. Francis Townsend and Senator Huey P. Long (the "Kingfish," as he called himself after the famous character on the *Amos 'n'*

Andy radio show) proposed various sorts of "share-the-wealth" programs (fig. 159), and Minnesota Governor Floyd Olson urged nationalization of key industries. The seven and one-half million people still out of work listened for the President's response.

Roosevelt took issues away from his opponents by moving farther to the left himself (fig. 160). He had rejected nationalization of the banks in 1933, but now he classed "business and financial monopoly, speculation, reckless banking, class antagonism, sectionalism, [and] war profiteering" as "old enemies of peace." "They had begun to consider the government of the United States as a mere appendage to their own affairs," he declared. "They are unanimous in their hatred for me—and I welcome their hatred."[7] Roosevelt's overwhelming reelection in 1936, then, was not the result of citizens returning votes for the few welfare dollars they had received, but rather was the reaction to a renewed belief that government might now provide the security and stability that had appeared so precarious only four years before (fig. 162). "Henceforth Democracy has its chief!" said *Paris-Soir*.[8]

Although the level of production had almost returned to the 1929 totals by 1937, Roosevelt realized that he had to take further steps to provide jobs for the millions still unemployed. He also realized, as a result of Supreme Court decisions in the NRA and AAA cases, that much of his program might be in danger of being declared unconstitutional. Taking steps to insure the safety of future legislation and to gain a measure of revenge on the old conservatives on the Court, Roosevelt unveiled his "court packing" plan that would permit the justices to retire at age seventy, but would add a new member (up to a maximum of fifteen) to the Court for every justice who did not retire at age seventy. The plan was widely regarded as a bluff and cartoonist C. K. Berryman expressed much of America's cynicism at the plan for an enlarged Supreme Court (fig. 163). But Roosevelt was serious and abandoned his idea only after conservative Judge Willis Van Devanter, who had been on the bench since 1911, announced his retirement. Other resignations followed, and Roosevelt was able to appoint four New Deal justices from 1937 to 1939.

Despite the continuing crisis at home, Roosevelt's time was gradually consumed by foreign affairs. Joseph Stalin was firmly entrenched in a Russia that President Roosevelt had formally recognized in 1933. Adolf Hitler (fig. 158) had systematically squelched democracy in Germany, and Italian dictator Benito Mussolini had invaded and occupied Ethopia in 1935 (fig. 159). The complexion of democratic Europe had changed radically. Aware of the growing militarism on the continent, Congress passed a series of "neutrality" acts permitting embargo of arms, prohibiting loans to belligerents, and (remembering the *Lusitania*) forbidding American citizens from traveling on ships of belligerents. "In times of so-called peace," said Roosevelt in 1937, "ships are being attacked and sunk by submarines without cause or notice. Nations are fomenting and taking sides . . . . Let no one imagine that America will escape . . . ."[9]

America did not take such warnings seriously. Men were still struggling to feed their families while European militarism was half a world away. "We shun political commitments which might entangle us in foreign wars," said the President. "We avoid connection with the political activities of the League of Nations . . . . We are not isolationists except insofar as we seek to isolate ourselves completely from war."[10] In this the nation supported Roosevelt; public opinon would not have permitted him to become involved. Isolationist sentiment was so strong that when a Japanese airplane intentionally sank a United States gunboat in Chinese waters in 1937, Congress almost passed the Ludlow Amendment that would have required a public referendum before Congress could declare war.

The inevitable conflict began when Germany blitzed hapless Poland on September 1, 1939. As Britain and France declared war on Germany, the United States announced its neutrality. But it was a pro-Allied neutrality based on Roosevelt's sure knowledge that if Germany controlled the eastern Atlantic and Japan the western Pacific, the United States would be isolated in world trade, subject to German and Japanese terms, and victim to their propaganda and sabotage at home. "We must be the great arsenal of democracy," Roosevelt told a 1940 audience as America armed itself (fig. 176). Goods were shipped to Britain on American vessels. Roosevelt allowed the Navy to help British ships locate the dreaded German submarines and cooperated with Britain in a freeze of Japanese assets in American- and British-held territory. Hitler "has every excuse in the world to declare war on us now, if he were of a mind to," the Chief of United States Naval Operations penciled in his diary.[11]

After the fall of France most Americans agreed that the United States could not allow Germany to win all of Europe, but were not yet willing to enter the war. Roosevelt and his advisors decided that if Japan attacked the East Indies the United States would enter the war, even if public opinion did not support the decision. America thus moved toward war in the same wavering, uncertain fashion as in 1917.

Realizing that war with the United States was a certainty, Japanese planners decided to strike first, believing that a crippling blow would further demoralize the United States and perhaps keep it out of the war altogether. The December 7, 1941, air raid on Pearl Harbor could hardly have been more successful: eight battleships were destroyed or damaged, three light cruisers, four other vessels, and 188 airplanes were rendered inoperative. More than 3,000 casualties were reported. But the Japanese had misjudged the American mentality (fig. 179). Facing a nation that only the day before had been isolationist, fragmented politically, and economically destitute, President Roosevelt predicted that this day "will live in infamy." "Hostilities exist," he told the now-united nation. "There is no blinking at the fact that our people, our territory and our interests are in grave danger. With confidence in our armed forces—with the unbounded determination of our people—we will gain the inevitable triumph—so help us God."[12]

All American industrial might was suddenly directed toward war. Never before had the United States so devoted all its productive capacity toward one goal. With fourteen million of its most able citizens serving in the armed forces, American factories still debouched more than ninety billions of dollars worth of war materials and supplies each year. The United States built the strongest army, navy, and air force the world has known, meanwhile increasing the standard of living and the level of consumption at home—an unprecedented feat (fig. 181). It is an accepted economic fact that production and employment are highest during wartime, but no nation had ever been able to produce as much.

American performance and ingenuity in the field matched the production at home. American commanders showed remarkable ability, their tactics consisting primarily of accumulating so many weapons and supplies for an offensive that the human risk was minimal (fig. 182). War had become basically an engineering problem. Over 400,000 Americans died during the war—a tragic figure—but more had perished during the Civil War almost 100 years before.

The most dramatic scientific breakthrough of the war was the successful construction of the atomic bomb. German scientists at work on nuclear fission for several years had proved that atoms of uranium when bombarded with neutrons "split" into atoms of other elements—a revolutionary discovery since it was widely assumed that elements were truly the lowest common denominator of matter and that an atom was its smallest part. If neutrons produced by splitting the uranium atom could be controlled and made to split still more atoms, a chain reaction would be set off, producing, according to Albert Einstein's famous formula ($E=mc^2$), an unprecedented amount of energy. (The energy released from the mass would be multiplied by the speed of light squared!)

The large number of German scientists who had fled or had been deported because they were "non-Aryan" pooled their discoveries with the superior laboratories and equipment of the Americans (fig. 178). Their new studies virtually convinced them that they could produce a bomb of untold power, and that the Germans were at least two years ahead of them in research. After Albert Einstein explained to President Roosevelt the possibilities and the potential assumed to be already in the hands of the Germans in 1939, the President established a committee on uranium.

After Pearl Harbor the government poured millions of dollars more into atomic research without being sure of the best method of splitting the atom (there were five known) or even if a bomb definitely could be produced. But in December, 1942, the Italian political refugee Enrico Fermi, working in a transformed squash court under the stands of Stagg Field at the University of Chicago, proved the neutrons could be controlled and a chain reaction sustained. It was a daring experiment in the midst of an urban center unaware of the potential danger, but from that point on scientists were confident that they could produce a bomb (fig. 186).

As the war in Europe drew to a close and the scientists realized that Germany was not going to develop the bomb, many of them became concerned about how it would be used. "This may sound fantastic," refugee scientist James Franck said in a statement to the President's committee, "but in nuclear weapons we have something entirely new in order of magnitude of destructive power, and if we want to capitalize fully on the advantage their possession gives us, we must use new and imaginative methods."[13] Franck and his colleagues wanted a demonstration of the bomb before representatives of the newly-organized United Nations; if the Japanese did not surrender then, perhaps it could be used against them. A majority of the atomic scientists opposed its surprise use.

With President Roosevelt's death in April, 1945, Harry S Truman inherited the awesome decision. Perhaps the most compelling reason to use the bomb against Japan was not to shorten the war and save American lives, as some have insisted, but rather to demonstrate to the Soviet Union that America was in possession of a dramatically new weapon capable of unprecedented destruction. Secretary of State James Byrnes favored this view and worried only how to justify such an expenditure before Congress. Truman gave the order to proceed, although as Alice Kimball Smith, a personal friend of many of the scientists, later observed, "To have called a halt, contrary to the advice of his most trusted associates, would have required an almost inconceivable exercise of individual initiative."[14] The power of a new age was unleashed on the Japanese cities of Hiroshima and Nagasaki in August, 1945 (fig. 184). Many of the German scientists had worked on the bomb until Hitler's defeat, then worried about the broader implications of their discovery. It was the Japanese fate, said one, to have to take Hitler's medicine (fig. 185).

The United States undoubtedly needed such an advantage because diplomatic blunders had cost the Allies strategic territory. One of the greatest tragedies, although it is far from certain that anything short of full-scale intervention would have turned the tide, was the handling of the Chinese situation (fig. 175). Because China was a potentially strong ally against Japan (fig. 180), American military advisors first wanted to take over Chiang Kai-shek's Nationalist army. When he refused, they urged him to form a coalition government with Mao Tse-Tung and the Communists. Chiang rejected the suggestion and the Americans withdrew, leaving him to eventual defeat and banishment to the offshore island of Formosa. The Communists, who had strong Soviet ties, occupied the Mainland. There was much recrimination and analysis after the Communist victory, but it soon became clear that Mao's forces were much stronger and Chiang's forces much weaker than American military strategists had estimated. No amount of diplomacy could have saved the Mainland for Chiang.

At the end of the war, two strong armies opposed each other in Europe and Asia. Russia had traditionally occupied territory along a line extending from the eastern Baltic Sea to the Black Sea. From time to time it also had controlled the helpless buffer states of Eastern Europe, but Germany had always been the balancing power. Now, the Russians occupied all the buffer states: Czechoslovakia, Yugoslavia, Hungary, part of Austria, and Germany to a line 100 miles west of Berlin. The rest of Europe lay prostrate, the American Army the only force standing between the Red Army and the English Channel. In Asia only American-occupied Japan and the Philippines challenged the expansion of the Chinese and Russians. At a time when monumental decisions were necessary, wrote British Prime Minister Winston Churchill, "The indispensable political direction was lacking. . . . The United States stood on the scene of victory, master of world fortunes, but without a true and coherent design."[15]

President Truman had presided as the world entered a new age. Now he watched in Fulton, Missouri, as Churchill defined the first epoch of the new age. "A shadow has fallen upon the scenes so lately lighted by the Allied victory," said the recently-retired Prime Minister. "From Stettin in the Baltic to Trieste in the Adriatic, an iron curtain has descended across the Continent. Behind that line lie all the capitals of the ancient states of Central and Eastern Europe. Warsaw, Berlin, Prague, Vienna, Budapest, Belgrade, Bucharest and Sofia, all these famous cities and the populations around them lie in what I must call the Soviet sphere, and all are subject in one form or another, not only to the Soviet influence but to a very high and, in many cases, increasing measure of control from Moscow. . . . Whatever conclusions may be drawn from these facts—and facts they are—this is certainly not the Liberated Europe we fought to build up. Nor is it one which contains the essentials of permanent peace."[16] The *Iron Curtain*—the name stuck. The Cold War had begun.

VII

1946–1975

THE COLD WAR and the continual threat of global annihilation were unfamiliar to Americans returning from the war convinced that they had justly defeated the enemy once and for all. They would have agreed with William Jennings Bryan that "destiny . . . is a matter of choice; it is not a thing to be waited for."[1] These Americans had chosen their destiny after being irrevocably provoked by the Japanese and they had won, but for the first time in history the absolute victor had achieved only an uneasy standoff in which the welfare of the country was more precarious than ever, as Daniel Robert Fitzpatrick, cartoonist for the St. Louis *Post-Dispatch*, depicted with his drawing of the awesomeness of atomic power (fig. 186).

Disillusionment and the new awareness had not come immediately; President Roosevelt had been optimistic about the post-war era and told the American people that his friendship with Joseph Stalin of the Soviet Union was built on a firm understanding and common goals. Even before Pearl Harbor a former American ambassador had pointed out that the Russians were fighting for a cause "vital to our security," and in 1943 *Time* magazine named Joseph Stalin, the Soviet dictator, "Man of the Year" as the Russians blunted the German eastward advance and began the long counterattack.[2]

The first disenchantment came when it became apparent that the Soviets would not live up to the terms of the Yalta agreement. Stalin, Roosevelt, and British Prime Minister Winston Churchill had agreed in February, 1945, that Eastern Poland would be awarded to Russia in return for Russia's entry into the Japanese war, but that free elections would be held throughout Poland. Large Polish communities in the United States and the Polish government-in-exile in London required that Roosevelt and Churchill concern themselves with Poland, and Poland, the first country to suffer the Nazi blitz, had become the symbol of liberty and determination throughout the West. "The Poles will have their future in their own hands, with the single limitation that they must honestly follow . . . a policy friendly to Russia," concluded Churchill in one of his more credulous moments. "This is surely reasonable."[3]

But Stalin was not that "reasonable." He did not understand the Americans' concern over Poland, a country not at all strategic to their defense. He had never concealed his goal of self-defensive expansion after the war and surely did not intend to permit free elections. In April a dying Roosevelt wrote Stalin of his "bitter resentment" over the dictator's "discouraging lack of application" of the agreements made at Yalta (fig. 188). In the months following Roosevelt's death, the new American President Harry S Truman (fig. 187) was only slowly disabused of his concept of Russia as the grand ally. Truman desperately chided Foreign Minister Vyacheslav Molotov, demanding that Stalin "carry out that [Yalta] agreement in accordance with his word." Finally realizing that the Russians did not intend to keep their promises, Truman pleaded for understanding: "But you *made* these agreements, didn't you? You *signed* them: Why on earth don't you *keep* them?" Molotov knew the American President had no alternative but to go to war, a decision neither he nor the American people were prepared to make in 1946. "If I had known then what I know now," Truman later remarked, "I would have ordered the troops to the western boundaries of Russia."[4] Even the atomic bomb had not deterred Stalin's effort to fill the power vacuum in Europe, a course so obvious that Alexis de Tocqueville had predicted as early as 1835 that although the United States and Russia were "different and their paths diverse . . . each seems called by some secret design of Providence one day to hold in its hands the destinies of half of the world."[5]

Awareness of the role America would be forced to play in post-war Europe came even more slowly, although before the war ended Stalin had told Harry L. Hopkins, Roosevelt's energetic diplomatic aide, that the United States "was a world power and would have to accept world interests" whether it "wished it or not." Europe was a "rubble-heap" of destroyed factories and farms, disrupted economy, and maimed and wounded people, said Churchill.[6] The once-great colonial powers had descended to second-rate and could no longer dominate or aid the rest of the world, or even protect themselves if the Red Army chose to march to the English Channel. Early in 1947 the British government warned President Truman that because of economic difficulty it could no longer support the Greek government against Communist rebels aided by the Moscow-backed regimes in Yugoslavia, Albania, and Bulgaria.

Truman realized that the Greek government could survive only with outside aid and that American interests were now unwittingly interwoven with European security. But the public would have to be educated. Coming on the heels of complete victory in Europe and the Pacific with abundant assistance from the Soviet Union, tired veterans would not be happy to learn that the one-time ally was now the enemy and that another European war threatened. Most of the Central European countries had already fallen to the Communists and Greece and Turkey appeared to be next, but isolationist Senator Robert Taft of Ohio, a likely candidate for the Republican presidential nomination in the upcoming election, would not be easily swayed. He wanted a return to the pre-war diplomatic simplicity which did not compel the United States to interfere in the affairs of other countries. Secretary of Agriculture Henry Wallace, on the other hand, counted the Soviet Union a genuine friend of America and did not want to damage that relationship.

Yet intervention was necessary to prevent further aggression. "Mr. President," advised Senator Arthur H. Vandenberg of Michigan, a veteran in dealing with the Soviets, "if that's what you want, there's only one way to get it. That is to make a personal appearance before Congress and scare hell out of the country." Meanwhile, the country was getting a good look at the new Soviet policy in action. Early in March the Russians rejected the American plan for sharing its atomic secrets, then demanded that the United States unilaterally destroy all its atomic bombs. Late in April Hungary succumbed to a Communist revolution. "I believe that it must be the policy of the United States to support free peoples who are resisting attempted subjugation by armed minorities or by outside pressure," President Truman told Congress on May 12.[7] Impressed with the ideological justification, Congress voted $400 millions to aid Greece and Turkey in their struggle. The Truman Doctrine, or the policy of containment, has dominated American foreign policy since that day.

In June Secretary of State George C. Marshall followed with a suggestion for restoring any European nation that would develop a plan and assist in its own recovery, even Russia itself. "The initiative . . . must come from Europe," he told a Harvard commencement audience. "The program should be a joint one, agreed to by a number, if not all, of the European nations." Poland and Czechoslovakia quickly accepted Marshall's proposal, but the Soviet Union forced them to withdraw from participation. Sixteen nations sent representatives to Paris to plan for their recovery, and Congress, overcoming initial objections in face of public opinion that now favored resistance to Communism, voted $13 billions for what was now called the Marshall Plan. Still loyal to the Soviet Union, Henry Wallace called it the "Martial Plan." "This is the turning point," said British Foreign Secretary Ernest Bevin, as yet another Communist *coup* pulled Czechoslovakia firmly into the Soviet sphere.[8]

Then American taxpayers received what was probably the rudest shock of all. The Truman Doctrine and the Marshall Plan were not enough; they were only the first steps. A series of crises soon proved that post-war America would have to be ever vigilant, ever mindful of the Communist threat around the world, and ever ready with aid. Hoping to assist European economic recovery, Britain, France, and the United States replaced Russian currency with their own in their three sectors of the occupied city of Berlin, which lay deep in the Russian zone of East Germany. The Soviet response was to shut off all land access to the city on June 19, 1948, threatening the more than two million Berliners with starvation and surrender to the Russians. But President Truman decided, in spite of pessimistic predictions from his Air Force advisors, to supply the city by air. Soon the American and British fliers were delivering 5,000 tons of supplies per day to the beleaguered city.

In addition to the foreign threats, there appeared to be serious security problems at home. In late 1948 Alger Hiss, a bright, young member of the Department of State, was accused of being an ex-Communist and was convicted of perjury in 1950. Between his indictment and conviction, President Truman announced that Russia had exploded its first atomic bomb. Had Hiss and others like him given our secrets to the Russians? The British supplied a partial answer in February, 1950, by announcing that Dr. Klaus Fuchs, an atomic scientist who had worked for both the Americans and the British, had admitted turning over top secret documents to the Russians. Not realizing that there were few atomic secrets to share and that the crucial factor in making a bomb is sophisticated technology and good equipment, Americans were incensed. In the ensuing investigation several Americans who had cooperated with Fuchs were arrested; Julius and Ethel Rosenberg were finally executed for their alleged part in the espionage.

Nor was the Asian front safe. The Chinese Nationalist government, long thought to be a powerful Asian ally of the United States, fled to the island of Formosa in the wake of the Communist takeover of the mainland in December, 1949, and in June, 1950, North Korean Communists crossed the thirty-eighth parallel and invaded South Korea, a government supported by the United States and the newly-founded United Nations.

The nation reeled from this series of confidence-shattering blows. Communist spies within, Communist aggression in Europe and Asia, and a government whose efforts to curb the menace were apparently ineffective. How had the most powerful nation on earth, the sole possessor of the doomsday weapon in 1945, come to this in 1950? Only one man was brash enough to supply simplistic answers. Joseph McCarthy, Republican senator from Wisconsin, made a speech to the Wheeling, West Virginia, Women's Republican Club in February (fig. 192). We were not suffering from weakness, McCarthy told the women. We were suffering from "the traitorous actions of those who have been treated so well by this nation"—men like Alger Hiss in the State Department and scientist Fuchs. Money was pouring into the bottomless pit of Europe, a result of the Marshall Plan; China had been "lost" after assistance totaling more than $3 billions, and now America had entered into an "entangling alliance" (the North Atlantic Treaty Organization, July 21, 1949) for the first time in history. Then, waving a piece of paper in his hand, McCarthy claimed to have the names of dozens of "card-carrying" members of the Communist Party who were at that moment employed by the State Department. "In my opinion the State Department . . . is thoroughly infested with Communists," he charged.[9] Actually he waved a letter from Secretary of State Byrnes to a congressman, making no mention of Communists, but McCarthy had found an insecure America willing to listen to his bombast. Within weeks he was the most talked-of senator in Washington.

For almost four years McCarthy virtually terrorized members of the Senate, Cabinet officers, and bureaucrats throughout the government (fig. 194). When a Senate committee chaired by Millard Tydings of Maryland found McCarthy's charges groundless, McCarthy "invaded" Maryland and helped defeat Tydings, who had seemed assured of reelection until McCarthy's intervention. When President Truman recalled General Douglas McArthur from Korea because of serious indiscretions, McCarthy ardently supported the General, then attacked Secretary of State Marshall for being a part of the Communist conspiracy. In February, 1953, he attacked the United States Information Agency, demanding that books by certain authors not be circulated in their overseas libraries, and some branches of the agency actually conducted book-burnings hoping that the senatorial tyrant would be placated. Then McCarthy turned his venom on the Army, claiming that a certain dentist, already honorably discharged, was a Communist. The Army responded that McCarthy had sought preferential treatment for one of his assistants who had been drafted, and the ensuing hearings were televised. When the nation saw the Senator try to discredit the Army's attorney by charging that a young member of the attorney's firm was a Communist, public opinion swiftly turned against him. The Senate ended his influence a few months later by voting to censure him, only the fourth senator to be censured in 167 years. Nor was the country comforted when the famous FBI counterspy, Herbert Philbrick, revealed at a press conference that the Communists felt that McCarthy had helped them considerably by undermining Americans' confidence in their government.

An advocate of a passive presidency that only carried out Congressional laws, newly-elected Dwight D. Eisenhower hoped to preside over peaceful years during which America restored its calm and confidence (fig. 195). It was his misfortune to be caught in an apparently never-ending arms race. Despite warnings of scientists as to the possible effects, President Truman had ordered in 1950 that work continue on the "so-called hydrogen or super-bomb" (fig. 189). Dr. Albert Einstein had replied that "General annihilation beckons," but the super-bomb had been developed before Eisenhower took office and became the foundation of his foreign policy. When the Russians announced that they, too, possessed the hydrogen bomb less than a year later, Eisenhower remarked that there was now "no real alternative to peace"[10] (fig. 202). Critics immediately questioned Secretary of State John Foster Dulles' policy of "massive retaliation." By sponsoring regional treaty organizations like NATO and by stockpiling nuclear bombs, Dulles hoped to control the small, "brushfire" wars such as the Korean conflict. Dubbed "brinkmanship" by its opponents, Dulles' policy called for massive retaliation against Moscow and Peking if either attempted to spread its influence by violent means. This would be a single and much cheaper deterrent in the long run than a massive defense mechanism spread around the world, he argued, and it would prevent the small conflicts that had proved so costly.

The problem, of course, was that both the United States and Russia had more than enough bombs to destroy the world, and neither would be able to use its atomic weaponry without provoking massive retaliation from the other (fig. 196). No President would start a nuclear war to prevent aggression against a non-strategic country, therefore Eisenhower was left without an alternative on several occasions. When the French were driven out of Vietnam in 1954, Eisenhower not only refused to attack Peking and Moscow, which the policy of massive retaliation would have dictated, he refused to do anything. When Russian tanks rolled into Budapest to quell the October, 1956, revolt, Eisenhower stood by powerless, unwilling to unleash a nuclear attack to free the Hungarian state from the Communist bloc despite pleas from several Hungarian officials for assistance. And when Egypt seized the Suez Canal, provoking an Israeli-British-

French invasion, Eisenhower demanded that they withdraw and leave the canal to the Egyptians. Thus the United States found itself in a costly arms race with the Soviet Union—hydrogen and atomic bombs, missiles, nuclear submarines, aircraft carriers, and long-range bombers—all directed toward a deterrent of doomsday proportions. The brushfire wars that Dulles had hoped to contain continued, forcing the nation to develop that capability too. Americans even became aware of Russia's superior rocket power when the Soviets launched the first unmanned satellite in 1957 (fig. 201).

Even then this fantastic, numbing string of crises did not stop. When Cuban dictator Fulgencio Batista fled leaving the country in the hands of Dr. Fidel Castro in 1959, Eisenhower immediately recognized the new regime, but Castro bitterly denounced the United States, nationalized American businesses, and established close ties with the Russians. A blundering 1962 invasion attempt—the Bay of Pigs (fig. 211)—failed, and Russia began sending medium-range nuclear missiles to the island. "The Americans had surrounded our country with military bases and threatened us with nuclear weapons," Soviet Premier Nikita Khrushchev later wrote in his memoirs, "and now they would learn just what it feels like to have enemy missiles pointing at you; we'd be doing nothing more than giving them a little of their own medicine."[11] President John F. Kennedy mobilized the National Guard and blockaded Cuba (fig. 212). For a few brief moments the world teetered on the "abyss of nuclear destruction and the end of mankind," wrote Attorney General Robert Kennedy.[12] The crisis defused just as quickly. When President Kennedy assured the Soviets that the United States would not invade Cuba, Khrushchev ordered the missiles removed.

Americans who sighed with relief at the termination of the "missile crisis" did not know that even then President Kennedy was considering sending more Americans to assist the South Vietnamese in "their war" (fig. 233). France and Britain had tried to solve the Vietnamese situation with the Geneva Agreement of 1954, which promised free elections in South Vietnam in 1956, but when President Ngo Dinh Diem refused to permit the elections the Communist rebels resumed their activity. By 1961 there were some 3,200 Americans in Vietnam as military advisors. That number increased to 16,000 by the end of 1963 and to more than 184,000 in another year. Meanwhile, President Lyndon B. Johnson had demanded and gotten a "blank check"—the Gulf of Tonkin resolution—from the Congress after North Vietnamese gunboats allegedly attacked American destroyers in international waters. Authorized to "repel any armed attack against the forces of the United States and to prevent further aggression," Johnson upped the commitment (fig. 225). More than 385,000 Americans battled Communist troops throughout South Vietnam by the end of 1965, more than 530,000 by 1969. Of course, Red China and Russia had increased their aid to North Vietnam, and the United States found itself in a full-scale conventional war in Vietnam—the dreaded land war in Asia that previous Presidents had warned against and that Johnson had promised to avoid during his 1964 campaign (fig. 226). Raw nerves were worn further when, at the height of the conflict, North Koreans seized the American spyship, USS *Pueblo*, threatening to renew the Korean conflict.

The Vietnamese intervention did not end until January, 1973, when President Richard Nixon's foreign affairs advisor, Dr. Henry Kissinger, reached agreement with North Vietnam's Le Duc Tho that established a cease-fire in Vietnam and allowed the United States to withdraw its troops (fig. 240). More explosives had been dropped on Vietnam between 1964 and 1968 than on Germany and Japan during all World War II. More than 46,000 Americans had died by 1973, and the war cost some $20 billions per year for the United States alone. Americans, meanwhile, were treated to the spectacles of a massacre of South Vietnamese civilians by American troops at My Lai, "tiger cage" prisons of South Vietnam, and the brutal television documentaries that brought this war closer to the American public than any other war. Kissinger and Le Duc Tho received the Nobel Peace Prize for their efforts, but the war was not finished. It had only stalled.

President Johnson tried to deal with difficult domestic crises simultaneously. In the midst of a massive civil rights movement, riots broke out on an unprecedented scale (fig. 223) in Los Angeles, Newark, Detroit—riots inspired by frustration and aimed toward nothing, riots triggered in one case by a white policeman stopping a black man for a traffic violation, in another case by the shocking assassination of civil rights leader Dr. Martin Luther King (fig. 216). As the nation began to adjust to another crisis, a short supply of oil, the greatest political scandal in the nation's history was unveiled before a disbelieving public (fig. 242).

Watergate, soon to become the code word for any kind of government bungling or corruption, began in 1972 with the "White House plumbers" burglary of the Democratic Party Headquarters in the Watergate apartment complex in Washington, D. C. (fig. 245). By the end of 1974 three cabinet officers, Nixon's two closest advisors, and a number of lesser officials including the acting head of the FBI had been convicted of perjury or obstructing justice or discredited, and Nixon himself had resigned. In an unrelated incident, Vice-President Spiro Agnew (fig. 234), the most outspoken law and order advocate with the possible exception of Alabama Governor George Wallace (fig. 238), pleaded guilty to income tax evasion and accepted a light sentence in exchange for his resignation. The "credibility gap" of the Johnson-Nixon years widened to include government officials on all levels—county, city, state, and federal—as Watergate dumbfounded even the most cynical observer. All government agencies, even prosecution of the Vietnam war, were affected by the backlash of this "third-rate burglary" that escalated into the greatest political scandal this country has known (figs. 245, 246, 247, 248, 249).

The public had not recovered from these unprecedented events when the Watergate-related investigations revealed many other "incidents." The giant International Telephone and Telegraph Company admitted giving Nixon's reelection campaign fund $400,000 in return for less vigorous prosecution in an antitrust case, and Attorney General Richard Kleindienst was convicted of perjury for testifying that Nixon had not pressured him to discontinue his ITT investigation. Several major airline companies confessed that they, too, had illegally contributed to the campaign fund and accepted fines. President Nixon's personal lawyer was convicted of forging the date on the document transferring Nixon's Vice-Presidential papers to the National Archives so Nixon could qualify for a huge tax deduction (Congress having since outlawed such deductions). Nixon then owed more than $500,000 in back taxes and interest (fig. 244).

Gerald Ford of Michigan, the man Nixon had appointed to replace Agnew according to the new twenty-fifth amendment, became President August 9, 1974 (fig. 250). One of his first acts was to grant Nixon a complete pardon, saying that the country had to be unified to face the important matters of the future. As President Ford struggled with an economy suffering from double-digit inflation (figs. 203, 204), rising health care costs, and increasing environmental problems (fig. 259), it became his duty to preside over the first American defeat in war—the fall of South Vietnam. Despite the 1973 agreement in Paris, both sides had violated the cease-fire, and President Nixon would have resumed bombing North Vietnam had he not been so involved in Watergate that he did not want to risk additional criticism. The Communist Viet Cong and North Vietnamese troops gradually tightened the circle around Saigon. When Congress turned down the Ford administration request for $722 millions in early 1975, there seemed no way that the South could hold out. President Ford brought American participation to a halt just days before the final collapse, telling a Tulane University audience that recriminations must cease. The war, he said, is "finished—as far as America is concerned."[13] Only Ford's dramatic rescue of the crewmen of the American merchant ship *Mayaguez*, captured by Cambodian gunboats, salvaged respect for proud Americans unused to losing a war.

The era from World War II until the present has been marked by the perpetual instant, the long-awaited instant that might bring holocaust, the instant captured on film that is preserved forever, the instant (as in the splitting of the atom) that seems to open eternal, infinite possibilities. Such discoveries obviously affect the work of sensitive artists. Fitzpatrick caricatured the threat (fig. 186), while Don Hesse captured the feeling of an endless quest for the ultimate energy (fig. 189); Garrett Price pictured the frustration of many Americans in dealing with modernism (fig. 218), and Benny Goodman (fig. 207) and Louis Armstrong (fig. 219) represent the return of the "good old days." The American spirit was captured by beatniks (fig. 206), hippies, and the apparently overwhelming desire to return to nature in an urban society—organic foods, the youth cult (figs. 229, 257), drug addiction (fig. 256), protection of the environment (figs. 259, 260): all seem to represent fairly simple desires twisted by a modern society.

The painter Jackson Pollock could have spoken for many of his fellow artists in 1950 when he pointed out that, "The modern painter cannot express this age, the airplane, the atom bomb, the radio, in the old forms of the renaissance or any other past culture." The search for new media has given us the photographic composition of Mark Podwall's Statue of Liberty (fig. 261) and Marisol's *LBJ* (fig. 220). The grind of the daily newspaper, meanwhile, has turned up numerous excellent draftsmen who bring the traditional talents of an artist to cartoons: Pat Oliphant (fig. 249), Draper Hill (fig. 245), and Paul Szep (fig. 231) are among the outstanding penmen publishing in daily newspapers, while Leslie Illingworth and David Levine display their unusually good drawing techniques and sharp wit in several newspapers and magazines. Perhaps John Cayea's *Eagle* is the most poignant, the drawing best capable of providing an icon for the 1970s (fig. 263).

Many questions remain unanswered as this great experiment moves toward its 200th birthday—almost imponderable questions that we might have turned away from because we feared the answer. What kind of balance will ultimately be achieved between personal freedom and modern society? Can a truly heterogeneous society, including radicals who would fight violently for their goals, survive under a Constitution intended for a homogeneous nation that originally worshipped the same God, was basically white, and was committed to peaceful settlement of differences? This potential was greatly acerbated with public knowledge that even a brilliant student could produce an atomic bomb.

Although these questions remain unresolved, the peaceful, democratic principles established by the founding fathers still survive. Cayea personifies in his strong drawing the confidence that the entire nation felt as the government peacefully changed hands in 1974. Few citizens even considered the possibility of armed resistance. After a long and eventful life, Thomas Jefferson concluded that "we can no longer say there is nothing new under the sun, for this whole chapter in the history of man is new." The "experiment of changing the constitution by assembling the wise men of the state, instead of assembling armies, will be worth as much to the world as the former examples we have given it." Benjamin Franklin was more modest: "We are making Experiments," he wrote a friend in 1786, but "we are . . . in the right Road of Improvement."[14]

RON TYLER
Curator of History
Amon Carter Museum

NOTES

I

[1]Arthur M. Schlesinger, *The Birth of the Nation* (New York: Alfred A. Knopf, 1969), 227.

[2]Henry Steel Commager, *Jefferson, Nationalism, and the Enlightenment* (New York: George Braziller, 1975), 12–13.

[3]Ibid., 159.

[4]Daniel J. Boorstin, *The Americans: The National Experience* (New York: Random House, 1965), 391.

[5]Dumas Malone, *Jefferson the Virginian*, Vol. 1 of *Jefferson and His Time* (5 vols.; Boston: Little, Brown and Company, 1948–1974), 388.

[6]Schlesinger, *Birth of the Nation*, 227.

[7]James Thomas Flexner, *Washington, the Indispensable Man* (Boston: Little, Brown and Company, 1974), 74.

[8]Harvey Wish, *Society and Thought in America* (2 vols.; New York: David McKay Company, Inc., 1950), I, 200; Adams to Jefferson, Aug. 24, 1815, in John Adams, *Works*, ed. by Charles Francis Adams (10 vols.; Boston: Little, Brown and Company, 1850–1856), X, 172.

[9]Commager, *Jefferson*, 20.

[10]Henry Bamford Parkes, *The American Experience* (New York: Vintage Books, 1959), 39–40.

[11]Commager, *Jefferson*, 39, 53.

[12]Daniel J. Boorstin, *The Americans: The Colonial Experience* (New York: Random House, 1958), 283.

[13]Commager, *Jefferson*, 176, 179.

[14]Oscar Handlin, *The Americans: A New History of the People of the United States* (Boston: Atlantic Monthly Press, Little, Brown and Company, 1963), 150.

[15]Commager, *Jefferson*, 44.

[16]Adrienne Koch (ed.), *The American Enlightenment* (New York: George Braziller, 1965), 188.

[17]Commager, *Jefferson*, 30, 85.

[18]Ibid., 153–154.

II

[1]Commager, *Jefferson*, 161–162.

[2]John A. Garraty, *The American Nation: A History of the United States* (New York: Harper & Row and American Heritage Publishing Company, Inc., 1966), 202.

[3]Boorstin, *The National Experience*, 221.

[4]Parkes, *The American Experience*, 43, 190.

[5]Koch, *The American Enlightenment*, 484.

[6]Richard Hofstadter, William Miller, and Daniel Aaron, *The American Republic* (2 vols.; Englewood Cliffs, New Jersey: Prentice-Hall, Inc., 1959), I, 395.

[7]Commager, *Jefferson*, 161.

III

[1]Contrary to traditional writing, slavery was profitable and rapidly expanding—Texas was the fastest growing slave state in the South—at the time of the Civil War. These slightly startling findings are thoroughly documented in Robert William Fogel and Stanley L. Engerman, *Time on the Cross: The Economics of American Negro Slavery* (2 vols.; Boston: Little, Brown and Company, 1974), I, 4–6.

[2]Kenneth M. Stampp (ed.), *The Causes of the Civil War* (Englewood Cliffs, N. J.: Prentice-Hall, Inc., Spectrum Books, 1959), 132.

[3]Ibid., 107.

[4]Robert W. Johannsen (ed.), *The Lincoln-Douglas Debates* (New York: Oxford University Press, 1965), 254.

[5]Ibid., 249.

[6]Monroe Lee Billington, *The American South* (New York: Charles Scribner's Sons, 1971), 136.

[7]Mrs. David Winningham, "Sam Houston and Slavery," *Texana*, III (Summer, 1965), 93–104.

[8]Hofstadter, Miller, and Aaron, *American Republic*, II, 7.

IV

[1]Alistair Cooke, *Alistair Cooke's America* (New York: Alfred A. Knopf, 1974), 259.

[2]Daniel J. Boorstin, *The Americans: The Democratic Experience* (New York: Random House, 1973), 3, 5.

[3]Garraty, *The American Nation*, 475.

⁴Boorstin, *The Democratic Experience*, 418.

⁵Mark Twain, "The Temperance Crusade and Women's Rights," in Charles Neider (ed.), *The Complete Essays of Mark Twain* (Garden City, N. Y.: Doubleday, 1963), 667.

⁶Boorstin, *The Democratic Experience*, 419, 504.

⁷Ibid., 504, 515.

V

¹Hofstadter, Miller, and Aaron, *American Republic*, II, 357.

²Ibid., II, 442.

³William E. Leuchtenburg, *The Perils of Prosperity, 1914–32* (Chicago: University of Chicago Press, 1958), 269.

⁴Hofstadter, Miller, and Aaron, *American Republic*, II, 386.

⁵Leuchtenburg, *Perils of Prosperity*, 12–13.

⁶Ibid., 13–14.

⁷Ibid., 142.

⁸Wesley M. Burnside, *Maynard Dixon: Artist of the West* (Provo, Utah: Brigham Young University Press, 1974), 65.

⁹Leuchtenburg, *Perils of Prosperity*, 104–105.

¹⁰Ibid., 58.

¹¹Hofstadter, Miller, and Aaron, *American Republic*, II, 427.

¹²Leuchtenburg, *Perils of Prosperity*, 219.

¹³Samuel P. Hays, *The Response to Industrialism, 1885–1914* (Chicago: University of Chicago Press, 1957), 73.

¹⁴Leuchtenburg, *Perils of Prosperity*, 214–215.

¹⁵Harold C. Syrett (ed.), *American Historical Documents* (New York: Barnes & Noble, Inc., 1960), 357.

¹⁶Maldwyn Allen Jones, *American Immigration* (Chicago: University of Chicago Press, 1960), 265, 275–276.

¹⁷Leuchtenburg, *Perils of Prosperity*, 188–189; Hofstadter, Miller, and Aaron, *American Republic*, II, 442.

¹⁸Leuchtenburg, *Perils of Prosperity*, 137, 201–202.

¹⁹Cooke, *America*, 327.

VI

¹Syrett (ed.), *American Historical Documents*, 362–365.

²Arthur M. Schlesinger, Jr., *The Crisis of the Old Order, 1919–1933* (Boston: Houghton Mifflin Company, 1957), 1.

³Ibid., 3–4.

⁴Ibid., 5.

⁵Arthur M. Schlesinger, Jr., *The Coming of the New Deal* (Boston: Houghton Mifflin Company, 1958), 13.

⁶Ibid., 13.

⁷Frank Freidel, "The New Deal in Historical Perspective," in Barton J. Bernstein and Allen J. Matusow (eds.), *Twentieth-Century America: Recent Interpretations* (New York: Harcourt, Brace & World, Inc., 1969), 256.

⁸Arthur M. Schlesinger, Jr., *The Politics of Upheaval, 1935–1936* (Boston: Houghton Mifflin Company, 1960), 656.

⁹Syrett (ed.), *American Historical Documents*, 379.

¹⁰Frank Freidel, *America in the Twentieth Century* (2nd ed.; New York: Alfred A. Knopf, 1965), 371.

¹¹Ibid., 384.

¹²Syrett (ed.), *American Historical Documents*, 391–392.

¹³Boorstin, *The Democratic Experience*, 589.

¹⁴Ibid., 590.

¹⁵Winston S. Churchill, *Triumph and Tragedy* (Boston: Houghton Mifflin Company, 1953), 455.

¹⁶Louis J. Halle, *The Cold War as History* (New York: Harper & Row, Publishers, 1967), 103–104.

VII

¹Boorstin, *The Democratic Experience*, 557.

²John A. Garraty, *The American Nation: A History of the United States* (2 vols.; New York: Harper & Row, 1975), II, 775.

³Ibid., II, 778.

⁴Herbert Agar, *The Price of Power: America Since 1945* (Chicago: University of Chicago Press, 1957), 14–15, 17–18, 59.

⁵Alexis de Tocqueville, *Democracy in America*, ed. by J. P. Mayer and Max Lerner, trans. by George Lawrence (New York: Harper & Row, 1966), 379.

⁶Agar, *Price of Power*, 19, 72.

⁷Ibid., 71.

⁸Ibid., 74.

⁹Ibid., 108.

¹⁰Ibid., 52.

¹¹Edward Crankshaw (Intro.), *Khrushchev Remembers*, trans. and ed. by Strobe Talbott (Boston: Little, Brown and Company, 1970), 494.

¹²Robert F. Kennedy, *Thirteen Days: A Memoir of the Cuban Missile Crisis* (New York: W. W. Norton & Company, 1969), 23.

¹³*The New York Times*, April 27, 1975, Sec. 4, p. 1.

¹⁴Koch, *American Enlightenment*, 105, 342.

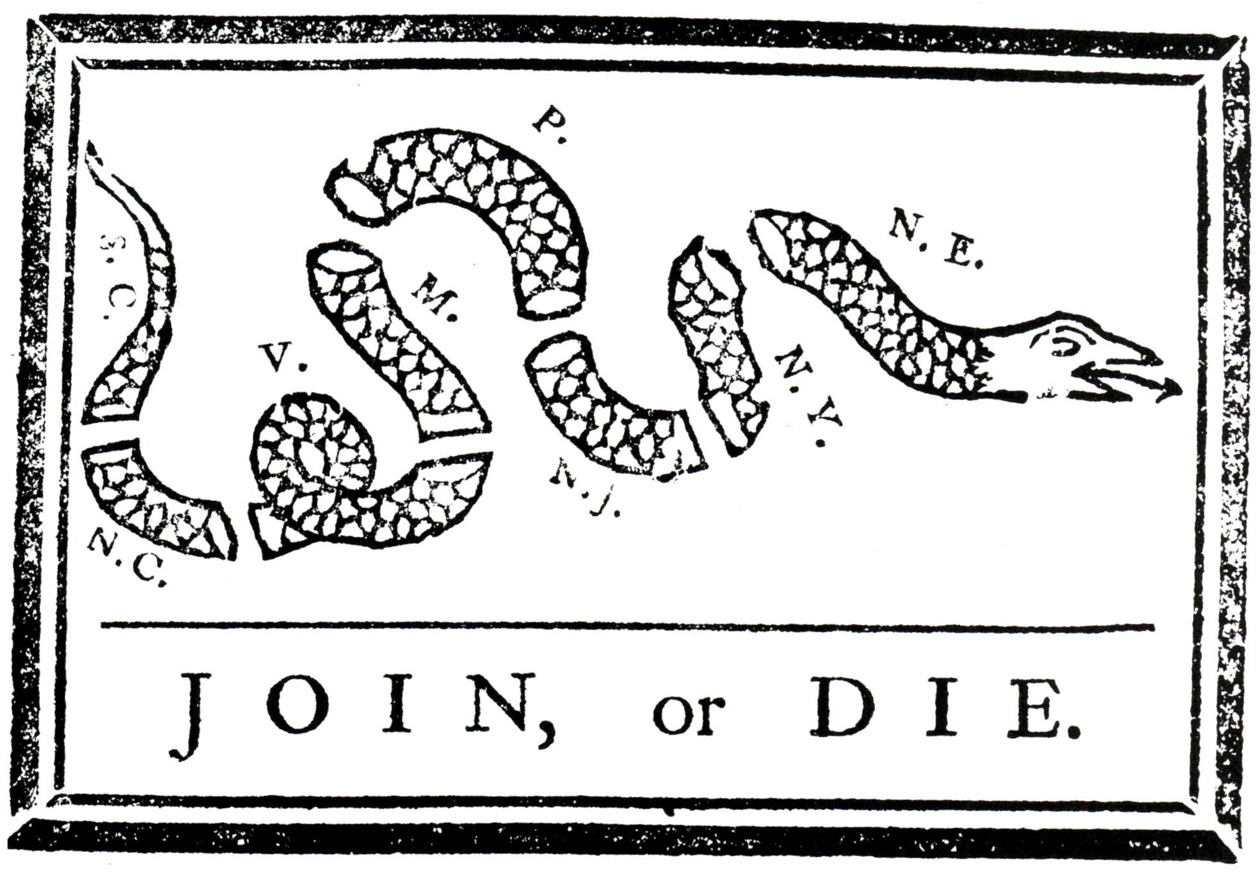

Fig. 1. *Join or Die*. Benjamin Franklin. May 9, 1754, in the *Pennsylvania Gazette*. Woodcut. 2 × 2 7/8 in. Courtesy Collections of The Library Company of Philadelphia.

As both French and Indian forces on the frontier threatened the colonies, and Britain appeared either incapable of or unwilling to help, Benjamin Franklin urged the delegates to the Albany Convention of 1754 to prepare for their own defense. In addition to some "short hints" for expansion, Franklin offered the delegates *Join or Die* to suggest forcefully that their destiny lay in their own hands. He urged an intercolonial council for defense with taxing powers, an army, fortifications, an expansion plan, and a Crown-appointed presiding officer. The individual colonies rejected his plan, but he believed until his death that its adoption would have prevented the Revolution. Widely thought to be the first cartoon appearing in an American newspaper, *Join or Die* was used again in 1765 (with Georgia added by Paul Revere) as Britain was trying to force the Stamp Act onto the colonists.

43

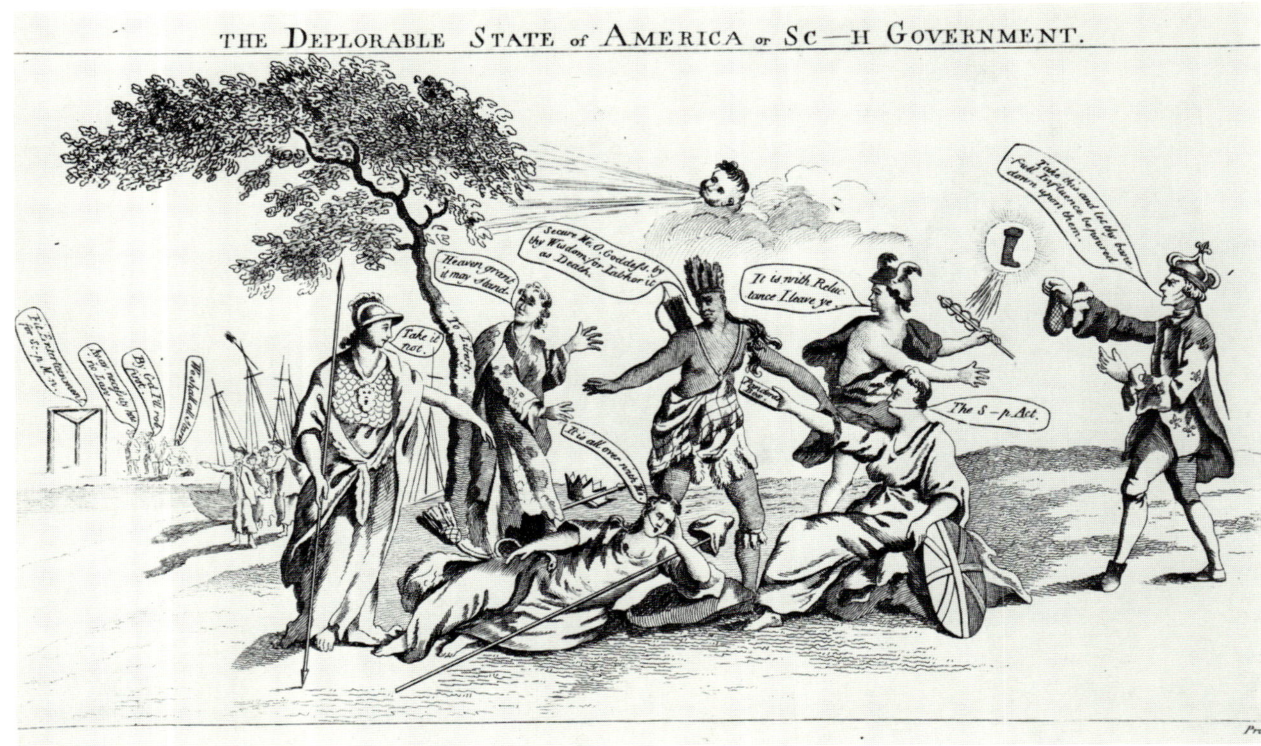

Fig. 2. *The Deplorable State of America or Sc---h Government.* Anonymous. 1765. Engraving. 9 5/16 × 15 1/4 in. Courtesy The Lilly Library, Indiana University, Bloomington.

This complicated cartoon depicts America as an Indian being offered the Stamp Act (in the form of Pandora's box) by Britannia. Minerva, the goddess of wisdom, advises America to "take it not," while Liberty is overcome by the serpent with the thistle attached (representing Scottish Lord Bute, former advisor to King George III) and a bystander prays that the Liberty Tree might be allowed to stand. In the left background the enraged American colonists describe the gallows as "Fit entertainment for St[am]p M[e]n." The "Sc---h" in the title suggests that Lord Bute still has influence over George III, although he was forced to resign because he accepted a French bribe.

44

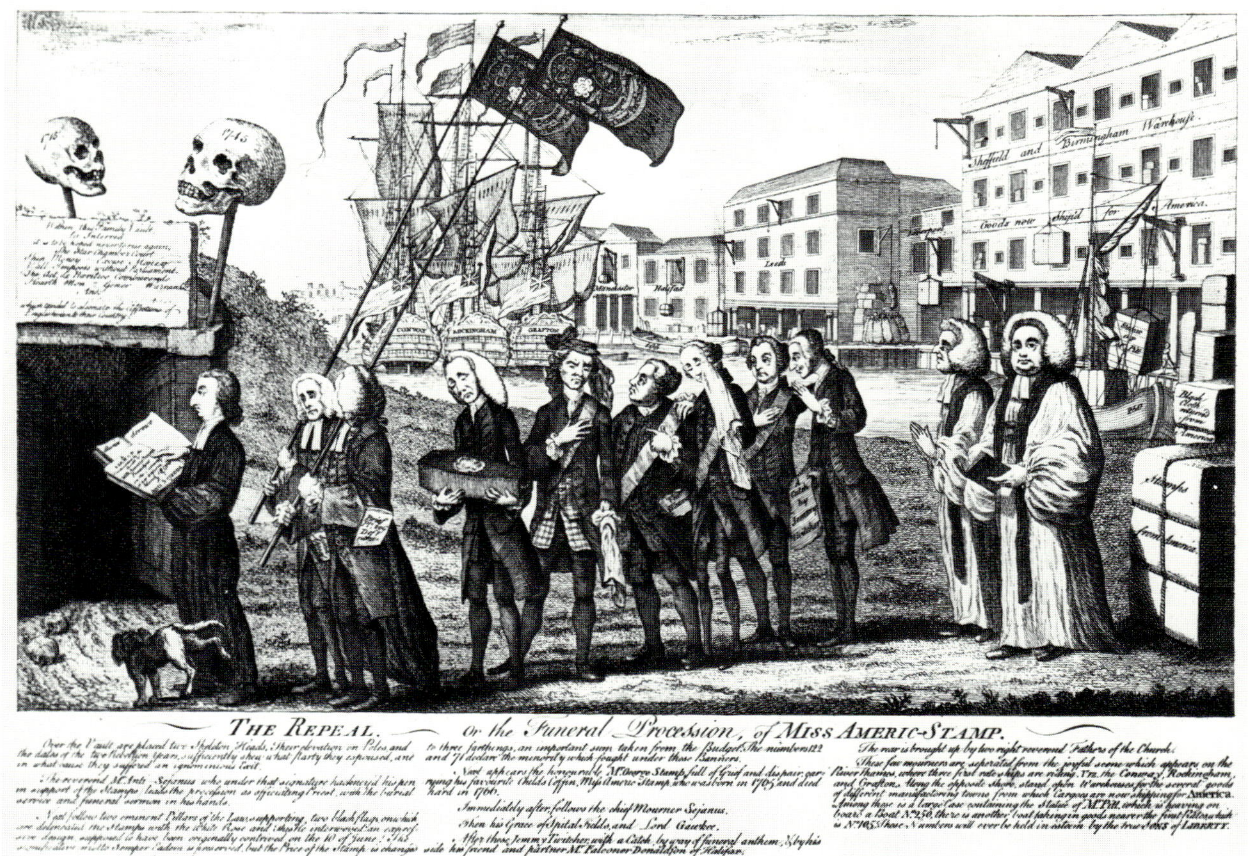

Fig. 3. *The Repeal. Or the Funeral Procession of Miss Americ-Stamp.* Anonymous. 1766. Etching. 11 3/4 × 18 1/4 in. Courtesy The Museum of Art, Carnegie Institute, Pittsburgh.

Colonial opposition to the Stamp Act was so violent that Parliament finally repealed it in 1766. This British print appeared within two weeks to haunt George Grenville, Chancellor of the Exchequer, who is shown taking his dead "child," the Stamp Act, to the Family Vault, surmounted by skulls dated 1715 and 1745, the dates of two unsuccessful Stewart rebellions and thus the burying place of other lost Whig-supported causes. The officiating priest is "Anti Sejanus" (Against Disunion), probably a reference to a pamphlet supporting the act published by Lord Bute, the mourner in the plaid vest, and the standards behind the priest parody the Stamp designs and show the Rose of England entwined with the Thistle of Scotland, another reference to the Scottish influence on George III.

45

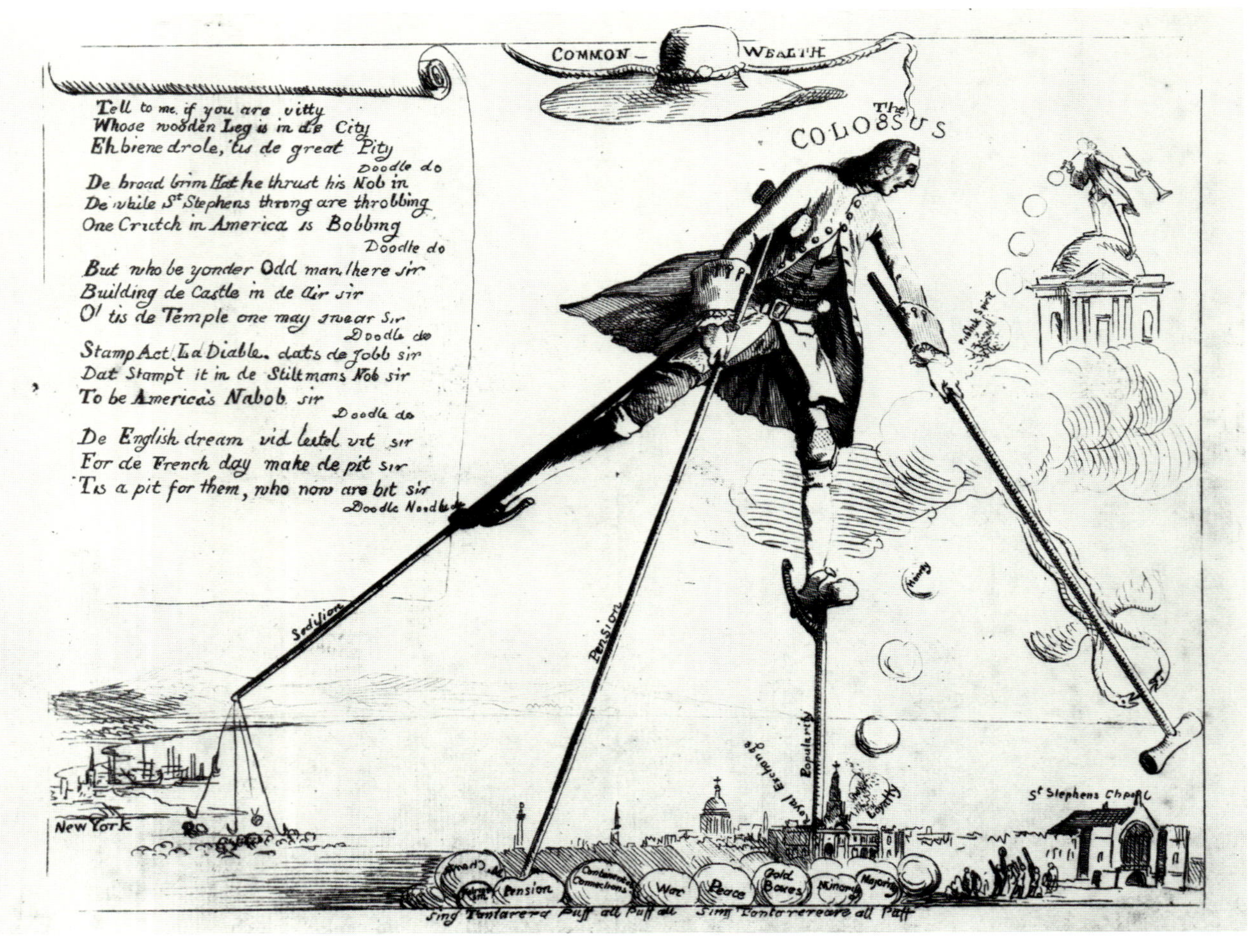

Fig. 4. *The Colossus*. Anonymous. 1766. Etching. 8 1/2 × 6 5/8 in. Courtesy American Antiquarian Society, Worcester, Mass.

With the repeal of the Stamp Act and the fall of the Grenville government, George III turned in 1766 to William Pitt (the Elder) to form a government. The "Great Commoner" had been known for his pro-American views, but the public widely accepted the rumors that he had agreed to serve as George's Prime Minister in return for a small pension (one of the main crutches shown in the cartoon). This cartoonist pictures Pitt caught in the middle of the debate: conservatives did not trust him because of his colonial views, thus one crutch is shown stirring up sedition in the colonies. Because of rumors that he had "sold out" to the king, and therefore turned against Parliament, he is shown about to crush St. Stephens Chapel, a euphemism for Parliament. The cartoonist also suggests that Pitt's popularity rests only with the "Royal Exchange," that is, with commercial interests, while bubbles of loyalty, honesty, and public spirit break upon it. The accompanying verse (to be said with a mock French accent) accuses Pitt of pro-American feelings only to make himself a nabob (millionaire who enriched himself in colonial dealings) there.

46

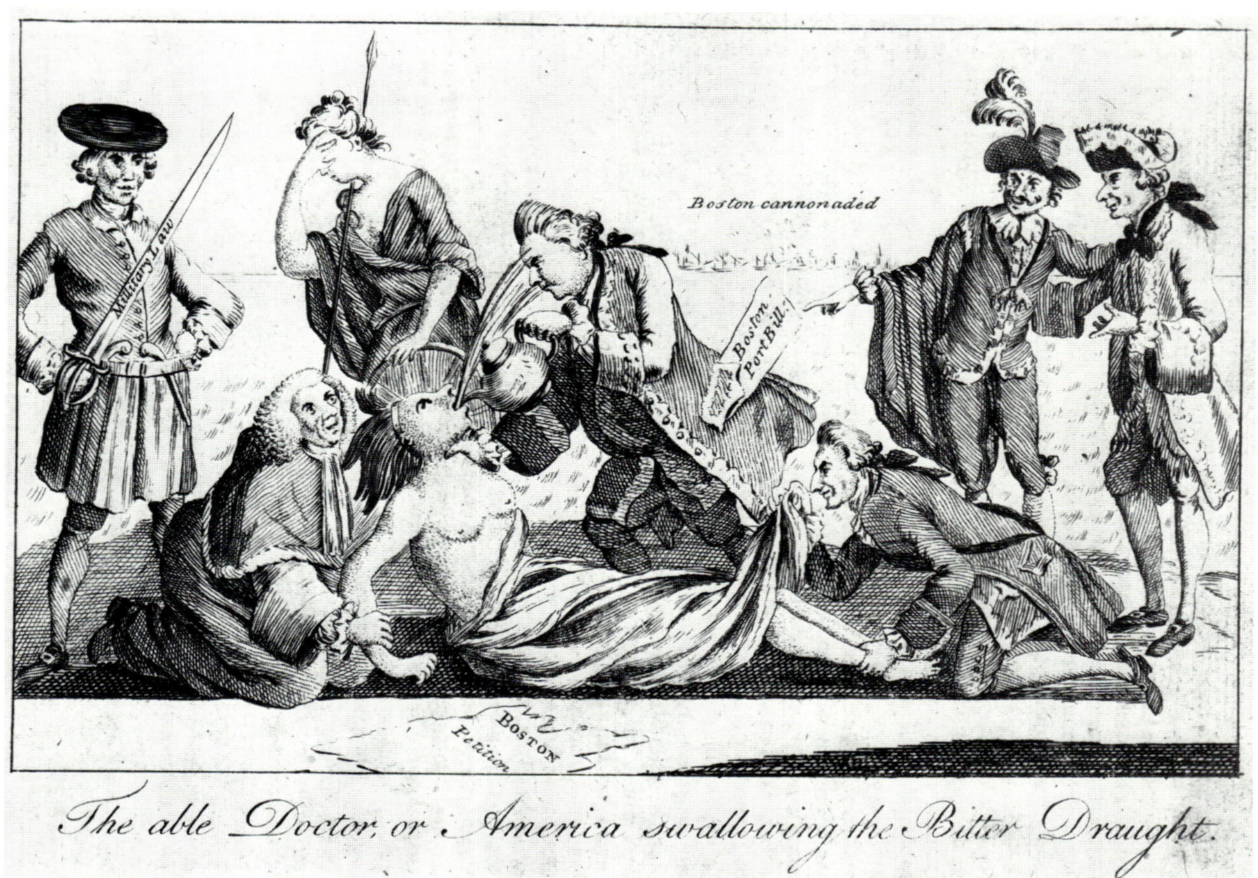

The able Doctor, or America swallowing the Bitter Draught.

Fig. 5. *The Able Doctor, or America Swallowing the Bitter Draught*. Anonymous. 1774. Engraving. 4 1/16 × 6 7/16 in. (sight). Courtesy The Newberry Library, Chicago.

In 1774 tea became the symbol for all British oppressions against the colonies. Lord North had hoped to rescue the East India Company from its financial difficulties by permitting it to sell directly to the colonies, but he imposed a tax on the tea, which the colonists rejected although they were then able to buy tea cheaper than Englishmen. This pro-American cartoon that first appeared in the *London Magazine* shows Lord North forcing tea down America's throat, while Chief Justice Peter Oliver holds America's hands and his brother, Lieutenant Governor Andrew Oliver, holds her feet. Governor Thomas Hutchinson of Massachusetts and King George III look on approvingly. The grim prediction "Boston cannonaded" in the background never came to pass. This English cartoon was copied in both Ireland and America (by Paul Revere); this is the Irish copy.

47

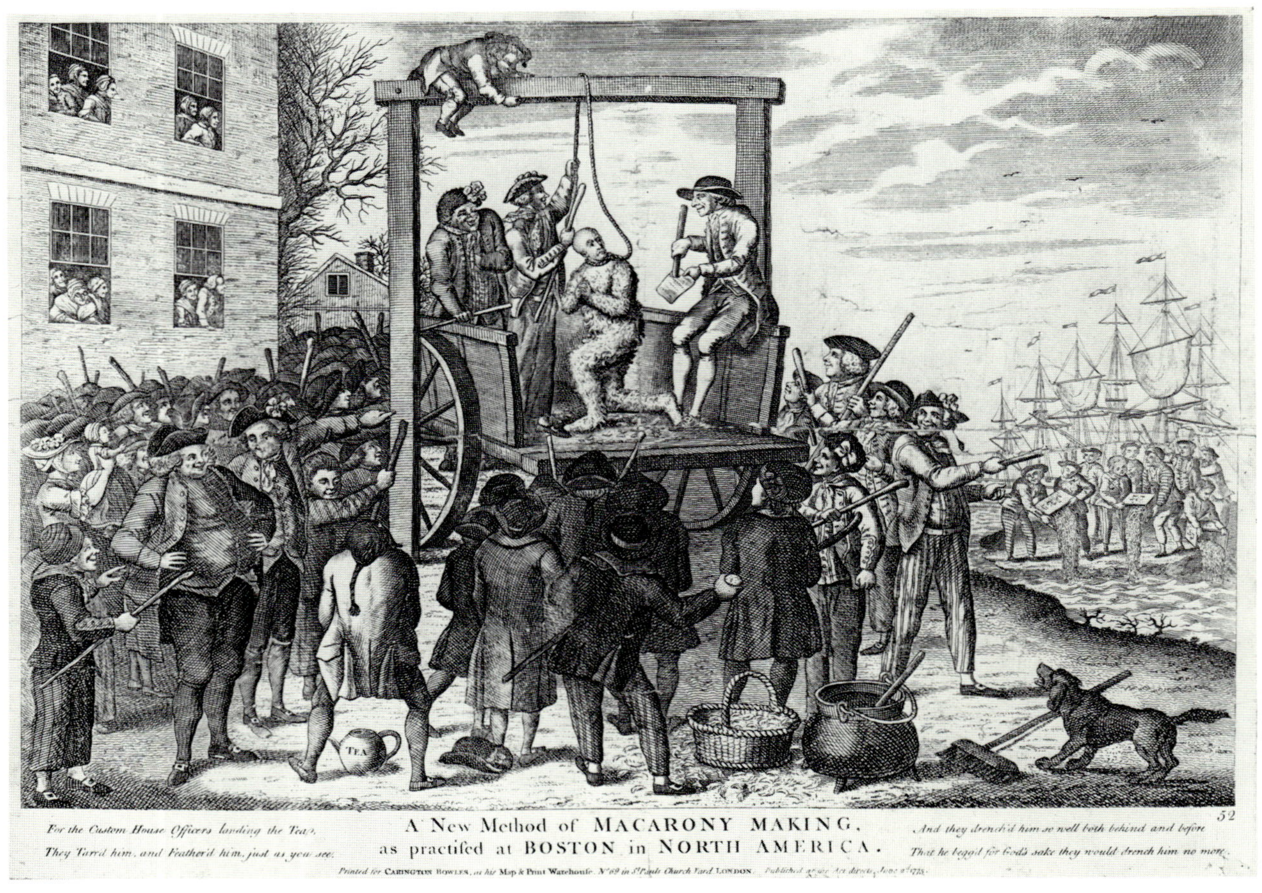

Fig. 6. *A New Method of Macarony Making as Practised at Boston in North America.* Caringon Bowles. 1774. Engraving and etching. 14 1/2 × 19 1/2 in. Courtesy The Museum of Art, Carnegie Institute, Pittsburgh.

48   When the Commissioner of Customs, John Malcomb, tried to collect customs duties in Boston, he was subjected to rough treatment, required to drink enormous quantities of tea, and threatened with hanging. The term "macarony" refers to the Italian word for dandy or fop, and Malcomb is being turned into a dandy "American style," that is, tar and feathers.

Fig. 7. *A Certain Cabinet Junto*. Paul Revere. 1775. Engraving. 3 15/16 × 6 1/2 in. Courtesy American Antiquarian Society, Worcester, Mass.

Britain did not abandon the idea of taxing the colonies with the repeal of the Stamp Act, nor the idea of punishing them with the failure of the Coercive Acts. Parliament declared the colonists in rebellion and voted in 1775 to send troops to quell the uprising. Inspired by a 1773 British print, Paul Revere saw the British action as part of a design whereby the colonists would be stripped of their "Civil & Religs liberty" and etched the "Cabinet Junto" for the *Royal American Magazine* in 1775. Liberty watches the proceedings from afar, praying to the Lord that "our hope is in thee."

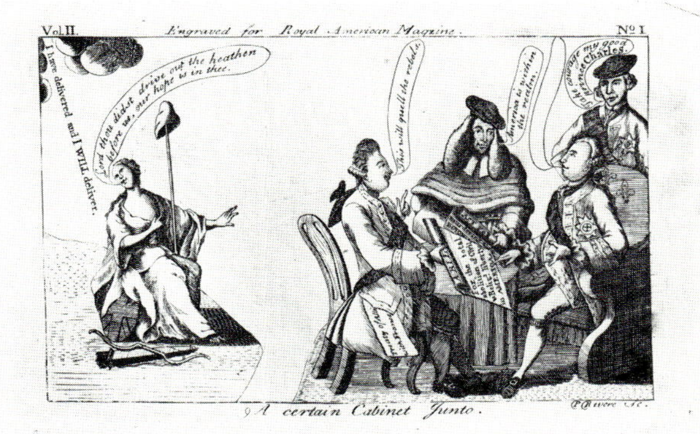

Fig. 8. *Poor Old England Endeavoring to Reclaim His Wicked American Children*. Anonymous. 1777. Etching. 9 3/4 × 13 3/4 in. Courtesy William L. Clements Library, University of Michigan, Ann Arbor.

A weak and crippled England is having a difficult time holding onto his American colonies in this cartoon, produced after the American successes at Trenton and Princeton. Old England is trying to bring them back under his influence, and the whip is ready to administer punishment should he succeed. Below the caption is a line from Shakespeare's *Henry IV*: "Thereby is England maimed and fain to go with a staff, but that my puissance holds it up," intended to suggest how weak and feeble England has become.

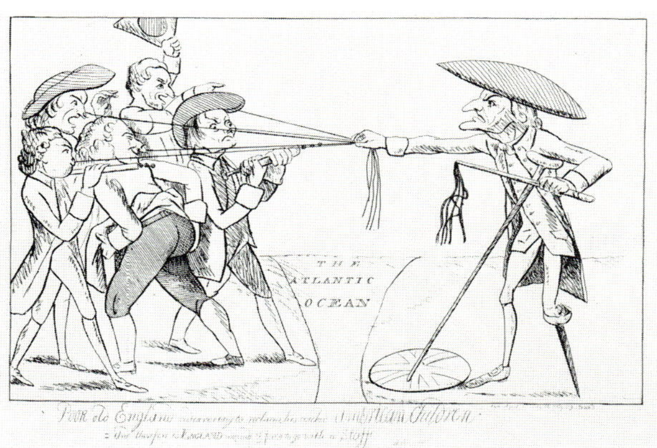

Fig. 9. *Loon Na Werk*. [Reward of Labor.] Anonymous. 1780. Mezzotint. 6 1/2 × 9 in. Courtesy James Ford Bell Library, University of Minnesota, Minneapolis.

This print was published in The Hague or Amsterdam in commemoration of the fact that John Paul Jones (known as John Paul until about 1773) was permitted to leave the Dutch port of Texel with his prizes of war. It shows France, Spain, and America whipping the English dog, while Holland holds the dog's tail with a forked stick. In the background, Jones is beating a crowned lady who is stripped to the waist and tied to a post. One of the most able American captains, Jones had just come from a successful encounter with HMS *Serapis*.

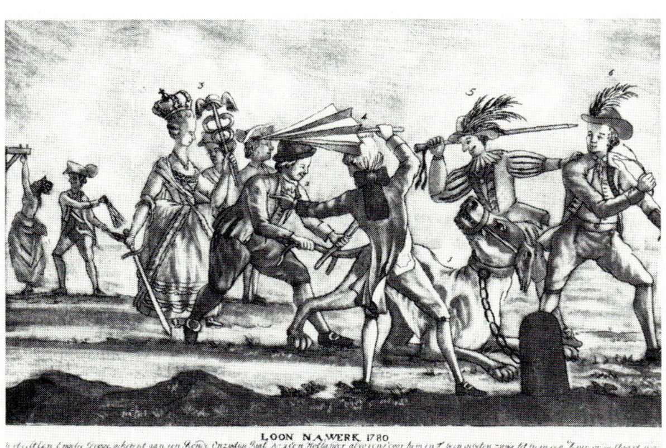

49

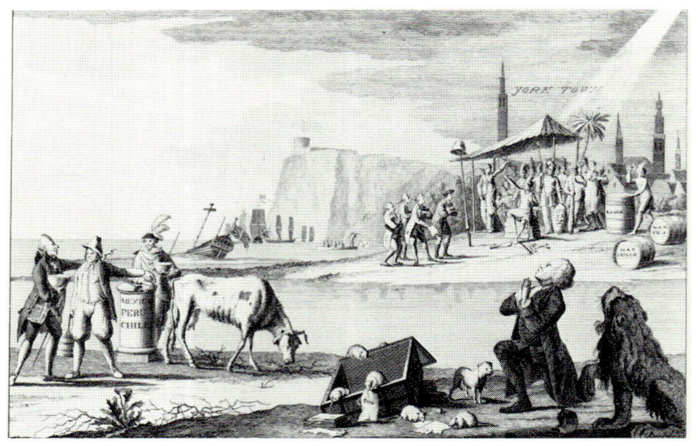

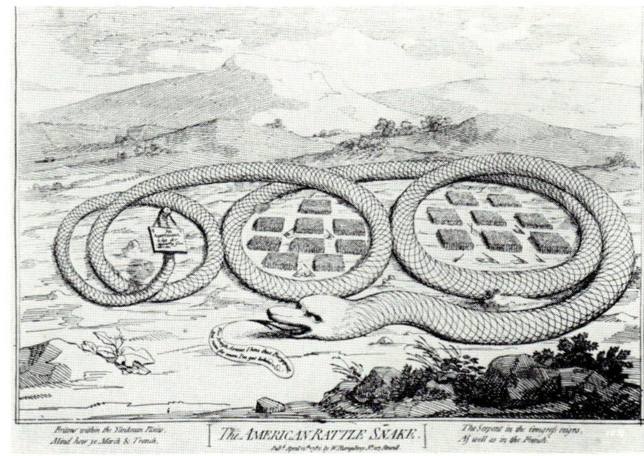

Fig. 10. [John Bull in despair as Cornwallis surrenders York-town.] Anonymous. 1781. Engraving. 6 13/16 × 10 1/2 in. Courtesy The Pierpont Morgan Library, New York City.

As Lord Cornwallis surrenders Yorktown to Washington's and Lafayette's combined forces in October, 1781, John Bull, in the foreground despairs over the defeat and over his empty war chest, the gold expended trying to hold onto the American colonies. This Dutch engraver also includes a reference to Europe's view of Britain, as the Frenchman, the Spaniard, and the Dutchman gesture derisively toward Britain's emaciated cow of commerce.

Fig. 11. *The American Rattle Snake*. James Gillray. Apr. 12, 1782. Etching. 9 5/16 × 12 11/16 in. Courtesy the Library of Congress, Washington, D.C.

This cartoon was published on the day the peace negotiations between America and Britain began in Paris. It shows the American rattlesnake coiled around two British armies, Burgoyne at Saratoga and Cornwallis at Yorktown, with yet a third "Apartment to lett."

50

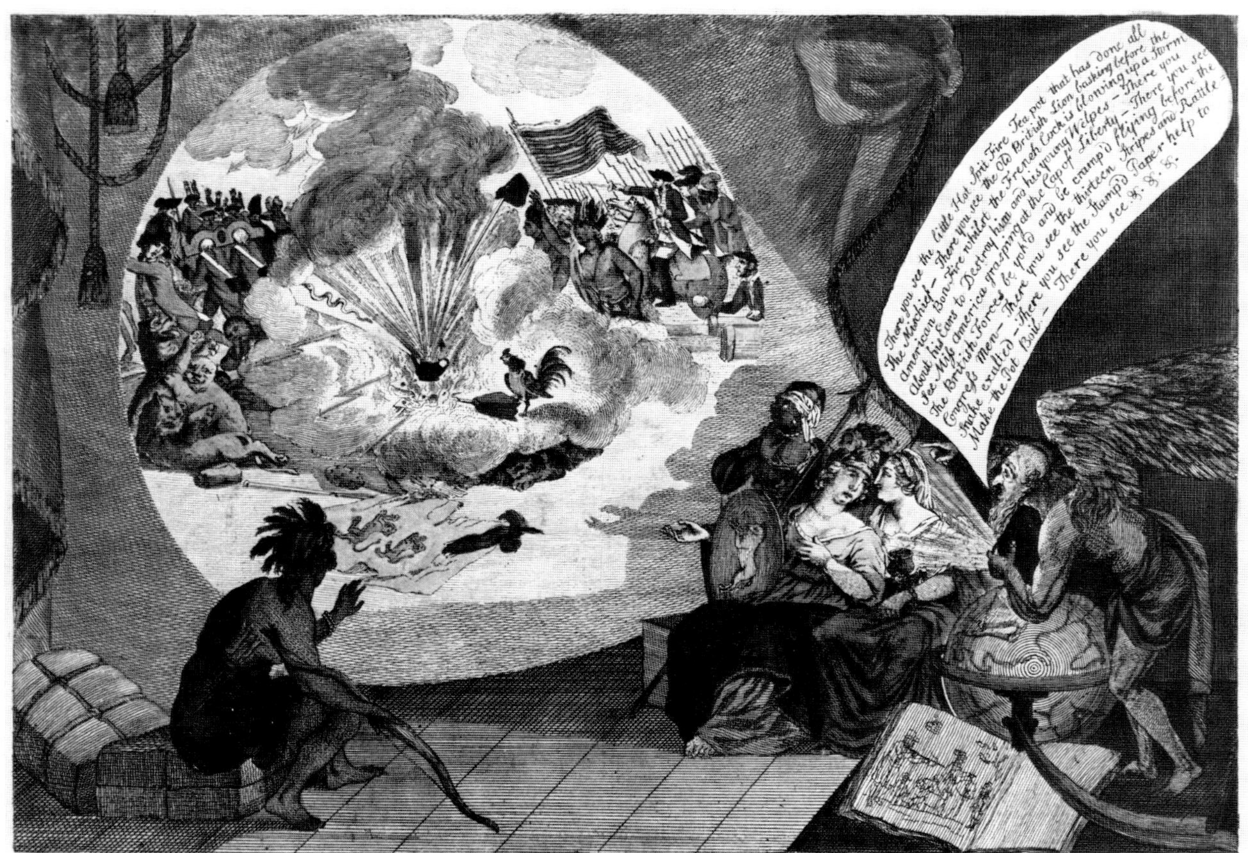

The *TEA-TAX-TEMPEST*, or *OLD TIME* with his *MAGICK=LANTHERN*.

Pub.ᵈ March 12 1783. by W.ᵐ Humphreys. N.º 227 Strand.

Fig. 12. *The Tea-Tax-Tempest, or Old Time with His Magick Lanthern*. W. Humphreys. 1783. Colored engraving. 9 15/16 × 13 15/16 in. Courtesy The Lilly Library, Indiana University, Bloomington.

In this elegant and sophisticated cartoon, Humphreys depicts Europe's view of the American Revolution. Using a magic lantern, Time is projecting a scene from the Battle of Saratoga onto the screen. In the center, tea being brewed on a fire of stamped paper has exploded as a French cock fans the fire. In the audience, Europe looks anguishingly toward Asia while Africa seems frightened. According to this print, most of Europe favored the new United States.

51

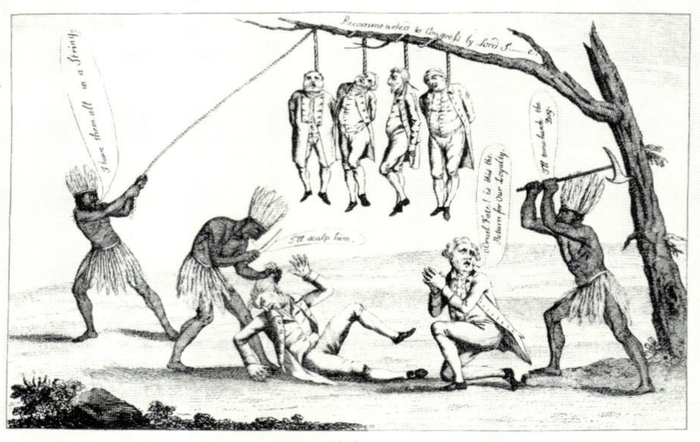

The General P—s, or Peace.

Fig. 14. *The General P--s, or Peace*. J. Barrum. 1783. Hand colored etching. 12 5/16 × 8 5/16 in. Courtesy the Library of Congress.

Fig. 13. *The Savages Let Loose, or the Cruel Fate of the Loyalists*. W. Humphreys. 1783. Engraving. 10 15/16 × 14 9/16 in. (sight). Courtesy The Newberry Library, Chicago.

Loyalists fared badly in the American Revolution; many returned to England. All the British negotiators were able to secure on their behalf at the peace conference were two provisions that proved unenforceable: that Congress would "recommend" to the states that property taken during the fighting be returned, and that further confiscation would cease. Lord Shelbourne's government fell because of public indignation over what most Britishers felt was abandonment of loyal subjects of the crown.

The Peace of Paris, which ended the American Revolution, was signed on November 3, 1782. It took effect when Britain and France, and Britain and Spain had signed separate agreements on January 20, 1783. James Rivington of New York published a broadside on March 25 proclaiming the treaty and explaining its terms. This English print also announced the "General Peace," as Britain, the Netherlands, the United States, Spain, and France have laid down their drums, swords, and flags. The poet has appended verse to call attention to the unusual event: "The belligerent powers, like good neighbours agree,/ A little time past Sirs, who would have thought this,/ That they'd so soon come to a general P---?"

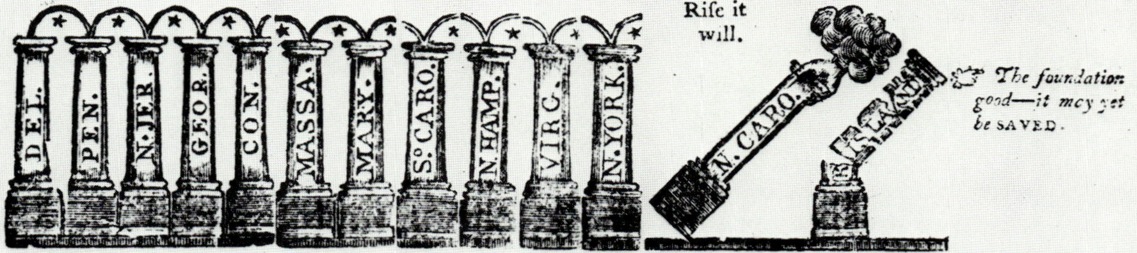

Fig. 15. *The Federal Edifice*. Anonymous. 1788. Engraving. 3 1/2 × 5 1/2 in. Courtesy The New-York Historical Society, New York City.

Having proved the unworkableness of the Articles of Confederation, the United States promulgated the Constitution in 1787. Delaware was the first to approve in December. Only nine states were required before the new document took effect, but for reasons of unity unanimous approval obviously was desired. This print was issued July 26, 1788, to commemorate New York's ratification of the Constitution. Although the two remaining pillars appear to be crumbling, the prophesies printed above each of them proved correct: of North Carolina the printer predicted "Rise it will." By Rhode Island, "The foundation good—it may yet be saved." Rhode Island finally made ratification unanimous in 1790.

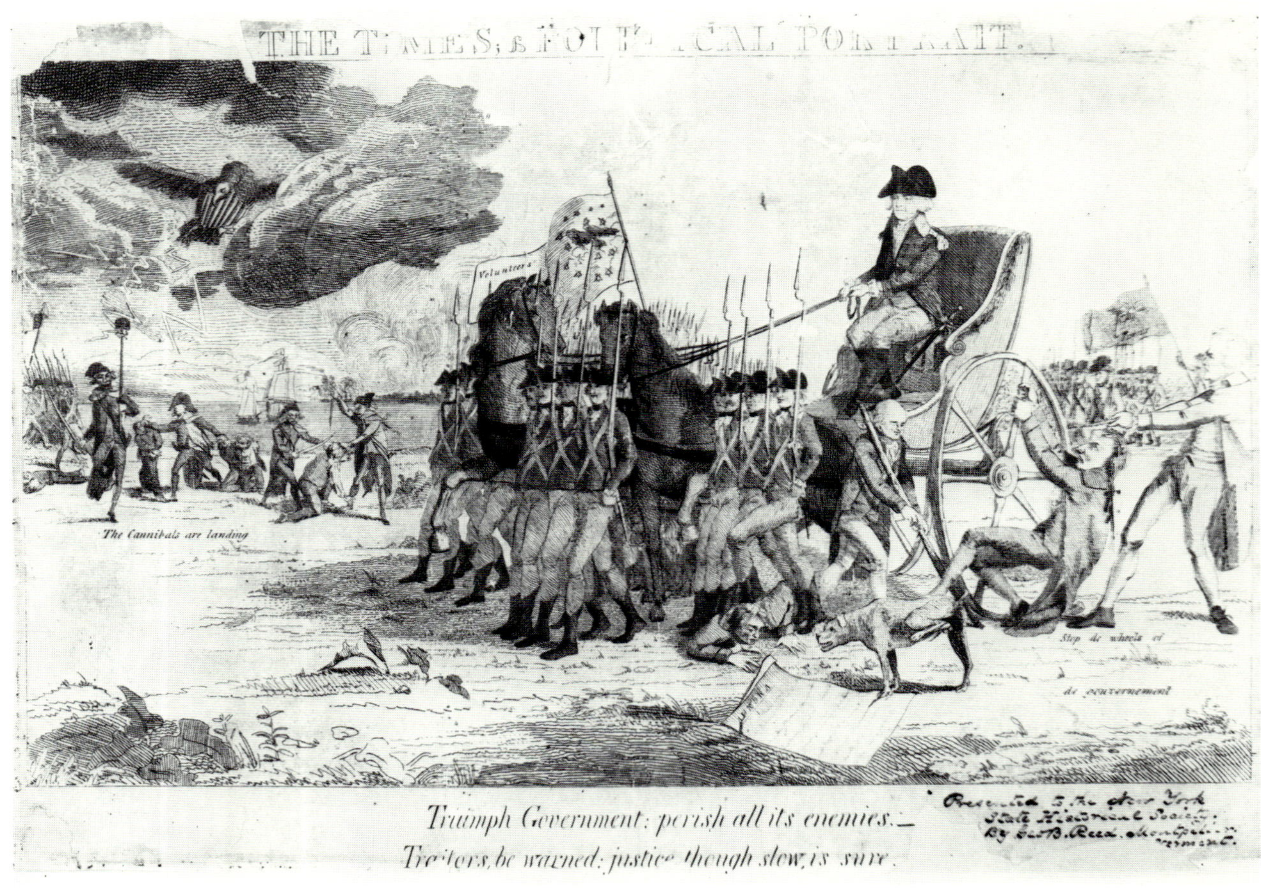

Fig. 16. *The Times; a Political Portrait*. Anonymous. c. 1795. Engraving. 12 1/4 × 17 3/4 in. Courtesy The New-York Historical Society, New York City.

Despite the unanimous approval of the Constitution, partisan politics during the formative years of our nation were as bitter as at any other time except the Civil War. Under Washington's able leadership two political factions formed: the Federalists, led by Alexander Hamilton, who believed in a strong central government; and the Democratic-Republicans, led by Jefferson, who favored a weaker central government. In this cartoon, probably one of many that were done about Washington, the President sits high atop the federal cabriolet leading the government, while Jefferson and his two pro-French supporters, Albert Gallatin and Citizen Edmond Genet, try to "stop de wheels of gouvernement." The partisanship demonstrated in this early cartoon is only representative of the fact that the founding fathers earnestly believed that the fate of the nation rested on their being in office at a particular time, to the exclusion of their political opponents.

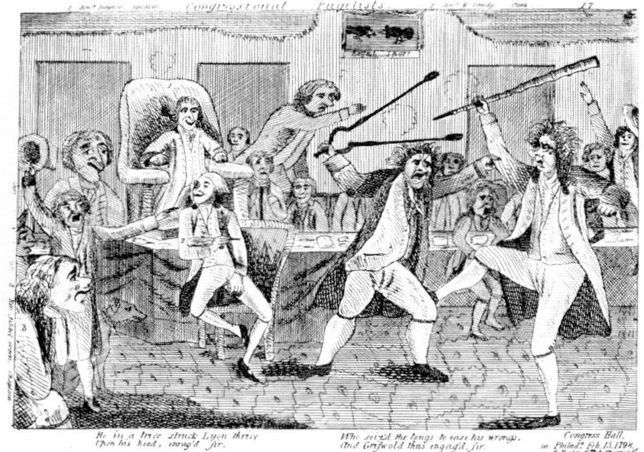

Fig. 17. *Congressional Pugilists*. Anonymous. 1798 (1864 restrike for *Historical Magazine*). Engraving. 10 3/16 × 12 15/16 in. Courtesy Independence National Historical Park Collection, Philadelphia.

When Congressman Roger Griswold of Connecticut spread an old rumor that Congressman Matthew Lyon of Vermont had been required to wear a wooden sword because of cowardice in the field, Lyon responded by spitting in Griswold's face. A fracas ensued after Congress failed to expel Lyon. The men were separated without dealing any real harm to each other, but they were not satisfied. A few days later they again fought, inspiring this cartoon. They were finally separated, and everyone was quite tired of the affair. Two other cartoons commemorate their altercations.

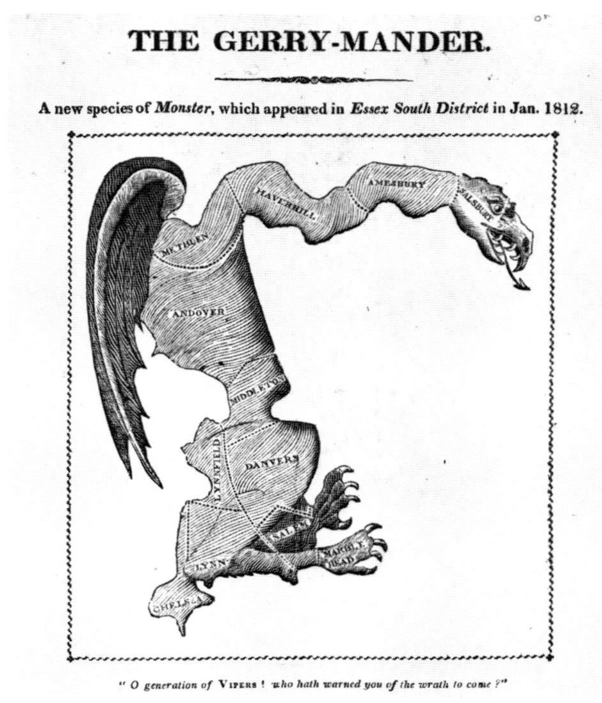

Fig. 18. *The Gerry-Mander*. Elkanah Tisdale. Mar. 26, 1812, in the Boston *Weekly Messenger*. Woodcut with set type. 19 1/2 × 9 1/4 in. Courtesy The New-York Historical Society, New York City.

When the Democratic majority arbitrarily realigned the voting district in Essex County, Massachusetts, so that the Republican vote in a single town (Marblehead) would outnumber the Federalist vote in eleven other towns, Tisdale designed a new American political monster, the ''gerry-mander.'' The cartoon is made by adding fangs, wings, and claws to a map of the voting district; the name comes from combining Republican Governor Elbridge Gerry's name with part of the word salamander. The district was redrawn the following year.

55

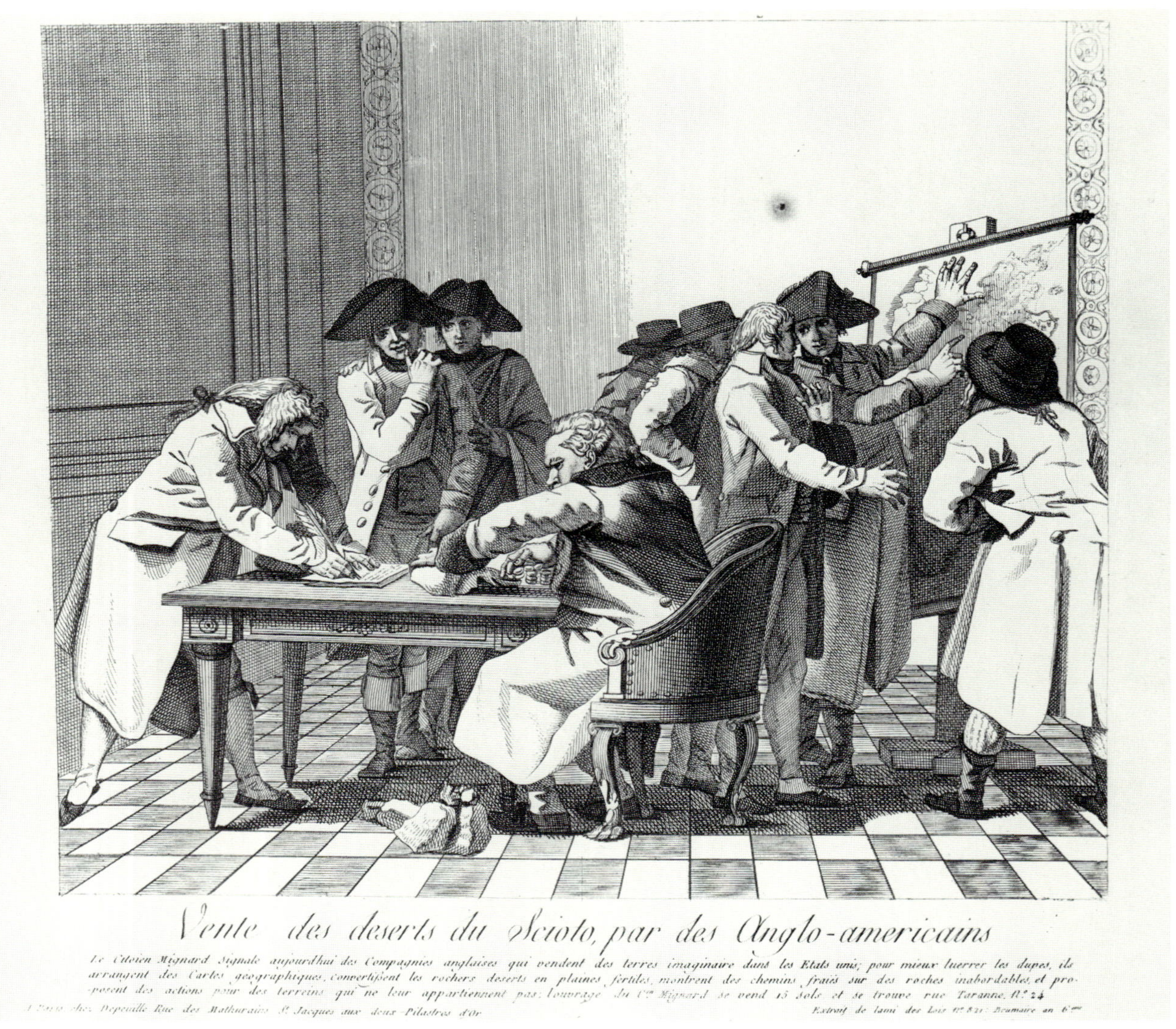

Fig. 19. *Vente des deserts du Scioto, par des Anglo-americains.* [Sale of the deserts of Scioto, by the Anglo-Americans.] Anonymous. Brumaire an 6eme. [Oct. 23 to Nov. 21, 1799.] Engraving. 11 1/2 × 12 7/8 in. Courtesy The Chicago Historical Society.

As the new United States began to spread into the land of the Old Northwest, land speculators invested in the virgin acres and turned quick dollars by selling to people unfamiliar with what they were buying. The caption of the cartoon explains that "Citizen Mignard signs today for some English companions who are selling imaginary lands in the United States. The better to ensnare dupes, they draw geological maps, converting rocky deserts into fertile plains, show roads cutting through impassable cliffs and offer shares in lands which do not belong to them."

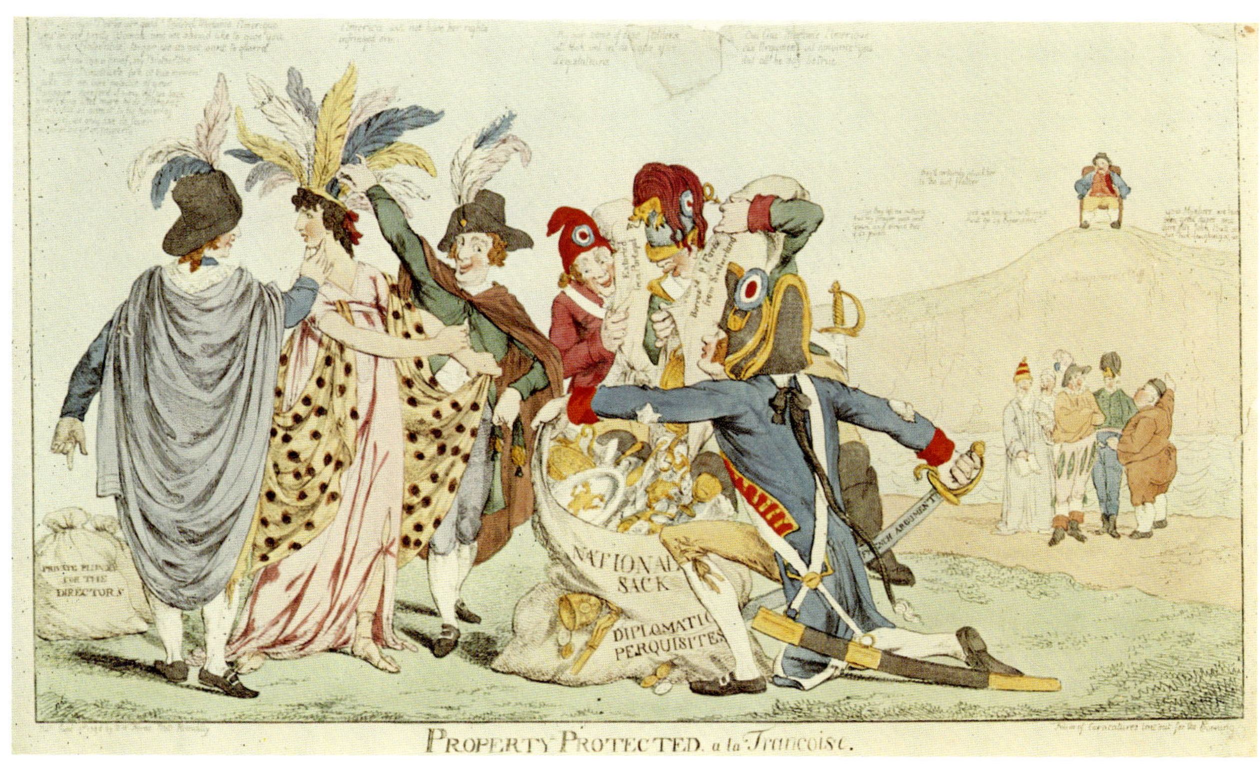

Fig. 20. *Property Protected, a la Francoise*. Ansell (?). 1798. Colored engraving. 10 3/8 × 17 1/16 in. Courtesy The Lilly Library, Indiana University, Bloomington.

When President John Adams sent three American envoys to Paris to assist Charles C. Pinckney in securing an improvement in American-French relations, Talleyrand, the French foreign minister, refused to receive them. Meanwhile, three of his unofficial agents contacted the Americans and suggested that a quarter of a million dollars gratuity for Talleyrand, a loan for France, and an indemnity for criticism that Adams had made against France would correct the problem. The Americans refused the terms, and Adams made the correspondence public, referring to the French officials as X, Y, and Z. This cartoon shows the lovely, young America being plundered by five Frenchmen representing the five Directors of the French government. John Bull (England) watches amused from "Shakespeare's Cliff," while the rest of Europe discusses the situation.

57

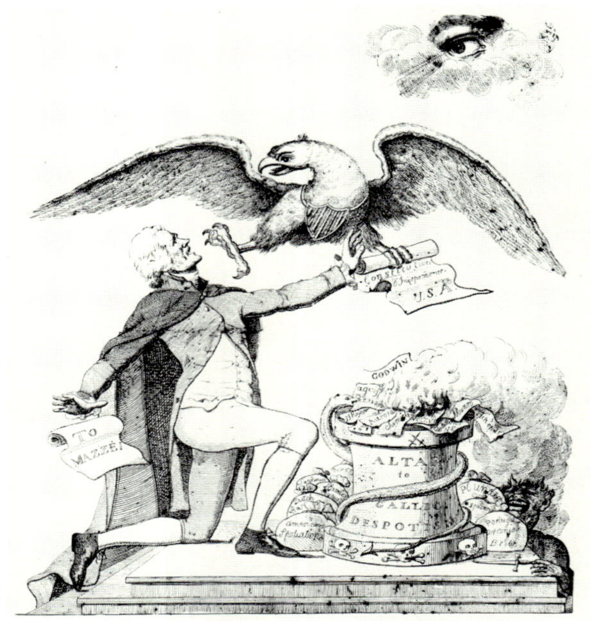

THE PROVIDENTIAL DETECTION

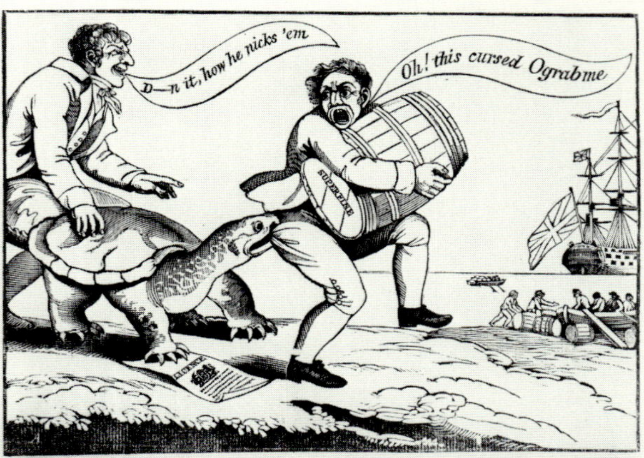

OGRABME, or. The American Snapping-turtle.

Fig. 21. *The Providential Detection*. Anonymous. 1800. Etching. 14 3/8 × 13 7/8 in. Courtesy American Antiquarian Society, Worcester, Mass.

While serving as Secretary of State under President Washington, Thomas Jefferson made no secret of his feeling that friendship with France was better for the young nation than alliance with Great Britain (friendship with both being impossible because they were established rivals). When Jefferson campaigned for the presidency in 1800, this Federalist cartoonist pictured his fear that Jefferson would prostrate the country before the French altar. The American Eagle has just taken the Constitution from Jefferson, who would have burned it just as he had certain classic works as well as the Federalist newspaper *Aurora*. In his right hand he holds the incriminating letter to his Italian friend Phillip Mazzei to whom he had written four years earlier that "an Anglican monarchical aristocratical party has sprung up, whose avowed object is to draw over us the substance, as they have already done the forms, of the British government."

Fig. 22. *Ograbme, or, the American Snapping-Turtle*. Alexander Anderson. 1807. Engraving. 7 1/2 × 9 1/2 in. Courtesy The New-York Historical Society, New York City.

During the Napoleonic wars, Britain and France sought to destroy each other's commerce on the high seas. While this was good practice in war, it was hard on neutral countries like the United States. In an effort to get them to stop harassing American shipping, Jefferson urged on Congress the Embargo (spelled backwards is "ograbme") Act in 1807. The embargo stopped virtually all foreign trade. Technically it did not prohibit imports, but few ships would bring goods to the United States if they could not return with a load, which the embargo prevented. Shippers and merchants were not ready to sacrifice so much and began smuggling (in the cartoon the "ograbme" has caught a tobacco smuggler) and otherwise disobeying the embargo. The ban was finally lifted in 1808 after disastrous economic results and virtually no diplomatic impact.

58

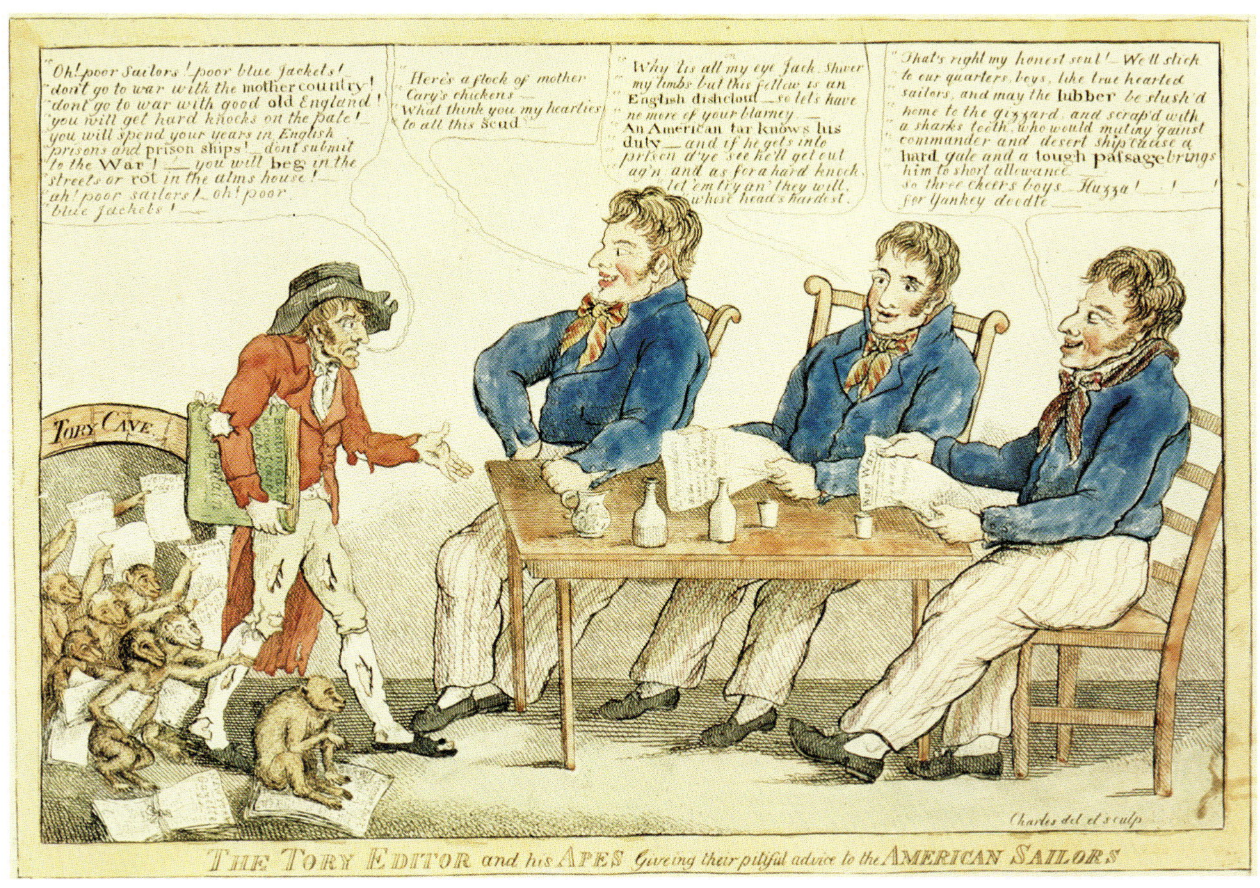

THE TORY EDITOR and his APES *Giveing their pitiful advice to the* AMERICAN SAILORS

Fig. 23. *The Tory Editor and His Apes Giveing Their Pitiful Advice to the American Sailors*. William Charles. 1813. Colored engraving. 11 1/4 × 15 1/16 in. Courtesy The Lilly Library, Indiana University, Bloomington.

As the Napoleonic wars dragged on, anti-British sentiment in the United States was rekindled because of the British impounding of cargoes and impressment of American sailors. Expansion-minded young Westerners like Henry Clay demanded war, but New England merchants counseled a neutral course. In this pro-war cartoon, strong American sailors are rejecting the advice of the ''Tory'' editor (with a copy of the Boston *Gazette* under his arm), who apparently has never recovered from the Revolution, as seen in his tired appearance and worn clothes. This cartoon also points out that American sailors were pro-war because they unrealistically envisioned easy victory over the British.

59

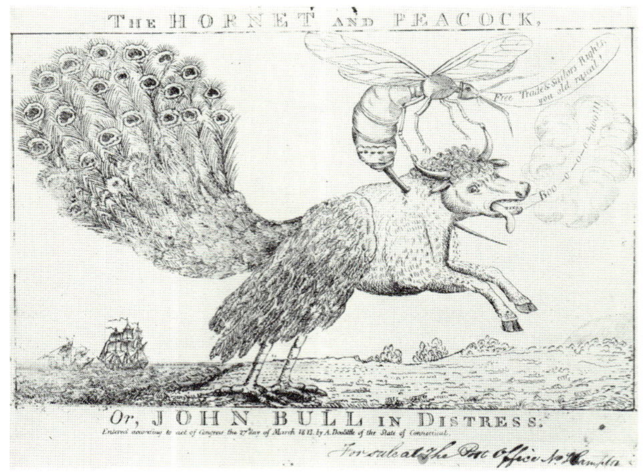
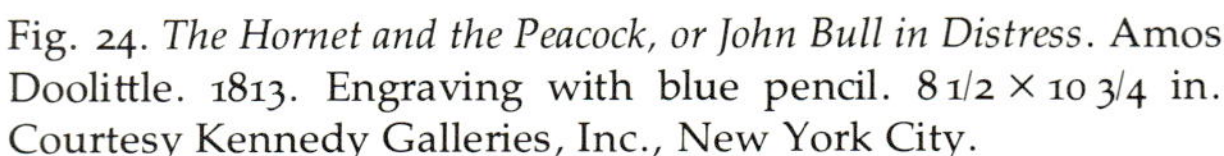

Fig. 24. *The Hornet and the Peacock, or John Bull in Distress*. Amos Doolittle. 1813. Engraving with blue pencil. 8 1/2 × 10 3/4 in. Courtesy Kennedy Galleries, Inc., New York City.

Naval rights—free trade and sailors' rights —were the main issues leading to the War of 1812, and even though the main part of the British navy was occupied fighting France, Britain could still put ninety-seven ships on the American side of the Atlantic to hold the sixteen American ships. By avoiding fleet action and concentrating on single ships, nevertheless, the Americans managed several naval victories. One of the most memorable American victories was the *Hornet's* defeat of the *Peacock*, depicted in this Doolittle cartoon.

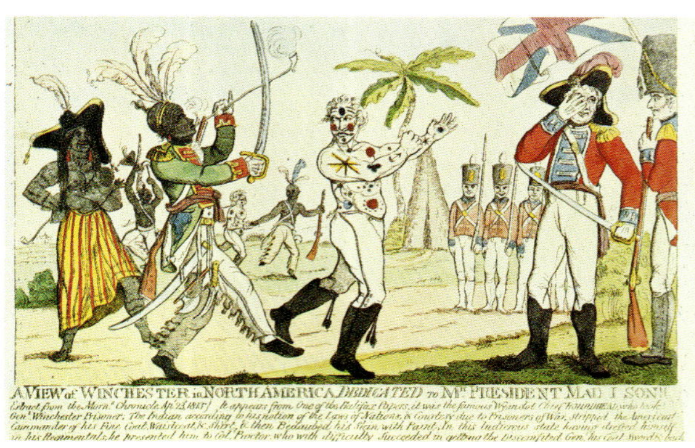

Fig. 25. *A View of Winchester in North America Dedicated to Mr. President Mad I Son!!* S. Knight. 1813. Colored engraving. 9 × 13 1/2 in. Courtesy The Lilly Library, Indiana University, Bloomington.

British Colonel Henry Proctor defeated American Brigadier General James Winchester during the first winter of the War of 1812. Hurrying to join General William H. Harrison at the Maumee Rapids, Winchester split his force to rescue some settlers and was unprepared for Proctor's attack. This cartoon depicts the meeting between Proctor and Winchester. Winchester was stripped of his uniform (being worn by one of Proctor's Indian allies), daubed with paint, and presented to the British commander. Winchester's defeat slowed General Harrison's plans to capture the Old Northwest Territory.

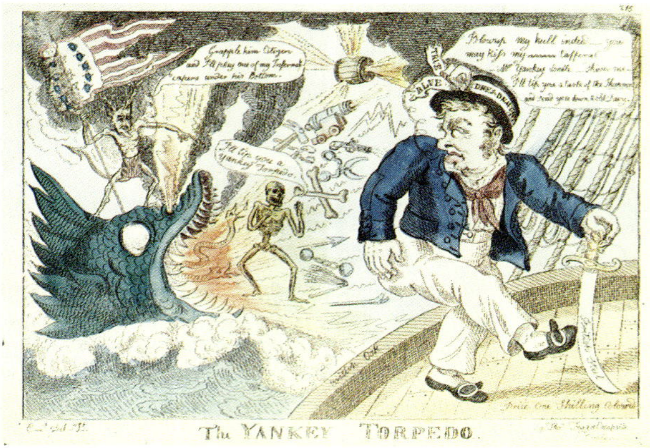

Fig. 26. *The Yankee Torpedo*. W. Elmes. 1813. Colored engraving. 10 5/8 × 15 7/8 in. Courtesy The Lilly Library, Indiana University, Bloomington.

The British did not take American threats made during the War of 1812 as seriously as the Americans intended them. On "British Oak" and leaning on a sword of "British Steel," this English sailor challenges the American sea-monster to "kiss my tafferal" (*i.e.*, taffrail, part of a ship's stern). He promises the monster "a taste of the *Shannon*," which defeated the USS *Chesapeake* in Boston Harbor, and a trip to Davy Jones' locker.

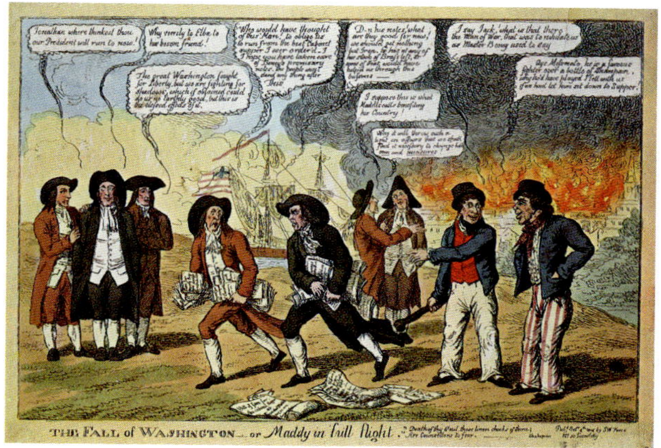 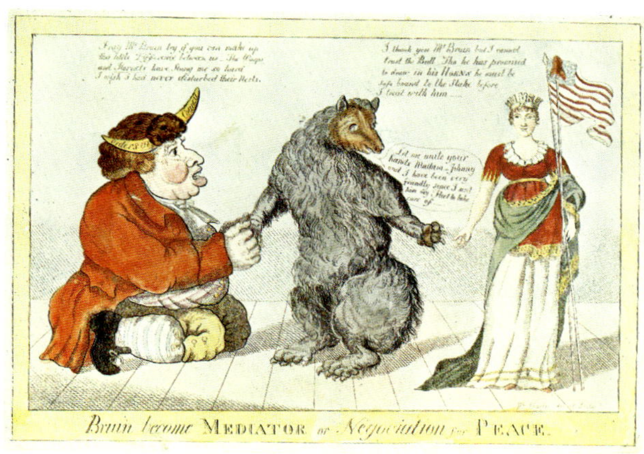

Fig. 27. *The Fall of Washington—or Maddy in Full Flight*. Williams. Oct. 4, 1814. Colored engraving. 14 1/2 × 10 in. Courtesy Anne S. K. Brown Military Collection, Brown University Library, Providence.

Hoping to divert attention from their Northern campaign, British forces struck at selected sites along the Eastern Coast in the summer of 1814. Although they were outnumbered, they easily pushed the badly prepared American forces back, leaving Washington, D. C., exposed. President James Madison had retired to Virginia by the time the British arrived. Two hundred Redcoats left "the Capitol wrapped in its winding sheet of fire," after feasting on food that Dolly Madison had prepared for the American troops before she also fled. Rear Admiral Sir George Cockburn and his men took whatever they wanted, then toasted the President with his own wine "for being such a good fellow as to leave us such a capital supper." The entire city might have burned had it not been for a violent thunderstorm that put out the fire.

Fig. 28. *Bruin Become Mediator or Negociation for Peace*. William Charles. c. 1813. Colored engraving. 10 11/16 × 14 3/4 in. Courtesy The Lilly Library, Indiana University, Bloomington.

Although the cartoon pictures John Bull, broken by victories of the American ships *Wasp* and *Hornet* at sea, pleading with the Russian bear to help settle the differences with the United States, the opposite situation was nearer the truth. President Madison had contacted Russian Tsar Alexander I in March, 1813, but the British refused the Tsar's offer of mediation. Negotiation finally began in August, 1814, and the Treaty of Ghent was signed in December. It restored all territory *status quo ante bellum*, granted amnesty for the Indian allies of the British, and provided for commissions to settle the boundary disputes. It did not mention impressment, neutral rights, or Canada and Florida, the main issues that had precipitated the war.

61

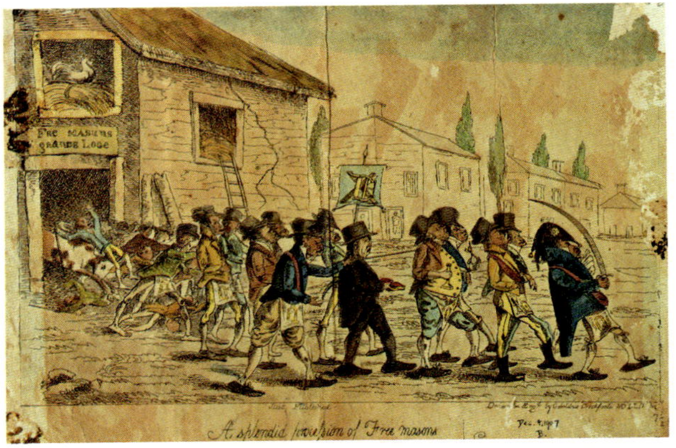

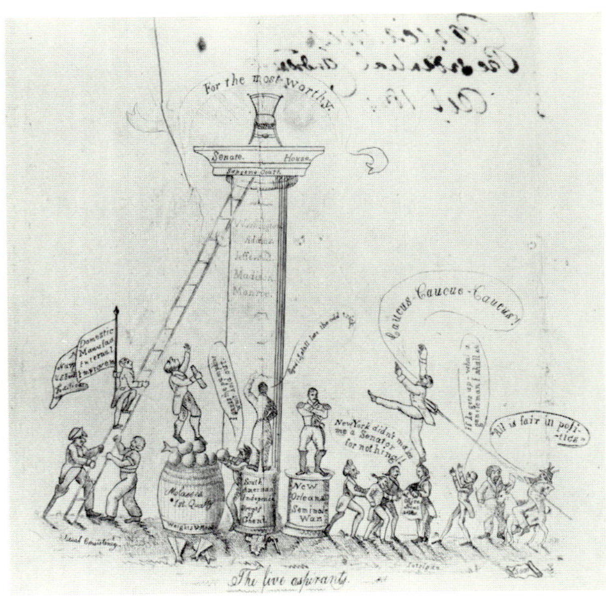

Fig. 30. *The Five Aspirants*. Anonymous. 1824. Etching. 7 3/4 × 8 7/8 in. Courtesy Houghton Library, Harvard University, Cambridge, Mass.

The election of 1824 was a rousing affair that marked the end of the politically inactive Era of Good Feelings. Five candidates presented themselves to the electorate—William H. Crawford, John C. Calhoun, Andrew Jackson, John Quincy Adams, and Henry Clay. Here Clay is shown basing his campaign on his support of South American independence and the Treaty of Ghent. Andrew Jackson's reputation rested on his victory over the British at New Orleans and his treatment of the Seminole Indians in Florida. Secretary of the Treasury William H. Crawford, the candidate of the Congressional Caucus, became an issue because the other candidates claimed that he had been nominated by a "secret" caucus instead of the people. John Quincy Adams is shown on the Molasses barrel while John C. Calhoun heads up the ladder toward the chair reserved "for the most worthy."

Fig. 29. *A Splendid Procession of Free Masons*. Gebobbus Crockforde (?). 1820s. Hand-colored engraving. 6 1/4 × 9 3/4 in. Courtesy Boston Public Library, Print Department.

The Masonic Order was popular early in the nineteenth century, and many influential Americans were members. Those out of power, hearing rumors of the international Masonic movement, immediately suspected a plot by Masons to take over the country. In an exceedingly ugly affair a Mason who was trying to desert the order and publish all its secrets was killed. An Anti-Mason Party was formed in protest and was particularly active in New York State. This cartoon is probably part of the anti-Masonic movement that flourished during the mid-1820s.

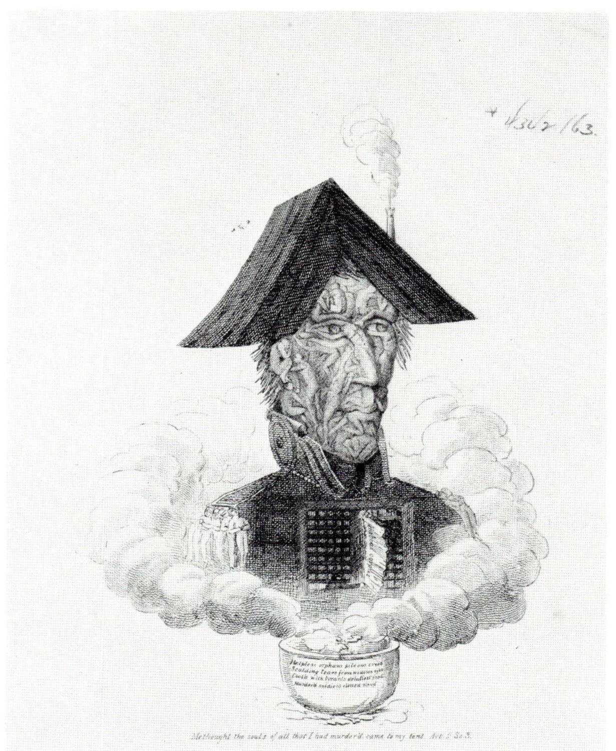

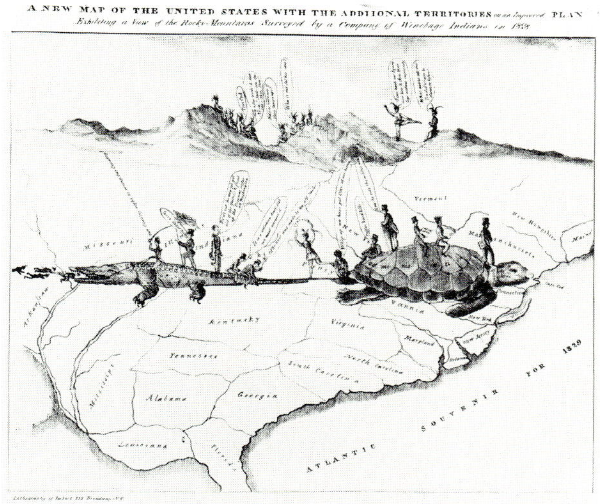

Fig. 32. *A New Map of the United States with the Additional Territories*. Anthony Imbert. 1828. Lithograph. 11 3/8 × 14 1/4 in. Courtesy Collections of The Library Company of Philadelphia.

When the election of 1824 was thrown into the House of Representatives for a decision, John Quincy Adams won with the support of Henry Clay. Jackson, who had accumulated the most popular votes, claimed that Adams and Clay had formed a "corrupt bargain," and immediately began preparations for the 1828 election. In this cartoon, the first lithographic cartoon produced in the United States, Jackson and his men are shown facing westward on the alligator; Adams and his supporters are on the tortoise facing eastward. Jackson's supporters venture the hope that he can "float up the Potomac as far as Washington," while the Indians behind the mountains in the background relate the developments they noticed during a recent visit into white man's culture.

Fig. 31. *Richard I.I.I.* David Claypool Johnston. 1828. Engraving with stipple. 8 1/2 × 5 3/4 in. Courtesy Boston Public Library, Print Department.

Andrew Jackson was the candidate with the most popular votes during the election of 1824, but the House of Representatives elected John Quincy Adams President. Jackson returned for the campaign of 1828, and David Claypool Johnston recalled his military record in presenting this portrait to the public. Johnston has taken the bodies of Indians and other symbols of Jackson's wartime accomplishments as integral parts of the picture.

63

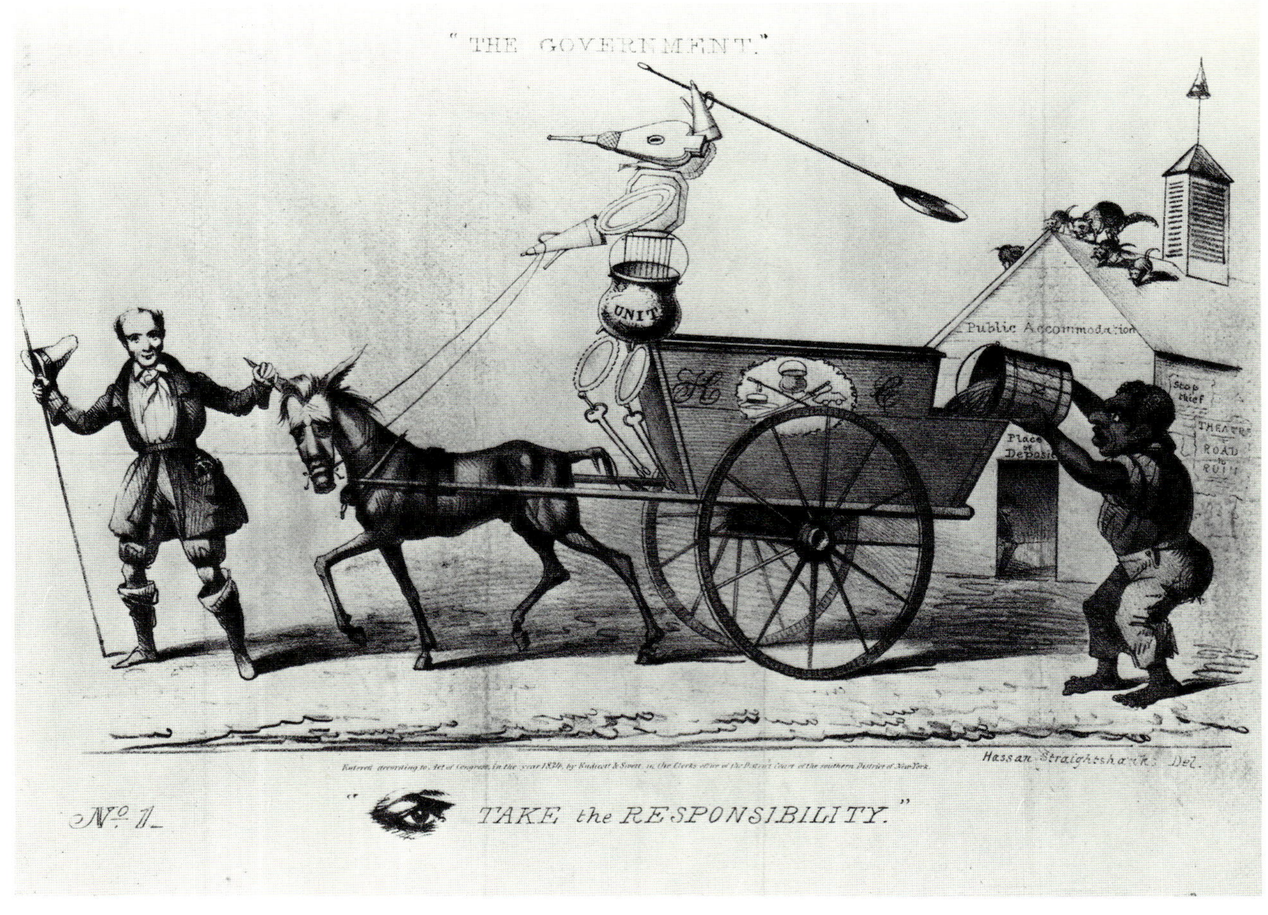

Fig. 33. *"The Government."* [I] *Take the Responsibility*. Hassan Straightshanks (pseud.). Endicott & Swett, pub. 1834. Lithograph. 8 1/2 × 13 1/8 in. Courtesy the Library of Congress.

Campaigning for the 1832 election was marked by processions of Democrats armed with sections of ''Old Hickory'' logs and villainous representations of Nicholas Biddle, president of the Bank of the United States. In this cartoon Straightshanks parodies these parades by showing the Jackson government as a garbage wagon pulled by a jackass (with the General's face) led by Martin Van Buren, Jackson's close confidant and chosen successor. The mechanical driver is a hodgepodge of kitchen appurtenances, perhaps symbolic of Jackson's famous Kitchen Cabinet, an informal body of advisors. The rats on the roof are probably a reference to another popular cartoon of the day, ''The Rats Leaving a Falling House,'' which showed Jackson's first cabinet, plagued by resignations and social scandal, deserting the wreckage of Jacksonian government.

64

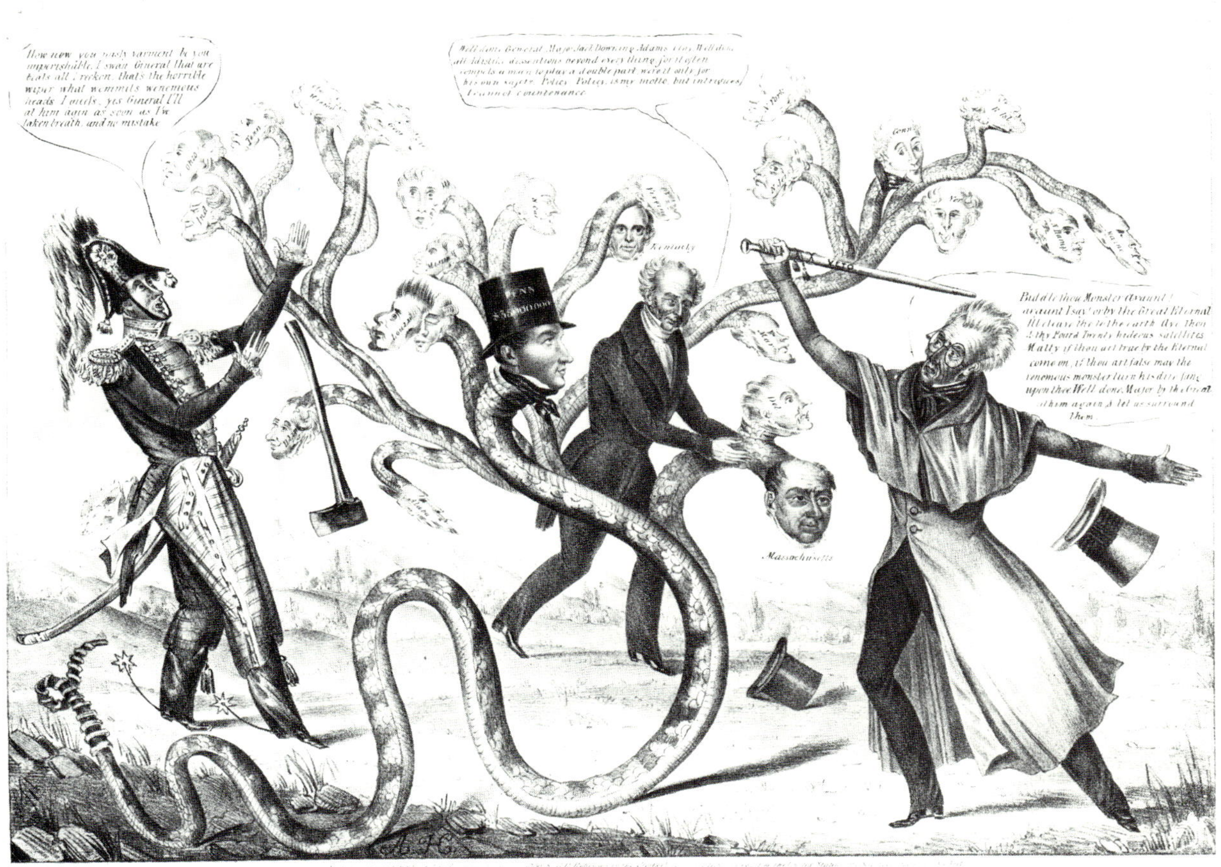

GENERAL JACKSON, SLAYING THE MANY HEADED MONSTER.

Published March 1836, by the proprietor, H. R. Robinson, 48 Courtland St. New York

Fig. 34. *General Jackson Slaying the Many-Headed Monster.* Anonymous. 1836. Lithograph. 13 3/4 × 18 1/2 in. Courtesy Smithsonian Institution, Harry T. Peters "America on Stone" Lithography Collection, Washington, D.C.

One of the major political battles of Jackson's presidency was his conflict with the Bank of the United States, which to him represented the plutocratic corruption that he so opposed. In this cartoon, Jackson, assisted by Martin Van Buren and Major Jack Downing (the comic character invented by Seba Smith), battles the bank, personified as the "Many-Headed Monster." Jackson killed the bank by withdrawing government money and depositing it in state banks, which became known as "pet" banks. He vetoed the bill that would have rechartered the bank in 1832, and the charter expired in 1836. I have "fixed my course as firm as the Rocky Mountain . . . Providence has a power over me, but frail mortals who worship Bale [sic] and the golden calf, can have none," he wrote Van Buren.

65

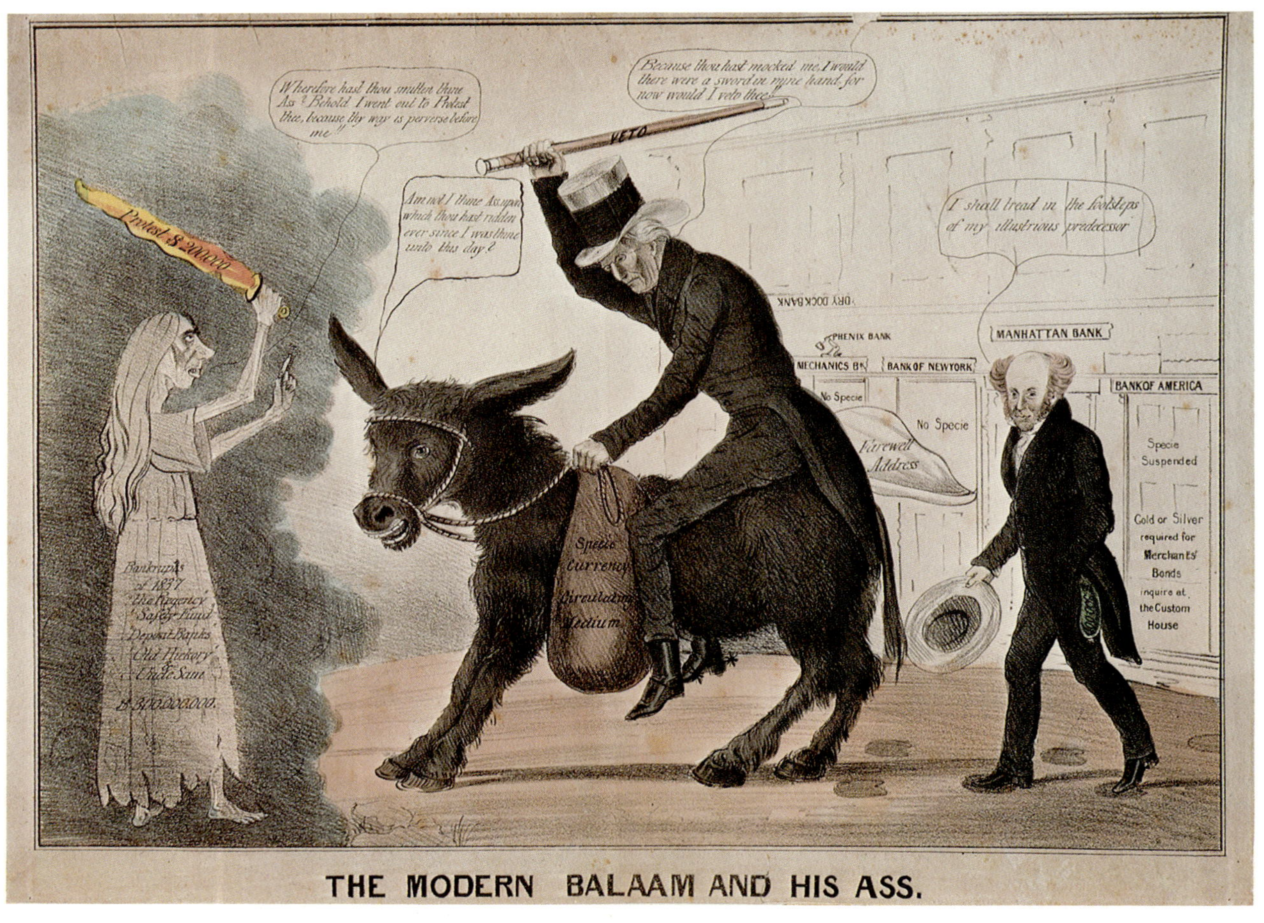

Fig. 35. *The Modern Balaam and His Ass.* Anonymous. 1837. Hand colored lithograph. 12 3/8 × 16 5/16 in. Courtesy the Library of Congress.

When land speculators began buying public lands with state bank currency at an unprecedented rate in 1835, President Jackson attempted to slow the sales by ruling in 1836 that only hard currency would be accepted for public land (the Specie Circular). Instead of driving the speculators from the market, it enhanced the value of the land they held, because only they would now sell for paper money. This cartoonist pictures Jackson as the Biblical Balaam who rides his jackass to deliver a message from God. Three times the ass sees an Angel and stops, each time Balaam beats him and urges him on. The cartoonist's suggestion is that the Specie Circular (the ass) is being urged on by Jackson despite the warnings of the angel (bank failures, as in the background of the print). The Specie Circular was finally repealed in 1838.

66

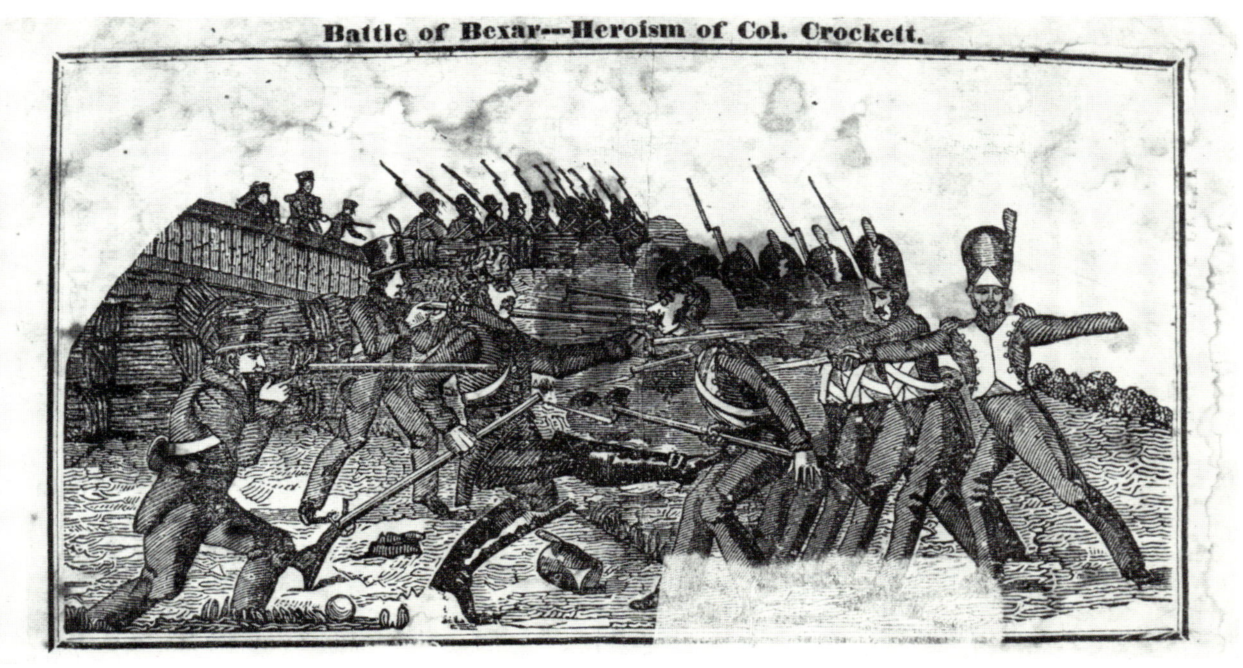

Fig. 36. *Battle of Bexar—Heroism of Col. Crockett*. Anonymous. 1837 in *Davy Crockett's Almanack*. Wood engraving. 6 1/2 × 3 1/2 in. Courtesy Archives Division, Texas State Library, Austin.

The son of a Revolutionary war veteran who ran away from home at age thirteen, David Crockett was elected to the Tennessee Legislature in 1821 and to the United States Congress when he accepted a friend's dare and campaigned for the office. He served three terms, but spent most of his time roaming the backwoods of Tennessee. He reportedly killed 105 bears during one nine-months period. He had little respect for "book-learning" or spell-ing, which he said were "contrary to nature." When he refused to "gee-woa-haw" to the tune of fellow Tennessean Andrew Jackson, Jackson's candidate defeated Crockett in the next congressional election, and Crockett was off to Texas, where he died heroically defending the "shrine of Texas liberty," the Alamo. Crockett's exploits—real or imaginary—were noted in the various issues of *Davy Crockett's Almanack,* which reached a wide audience whose appreciation of the stories was enhanced by the pictures, such as this humorous portrayal of the tragic defense of the Alamo.

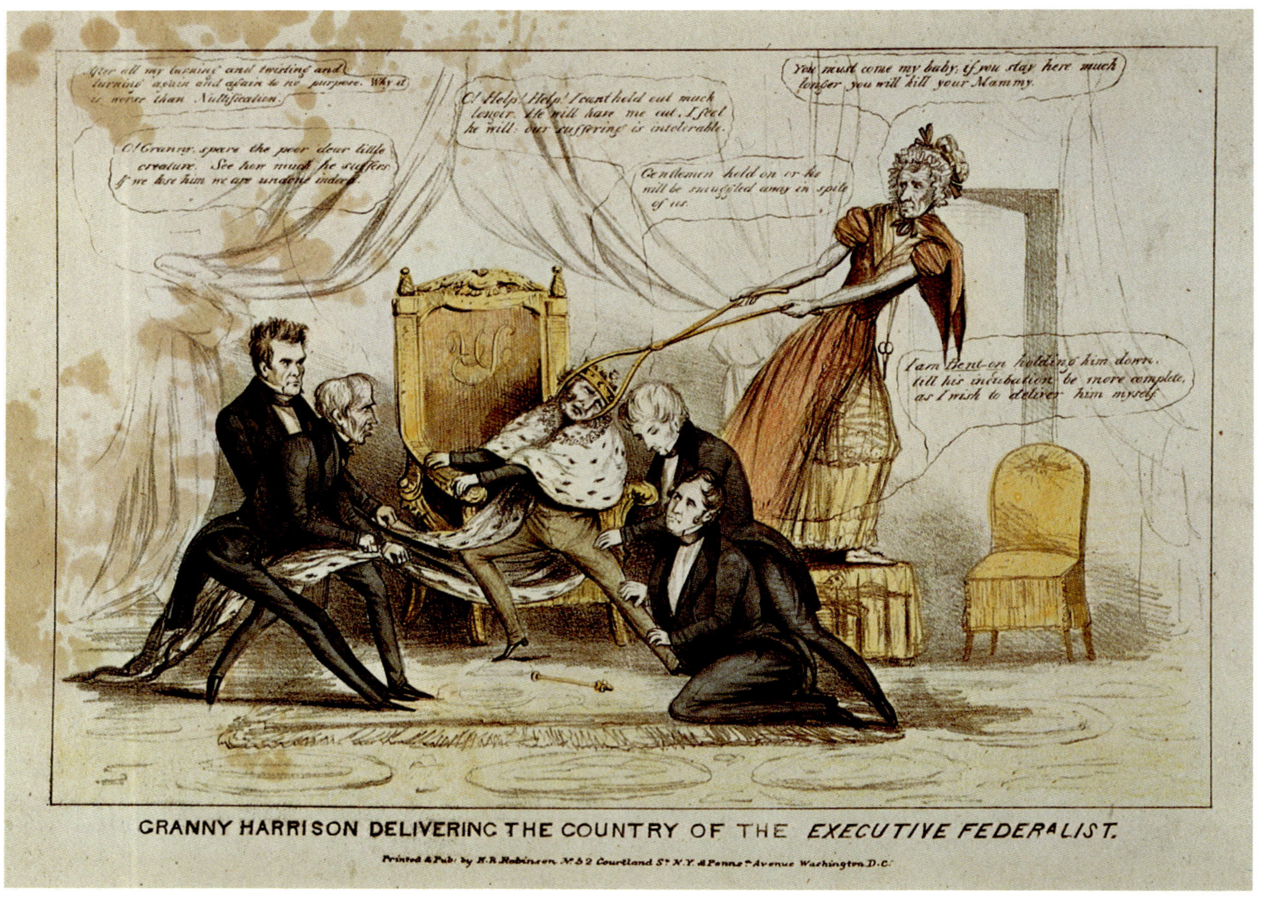

Fig. 37. *Granny Harrison Delivering the Country of the Executive Federalist*. H. R. Robinson. 1840. Colored lithograph. 12 15/16 × 18 1/8 in. Courtesy Smithsonian Institution, Harry T. Peters "America on Stone" Lithography Collection, Washington, D.C.

The Jacksonian Democrats had held onto the presidency for twelve years when General William H. Harrison, called "Granny" because of his sixty-seven years, managed to unseat Martin Van Buren, Jackson's protégé and successor. In this cartoon, John C. Calhoun, Jackson himself, and Thomas Hart Benton attempt to keep Van Buren in the office, while Harrison is successfully pulling him out. Harrison was unable to enjoy his victory, however, as he became ill as a result of the campaign and died after only a month in office.

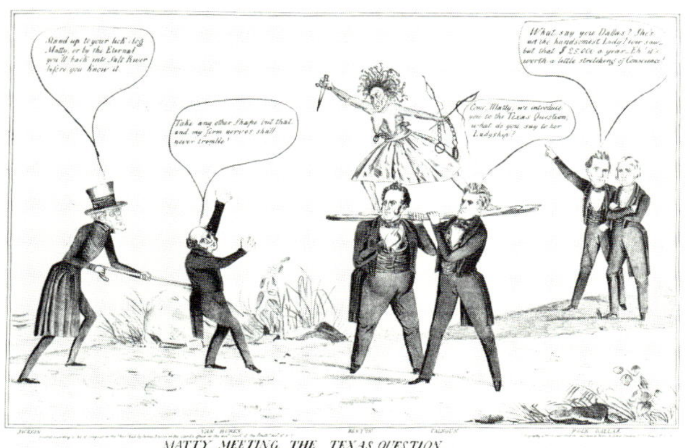

MATTY MEETING THE TEXAS QUESTION.

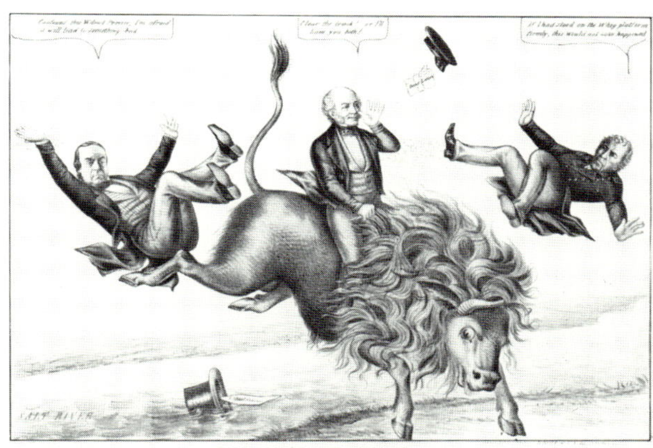

THE BUFFALO HUNT.

Fig. 38. *Matty Meeting the Texas Question*. James Baillie. 1844. Lithograph. 13 1/4 × 19 7/16 in. Courtesy Amon Carter Museum, Fort Worth.

Fig. 39. *The Buffalo Hunt*. H. R. Robinson. 1848. Lithograph. 10 3/8 × 15 1/2 in. Courtesy Smithsonian Institution, Harry T. Peters "America on Stone" Collection, Washington, D.C.

Americans had been colonizing the Mexican province of Texas ever since the 1820s. Although they originally intended to become loyal citizens of Mexico, a series of incidents led to their rebellion in 1836 and to the Republic of Texas, which immediately made itself available for statehood. Because of the slavery issue, and not wanting to anger Mexico, President Jackson did nothing about Texas. By the 1844 election, Texas was a potent political question. Jackson is urging Van Buren to "stand up to your lick-log" and accept Texas, while Polk and Dallas, his Vice-Presidential candidate, decide that Dame Texas might not be the worst ally they could find. Polk entered the campaign calling for the annexation of Texas.

The 1848 election was a confused affair with several parties nominating candidates. The Whigs chose war hero Zachary Taylor to bear their banner; the Democrats picked Lewis Cass. Former President Martin Van Buren received support and nomination from the Barnburner and Free-Soil branches of the Democratic Party in a Buffalo, New York, convention. Thus he is shown here astride a buffalo thumbing his nose at Cass and Taylor, something which did not happen, for he received only about ten percent of the total vote cast.

69

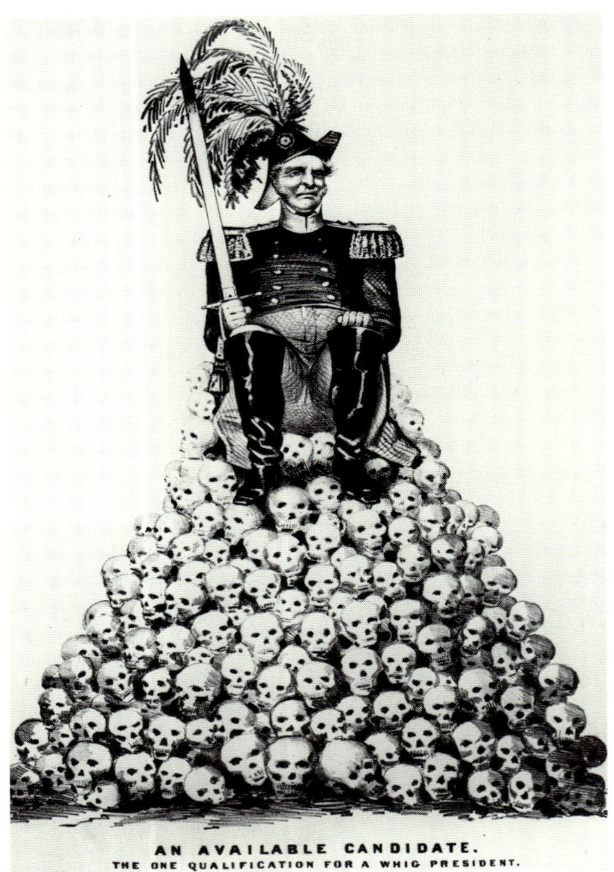

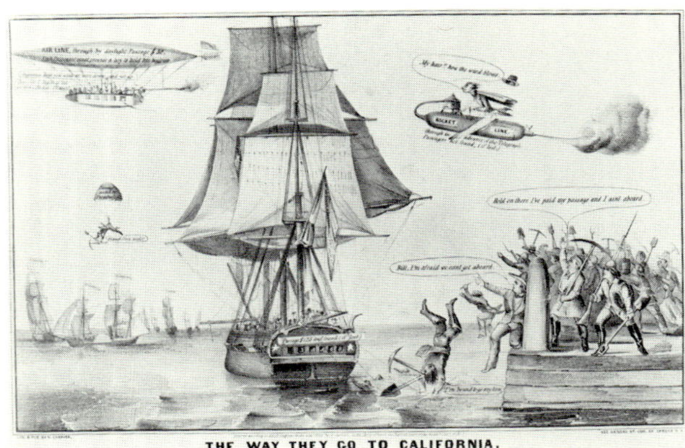

Fig. 40. *An Available Candidate*. [N. Currier?] 1848. Lithograph. 16 × 11 in. Courtesy the Library of Congress.

Political candidates readily acknowledged that a military background helped garner votes. Recalling that the country already had elected Washington, Jackson, and Harrison, President James K. Polk feared the ambitions of General Zachary Taylor and therefore appointed General Winfield Scott to lead the march into Mexico City during the war with Mexico. Still, the fame that Taylor had gained in victories at Palo Alto, Monterrey, and Buena Vista thrust him into the forefront of Whig Party politics, and he received the 1848 nomination, despite this Democratic lithographic comment.

Fig. 41. *The Way They Go to California*. Nathaniel Currier. 1849. Lithograph. 14 × 21 in. Courtesy The Chicago Historical Society.

When it became generally known that John A. Sutter had discovered gold on the American River in California, "forty-niners" began immediate emigration to the West Coast. Because there were no transcontinental roads, they got there the best way they could: overland through the Rocky Mountains, the Southwestern trail through northern Mexico, ship via the Isthmus of Panama, and ship around the Horn. Currier is suggesting even more inventive ways of getting there in this print, while he shows that the conventional means of transportation were full.

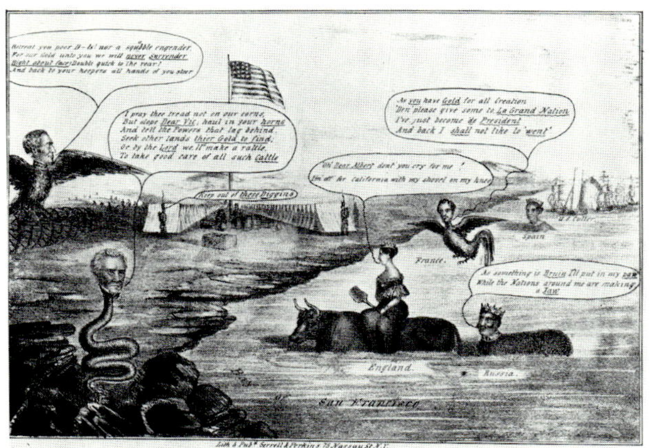

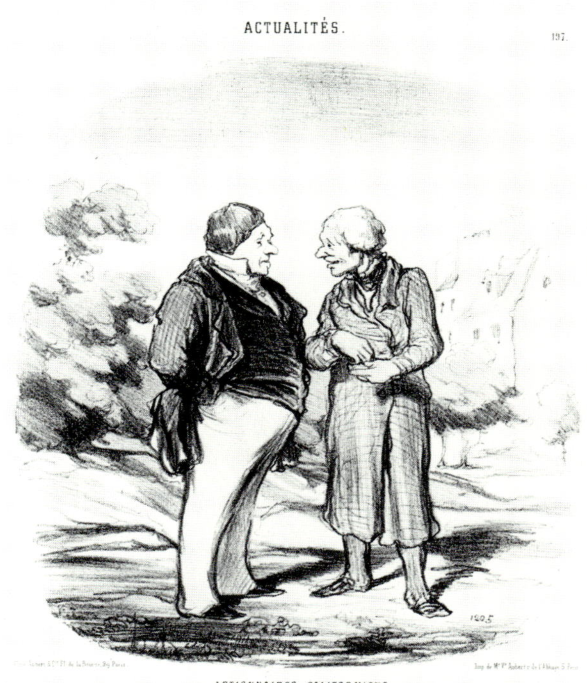

Fig. 42. *Defence of the California Bank*. Serrell & Perkins. 1849. Lithograph. 10 3/8 × 14 1/2 in. Courtesy the Library of Congress.

Once Americans had made the long trek to the California gold-fields, they became jealous of their opportunity, particularly against foreigners. This cartoon shows Queen Victoria, Louis Napoleon, the Russian Tsar, and a Spaniard coming into San Francisco Bay as a soldier on the shore shouts for them to "keep out of these Diggins." Although the majority of the gold hunters were Americans, Mexicans, Australians, Hawaiians, English, Irish, Chinese, and French also crowded the goldfields.

Fig. 43. *Actionnaires Californiens*. Honoré Daumier. 1850. Lithograph. 9 9/16 × 8 1/2 in. Courtesy Boston Public Library, Print Department.

The gold discovery in California, one of the largest finds of the nineteenth century, attracted attention around the world. Here Daumier pictures two Frenchmen discussing purchase of land in California along the Sacramento River in the gold country. "I invested all the money I owned," says one would-be entrepreneur.

71

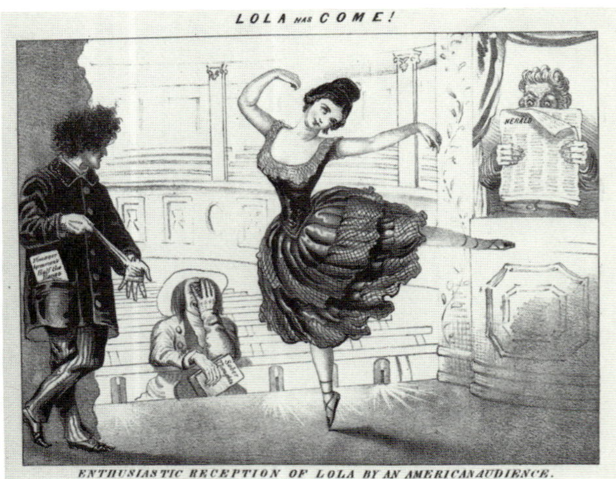

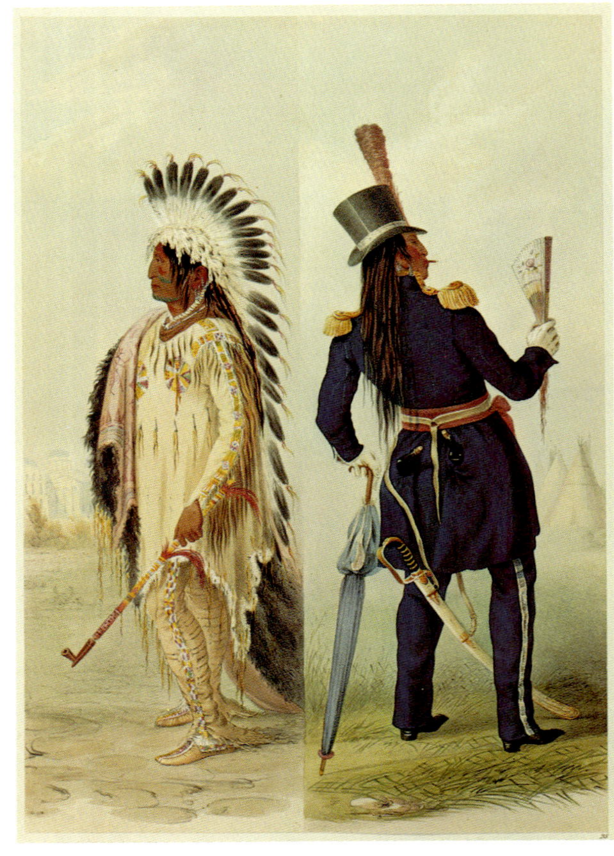

Fig. 44. *Lola Has Come!* Anonymous. 1852. Lithograph. 7 1/8 × 11 in. Courtesy Hoblitzelle Theatre Arts Collection, Humanities Research Center, University of Texas, Austin.

A celebrated figure in the nineteenth century, Lola Montez made the most of a confused parentage to play up her supposedly exotic European background, becoming the mistress of, among others, Franz Liszt, Alexandre Dumas, and King Leopold of Bavaria, who made her Countess of Landsfeld and who was forced to abdicate after his attentions toward her were made public. With this reputation preceding her, she arrived in the United States in 1852 billing herself as a Spanish dancer. This cartoon shows Lola dancing in a nearly empty theater (although she most often had a full house). A Quaker peers at her hypocritically from behind spread fingers, while a gentleman reading the New York *Herald* (which gave Lola lots of press) gazes from his box.

Fig. 45. *Wi-Jun-Jon*. George Catlin. 1844. Colored lithograph. 18 1/2 × 23 1/2 in. Courtesy Amon Carter Museum, Fort Worth.

Artist Catlin found *Wi-jun-jon* (as he recorded the name; *Ah-jon-jon* it should have been) along the Upper Missouri River, a proud warrior with great respect among his people, and took him to Washington to meet President Jackson. The Indian quickly assimilated the white man's ways and became a caricature of his former self. "He had . . . exchanged his beautifully garnished and classic costume for a full dress *en militaire*," said Catlin. When he returned to his village his friends and relatives hardly recognized him. Gradually he began to tell stories of his adventure. So preposterous were his tales that his tribesmen killed him as a liar after several months.

72

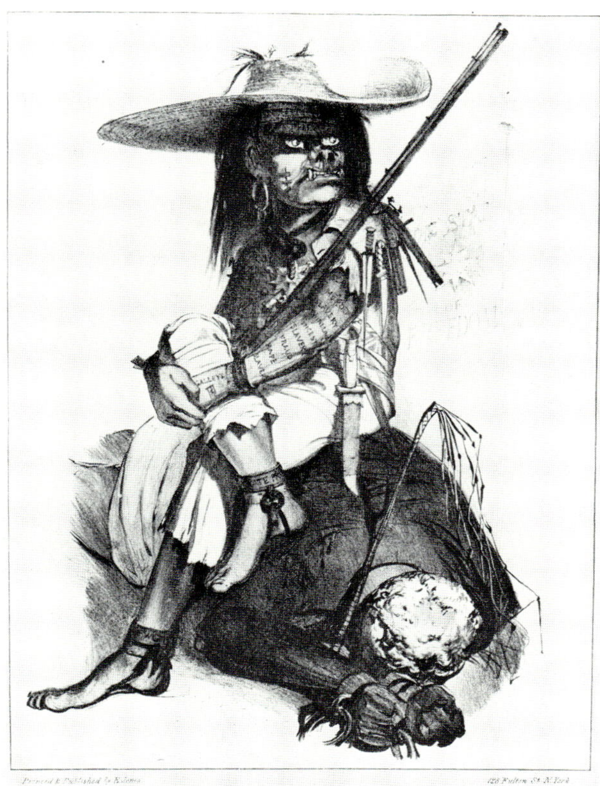

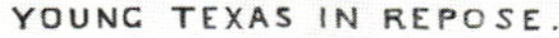

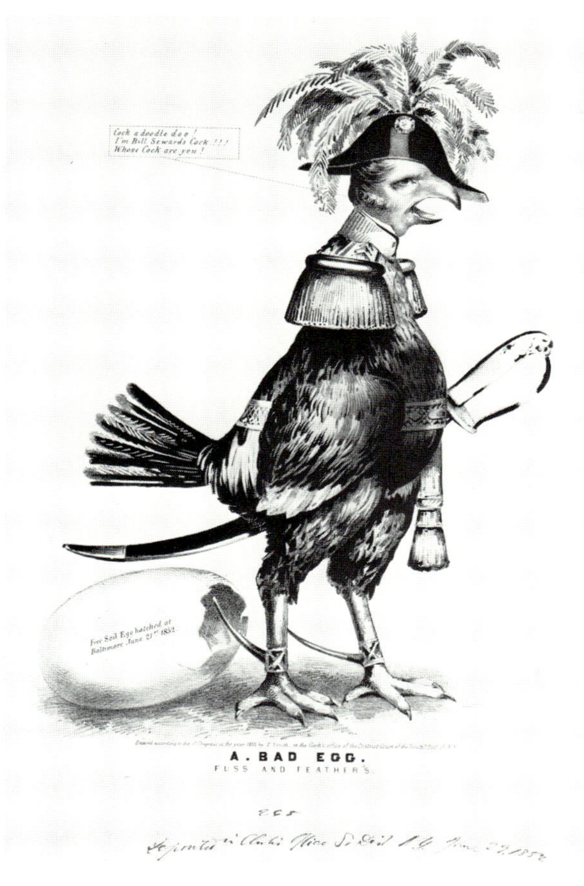

Fig. 46. *Young Texas in Repose*. E. Jones. 1852. Lithograph. 14 1/16 × 9 13/16 in. Courtesy Arts of the Book Collection, Yale University Library, New Haven.

The primary political issue of the 1850s was expansion of slavery into Kansas and other territories. Texas was considered a particularly depraved slave-holding state by abolitionists because they felt the 1836 Revolution to be a slave-holder plot to get another slave state into the Union and because it was the fastest growing slave state in the Union throughout the 1850s. Thus this particularly brutal young man sitting on a slave who bears a strong resemblance to a bale of cotton is labeled "Young Texas."

Fig. 47. *A Bad Egg. Fuss and Feathers*. P. Smith. [N. Currier]. 1852. Lithograph. 16 3/8 × 11 in. Courtesy the Library of Congress.

The election of 1852 further cemented the tie between military success and the presidential nomination, with two Mexican War generals, Winfield Scott and Franklin Pierce leading the Whigs and the Democrats respectively. Scott was also supported by the Free Soil Party (thus the "Free Soil Egg" hatched in Baltimore). Fearful that Scott would be influenced by abolitionist William Seward, Southerners were deserting the party. In an effort to stop the desertion, Seward announced that he would accept no favors from Scott, but the cartoonist obviously does not agree.

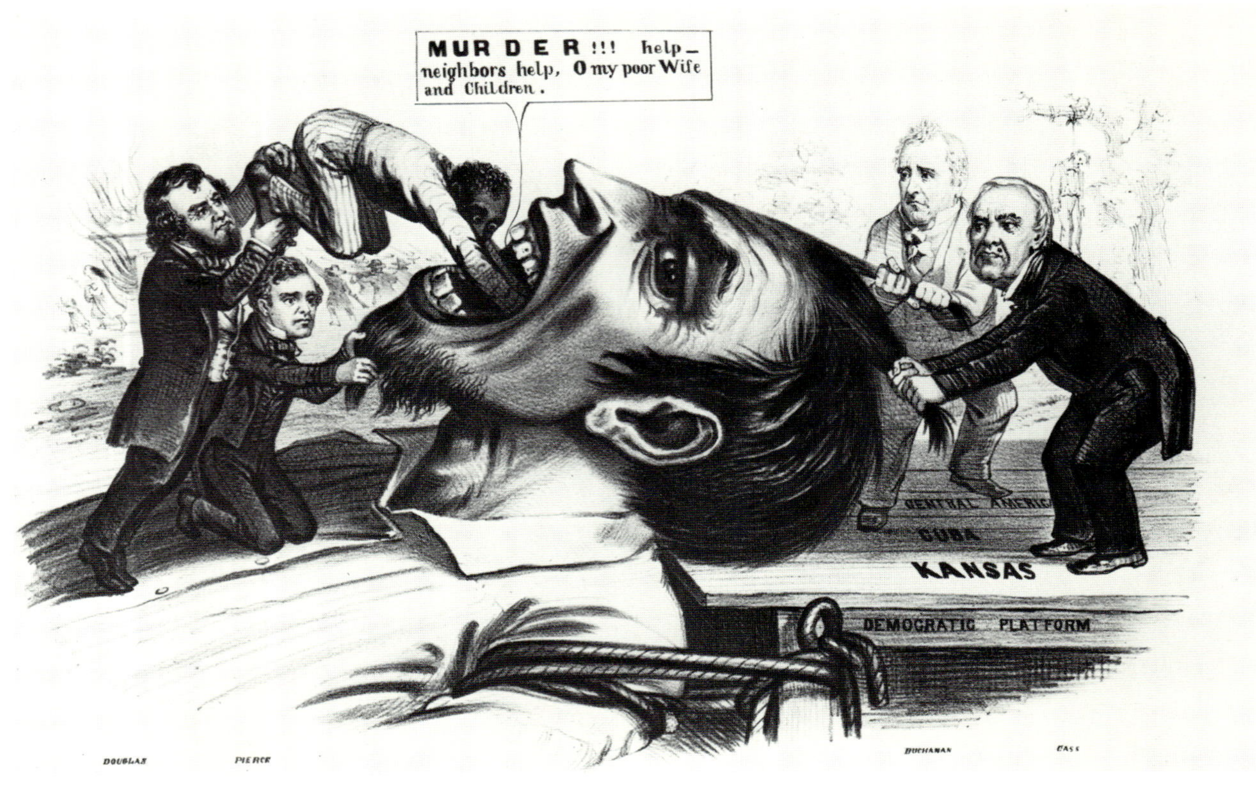

Fig. 48. *Forcing Slavery Down the Throat of a Free-Soiler.* Anonymous. 1856. Lithograph. 12 × 15 3/4 in. Courtesy The New-York Historical Society, New York City.

By 1856 the issue of slavery dominated politics. Senator Stephen A. Douglas of Illinois, a leading Democratic contender, tried to sidestep the issue by leaving it up to the voters of each territory, but this cartoonist sees Douglas' position as one of forcing slavery onto the territories (Kansas, in this instance) because of the effort pro-slavery forces would make to win the elections. James Buchanan is shown holding the free-soiler while Douglas administers the force, a prediction of Buchanan's leaning since he had been away as Minister to England and no one really knew where he stood on the issue.

74

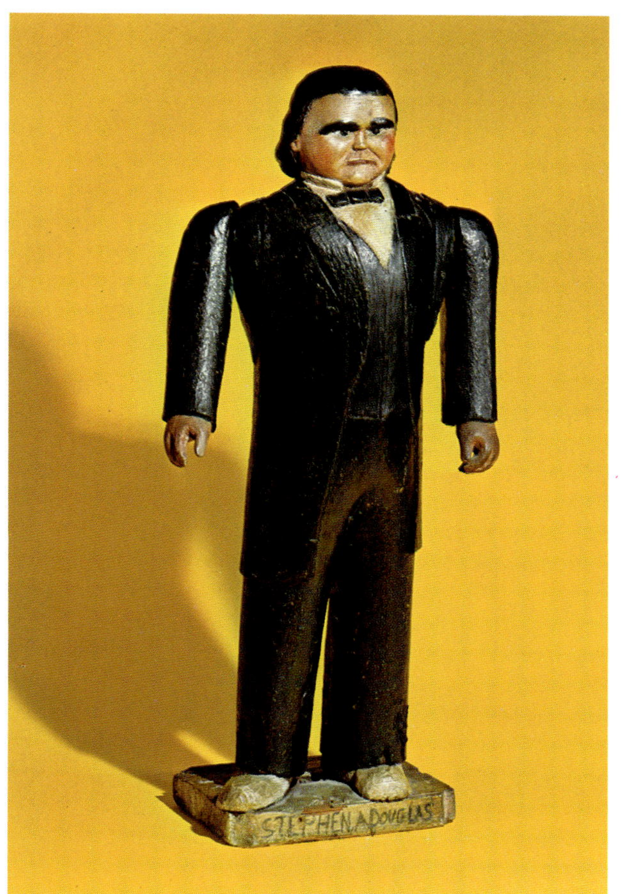

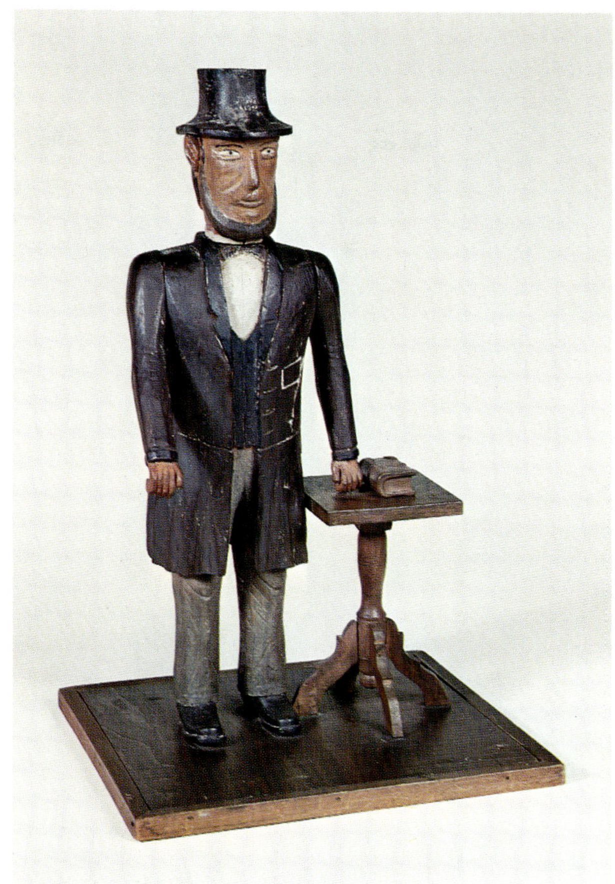

Fig. 49. *Stephen Arnold Douglas*. Anonymous. 1858. Wood sculpture, polychromed. 18 in. high. Courtesy National Portrait Gallery, Smithsonian Institution, Washington, D. C.

The "Little Giant," as Stephen Douglas was fondly called, was a powerful politician and presidential aspirant during the 1850s. Perhaps most famous for his debates with Abraham Lincoln during the 1858 senatorial campaign, Douglas espoused "popular sovereignty," which held that the states themselves should decide the future of slavery within their boundaries. He ran for President in 1860 as a Democrat but lost much support because the Democratic Party split into northern and southern branches. He died at age 48 of typhoid fever.

Fig. 50. *Abraham Lincoln*. Anonymous. c. 1863. Wood sculpture, polychromed. 17 3/4 in. high. Courtesy Missouri Historical Society, St. Louis.

President Lincoln's leadership during one of the severest crises the country has known endeared him to Americans and made him one of the great figures in our country's history. This anonymous carver seems to have captured Lincoln's dignity and forthrightness. He also tells something about Lincoln by having him pose with his hand near the Bible, which Lincoln often quoted during his speeches.

75

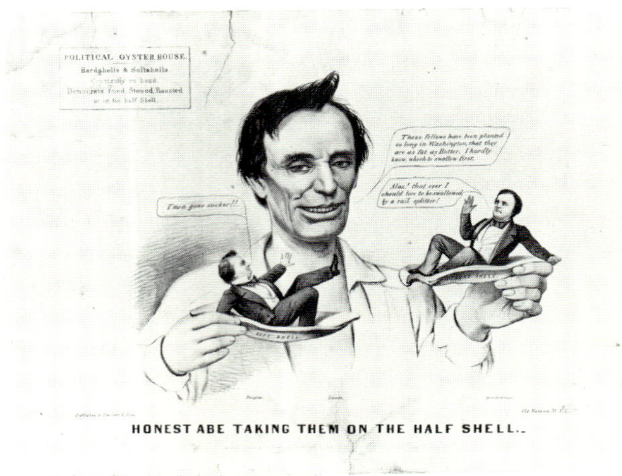

Fig. 51. *Honest Abe Taking Them on the Half Shell*. Currier & Ives. 1860. Lithograph. 13 9/16 × 18 1/16 in. Courtesy The Lilly Library, Indiana University, Bloomington.

Northerners classified Democrats as either "hard-shell" (pro-slavery) or "soft-shell" (moderate on slavery). In this cartoon, the Republican Lincoln is about to swallow his hard-shell and soft-shell Democratic opponents. The sign in the background indicates that this is a Republican "Political Oyster House," where Democrats are served "fried, Stewed, Roasted or on the half Shell."

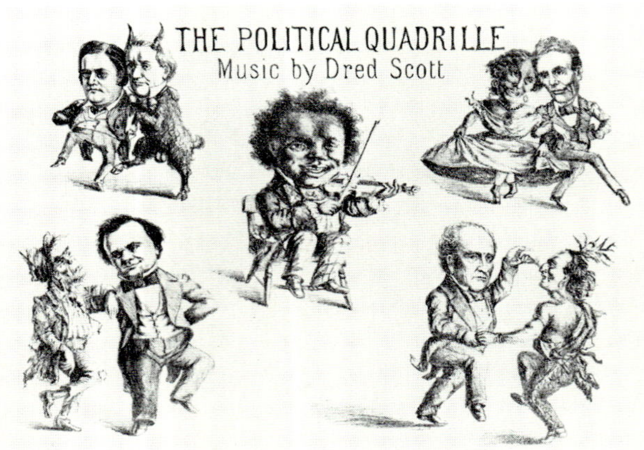

Fig. 52. *The Political Quadrille. Music by Dred Scott*. Anonymous. 1860. Lithograph. 12 3/4 × 17 7/8 in. Courtesy the Library of Congress.

Dred Scott was a slave whose master had taken him into free territory, then back into slave territory. Scott sued for his freedom, claiming that his sojourn in free territory made him a free man. Chief Justice Roger B. Taney, in his opinion, stated that Scott was a slave and therefore had no right to sue in federal court. Further, he ruled that Scott was property and the slave owner could not be deprived of his property without "due process." This meant that the Missouri Compromise of 1820 was unconstitutional, because it had established certain free territory in which slavery could not exist. Shown in this cartoon are the candidates in the 1860 election, Abraham Lincoln, John Bell, Stephen A. Douglas, and John C. Breckinridge.

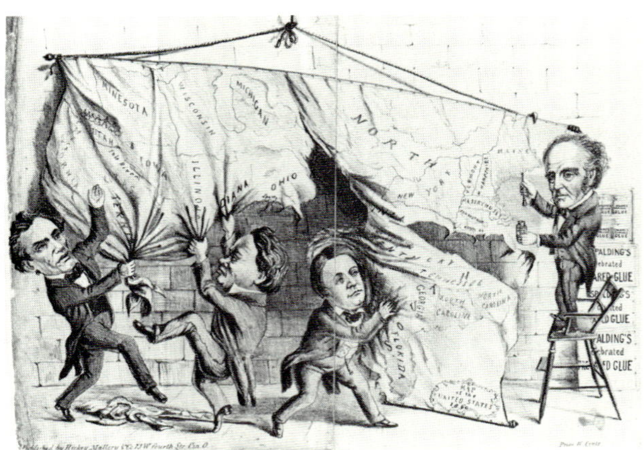

Fig. 53. *Dividing the National Map*. Rickey, Mallory & Company. 1860. Lithograph. 13 11/16 × 19 1/4 in. Courtesy The Lilly Library, Indiana University, Bloomington.

Political parties were badly divided as they entered the campaign of 1860. Sectional issues had split the Democrats into Northern and Southern branches, Stephen A. Douglas leaning toward the Northerners and John C. Breckinridge of Kentucky the Southerners' candidate. Remnants of the Whig and Know-Nothing parties united under the Constitutional Union Party banner and nominated John Bell. Lincoln was the candidate of a united but Northern Republican Party. This cartoon shows Lincoln and Douglas struggling for the western section of the map, while Breckinridge captures the South and Bell tries to repair the damage.

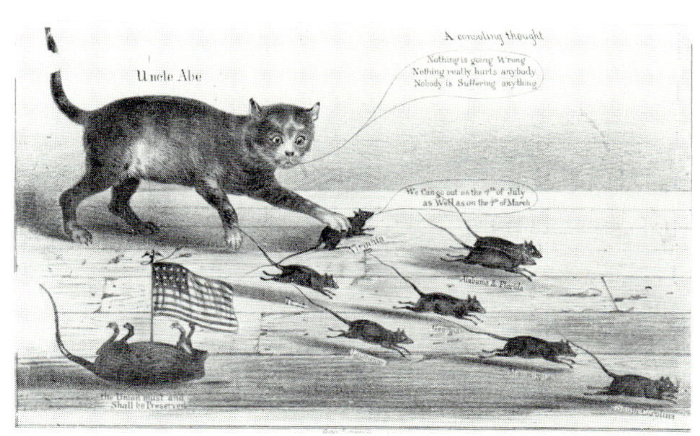

Fig. 54. *Virginia Paw-sing*. Anonymous. 1861. Lithograph. 8 1/2 ×
14 in. Courtesy The Chicago Historical Society.

Produced in Richmond as the Southern states were seceding,
this cartoon shows the order in which the states left the Union,
with South Carolina leading the way. It also graphically shows
that President Lincoln tried to keep them from leaving. The
popular Northern belief that ''the Union must and Shall be
Preserved'' is shown as a dead issue—a decapitated rat.

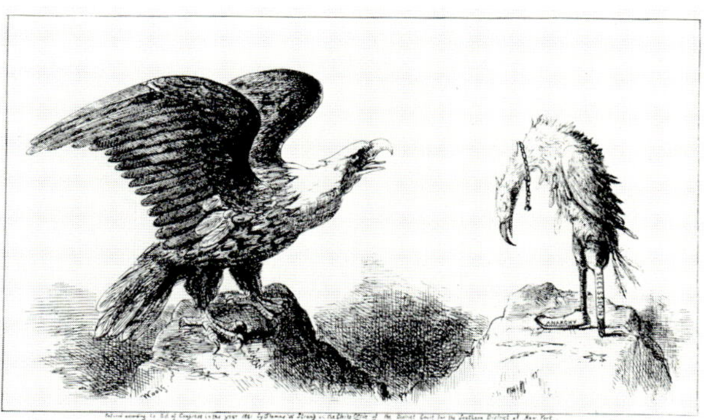

Fig. 55. *Our National Bird As It Appeared When Handed to James
Buchanan. March 4, 1857. The Identical Bird As It Appeared A. D.
1861*. Michael Angelo Woolf. 1861. Lithograph. 7 5/8 × 13 in.
Courtesy Boston Public Library, Print Department.

It was President James Buchanan's misfortune to serve during
four of the most hectic years our country has known. While it
is unlikely that any man could have preserved the Union in
1861, Buchanan had made his share of blunders. He began by
announcing that he intended to serve only one term, lessening
his influence immediately. He continually called for preservation
of the Union, but instituted no measures directed toward that
end. In a typical remark, he told Congress that secession was
unconstitutional, but that neither the President nor Congress
had the power to prevent it.

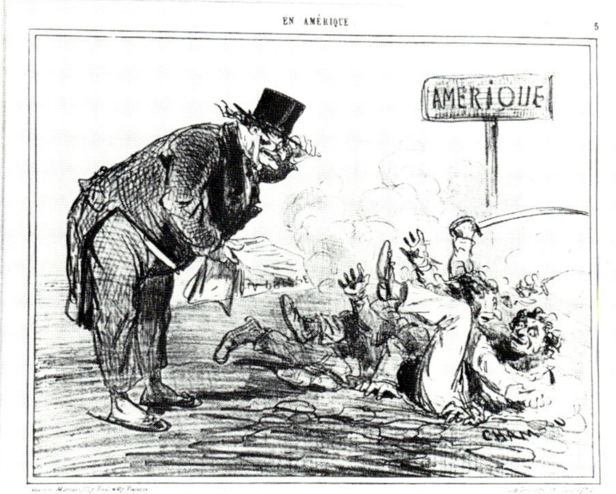

Fig. 56. *En Amerique*. Cham (?). c. 1862. Lithograph. 10 3/4 ×
14 3/16 in. Courtesy Louisiana State Museum, New Orleans,
1956.

To a middle class Frenchman it must have been difficult to tell
the difference between the North and the South, for their differences were small by comparison with the peculiarities of France,
or Europe in general. Without slavery there would have been too
few differences to provoke a bloody Civil War, as this Frenchman
seems to understand: "Ah! Devil! I am starting to get mixed up in
all this," he says. "Which one is the North? Where is the South?
I don't understand anything any more."

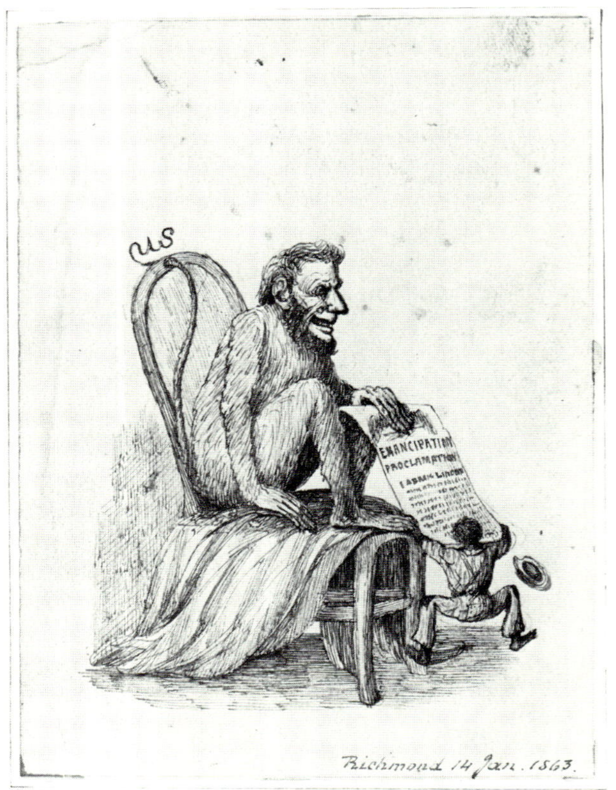

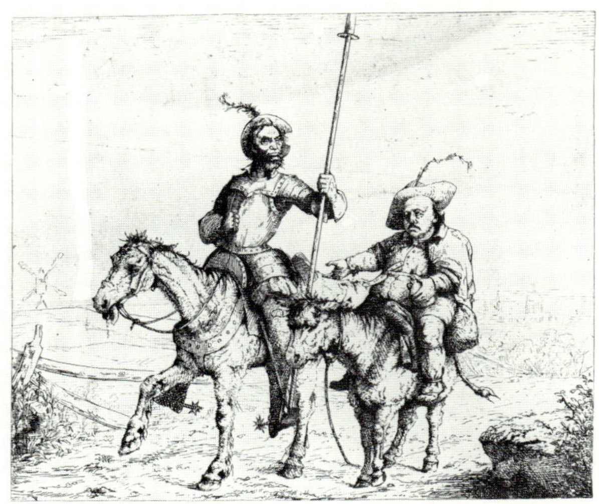

Fig. 57. [Lincoln as a Monkey.] David H. Strother [attrib.] Jan. 14, 1863. Pencil on paper. 8 13/16 × 5 1/4 in. Courtesy The Lilly Library, Indiana University, Bloomington.

On March 2, 1862, President Lincoln suggested to Congress a plan whereby slaves in loyal states would be given their freedom and their owners compensated up to an average of $400. Congress took no action regarding the loyal states, but on January 1, 1863, Lincoln issued the Emancipation Proclamation, which granted freedom to slaves in the rebellious states. Few slaves were actually freed until after the war, because Lincoln obviously did not possess the power to free slaves in Confederate-held territory unless the individual slaveholders decided to cooperate. At the conclusion of the war, the Union Army freed slaves as it took possession of territory. Lincoln had feared the Proclamation would be declared unconstitutional, but instead it was validated by the thirteenth amendment.

Fig. 58. *Lincoln and Butler as Don Quixote and Sancho Panza.* Adalbert Volck. 1863. Etching. 6 1/2 × 7 1/2 in. Courtesy The New-York Historical Society, New York City.

Adalbert Volck, a Baltimore dentist and artist, did a number of etchings to accompany verse satirizing the military career of General Benjamin F. Butler, along with Lincoln among the most hated men in the South. Today it may be difficult to understand Butler's prominence in the cartoons of the era, but he was a well-known figure whom many Southerners had thought would fight with them. When he chose to remain with the Union, they considered him a traitor. His command of the Union occupation forces in New Orleans earned him the nicknames "Beast" and "Butcher" before he was finally removed from the command in December, 1862.

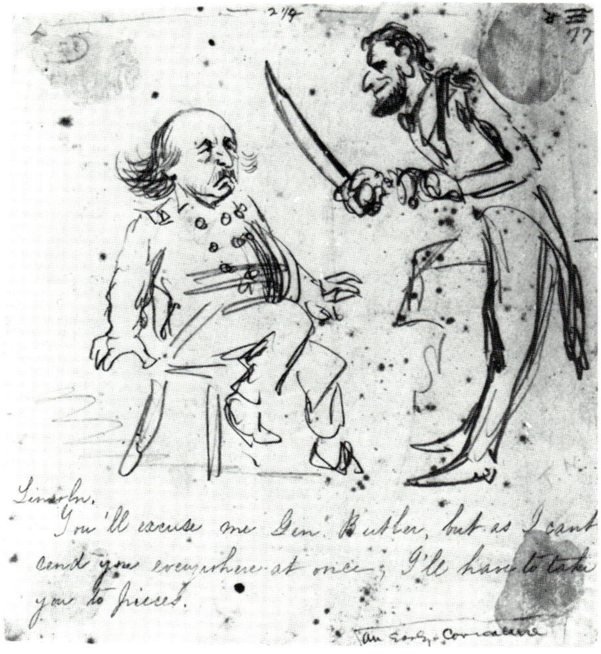

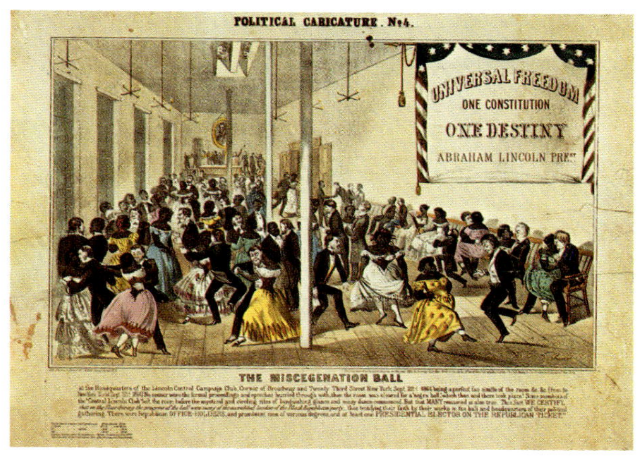

Fig. 59. *Lincoln. You'll excuse me Gen. Butler, but as I cant send you everywhere at once, I'll have to take you to pieces.* Thomas Nast [attrib.] n.d. Pencil on paper. 5 7/8 × 6 11/16 in. Courtesy The Lilly Library, Indiana University, Bloomington.

Perhaps Thomas Nast, a loyal Unionist, attempted to answer the Southern caricatures of General Butler with this drawing which seems to say that Butler is so important to Lincoln that the President would like to cut him up and send him to several different locations at once. He was such a poor general, however, Nast might have intended exactly the opposite meaning for his cartoon. Because of Butler's large personal following, Lincoln could not afford to alienate the general and was obliged to give him a field command. Perhaps only in this Nast drawing did Lincoln reveal his true feelings toward Butler.

Fig. 60. *The Miscegenation Ball*. Anonymous. 1864. Colored lithograph. 19 × 23 3/4 in. Courtesy Smithsonian Institution, Harry T. Peters "America on Stone" Collection, Washington, D.C.

Bromley & Company of New York City did several anti-abolitionist cartoons during the Civil War. This one ridicules a Lincoln campaign ball, showing blacks and whites dancing together and in various stages of embrace. Some of the political leaders left the room before the ball began, says Bromley, but many stayed for the party. This print, he claims, is a "perfect facsimile of the room &c. &c."

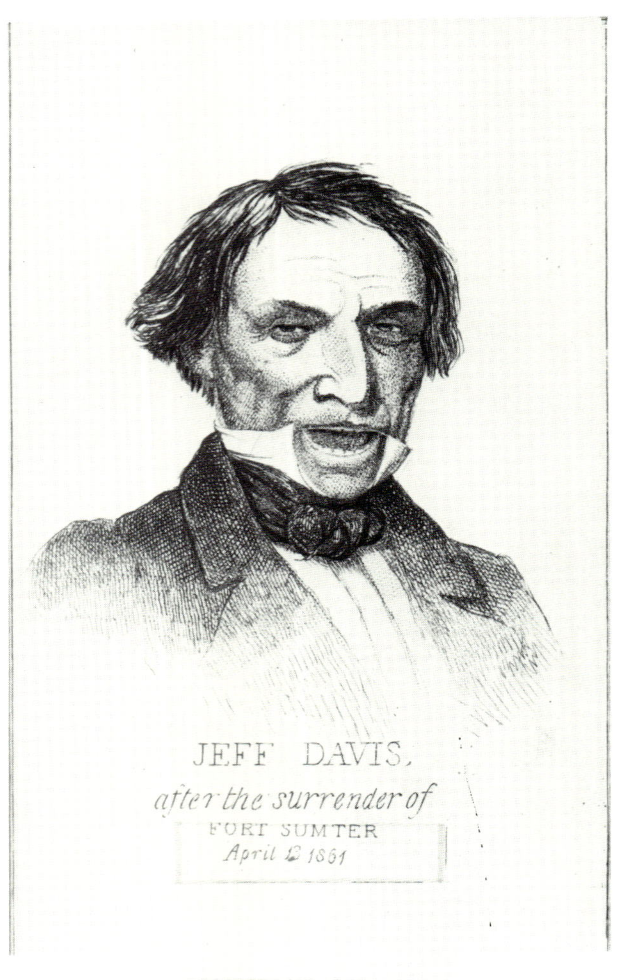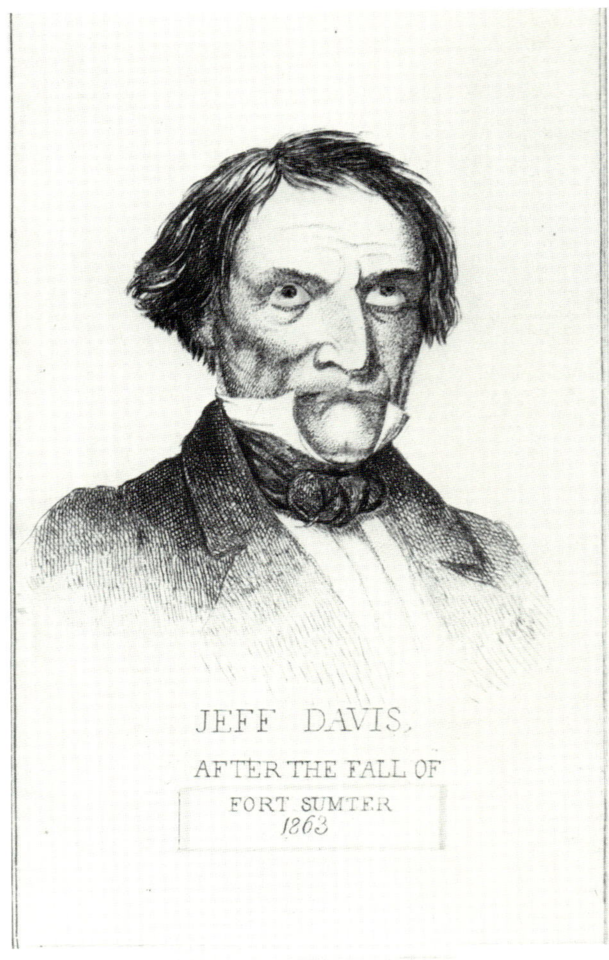

Fig. 61. *Jeff Davis After the Surrender of Fort Sumter, April 13, 1861. Jeff Davis, After the Fall of Fort Sumter, 1863*. David Claypool Johnston. c. 1863. 4 1/2 × 2 3/4 in. and 4 1/2 × 2 3/4 in. Courtesy Mr. and Mrs. Draper Hill, Memphis, Tenn.

Jefferson Davis, the President of the Confederate States, was frequently caricatured in the North, particularly after a Northern victory, such as the one alluded to here by Johnston. Fort Sumter was the first Union fort to fall to the rebels as the Civil War began. It was a symbolic victory when the Union won it back in 1863. Shown here are two postcards which can be moved so that Davis is either smiling or frowning. The event shown below the title also changes as the card is maneuvered.

80

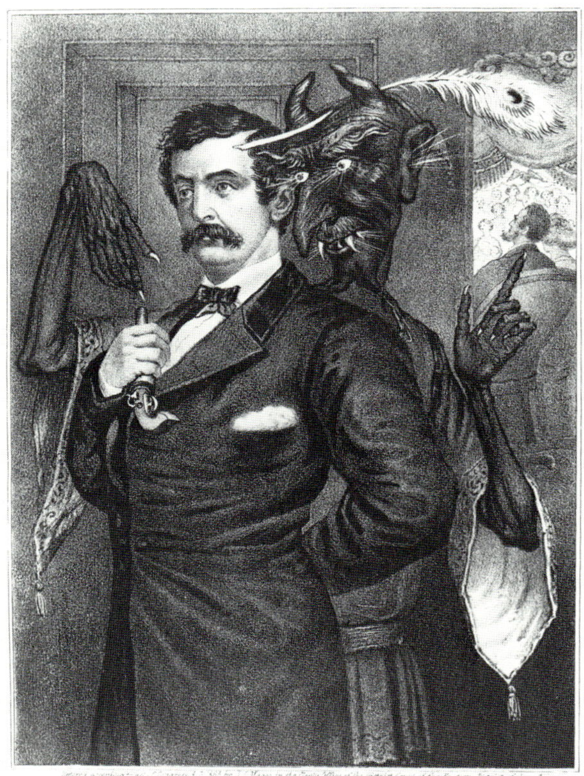
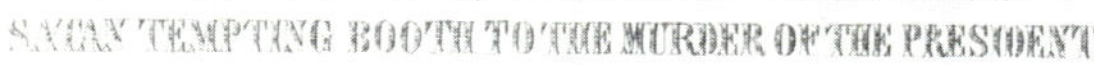

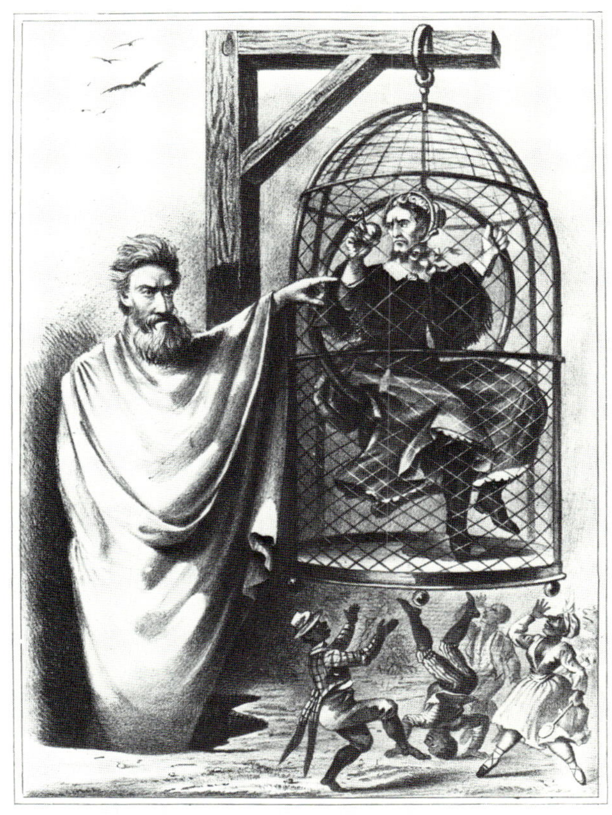

Fig. 62. *Satan Tempting Booth to the Murder of the President*. J. L. Magee. 1865. Lithograph. 10 1/2 × 8 3/4 in. Courtesy Collections of The Library Company of Philadelphia.

On the afternoon of April 14, 1865, President Lincoln told his cabinet that, ''I hope there will be no persecution, no bloody work after the war is over. No one need expect me to take any part in hanging or killing those men, even the worst of them. . . . We must extinguish our resentments if we expect harmony and union.'' That night he was assassinated by actor John Wilkes Booth, a demented Southern sympathizer, as he relaxed at Ford's Theater in Washington.

Fig. 63. *John Brown Exhibiting his Hangman*. G. Querner. 1865. Lithograph. 16 3/8 × 12 1/4 in. Courtesy The New-York Historical Society, New York City.

John Brown, an abolitionist who had incited rebellion and murdered five slave owners, had been hung for his excesses in 1859 by the State of Virginia. Embittered and enraged by the Civil War experience many Northern sympathizers came to liken Brown to an Old Testament prophet who called violence down upon the heads of the sinful, slaveholding South. This cartoon, executed soon after the war, depicts Brown as a vengeful spirit pointing an accusing finger at Jefferson Davis. Davis is depicted as a woman holding Eve's apple of sin and is suspended above the heads of the emancipated slaves for their ridicule.

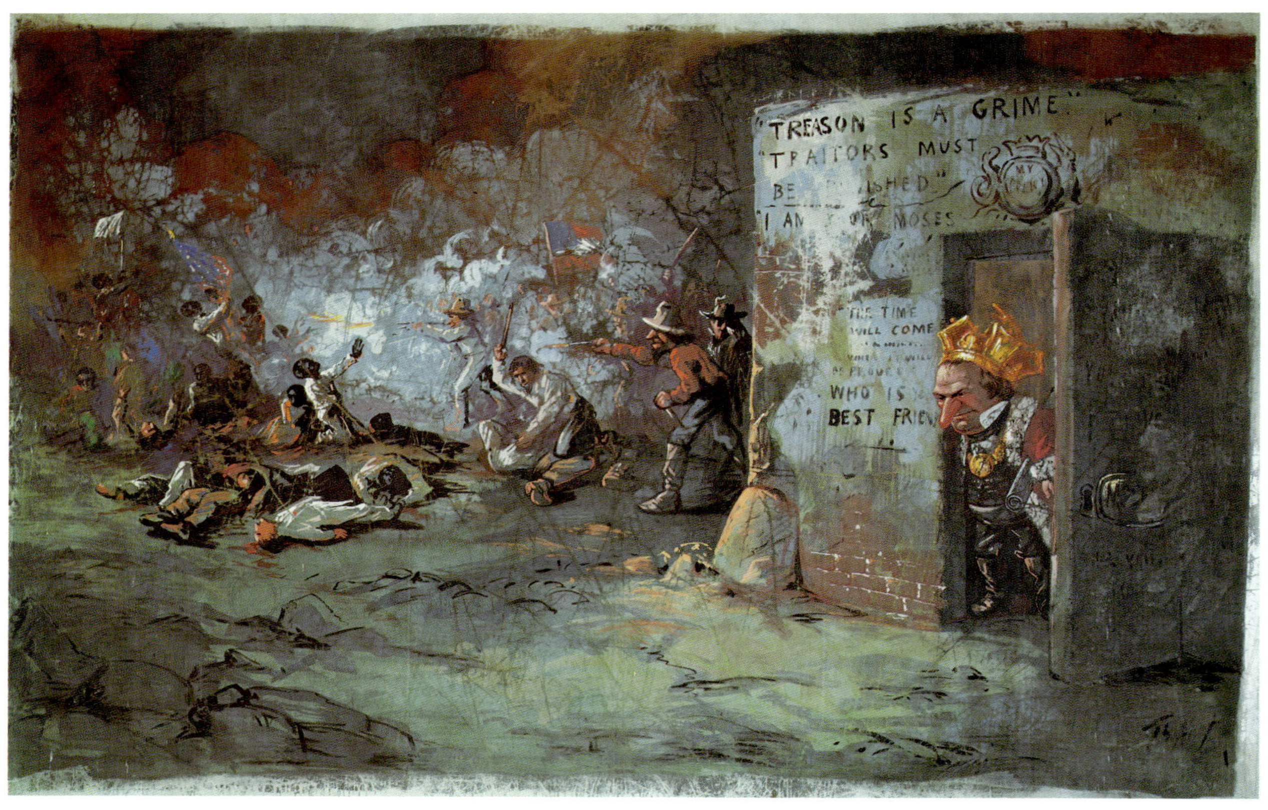

Fig. 64. *The Massacre at New Orleans*. Thomas Nast. 1867. Oil on canvas. 7 ft. 10 3/4 in. × 11 ft. 6 1/2 in. Courtesy The Swann Collection of Caricature and Cartoon, New York City.

In the summer of 1867 Thomas Nast, by then a well known cartoonist for *Harper's Weekly*, began work on his Grand Caricaturama, which was exhibited in Dodworth Hall, New York City, in December, 1867. The Caricaturama consisted of thirty-three "Grand Historical Paintings." Shown here is his depiction of the New Orleans riot of July 30, 1866, in which thirty-seven Negroes and three white sympathizers were killed. The riot started when police attacked a number of Negroes participating in a Radical Republican meeting, which was designed to help the Radicals take over the state from the Johnson Republicans. Combined with riots in Memphis and Vicksburg, the New Orleans riot gave Northerners the impression that Southerners were taking out their frustration on the Negroes, and Nast blamed President Johnson.

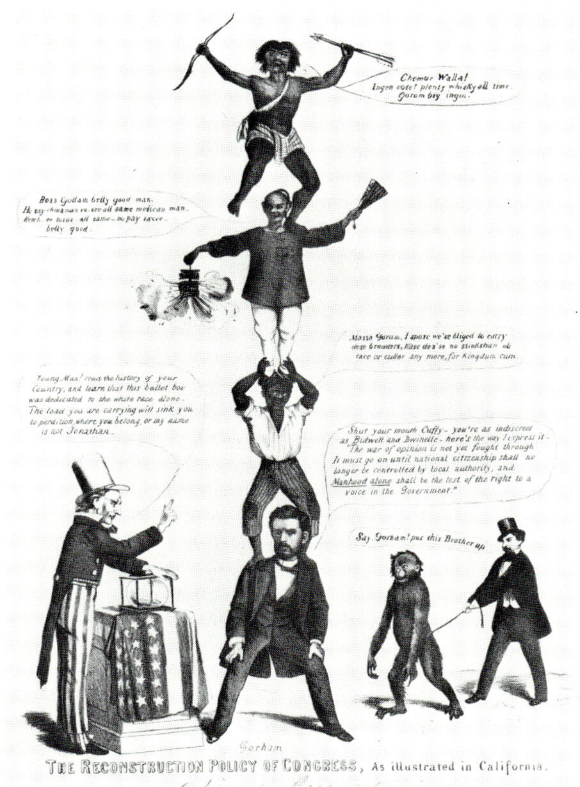

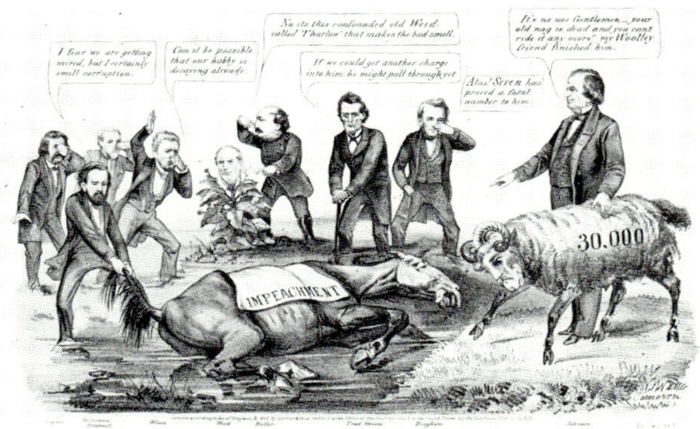

Fig. 66. *The Smelling Committee*. John Cameron. 1868. Lithograph. 8 1/2 × 14 1/2 in. Courtesy Boston Public Library, Print Department.

During March, April, and May of 1868 the Senate sat as a jury in the impeachment trial of President Andrew Johnson, who faced eleven charges of high crimes and misdemeanors in office. When the first ballot was taken, the Radical Republicans who had instigated the impeachment proceedings were shocked to find that they had lost by one vote. They recessed for ten days to try to marshal the votes necessary for conviction, but when they reconvened, they were again defeated. Seven Republicans (the "fatal number") voted with the Democrats to acquit Johnson. The impeachment managers, John A. Logan, T. Williams, George S. Boutwell, J. F. Wilson, Ben Butler, Thaddeus Stevens, and J. A. Bingham, encircle a dead horse, "Impeachment," in this cartoon. Butler suggests that Thurlow Weed, Republican political boss of the 1840s who sanctioned bribery and legislative trading as legitimate political tools, is causing the bad smell. But Johnson, at right, corrects him by pointing out that it is impeachment that is dead and decaying.

Fig. 65. *The Reconstruction Policy of Congress, as Illustrated in California*. Anonymous. 1867. Lithograph. 14 3/8 × 10 1/2 in. Courtesy the Library of Congress.

In 1867 George C. Gorham was nominated for governor of California by the Republican Party convention. A man who made no secret of his ambitions, Gorham is here satirized as a tool of the Radicals who uses the "machine" votes of Negroes, Chinese, and Indians to gain election. There was so much protest over his selection that the Republicans held another convention and the nomination was offered to John Bidwell, who turned it down. Finally, Caleb T. Fay was nominated, but he was beaten by Democrat H. H. Haight.

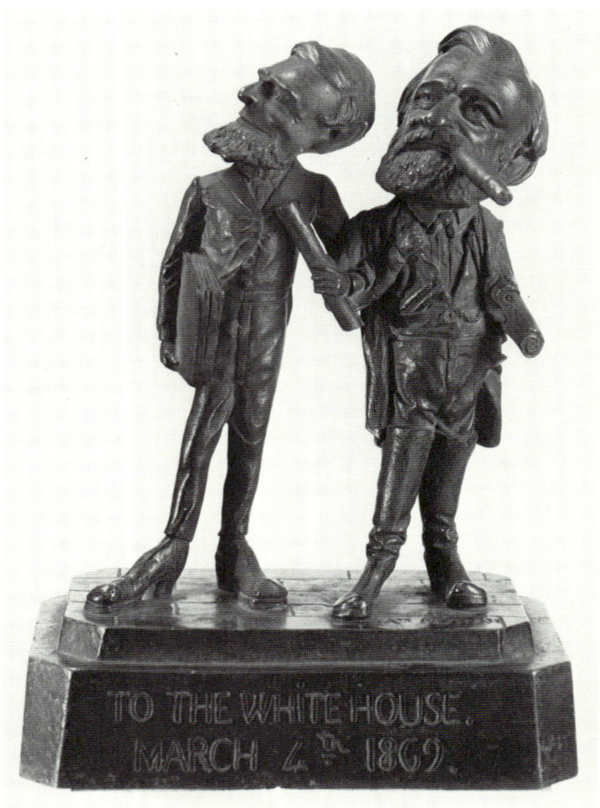

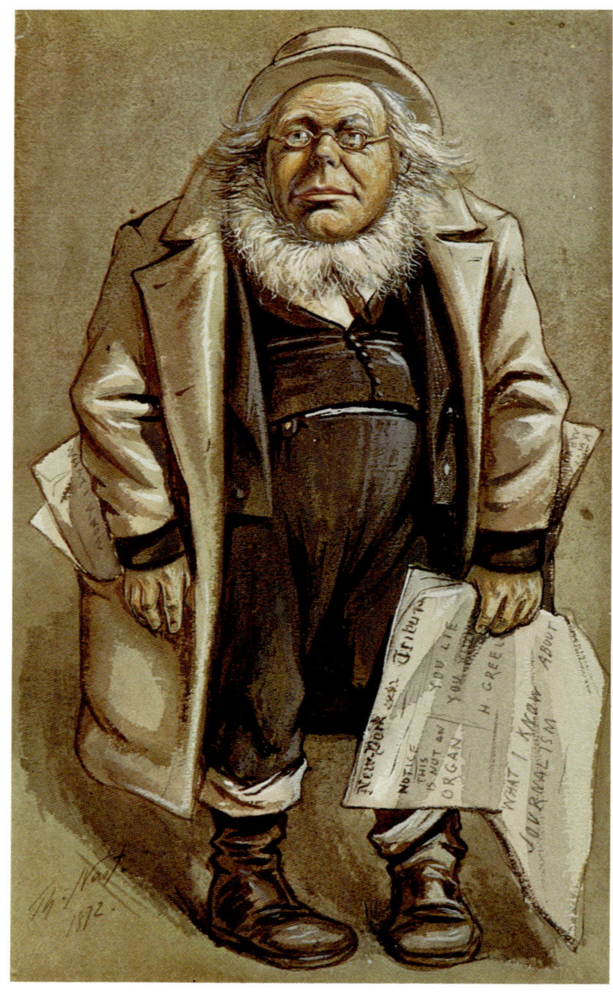

Fig. 68. *Horace Greeley*. Thomas Nast. 1872. Watercolor on paper. 12 1/8 × 7 1/4 in. Courtesy National Portrait Gallery, Smithsonian Institution, Washington, D. C.

Perhaps most famous for his admonition to young men to "Go West," Horace Greeley was the influential founder and editor of the New York *Tribune* and a candidate for president in the controversial 1872 election, which also included the first woman candidate for that office (fig. 71). He had been a supporter of Grant, but later denounced that corrupt administration, split from the Republican Party, and helped form the Liberal Republican Party. More a social reformer than a politician, Greeley actually thought he had a good chance to be elected. Overwhelmed by Grant's crushing victory, Greeley died a short time after the election.

Fig. 67. *To the White House, March 4th 1869*. Auguste Peyrau. 1869. Bronze. 10 5/8 in. high. Courtesy Museum of Fine Arts, Boston: M. and M. Karolik Collection.

The Civil War hero Ulysses S. Grant was elected President in 1868 to succeed the ineffective Andrew Johnson. Grant's Vice-President was Schuyler Colfax.

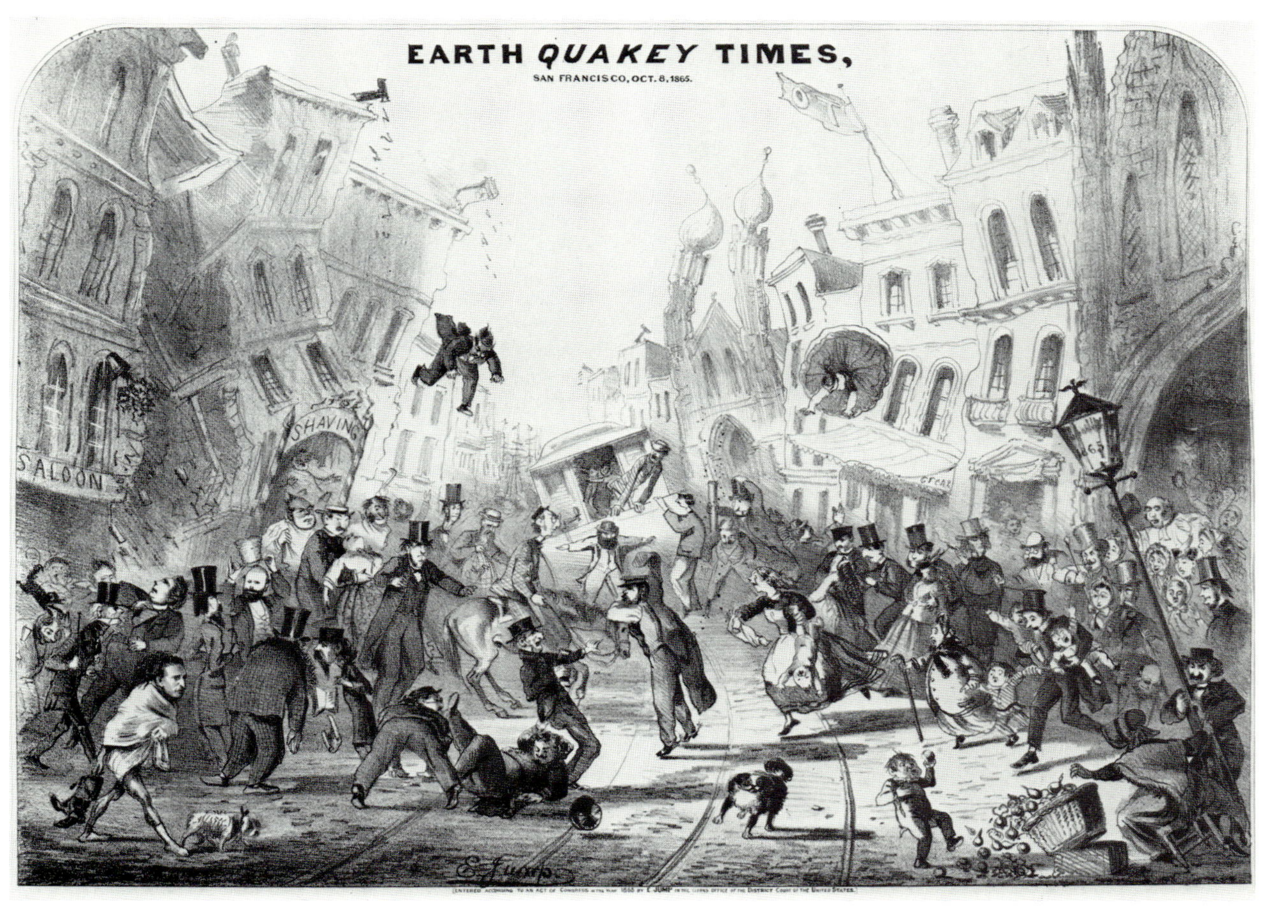

Fig. 69. *Earth Quakey Times, San Francisco, Oct. 8, 1865*. Edward Jump. 1865. Lithograph. 14 3/16 × 19 7/8 in. Courtesy Collections of the California Historical Society, San Francisco.

This print "celebrates" the earthquake that shook San Francisco on October 8, 1865. Jump has taken a tragic situation and by means of skillful pen and imagination turned it into a humorous lithograph with eccentric people and buildings braving the quake.

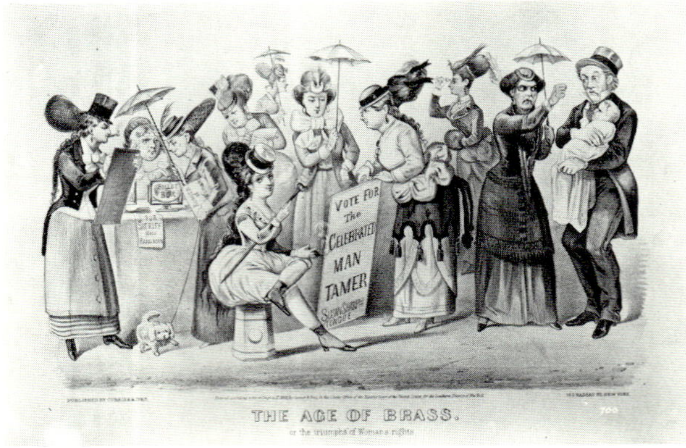

Fig. 70. *The Age of Brass. Or the Triumphs of Woman's Rights*. Currier & Ives. 1869. Lithograph. 18 3/4 × 13 3/8 in. Courtesy the Library of Congress.

Woman's crusade for equal rights predates this Currier & Ives print, but the Civil War made the issue timely again. Women took on many roles that were not necessarily theirs by routine during the war—running farms or plantations, organizing charities, hospitals, etc. on the home front. After the war they were not anxious to give up their newly won privileges, privileges they proved they could handle during the war. Currier & Ives are only predicting what most men thought would be the logical end of such nonsense.

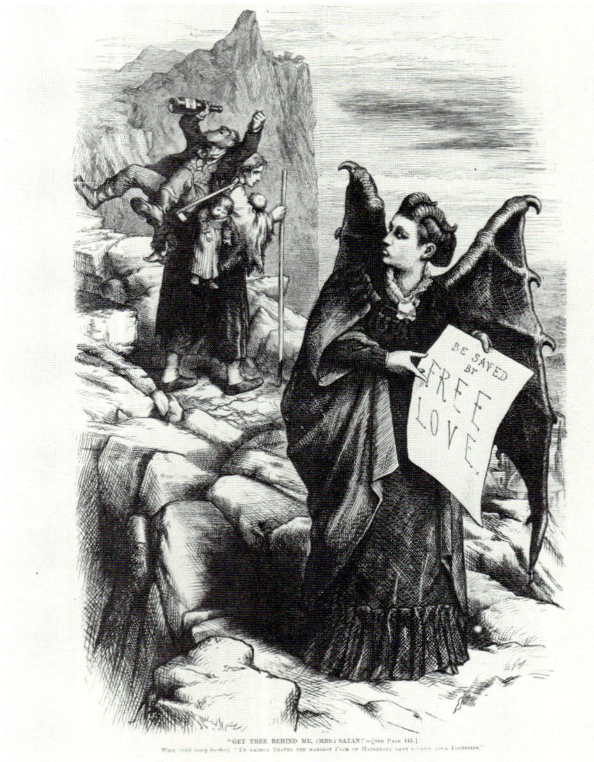

Fig. 71. *"Get thee behind me, (Mrs.) Satan!"* Thomas Nast. Feb. 17, 1872 in *Harper's Weekly*. Wood engraving. 15 15/16 × 11 in. Courtesy Amon Carter Museum, Fort Worth.

Victoria Claflin Woodhull was an unconventional woman's rights agitator whose antics continually shocked and disturbed nineteenth century America. She was alleged to be the offspring of a one-eyed backcountry drifter and an Ohio saloonkeeper's daughter. At age fifteen Victoria married the elderly Dr. Canning Woodhull. They separated, and she divorced him to marry Col. James Harvey Blood. With Col. Blood she became involved in the nineteenth century fad of spiritualism, a profession which introduced her to railroad magnate Cornelius Vanderbilt. With Vanderbilt's money and advice Victoria and her sister, Tennessee, established a prosperous brokerage firm. The next male bastion the intrepid Mrs. Woodhull assaulted was politics. In her *Origin, Tendencies and Principles of Government*, first printed as articles in the New York *Herald* in 1870, she espoused free love and communal property. On April 2, 1870, buoyant on the waves of her notoriety, she declared her candidacy for President of the United States. Her highly unconventional views and colorful background made her appear in most Victorian eyes as a female antichrist rather than a potential national leader.

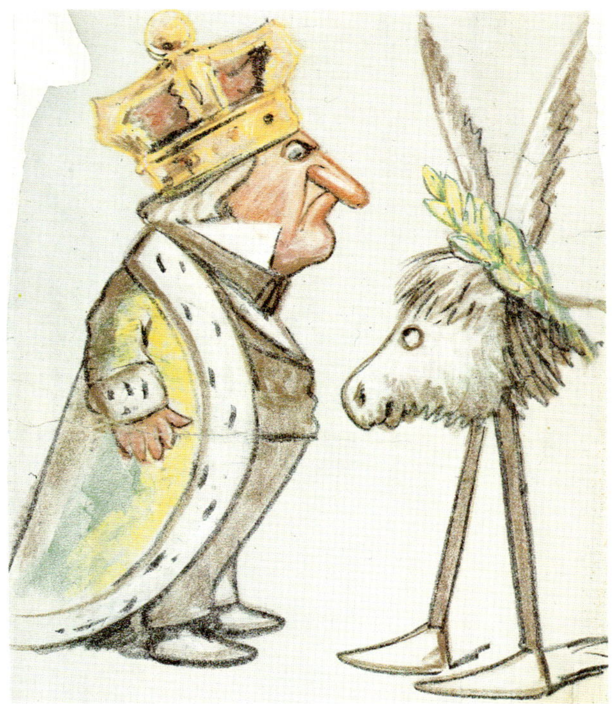

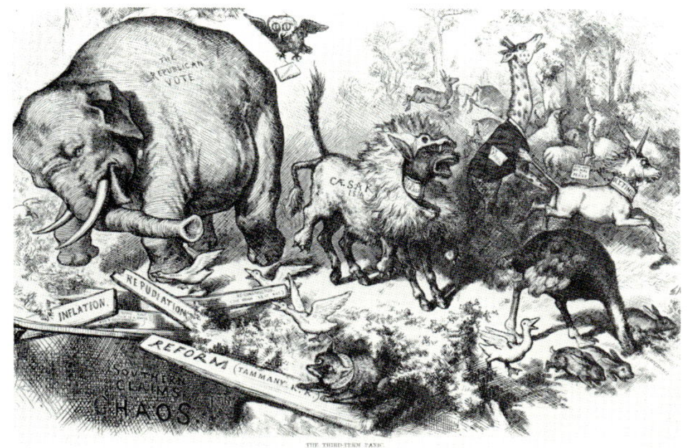

Fig. 72. [Andrew Johnson caricature with a donkey]. Thomas Nast. c. 1876. Pastel on paper. 51 1/2 × 40 1/2 in. Courtesy National Portrait Gallery, Smithsonian Institution, Washington, D. C.

To Nast Andrew Johnson represented tyranny in the Executive Office. "King Andy" as Nast portrayed him, is confronted here with the whimsical donkey scarecrow, which Nast used to symbolize President Grant's alleged "Caesarism." Throughout Grant's second term the press had accused him of arrogance and vaunting political ambition, speculating that he would seek a third term to satisfy this lust for power. Nast, ever defensive of Grant despite the scandals and political debacles of his administration, portrayed this supposed threat as a make-believe jackass, thus juxtaposing the "real" tyrant Johnson (in Nast's opinion) with the unreal threat of Grant's Caesarism created by the hostile press.

Fig. 73. *The Third-Term Panic*. Thomas Nast. Nov. 7, 1874, in *Harper's Weekly*. Wood engraving. 11 × 15 15/16 in. Courtesy Amon Carter Museum, Fort Worth.

While continuing to counter the charge of President Grant's "Caesarism," Nast inadvertently invented the Republican elephant. In this cartoon the New York *Herald*, which had been vociferously denouncing what it thought were Grant's intentions of running for a third term, is shown as an ass masquerading in a lion's skin scaring off all the other newspapers (the frightened animals, in this reference to one of Aesop's fables). The elephant symbolizes the massive Republican vote, which Nast fears is about to be duped by the *Herald's* charges (portrayed by the trap the elephant is about to fall into). The Democratic Party is the fox in this picture, the donkey having been assigned to the *Herald*.

87

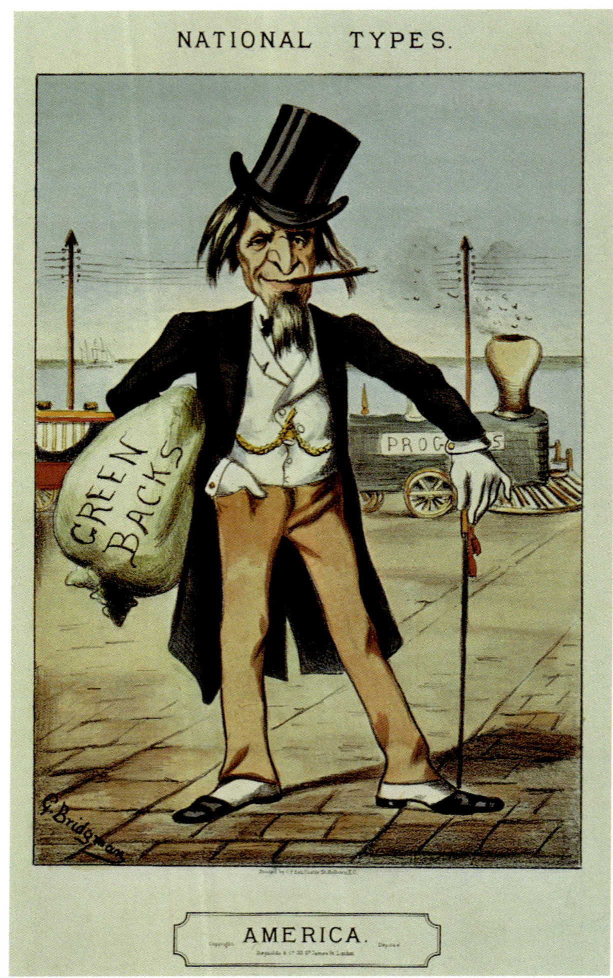

Fig. 74. *America*. G. Bridgman. 1870s. Hand-colored lithograph. 16 1/2 × 10 15/16 in. Courtesy Amon Carter Museum, Fort Worth.

The American businessman of the 1870s confronted the world, confident of his ability, riding the railroad of ''Progress,'' and spreading ''Greenbacks'' wherever he traveled in search of new materials and markets. The greenbacks owed their popularity to the political party of the same name, which campaigned in 1876 for the issue of more paper money. Peter Cooper ran for president, but received only 80,000 votes. Two years later the party drew more than two million votes, but in the following years merged itself with other inflationist groups and disappeared. Bridgman's caricature of the American businessman represents the vigor with which the new merchants hit the world's economy following the Civil War and the expansive period of industrialization in this country.

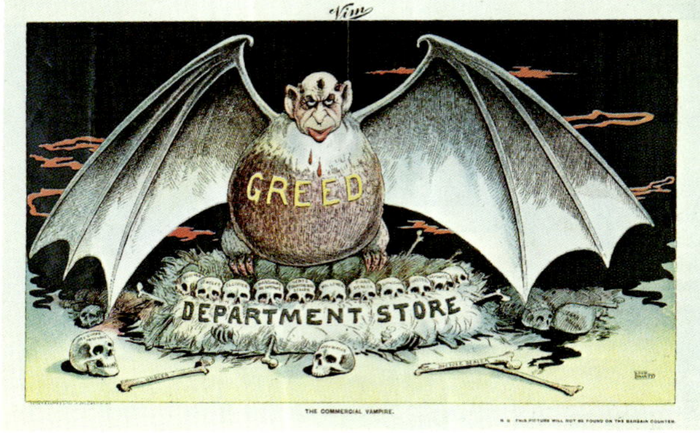

Fig. 75. *The Commercial Vampire*. Leon Barritt. 1898 in *Vim*. Chromolithograph. 11 1/4 × 18 in. Courtesy The Chicago Historical Society.

Known as ''Palaces of Consumption,'' the department stores revolutionized consumerism in the United States at the turn of the century. By locating in large buildings, the department stores were able to centralize distribution of associated merchandise and lower the price to a set, non-negotiable figure. Barritt shows, by the skulls and bones of bankrupt dry goods merchants, bicycle dealers. and ''segar'' dealers, that the department stores drove many smaller merchants and clerks out of business. ''N. B.,'' he adds to the caption, ''This picture will not be found on the bargain counter.''

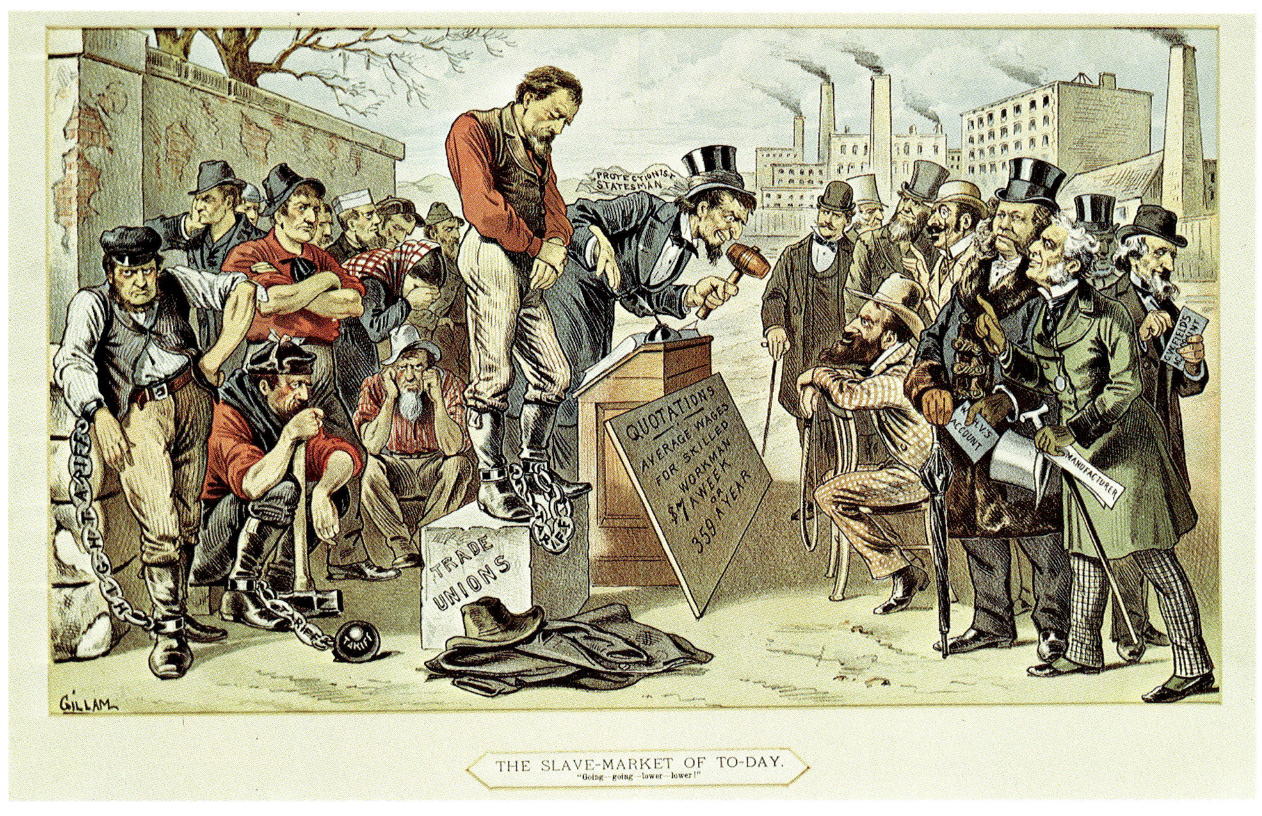

THE SLAVE-MARKET OF TO-DAY.
"Going—going—lower—lower!"

Fig. 76. *The Slave Market of Today*. Bernhard (?) Gillam. Jan. 2, 1884, in *Puck*. Chromolithograph. Approx. 14 1/2 × 20 1/2 in. Courtesy The Chicago Historical Society.

One of the raging issues of the 1880s was whether the United States would adopt a high tariff on foreign goods. Throughout most of the decade the country did erect a protectionist shield, behind which labor struggled to organize but was virtually at the mercy of industry. "Surely there should be some consideration for the workman, who, although he may not be aware of it, is nevertheless bound hand and foot, and is of necessity the abject slave of the Protectionist," commented the *Puck* editors.

89

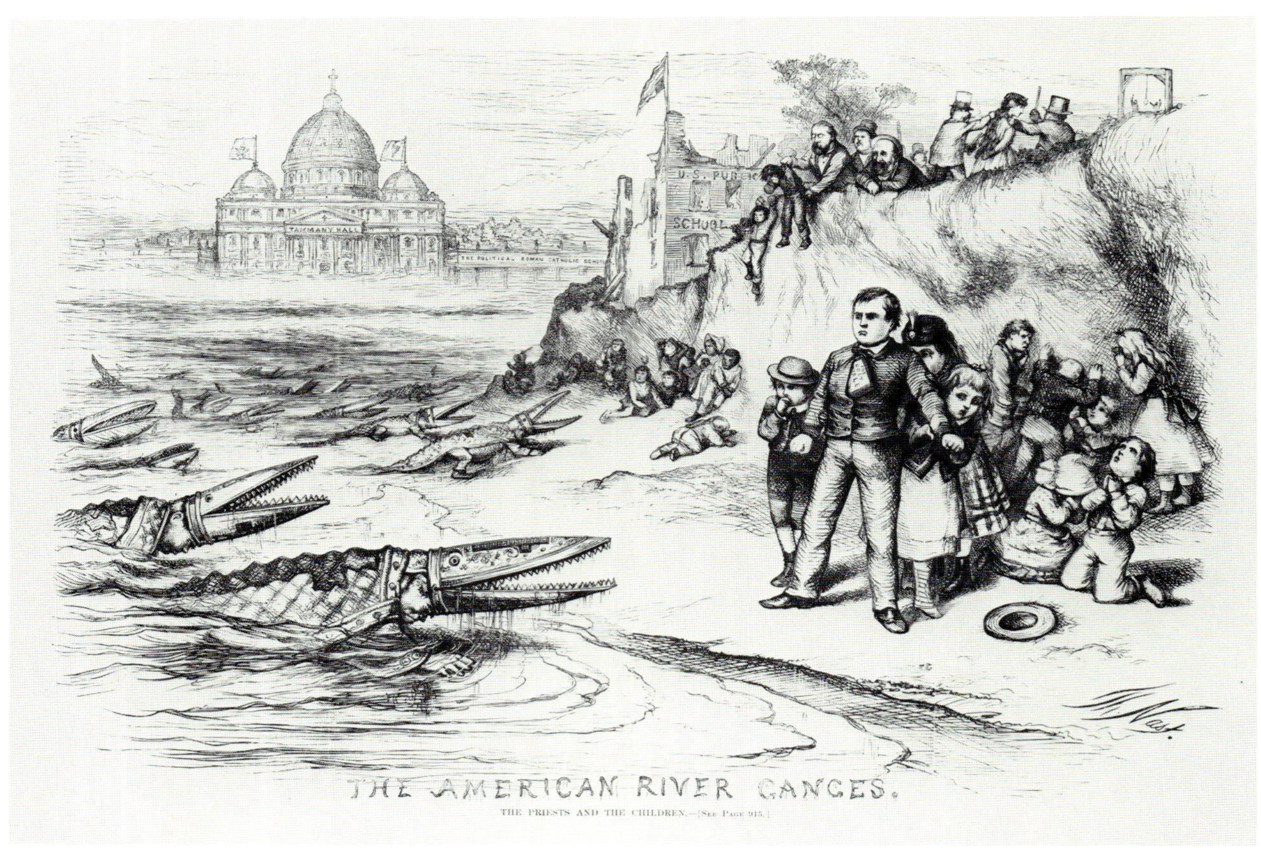

Fig. 77. *The American River Ganges. The Priests and the Children.* Thomas Nast. Sept. 30, 1871, in *Harper's Weekly.* Wood engraving. 11 × 15 7/8 in. Courtesy Amon Carter Museum, Fort Worth.

A common fear throughout the nineteenth century on the part of "Americans" was that their standards would be lowered by the horde of immigrants. The article accompanying this powerful Nast cartoon bemoans the decline in the public school system because of Irish Catholic influence. "To destroy our free schools, and perhaps our free institutions, has been for many years the constant aim of the extreme section of the Romish Church." Some even believed that the radical Catholics in New York City wanted to deliver that city into the Pope's hands because they controlled the elected and appointed governing offices (through Tammany Hall). Strongly anti-Catholic himself, Nast shows the Catholic assault on "our children" in this cartoon.

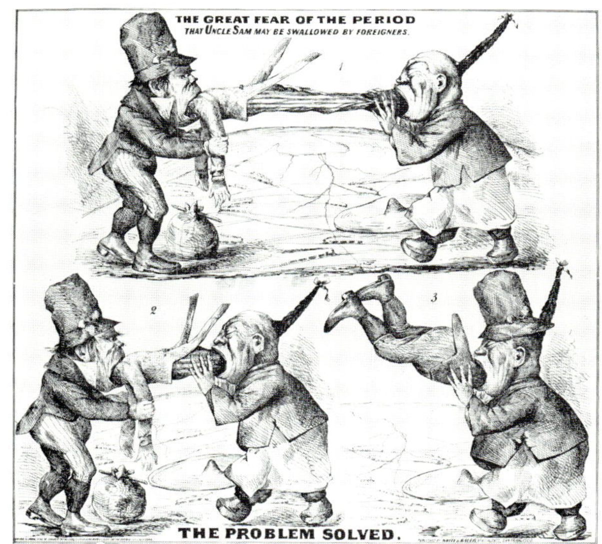

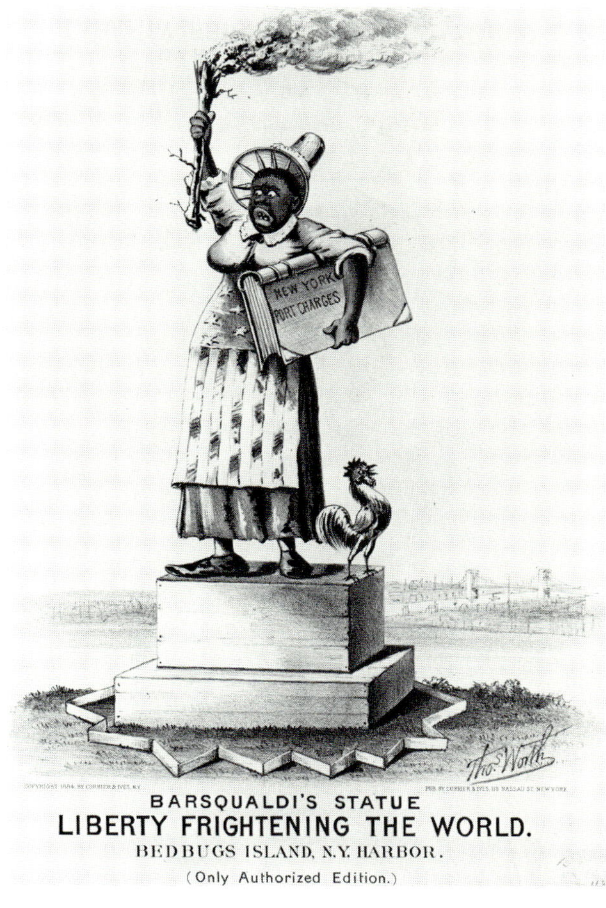

Fig. 78. *The Great Fear of the Period: That Uncle Sam May be Swallowed by Foreigners*. White and Bauer, pubs. 1860s. Pen lithograph. 23 1/8 × 25 in. Courtesy the Library of Congress.

Several years of free immigration into the United States led many "natives" to fear that they would be overcome by the newcomers. Immigration into California was particularly large as a result of the gold rush. Friction between the "natives" and the immigrants was a regular feature, with some 300,000 Chinese being tormented, mobbed, stoned, and their businesses burned by laborers who feared that the industrious Chinese would drive them out of work. The Exclusion Act of 1882 limited immigration, as did the ban on importation of contract labor in 1885. Limitation of immigration continued to be popular until the twentieth century, supported by organizations like the American Protective Association, established in 1887.

Fig. 79. *Barsqualdi's Statue. Liberty Frightening the World. Bedbugs Island, N. Y. Harbor*. Thomas Worth. 1884. Lithograph. 15 3/8 × 10 1/8 in. Courtesy the Library of Congress.

The many corruptions in the administration of New York Harbor led Thomas Worth to produce this racist picture for Currier & Ives showing Liberty as a symbol of the corruption and the abusive treatment of immigrants rather than the symbol of freedom to all the world.

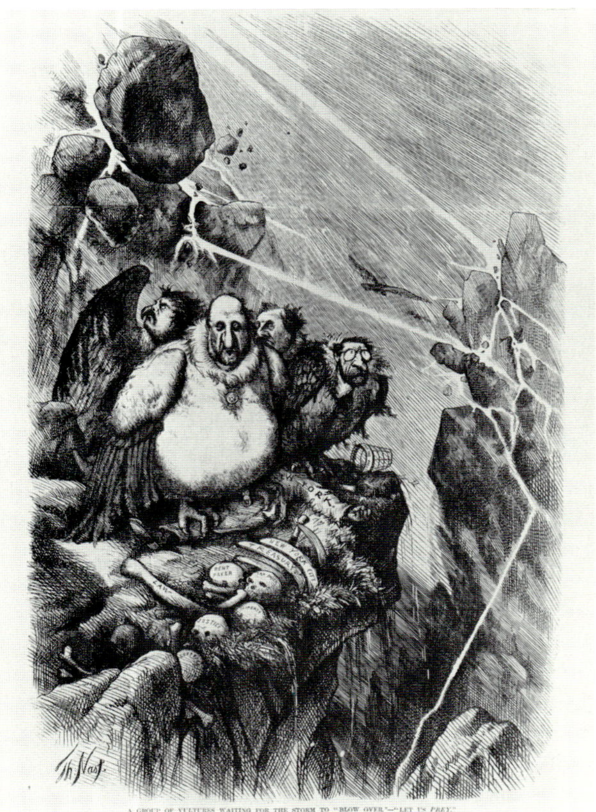

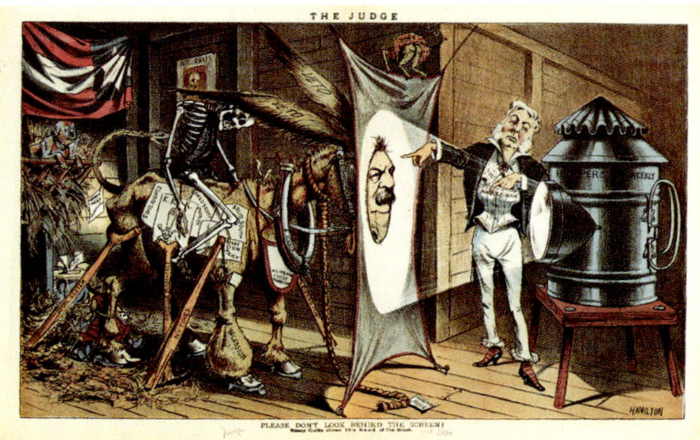

Fig. 80. *A Group of Vultures Waiting for the Storm to "Blow Over."*
—"*Let Us Prey.*" Thomas Nast. Oct. 1871, in *Harper's Weekly*.
Wood engraving. 15 15/16 × 11 in. Courtesy Amon Carter Museum, Fort Worth.

Thomas Nast undertook his most famous crusade in 1871 when the corruption in the Court House of New York City became known. William M. Tweed, the Tammany Hall boss, had been doling out millions of dollars to himself and his cronies for several years. When the corrupt practices became known, 31-year-old Nast began a series of cartoons that literally ran Tweed out of town. After the scandal had become public, Tweed and his henchmen hoped the storm would blow over, but Nast kept the public aware of the crime with his pictures. In a famous statement, Tweed commented that he did not care what the newspapers wrote, because most of his supporters could not read. But "them damn pictures," which they could understand without reading were hurting him.

Fig. 81. *Please Don't Look Behind the Screen*. Grant Hamilton. Oct. 18, 1884, in *Puck*. Chromolithograph. 13 5/8 × 20 3/4 in. Courtesy The Chicago Historical Society.

When Grover Cleveland was proposed as a presidential candidate, the editors of *Puck* quickly let it be known that they were against him. Even his friends admitted that he had no outstanding record of achievement, commented the editors, but they did propose him as "the great moral reformer." After investigation, however, even that disappeared. "Then . . . came the terrible story of Maria Halpin to scatter all his pretentions of morality to the winds," charged the editors. One of the most memorable campaign slogans of our history came out of Cleveland's alleged involvement with Miss Halpin: "Ma, Ma, where's my pa?"

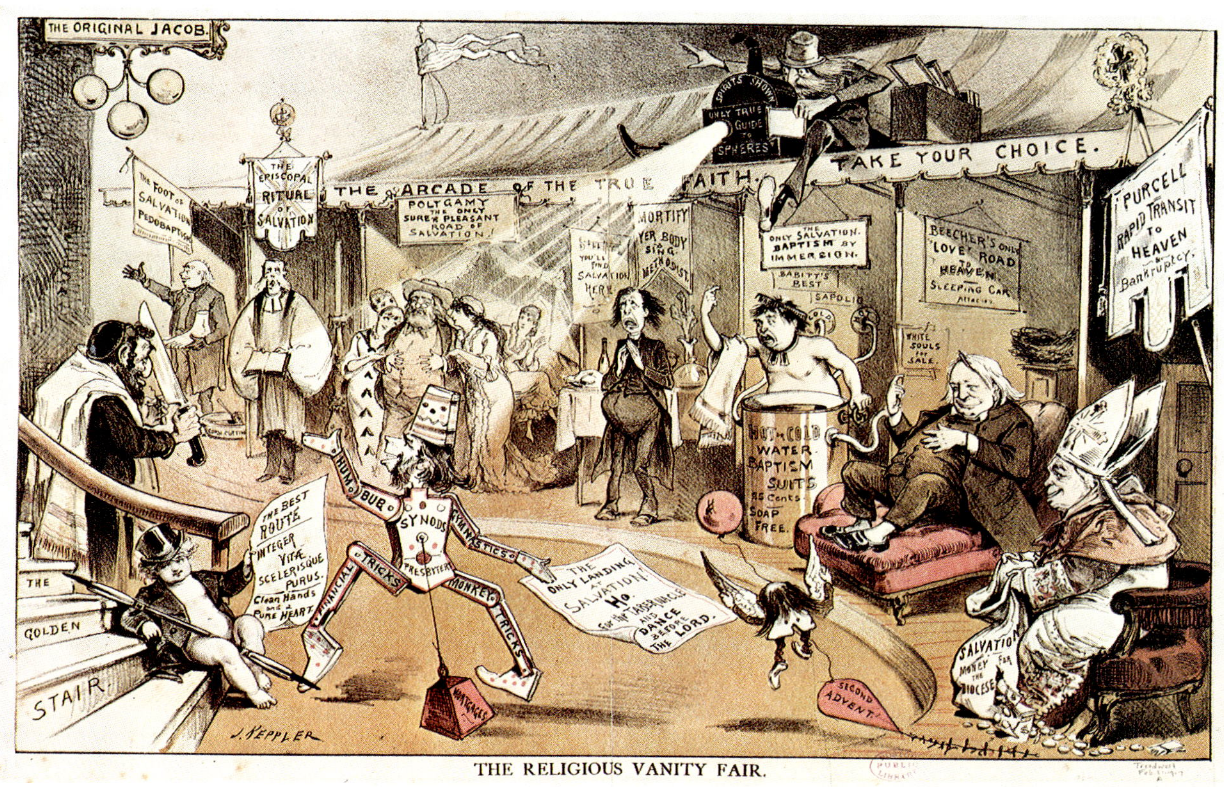

Fig. 82. *The Religious Vanity Fair.* Joseph Keppler. Oct. 22, 1879, in *Puck.* Chromolithograph. 12 × 18 1/2 in. Courtesy Boston Public Library, Print Department.

Indigenous American religious movements, combined with the varieties of religious practice imported with the immigrants, produced a true "Vanity Fair" of religion in the last quarter of the nineteenth century. Here the *Puck* editors comment that one can consult *Cook's Tourist Guide* to find any spot on the globe, but when one seeks "to soar beyond this habitable sphere" the "routes and guides are so many, so contradictory, and so confusing, that the poor man, who would be *en route* for Heaven gets himself completely mixed and finds himself at a standstill." This Keppler print exaggerates the religious situation of the day, but makes reference to several of the newsworthy events of the day such as "Beecher's only love road to Heaven."

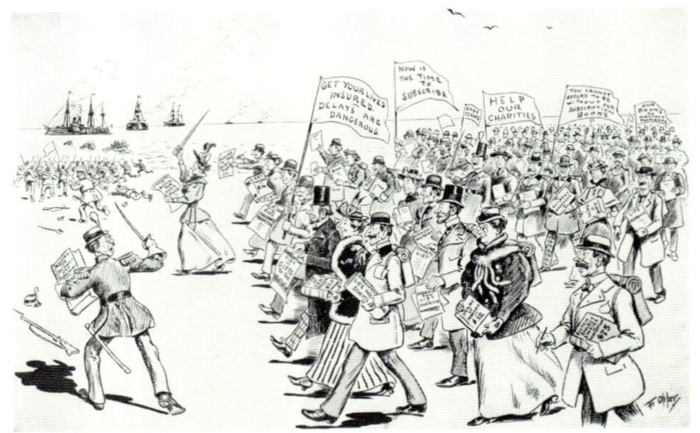

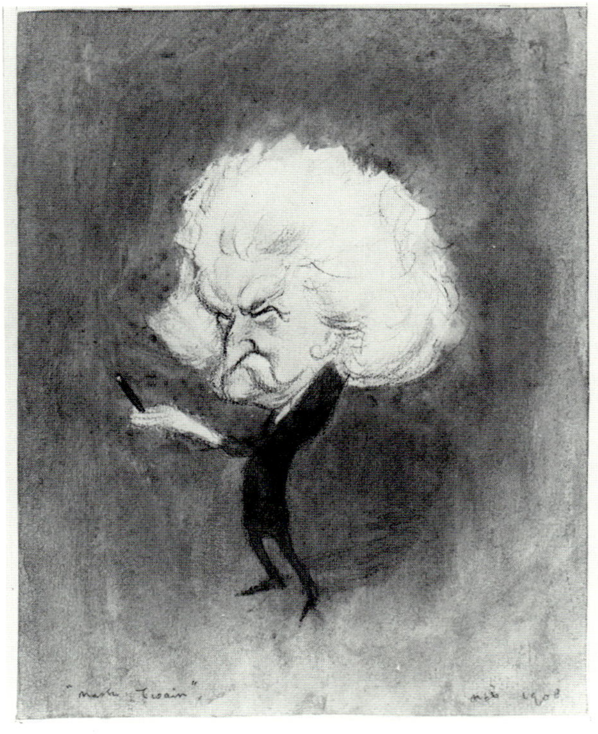

Fig. 84. *"Mark Twain."* Max Beerbohm. 1908. Pencil and water-color on paper. 8 1/4 × 6 3/8 in. Courtesy The Iconography Collection, Humanities Research Center, University of Texas, Austin.

Mark Twain (whose real name was Samuel Langhorne Clemens) was one of the leading writers and humorists of the nineteenth and early twentieth centuries, and one of America's greatest prosemen. Immortalizing his boyhood on the Mississippi River in such works as *Life on the Mississippi* (1883), *The Adventures of Tom Sawyer* (1876), and *The Adventures of Huckleberry Finn* (1884), he was a respected critic and literary figure whose opinions were widely sought and published. Today he is one of the most recognizable American literary figures around the world.

Fig. 83. *Parade for Causes*. Frederick Opper. c. 1890. Pen and ink on paper. 17 × 25 in. Courtesy The Swann Collection of Caricature and Cartoon.

As Americans became aware of the problems of their society, and as society itself became more complex, reforms defending virtually any group or cause organized to achieve their ends, as Opper illustrates here.

94

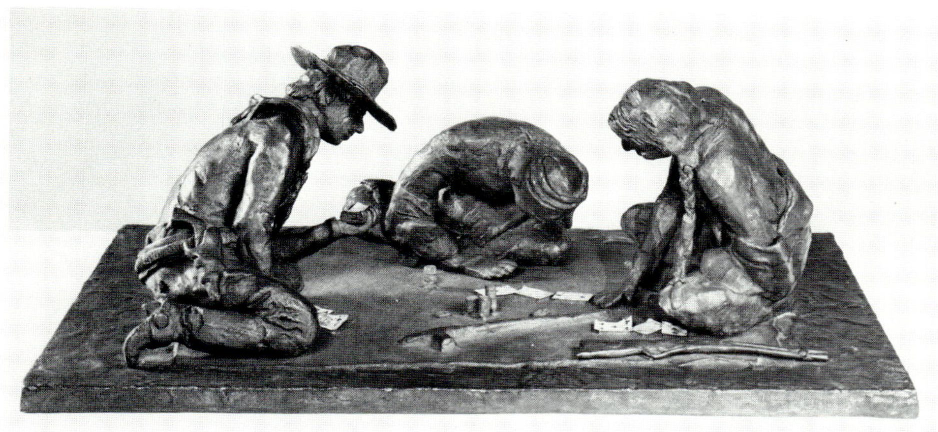

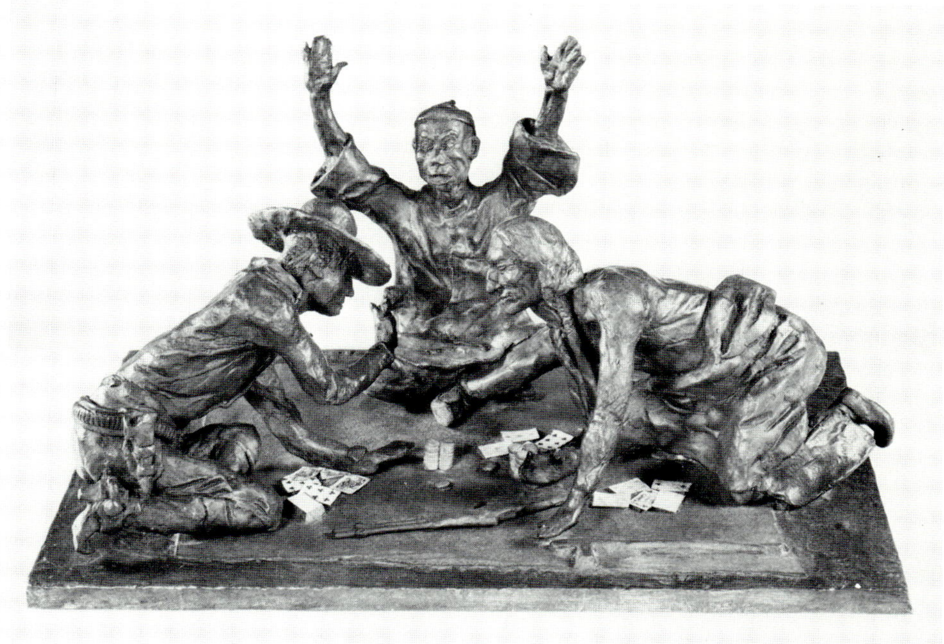

Fig. 85. *The Poker Game* and *Not a Chinaman's Chance*. Charles M. Russell. 1893. Bronze (cast in 1966). 6 3/4 in. high. 10 1/2 in. high. Courtesy Amon Carter Museum, Fort Worth.

Charlie Russell, the "cowboy artist," delighted in caricaturing the stereotypes of the West. Here he shows a cowboy, an Indian, and a Chinese playing poker. According to the Helena, Montana *Weekly Herald* (Dec. 28, 1893), "The Chinaman has the best of the layout as far as the game has progressed." In the second sculpture, the cowboy has pulled a gun on the Oriental and is raking in the stakes. "The observer can only conjecture whether the wily Oriental was caught dealing from the bottom of the deck or had an ace up his sleeve, but it is obvious that 'he didn't have a Chinaman's chance' against two such adversaries." The editor of the newspaper did not suggest that the cowboy might have lost the game and pulled the gun to recoup his losses.

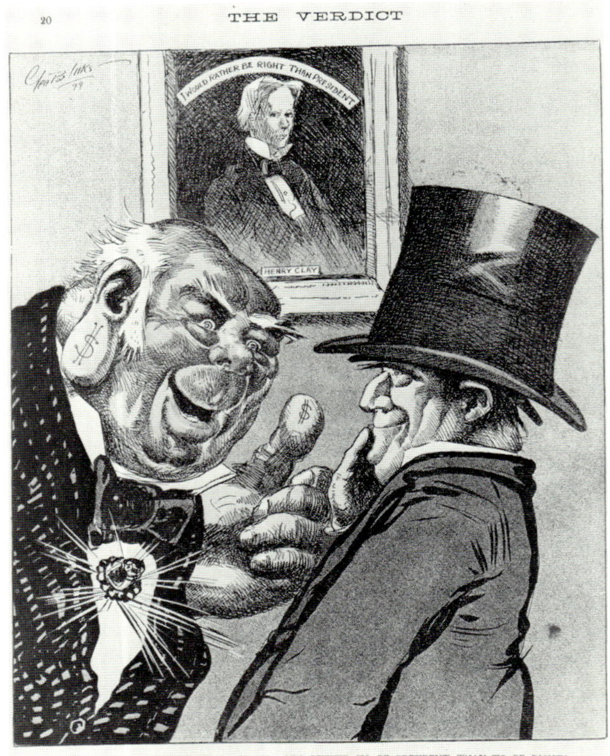

Fig. 86. *Hanna: That Man Clay was an Ass. It's Better to be President than to be right!* George Luks. 1899 in *The Verdict*. Lithograph. Courtesy the Library of Congress.

A Cleveland coal, iron, and newspaper millionaire, Marcus A. Hanna, was a shrewd power broker who early spotted William McKinley as a vote-getter. Coaching McKinley to stay at home and make only carefully-rehearsed speeches to selected visitors, Hanna carried on the battle against Democratic nominee William Jennings Bryan from his New York office. Assessing corporations and big banks one quarter of one percent of their capital funds, shaking down insurance companies and railroads, he amassed one of the largest campaign funds in history. With his money Hanna hired an army of 1,400 speakers to follow Bryan around the country and refute his speeches; he mailed more than 100 million pieces of campaign literature; and sponsored a ''sound money'' parade in New York the Sunday before the election. The Democrats countered as best they could. *The Verdict*, a quarto-size magazine published by Alfred Henry Lewis with brilliant cartoonists such as George Luks, was one of the more effective publications they issued for the campaign of 1900. Hanna is actually reported to have made the remark that Luks attributes to him in the cartoon.

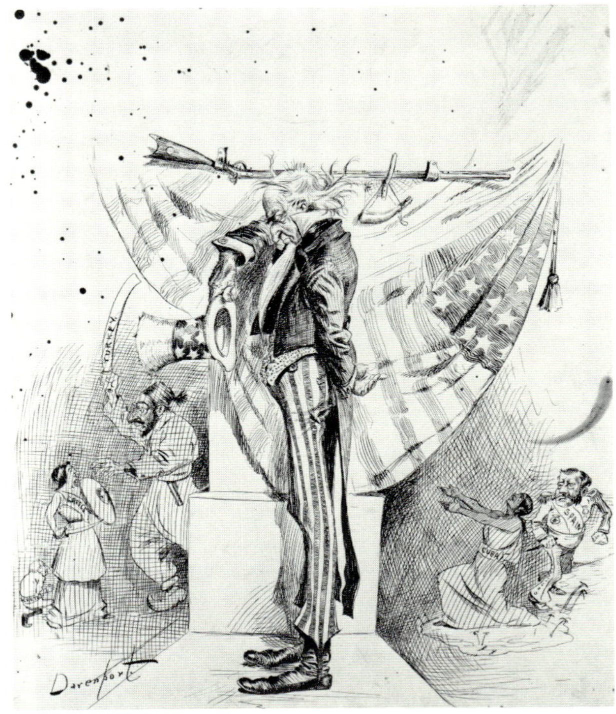

Fig. 87. *A Cry for Help*. Homer Davenport. 1890s. Ink on paper. 22 × 21 9/16 in. Courtesy the Library of Congress.

America's moral conscience was active during the reform years following the Civil War and settlement of its corruption. With liberties firmly entrenched at home, Americans looked around the world and saw the home of liberty, Greece, threatened by Turkey, and Cuba, an island that always would have made a profitable annexation, plundered and enslaved by the Spaniards. Davenport is suggesting that Uncle Sam cannot hold up his head until he takes the musket down from the wall and defends liberty wherever it is threatened.

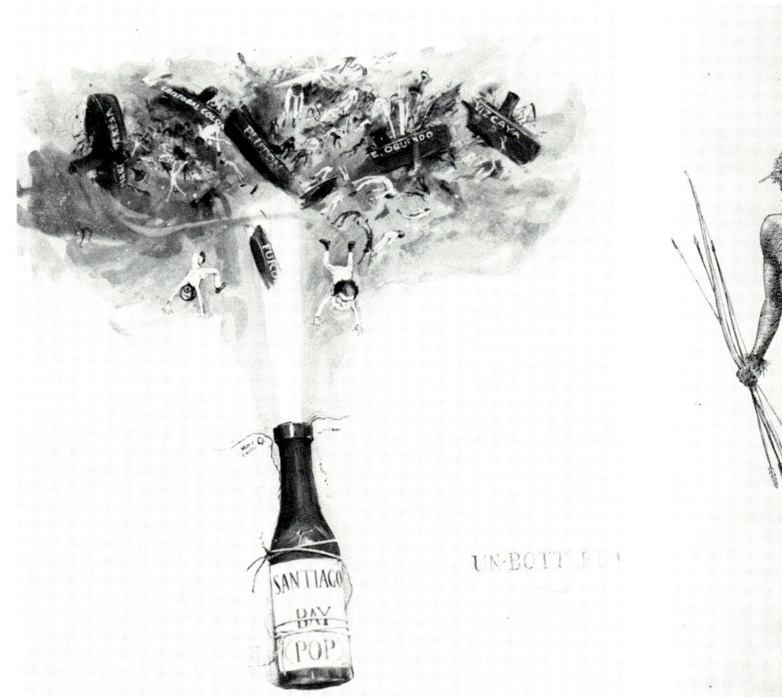

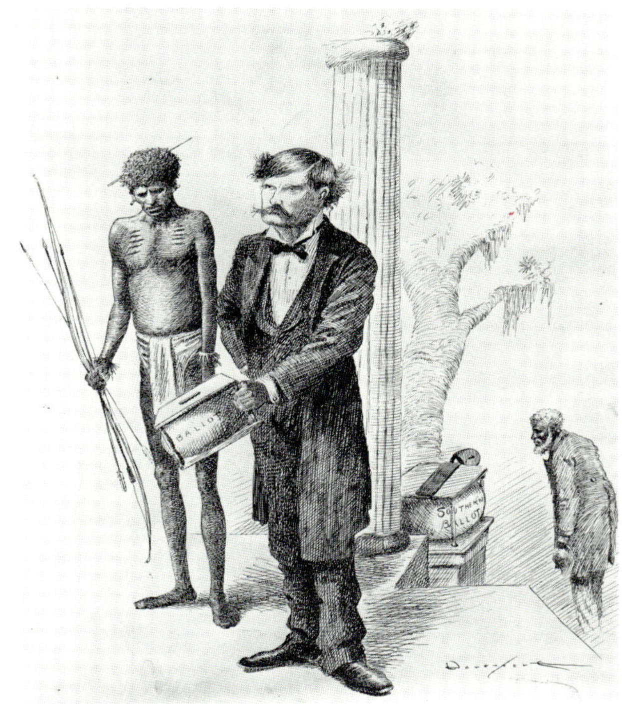

Fig. 88. *Santiago Bay Pop*. Anonymous. 1898–1901. Gouache on paper. 26 × 22 in. Courtesy the Georgia Historical Society, Savannah.

The last major battle of the short Spanish-American War was the destruction of the Spanish fleet in Santiago Harbor. With the battleships *Indiana*, *Iowa*, *Massachusetts*, *Oregon*, and *Texas*, and cruisers *New York* and *Brooklyn*, Rear Admiral William T. Sampson had trapped Spanish Admiral Pascual Cervera y Topete's fleet in Santiago Bay. When the *Infanta María Theresa*, the *Cristobal Colón*, the *Furor*, the *Plutón*, the *Admirante Oquendo*, and the *Vizcaya* tried to escape on the morning of July 3, 1898, Admiral Sampson's ships destroyed them. "If I were to live a thousand years and a thousand centuries never should I forget that 3d day of July 1898," said one of Cevera's officers, "nor do I believe that Spain will ever forget it."

Fig. 89. *Who Gets the Ballot, Philippines or Negro?* Homer Davenport. 1900. Ink on paper. 25 7/16 × 21 7/8 in. Courtesy the Library of Congress.

As a result of the Spanish-American War, the United States acquired the Philippine Islands. There was much discussion as to what kind of colonial policy the country should develop, with Senator Albert J. Beveridge speaking out strongly in favor of territorial expansion: "[God] has made us . . . the master organizers of the world to establish system where chaos reigns . . . He has made us adept in government that we may administer government among savage and senile peoples. . . . And of all our race, He has marked the American people as His chosen Nation to finally lead in the regeneration of the world." Davenport is obviously puzzled by the person who would extend the vote to the recently dominated natives of the Philippines and not to the American Negro of the South, who at that time was suffering from widespread moves to disenfranchise him.

97

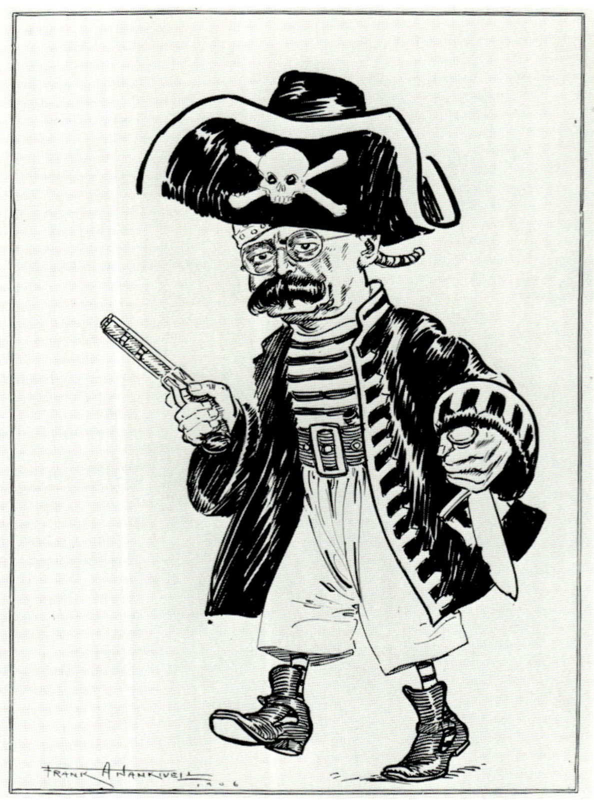

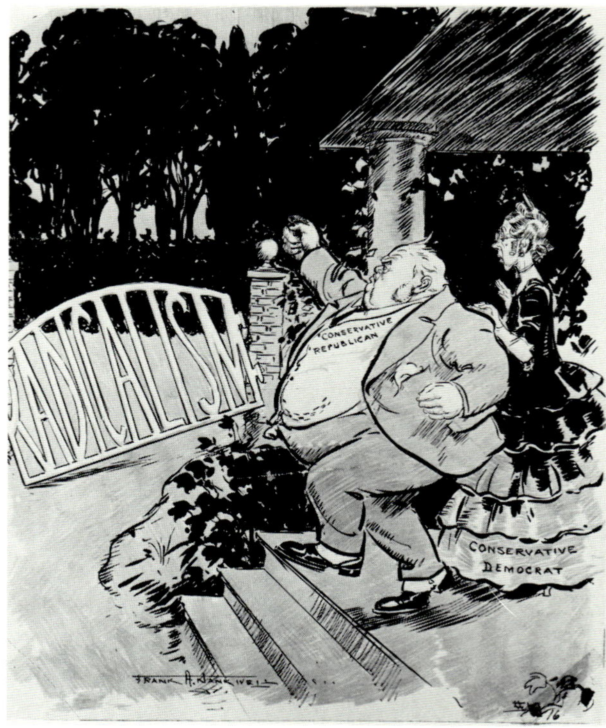

Fig. 90. [Teddy Roosevelt as a pirate.] Frank A. Nankivell. 1906. Ink on paper. 22 1/2 × 13 5/8 in. Courtesy The Swann Collection of Caricature and Cartoon.

When President William McKinley was assassinated, Theodore Roosevelt, who called the office a ''bully pulpit'' and soon ''preached from it,'' became President. His image as a courageous and adventuresome leader was enhanced when, during the 1904 Republican Convention, he responded swiftly to ransom demands from a Moroccan bandit named Raizuli who had captured an American citizen, Ion H. Perdicaris. ''We want Perdicaris alive or Raizuli dead,'' Roosevelt ordered. The convention talked of nothing else for days as Roosevelt was overwhelmingly nominated for a second term. His popularity increased even more when Perdicaris was safely returned to the American consul. Perhaps it was the aura of the Barbary Coast that led Nankivell to picture Roosevelt as a pirate.

Fig. 91. *It's That Roosevelt Kid Again*. Frank A. Nankivell. 1906. Ink on paper. 19 7/8 × 16 5/8 in. Courtesy The State Historical Society of Missouri, Columbia.

Although Roosevelt talked much about breaking up the trusts, thereby disturbing the conservative elements in both parties, he really did little to disrupt them, trying instead the countervailing power of government to keep them from abusing their privileges. Until businessmen learned that they had little to fear from him, they considered him an upstart and something of a radical.

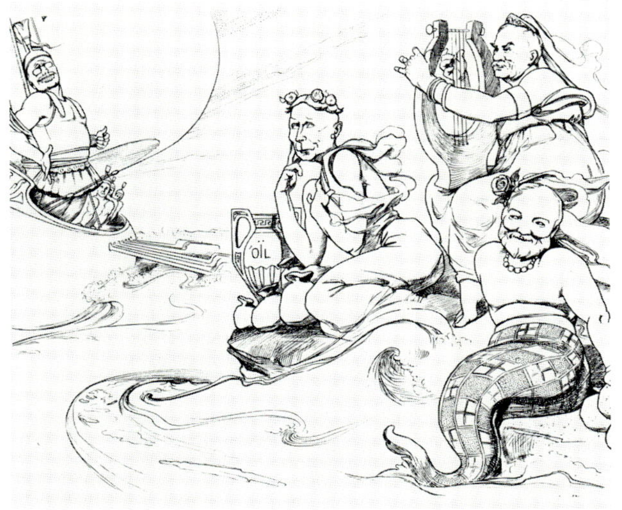

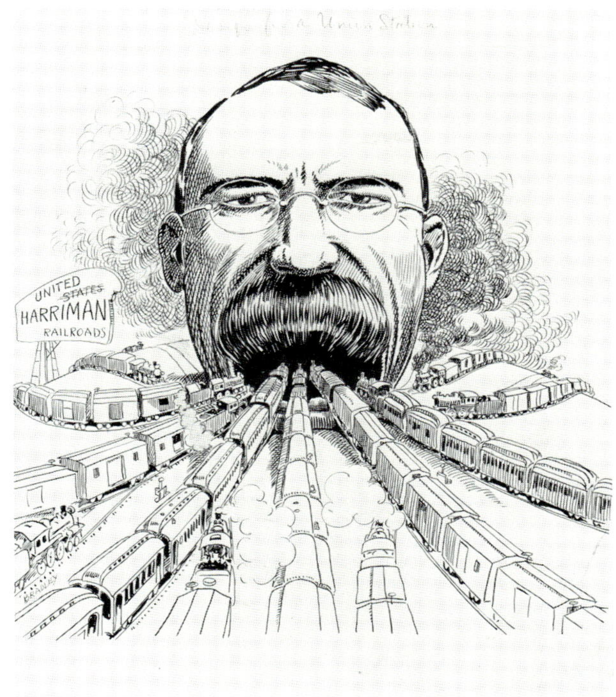

Fig. 92. *The Teddyssey*. Otho Cushing. May 16, 1907, in *Life*. Ink on paper. 18 7/8 × 22 1/4 in. Courtesy The State Historical Society of Missouri, Columbia.

One of a series of drawings done for the original *Life* magazine, *The Teddyssey* depicts Roosevelt as Ulysses tied to the mast of his ship while the sirens, John D. Rockefeller, J. P. Morgan, and Andrew Carnegie, three of the wealthiest men in the world in 1907, try to lure him from his stated policy of regulation of trusts. Like Ulysses, Roosevelt might have thought that such a close encounter with the sirens would strengthen him.

Fig. 93. *Design for a Union Station*. Luther Daniels Bradley. 1907. Ink on paper. 17 × 13 7/8 in. Courtesy The Swann Collection of Caricature and Cartoon.

Edward H. Harriman was one of the ablest and most practical railroad men of his generation. The son of a clergyman, he started in business as a runner on Wall Street, and owned a seat on the Stock Exchange by age 22. Entering railroading seriously, he revamped the weak Illinois Central, then turned his attention to the near-bankrupt Union Pacific. In 1901 he bought the Southern Pacific, gaining control of the principal system of transportation between Kansas City and California. Here Luther D. Bradley, a brilliant cartoonist for the Chicago *Daily News*, graphically depicts Harriman's one-man control of the railroads.

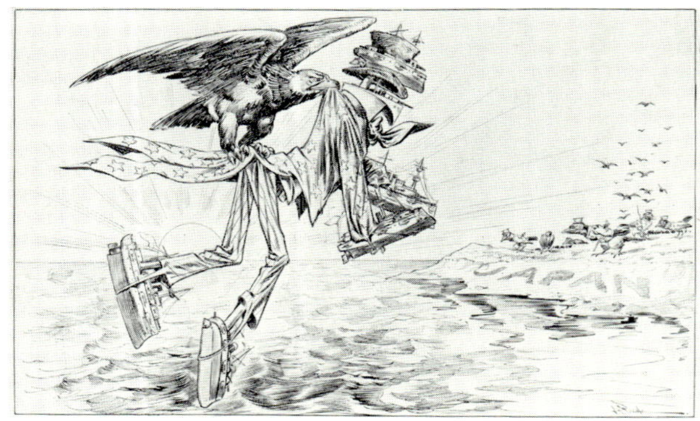

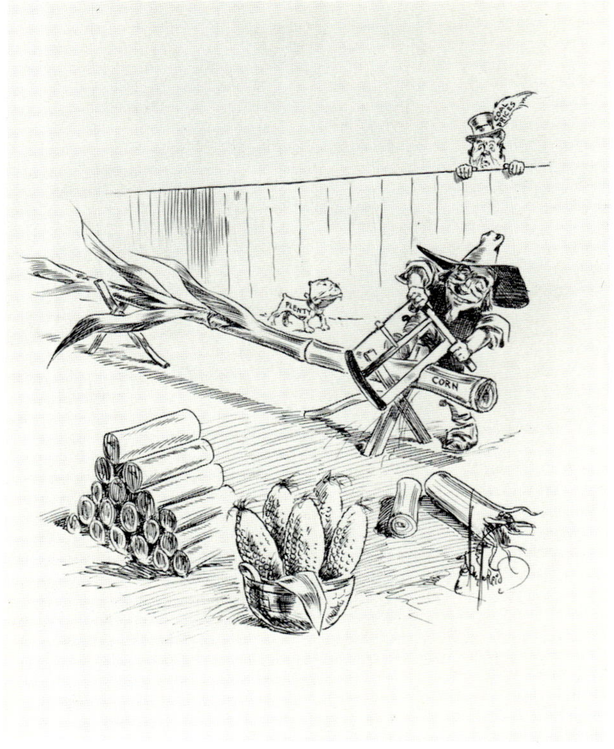

Fig. 94. *Scarecrow of the Pacific*. John S. Pughe. Oct. 16, 1907, in *Puck*. Pen, ink, blue chalk on paper. 17 1/2 × 27 1/2 in. Courtesy The Metropolitan Museum of Art, Fletcher Fund, 1942.

In 1907 amid anti-American agitation in Japan and anti-Japanese demonstrations on the West Coast of the United States, President Roosevelt announced that the entire American fleet would move from the Atlantic to the Pacific, stimulating rumors that hostilities between the United States and Japan were about to begin. As the fleet reached the Pacific, however, Roosevelt talked of a "good will cruise" and soon announced that the "Great White Fleet" would actually visit Japan. The show of force had its effect, as the Japanese welcomed the Americans, and anti-Japanese and anti-American demonstrations ceased. The "big stick" had carried the day again.

Fig. 95. *That Western Corn. The Western Farmer—"Wot'd' I care about the price of coal?"* Albert T. Reid. Aug. 29, 1902, in the Kansas City *Journal*. Pen and ink on paper. 18 × 11 5/8 in. Courtesy Kansas State Historical Society, Topeka.

By the turn of the century the urban centers of the nation had developed serious problems directly traceable to overcrowding, sanitation, and high prices. With thousands of people leaving the farms for the cities, a feeling of competition between farm and city developed. Albert T. Reid, the famous Missouri cartoonist, has captured that feeling of competition as the prosperous farmer counts his blessings compared to the tribulations of the city-dwellers. This situation did not last long, for the farmers were among the first to feel the effects of the depression that eventually engulfed all the world in 1929.

100

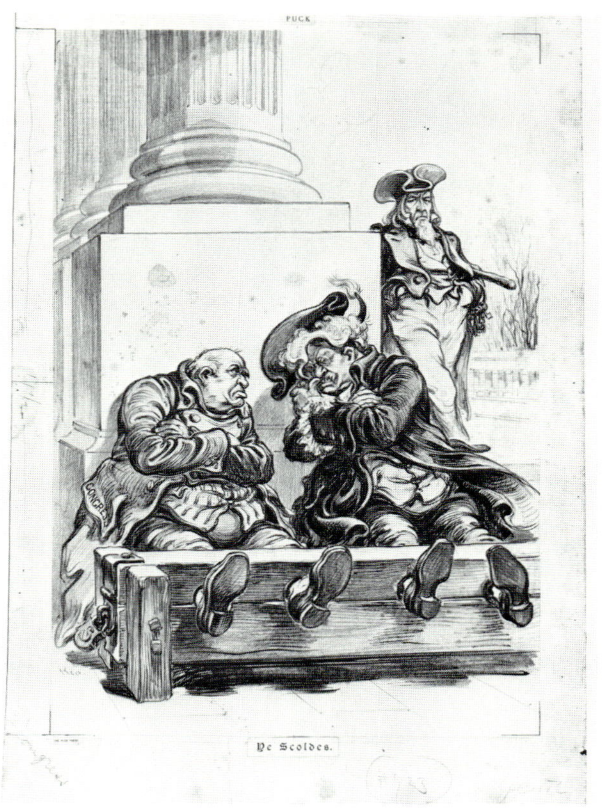

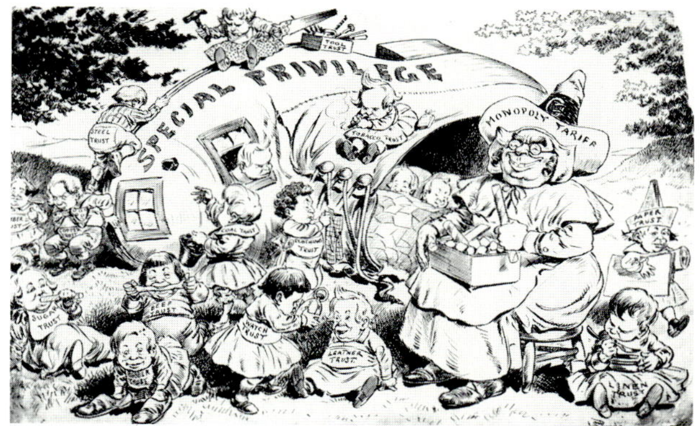

Fig. 96. *Ye Scoldes*. Joseph Keppler, Jr. 1908 (?) in *Puck*. Ink and crayon on paper. 22 1/8 × 14 3/8 in. Courtesy The Swann Collection of Caricature and Cartoon.

Fig. 97. *The Old Woman and the Shoe*. John S. Pughe. March 25, 1908 in *Puck*. Ink on paper. 17 × 17 in. Courtesy The Swann Collection of Caricature and Cartoon.

During his last term in office, Roosevelt had a Congress more conservative than himself. A good democratic politician, he had been watching the rise of liberalism throughout his career, feeling in 1908 that the socialist movement was more significant than the Populists. As he was going out of office in January, 1908, Roosevelt sent Congress the most radical message of his entire eight years. He blasted the federal courts (one of his measures had just been declared unconstitutional) and big business, and demanded regulation of Stock Market ''gambling,'' which he claimed was no different from gambling with machines or cards. Roosevelt did not long remain locked in the stocks with Congress, for his term ended when he turned the presidency over to William Howard Taft in 1909.

The enormous industrial capacity the United States had developed during the nineteenth century was organized under such wizards of industry as Morgan, Rockefeller, Carnegie, and Vanderbilt in the early twentieth century into trusts and monopolies. Little had been done to insure free exchange, but the legal machinery existed: the Sherman Antitrust Act, 1890. Roosevelt recognized that the ''tremendous and highly complex industrial development'' presented the country with ''very serious social problems,'' and he got indictments against forty-two trusts during his eight years in office. In four years, however, Taft prosecuted even more trusts than Roosevelt had.

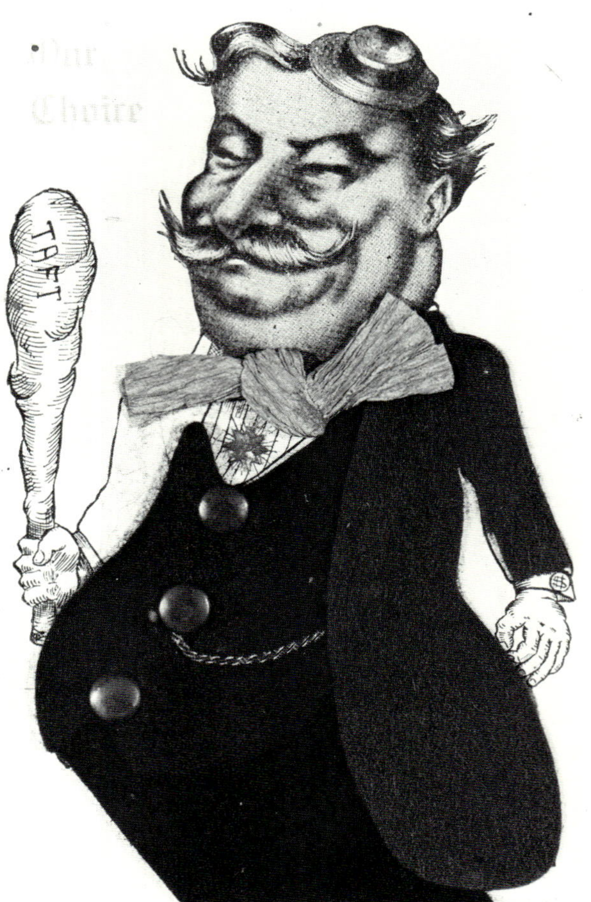

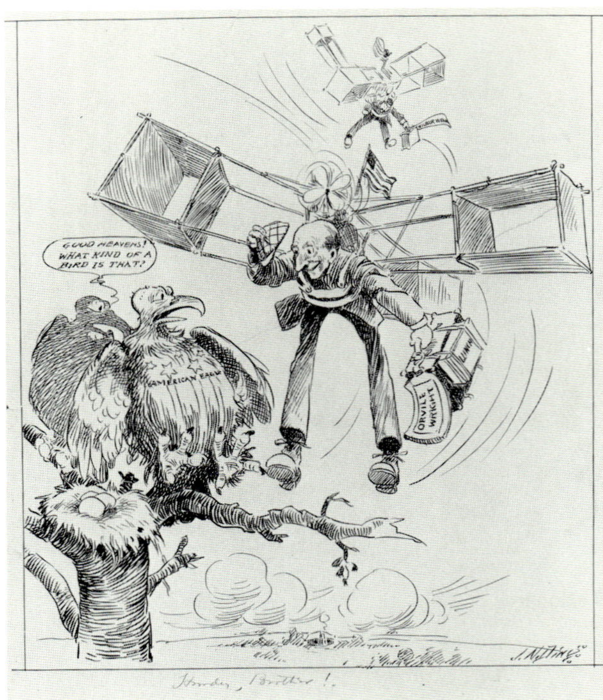

Fig. 98. [William Howard Taft.] Anonymous. c. 1908. Printed postcard, cloth, paper and brass. 5 1/2 × 3 1/2 in. Courtesy University of Hartford, DeWitt Collection, West Hartford, Conn.

A huge man of conservative mind, William Howard Taft only desired a seat on the Supreme Court. Three times Roosevelt offered that seat to him, but three times he declined, the last time because Mrs. Taft so badly wanted her husband to be President. When Roosevelt decided not to seek a third term, he chose Taft as his successor. Taft had been a loyal administrator under Roosevelt, but his own views were more conservative, and he did not trust the progressives and reformers who gathered around Roosevelt. Naturally the Taft administration was more conservative than Roosevelt's, leading Teddy to repudiate his hand-picked successor and seek reelection on his own in 1912.

Fig. 99. *Howdy, Brother!* Jay Norwood Darling (''Ding''). May 9, 1909, in the Des Moines *Register*. Pen and ink on paper. 22 1/2 × 18 1/2 in. Courtesy The University of Iowa Libraries, Iowa City.

American pride soared with the Wright brothers, Orville and Wilbur, when they successfully tested their four-cylinder engine with a twelve-second flight at Kitty Hawk, North Carolina, in 1903. By 1905 they had made a twenty-four mile flight from Dayton, Ohio. In 1909 their patented machine was adopted by the United States Army in time to have planes ready for the Mexican intervention in 1916 and World War I in 1917. Wilbur died in 1912 at age forty-five, but Orville lived until 1948 and reigned as the elder statesman of aviation.

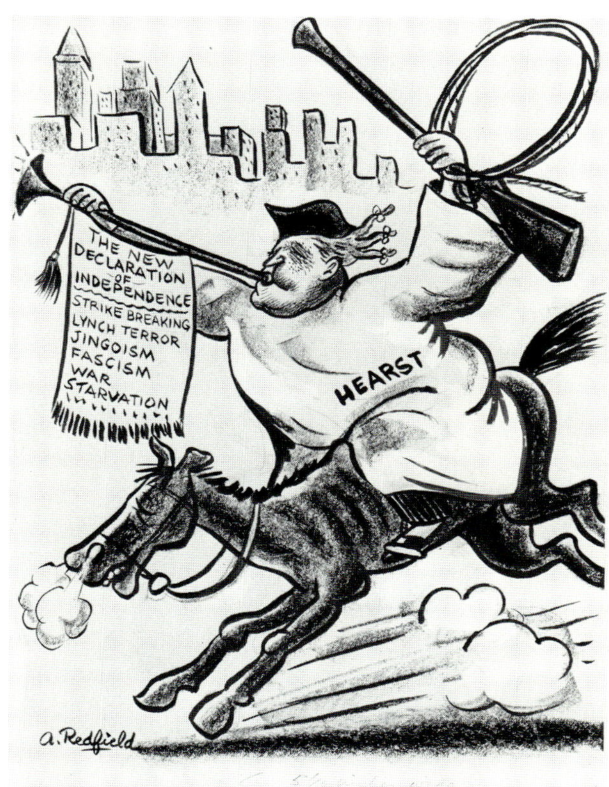

Fig. 100. [William Randolph Hearst.] A. Redfield. n. d. Ink on paper. 15 × 11 1/8 in. Courtesy Collection of Morris George Hecht.

An ambitious young man who had taken over his father's failing San Francisco *Examiner* in 1887, William Randolph Hearst realized the success of Joseph Pulitzer's New York *World* could also be his. He bought out the New York *Journal* and began to out-sensationalize Pulitzer. With colored comic strips, bold headlines trumpeting the day's news, and full-page editorials, Hearst soon attracted attention. He provoked much of the public sentiment behind the Spanish-American War, calling it "the *Journal's* war." His estimated worth in 1935, the depths of the depression, was more than $200 millions, and he built an extravagant castle, San Simeon, in California. He died in 1951.

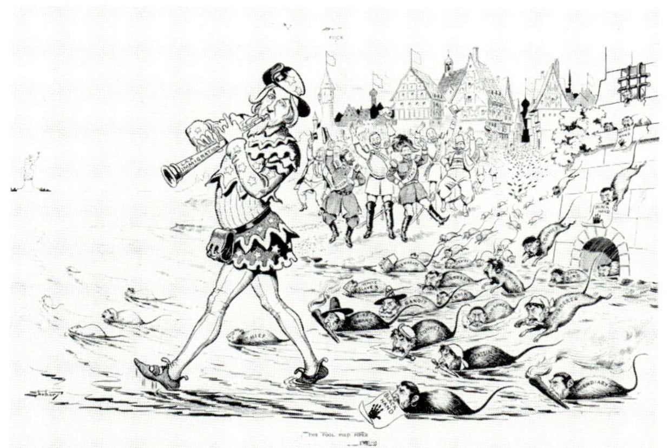

Fig. 101. *The Fool Pied Piper*. Ehrhart. June 2, 1909, in *Puck*. Ink on paper. 16 3/4 × 27 1/2 in. Courtesy The State Historical Society of Missouri, Columbia.

Much of the anti-immigration feeling of the early twentieth century was attributable to the belief that most immigrants were associated with the Black Hand, a secret society which began in Italy in 1868 and apparently bore some resemblance to the present-day Mafia. It turned up in Spain and Serbia associated with anarchists and nationalists. Here Ehrhart shows Europe glad to be rid of the bad elements of society that Uncle Sam, in the form of the Pied Piper, is not only accepting but luring away.

103

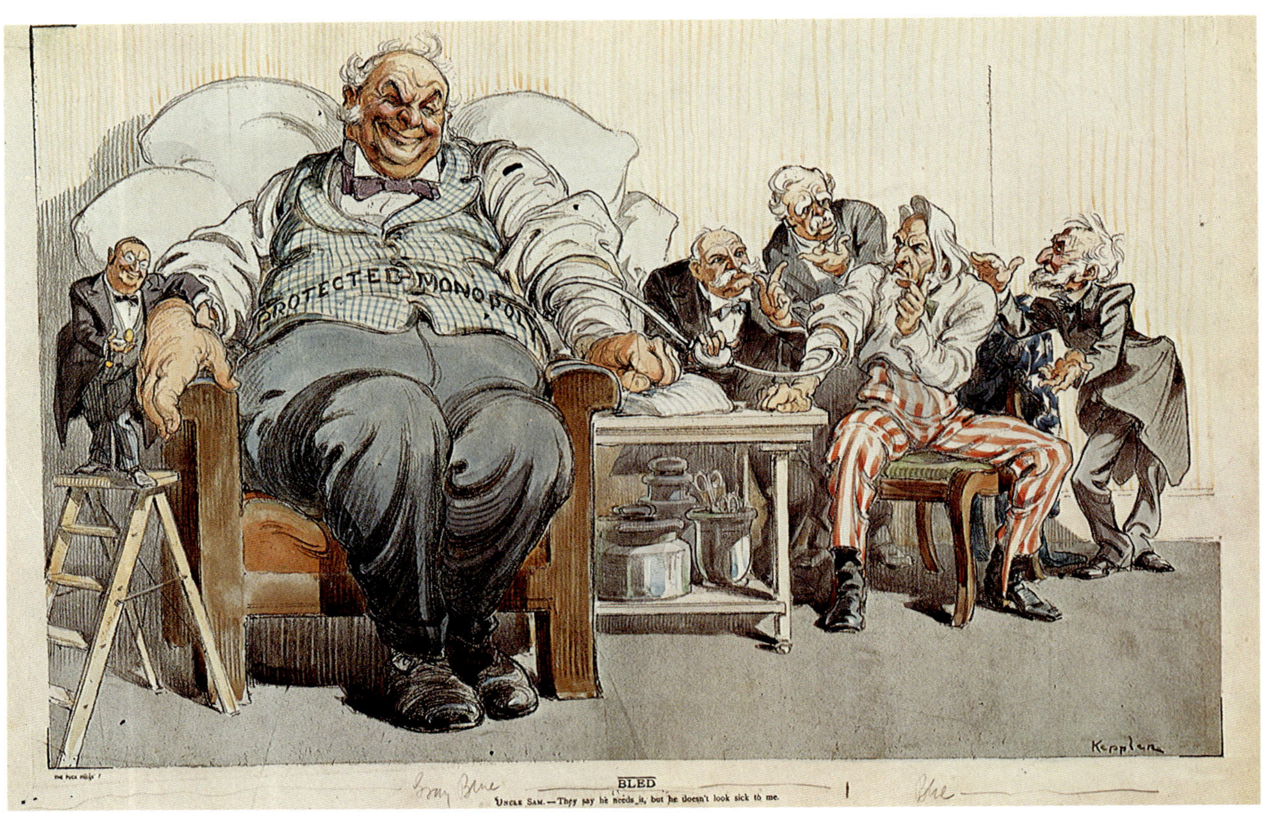

Fig. 102. *Uncle Sam: "They say he needs it, but he doesn't look sick to me."* Joseph Keppler, Jr. Mar. 17, 1909, in *Puck*. Crayon on paper. 13 1/2 × 19 3/4 in. Hand colored print. 14 1/4 × 20 1/4 in. Courtesy The Murray A. Harris Collection of Graphic Art, North Hollywood, Calif.

America has traditionally been a high-tariff nation, favoring home industry and passing laws favorable to its development. The tariffs rose from 1861 until 1909, when the hugeness of the trusts finally made politicians realize that American business no longer needed protection. A protective tariff is nothing more than "a tax on commerce, forcing the body of citizens to pay tribute to producers at home," said David Starr Jordan, president of Indiana University and later Stanford University. "To guarantee anyone a reasonable profit is to do so at the expense of the rest." Both the Democrats and the Republicans campaigned for lower tariffs in 1908. Exhibited here are the original drawing and the proof made for *Puck*.

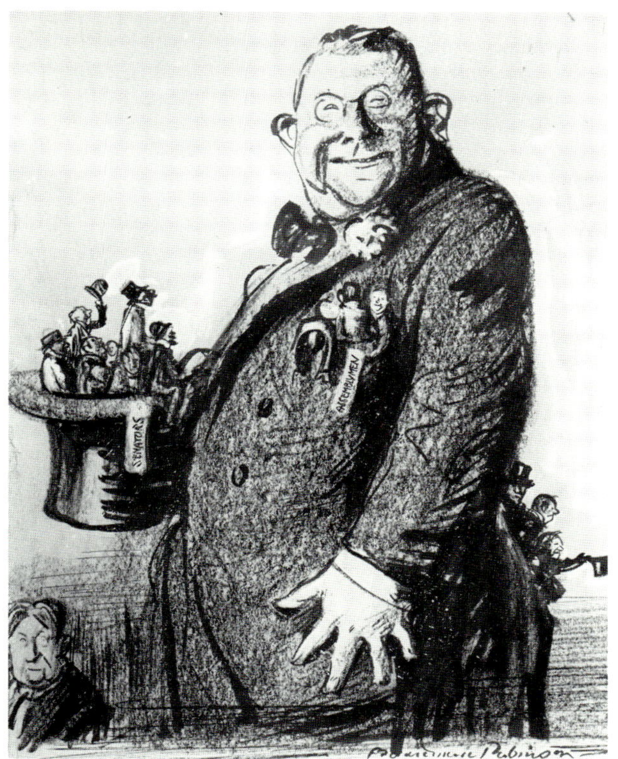

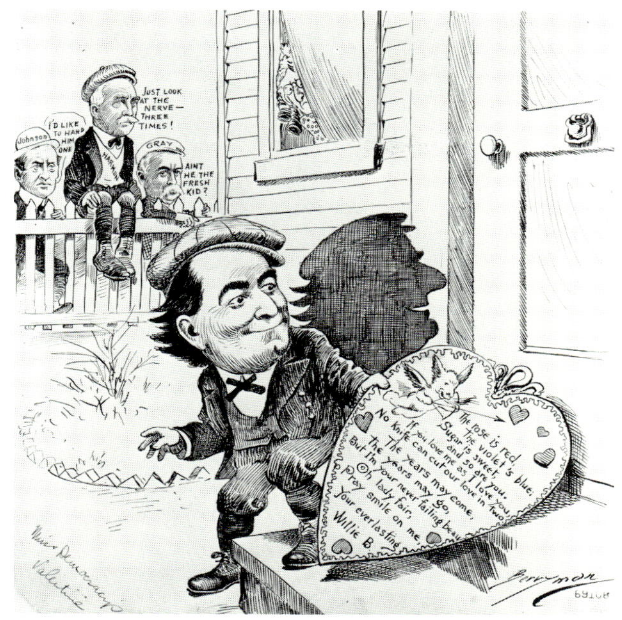

Fig. 103. *I'm Not a Member of the Legislature*. Boardman Robinson. c. 1912. Black crayon, ink wash, white highlights on paper. 19 1/2 × 14 1/2 in. Courtesy Grunwald Center for the Graphic Arts, University of California, Los Angeles.

The thousands of non-English-speaking immigrants who entered the country each year participated in politics by means of the "boss system," that is, a neighborhood boss took care of them, provided them with a job, insured that their needs were fulfilled in return for their votes. New York City built the most durable political machine, Tammany Hall, which controlled an annual city payroll of more than $12 millions after 1880. Charles Francis Murphy led Tammany from 1902 to 1924, controlling the state legislature and lining his pockets with what Richard Croker called "honest graft"—taking advantage of inside knowledge to buy the right stocks, real estate, etc., and kickbacks, which were illegal.

Fig. 104. *Miss Democracy's Valentine*. C. K. Berryman. 1912. Ink on paper. 14 15/16 × 14 1/8 in. Courtesy the Library of Congress.

William Jennings Bryan had led the Democratic Party to national defeat three times before 1912. He was the titular head of the party as the 1912 election approached, but most of the country felt the party had to be reorganized to get some new faces before the electorate to try to stop the Republican sweep, which had lasted since 1896. Bryan is leaving his "valentine" in front of Miss Democracy's door, but Hiram W. Johnson, Judson Harmon, and George Gray, watching from behind the fence, remark on his persistence. They plan to unseat him as head of the party.

105

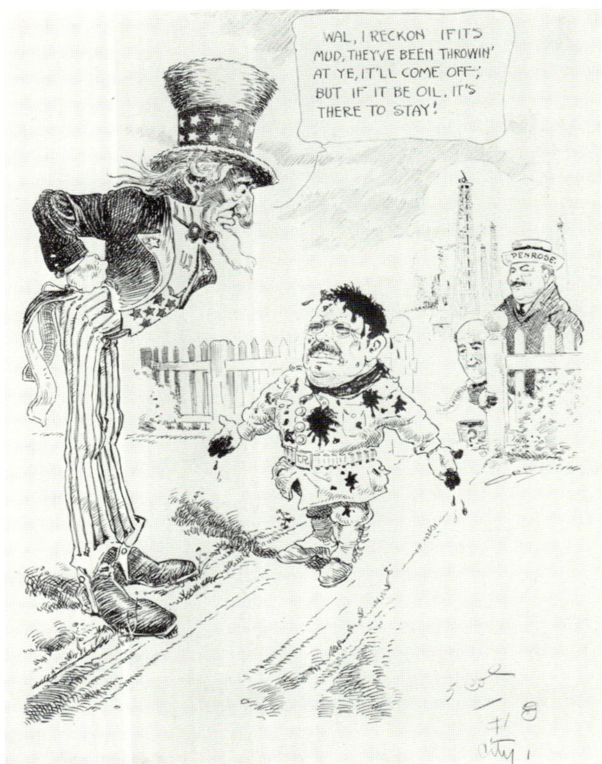

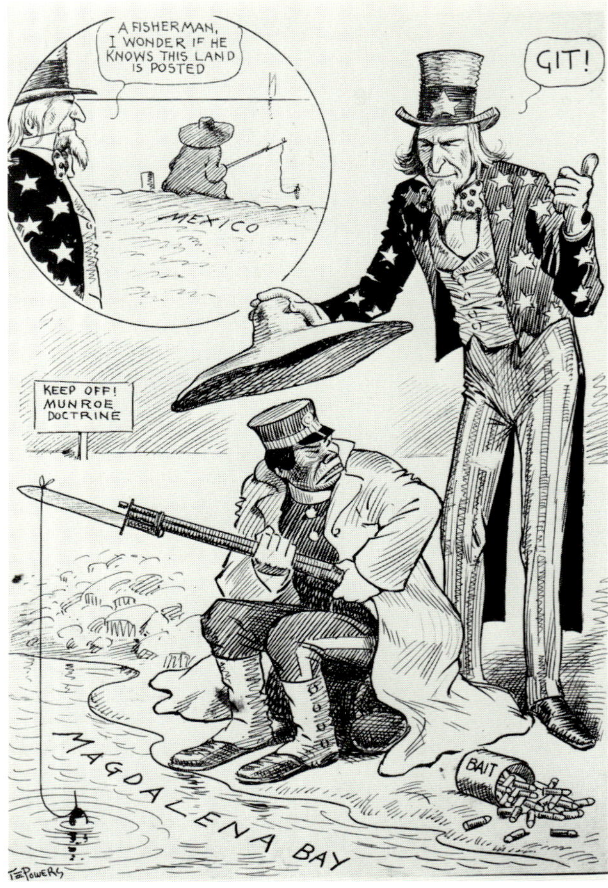

Fig. 105. *Time Will Tell*. Carey Orr. 1912. Ink on paper. 24 3/4 × 18 in. Courtesy Jonson Collection, University of New Mexico, Albuquerque.

In September, 1912, the Senate Committee on Privileges and Elections conducted hearings on Roosevelt's political campaign contributions in the elections of 1904, 1908, and 1912. Allegedly involving John D. Archibold of Standard Oil Company, the investigations held potential embarrassment for Roosevelt, although nothing was ever proved. Senator Boies Penrose was one of the sponsors of the resolutions sponsoring the hearings in the Senate.

Fig. 106. *Keep Off! Munroe Doctrine*. T. E. Powers. 1912. Ink on paper. 14 1/2 × 10 3/4 in. Courtesy The Swann Collection of Caricature and Cartoon.

When Americans realized in 1911 that a Japanese syndicate was negotiating for purchase of a large tract of land along the West Coast of Mexico on Magdalena Bay, Baja California, the State Department registered its disapproval and Senator Henry Cabot Lodge introduced legislation in the Senate stating that the United States viewed with "grave concern" the possession of strategic areas in the Americas by any foreign country or company. This became the Lodge Corollary to the Monroe Doctrine.

Fig. 107. [Uncle Sam shooting dice with Carranza.] C. K. Berryman. Jan. 4, 1917, in the Washington *Evening Star*. Ink on paper. 12 1/8 × 14 1/16 in. Courtesy the Library of Congress.

When Mexican bandits under Pancho Villa raided the town of Columbus, New Mexico, on the night of March 9, 1916, President Woodrow Wilson ordered General John J. Pershing and 7,000 American troops to pursue the bandits into northern Mexico. Pershing marched more than 300 miles into Mexico in what to President Venustiano Carranza was an invasion. He vehemently protested, threatening even to attack the Americans unless they were immediately withdrawn. Soon more than 100,000 American troops and National Guardsmen lined the border to prevent another raid.

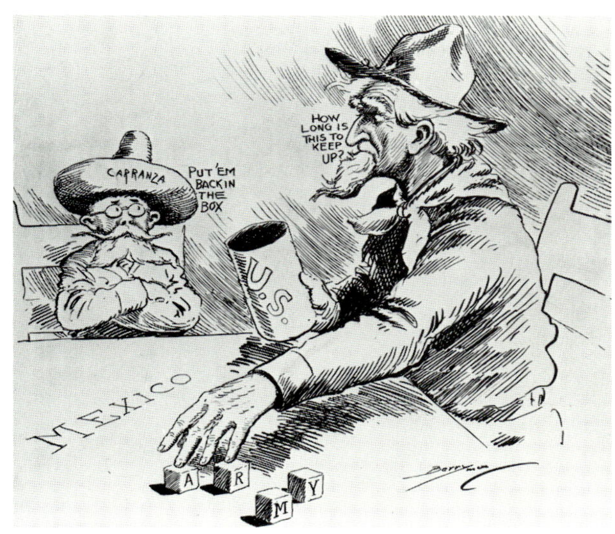

Fig. 108. *A Quieter Spot for Him*. Luther Daniels Bradley. c. 1915. Ink on paper. 13 1/4 × 21 3/4 in. Courtesy The Swann Collection of Caricature and Cartoon.

When the British transatlantic steamer *Lusitania* was sunk by a German U-boat off the Irish coast on May 7, 1915, 128 Americans were killed. President Wilson drafted a protest note for Secretary of State William Jennings Bryan's signature, demanding that Germany abandon unrestricted submarine warfare, disavow the sinking of the *Lusitania*, and pay reparations for the loss of American lives. Wilson regarded the response as evasive and drafted another note, which Bryan refused to sign because he felt it might provoke Germany to war. The pacifist Bryan resigned on June 7.

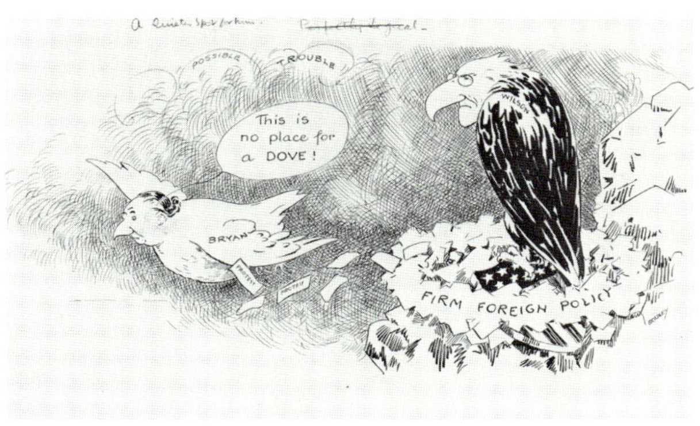

Fig. 109. *In the White House Attic—a Find*. Luther Daniels Bradley. 1916. Ink on paper. 13 × 22 1/4 in. Courtesy The Swann Collection of Caricature and Cartoon.

President Roosevelt not only talked about a "big stick," but he wielded one while he was in office. Woodrow Wilson hoped for a different approach. "Many of us thought that peace could be achieved by processes which would permit us to split the big stick into kindling for the hearth fire, or cut it into gavels for purposes no more belligerent than registering decisions at meetings," commented Mark Sullivan (*Our Times, 1900–1925* [New York: Scribner, 1936], IV, 136). But as German aggression continued, even Wilson realized that the big stick was useful.

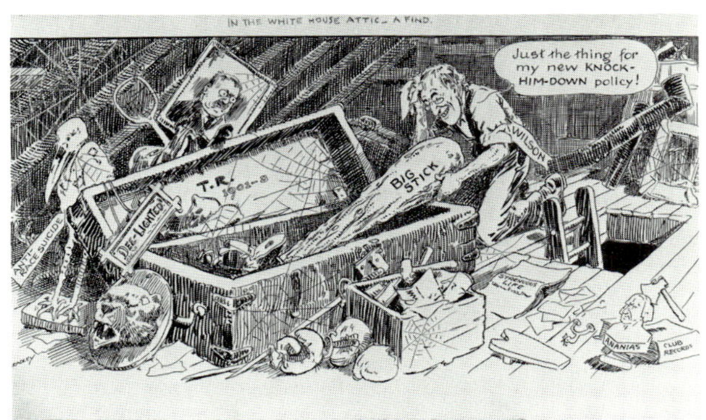

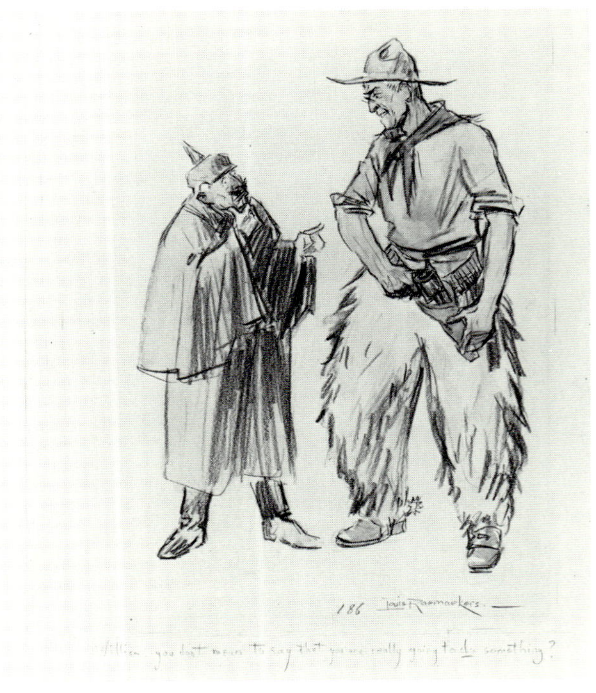

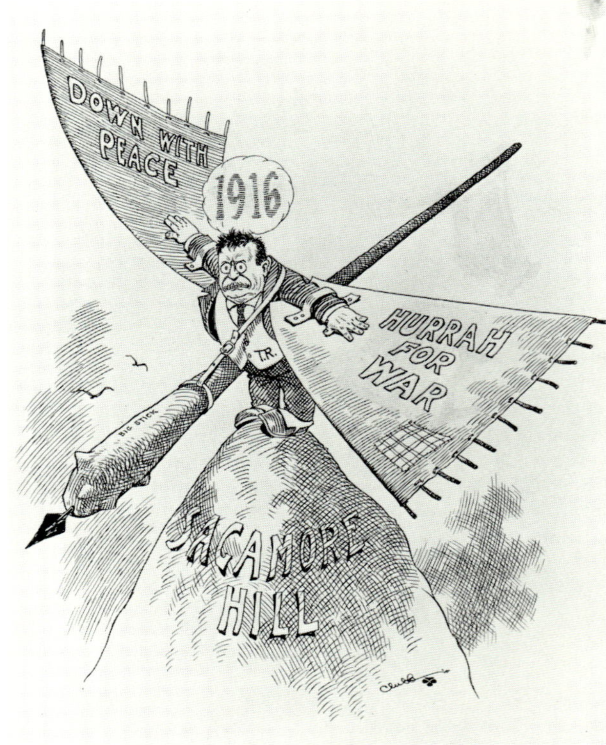

Fig. 110. *William, you dont mean to say that you are really going to* do *something?* Louis Raemaekers. 1917. Pencil and watercolor on paper. 17 × 13 in. Courtesy Hoover Institution on War, Revolution, and Peace, Stanford University, Palo Alto, Calif.

Had the Kaiser been more familiar with the chivalrous "code of the American West," he might not have been so surprised at President Wilson. In asking Congress for a declaration of war on April 2, 1917, Wilson couched his message in the moralistic, idealistic terms so pervasive in American society: "The world must be made safe for democracy. Its peace must be planted upon the tested foundations of political liberty. We have no selfish ends to serve. We desire no conquest, no domination. We seek no indemnities for ourselves, no material compensation for the sacrifices we shall freely make. We are but one of the champions of the rights of mankind. . . . We shall . . . observe with proud punctilio the principles of right and of fair play we profess to be fighting for."

Fig. 111. *White House or Bust*. John Clubb. 1916. Ink on paper. 19 × 14 in. Courtesy The Swann Collection of Caricature and Cartoon.

Lusting for office and detesting Wilson's 1916 slogan, "He Kept Us Out of War," Roosevelt tried to arrange for the Republican Party to draft him for the nomination. But the Republicans were not interested in the Bull Moose Party candidate of 1912 and chose instead Charles Evans Hughes. Convinced that Hughes was overcautious, Roosevelt nevertheless decided to support him rather than split the Republican vote by again seeking office on a third party ticket. He might have exercised more real influence in the party and the election if he had remained the aloof elder statesman in retirement at his home at Sagamore Hill.

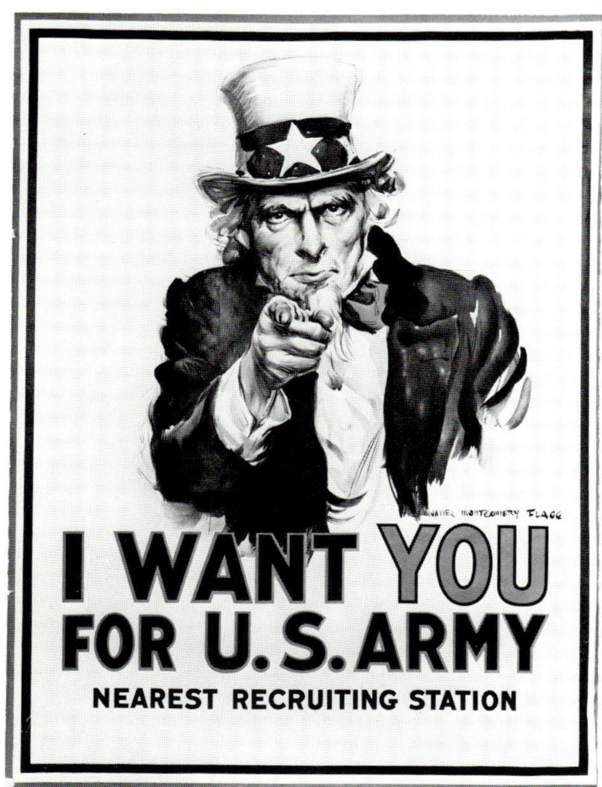

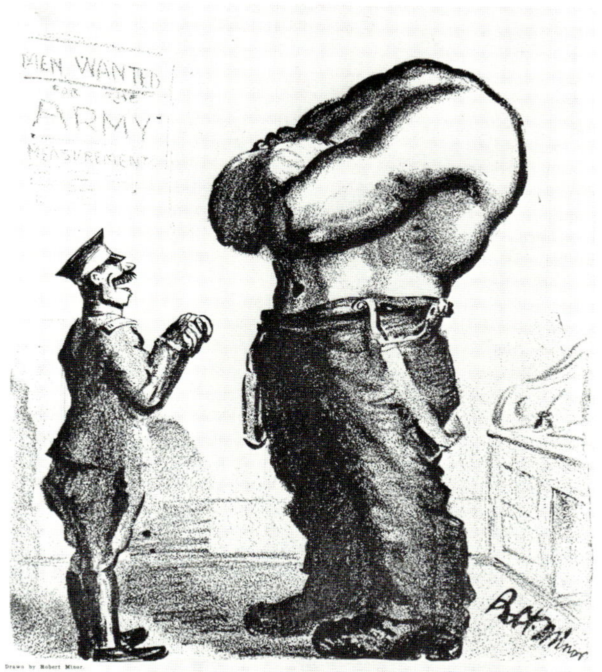

Army Medical Examiner: "At last a perfect soldier!"

Fig. 113. *Army Medical Examiner: "At Last a Perfect Soldier."* Robert Minor. July, 1916, in *The Masses*. Magazine page. 12 1/2 × 10 in. Courtesy Ben Goldstein, New York City.

Fig. 112. *I Want You for U. S. Army*. James Montgomery Flagg. 1917. Colored poster. 40 × 29 3/16 in. Courtesy the Library of Congress.

The classic image of Uncle Sam is this Flagg poster that was published for World War I recruiting. It has been revived numerous times and used by the Army. It is probably a self-portrait of Flagg.

Robert Minor was among the small number of liberal artists who contributed cartoons to the outspoken leftist magazine *The Masses*, which actually was banned from the mail by the Postmaster General during World War I. This cartoon is representative of a number of pacifist caricatures which appeared in the United States prior to America's entry in the war and that pointed out the degradation of the intellect and the personality by the military and by war.

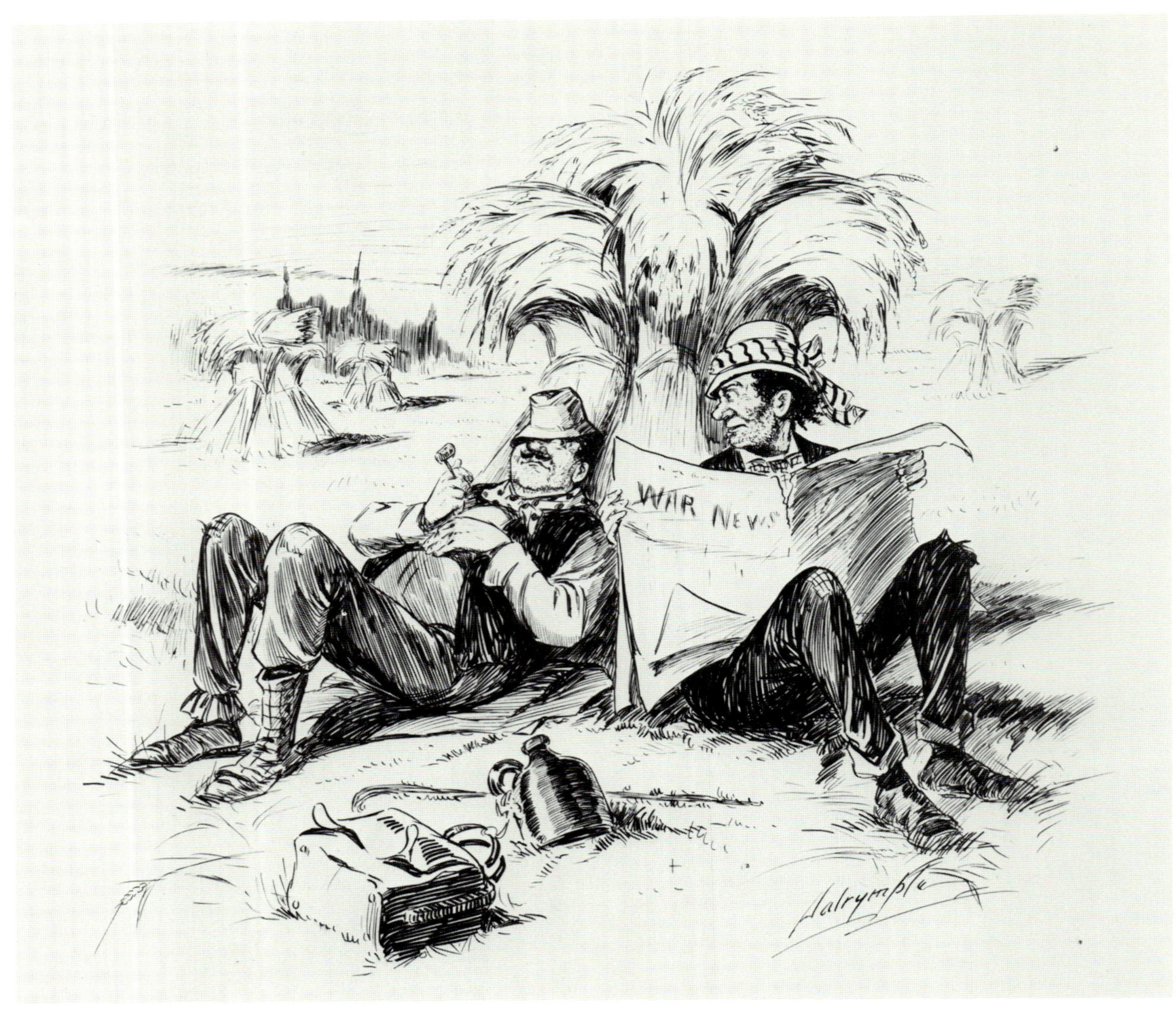

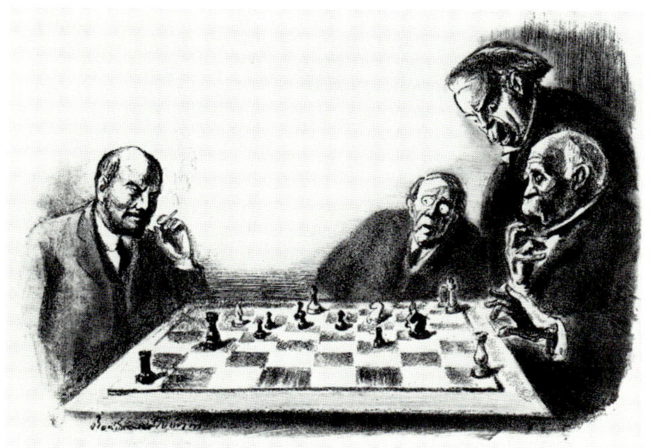

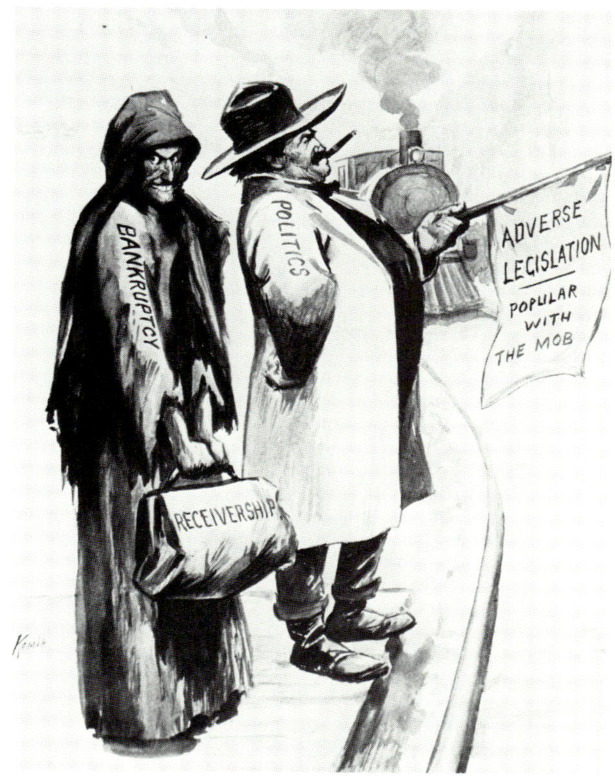

Fig. 116. *The Hold-Up*. Edward Kemble. 1919. Ink wash on paper. 15 1/8 × 12 1/8 in. Courtesy The Swann Collection of Caricature and Cartoon.

Fig. 115. *Chess Players*. Boardman Robinson. [1917.] Lithograph. 8 3/16 × 11 13/16 in. Courtesy Fogg Art Museum, Harvard University, Cambridge, Mass., Gift of James N. Rosenberg.

Although Lenin, Wilson, Lloyd George, and Georges Clemenceau never met in a four-way conference, this Boardman Robinson cartoon probably expresses the threat the Allied leaders felt as Lenin was negotiating a separate peace with Germany in March, 1918, freeing the Germans to fight only on the Western front. The international Communist movement threatened the United States, Britain, and France, giving Lenin the somewhat sinister air associated with the "Bolshevik Menace."

The return of the railroads to private hands after World War I was a controversial problem. To facilitate prosecution of the war the government had taken over the railroads. The Transportation Act of 1920 returned the roads to private companies, but also widened the powers of the Interstate Commerce Commission, enabling the Commission to consolidate the railroads into a small group of companies exempt from antitrust laws. The companies claimed that the government had not kept up the roads during the War, that they would be required to spend millions of dollars to put them back in order, etc. Many of today's railroad problems might be traced to the ill-will resulting from the government takeover of World War I.

111

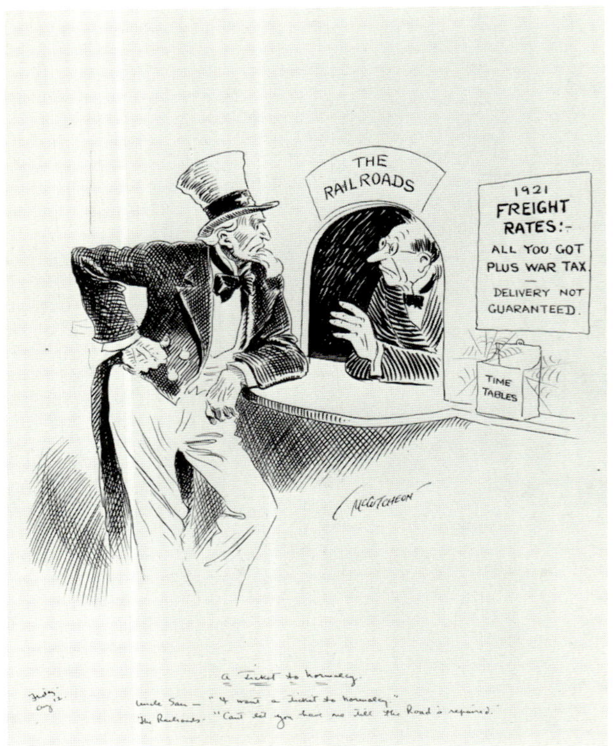

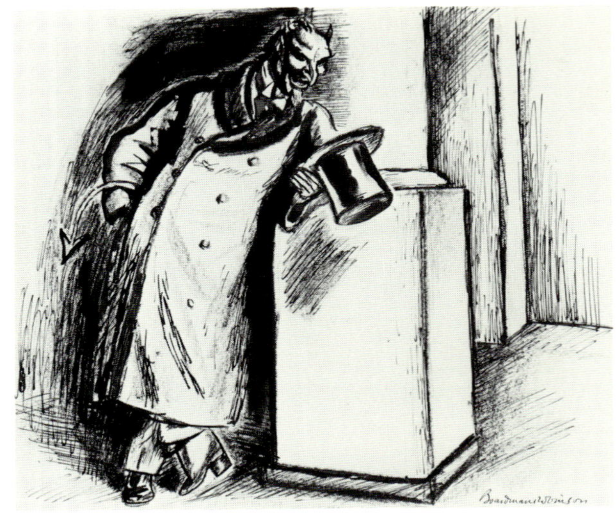

Fig. 117. *A Ticket to Normalcy*. John Tinney McCutcheon. Aug. 12, 1921. Ink on paper. 23 1/4 × 14 5/8 in. Courtesy The Lilly Library, Indiana University, Bloomington.

Employing President Harding's famous phrase "normalcy," a term he used in his 1920 presidential campaign to indicate a swift national recovery from World War I and a return to life and business as usual, John McCutcheon calls attention to the plight of the railroads following government operation of them during the war. "I want a ticket to Normalcy," says Uncle Sam. "Can't let you have one till the Road is repaired," answers the stationmaster.

Fig. 118. *Washington Conference*. Boardman Robinson. 1921. Ink and pastel on paper. 14 1/2 × 15 in. Courtesy The Swann Collection of Caricature and Cartoon.

President Harding at the request of Senator Borah issued a call to all major powers, except Russia, to attend the Washington disarmament conference in August, 1921. Secretary of State Charles Evans Hughes startled the conferees in his opening remarks by suggesting that they not only limit future armaments, but scrap large portions of those already constructed. Under Hughes' skillful leadership the delegates agreed to a limit for future construction along with a host of other treaties regarding warfare and colonial disagreements. The tonnage of capital ships in the future was limited to the ratio of five for the United States and Britain, three for Japan, and 1.67 for France and Italy.

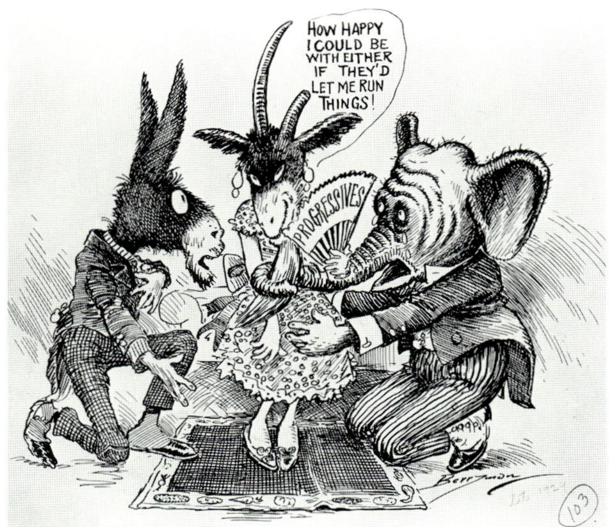

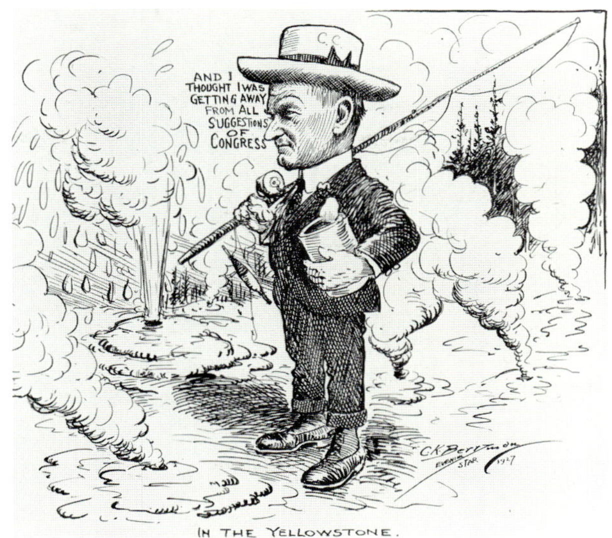

Fig. 119. *How Happy I Could Be with Either if They'd Let Me Run Things*. C. K. Berryman. 1924. Ink on paper. 12 3/16 × 14 3/16 in. Courtesy the Library of Congress.

Perhaps the most ardent Progressive of all was Robert M. La Follette, Senator from Wisconsin, who entered the 1924 election as the head of a third party, the Progressive Party. Berryman is pointing out in this cartoon that La Follette would have worked with either party if they had turned more toward progressivism, and that either party would have liked to have had La Follette's progressive followers vote for them.

Fig. 120. *In the Yellowstone*. C. K. Berryman. 1927, in the Washington *Evening Star*. Ink on paper. 13 1/2 × 14 1/4 in. Courtesy National Park Service Archives. Harper's Ferry, W. Va.

An aloof and austere man who made a point of honesty and propriety, President Calvin Coolidge loved the simple things of life. He was on a fishing trip with his father in Vermont when President Harding died in San Francisco. Coolidge was also well known for being a man of few words, a virtue that Berryman obviously thinks Coolidge would have appreciated in Congress.

113

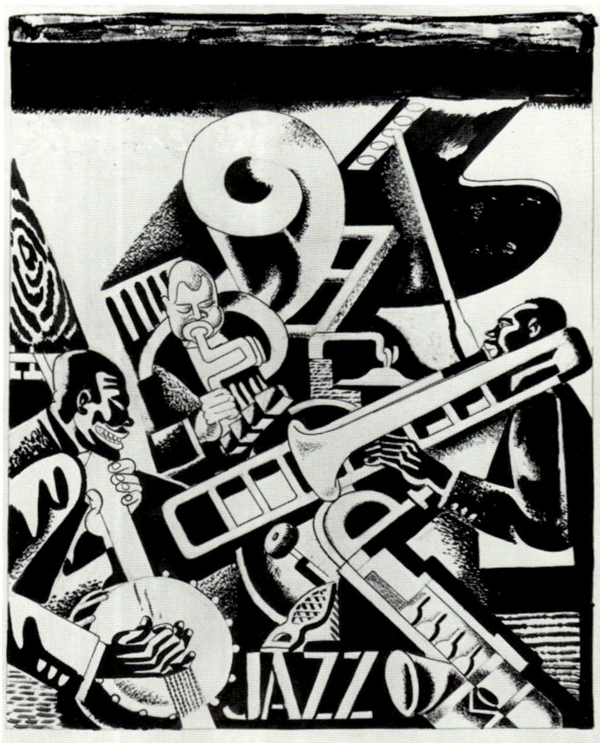

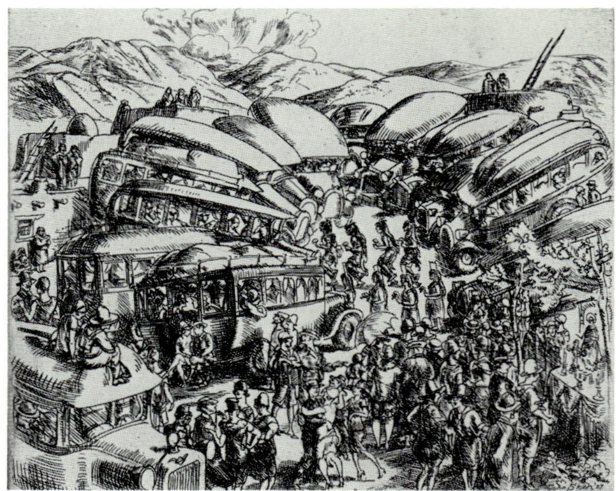

Fig. 121. *Negro Jazz Band*. Jan Matulka. 1920s. Black ink, pencil and white highlights on paper. 25 × 19 1/8 in. Courtesy St. Louis Art Museum: Friends of the St. Louis Museum Fund.

Nothing expresses the spirit of the 1920s better than jazz. It began to emerge from the Black enclaves of America's cities during the early years of World War I and burst onto the national scene along with bobbed hair, short skirts and joy rides. This vital expression of the emotional extremes of Black life is one of America's most important contributions to twentieth century music and is destined to endure, according to Leopold Stokowski, "because it is an expression of the times, of the breathless, energetic, superactive times in which we are living. . . ."

114

Fig. 122. *Indian Detour*. John Sloan. Sept. 24, 1927. Etching. 9 13/16 × 12 5/8 in. Courtesy Amon Carter Museum, Fort Worth.

The tourists have crowded around the corn dance at Santo Domingo Pueblo. In this print Sloan is satirizing the Fred Harvey Indian Tour. "Busses take the tourists out to view the Indian dances, which are religious ceremonials and naturally not understood as such by the visiting crowds," he wrote.

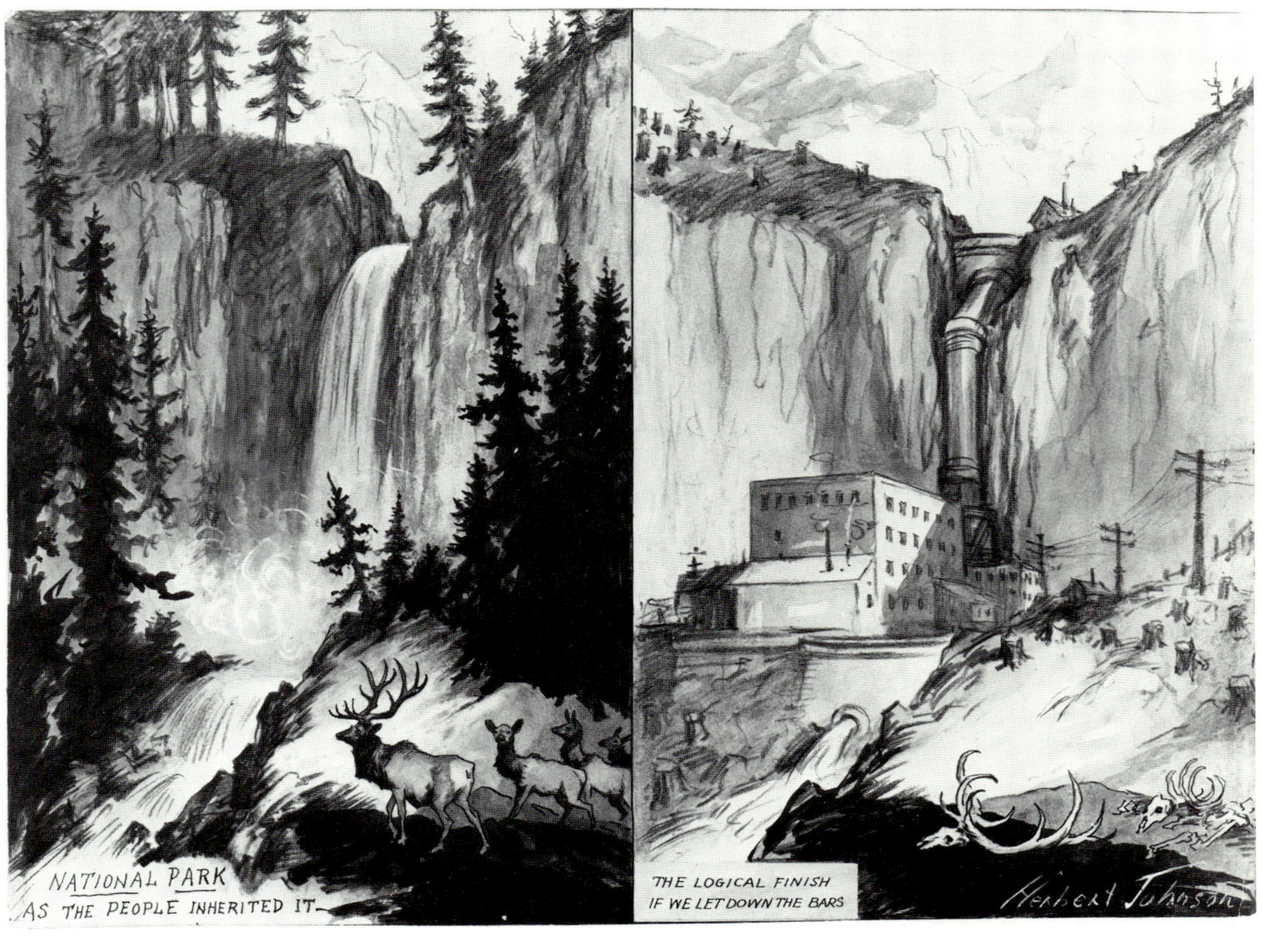

Fig. 123. *National Park as the People Inherited It*. Herbert Johnson. 1920s. Ink, gouache, crayon on paper. 13 1/2 × 18 in. Courtesy National Park Service Archives.

Industry and manufacturing were growing with phenomenal speed during the decade of the twenties, and in many cases this growth was labeled as ''progress'' in spite of detrimental effects it might have had on the environment. Here Herbert Johnson expresses the fear that, unless checked, these industries could end up destroying all the beautiful areas set aside as national parks.

115

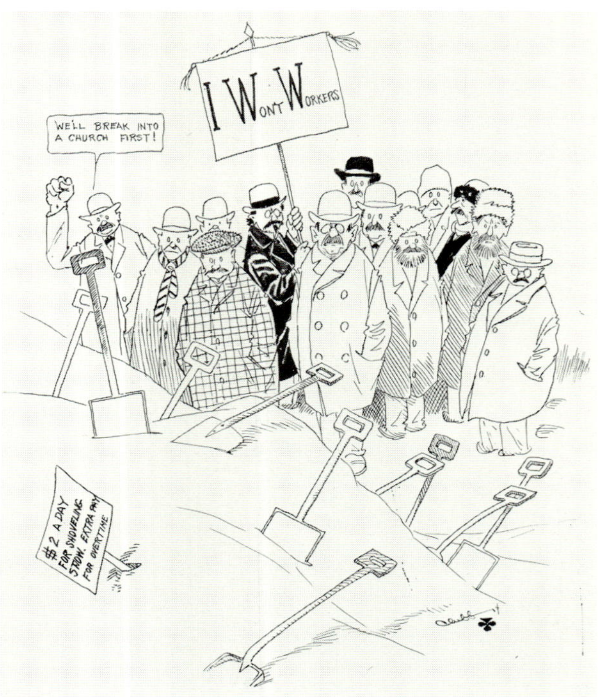

Fig. 124. *I Won't Workers*. John Clubb. 1914. Ink on paper. 17 3/4 × 13 5/8 in. Courtesy The Swann Collection of Caricature and Cartoon.

One of the more radical labor unions in America's history, the Industrial Workers of the World was founded in June, 1905, in Chicago. Advocating abolition of the wage system and formation of industrial unions, the I. W. W. opposed America's entry into World War I, but was itself eliminated as a powerful labor force in the West between 1918 and 1920 by government prosecution. Their most influential leader, William D. ("Big Bill") Haywood, led them in several successful strikes when laborers were badly needed in the expanding economy, but was himself jailed during the war.

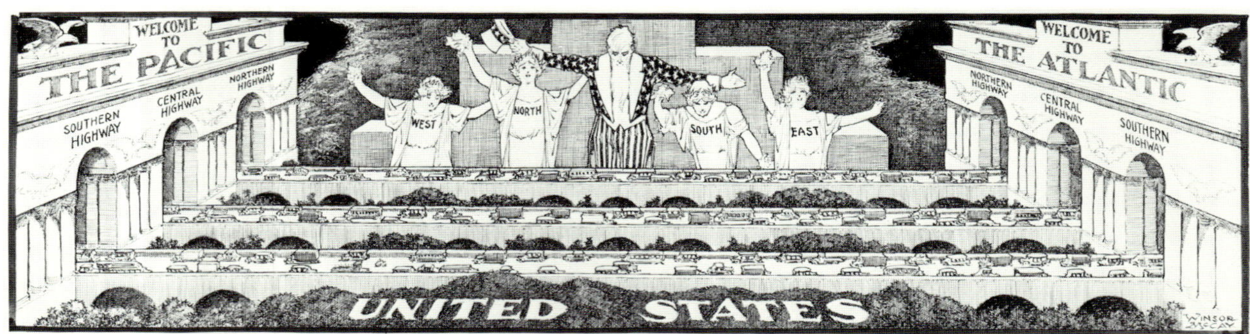

Fig. 125. *Celebration of Highways*. Winsor McCay. n.d. Pen and ink on paper. 6 7/8 × 23 in. Courtesy The Chesler Collection, Library, Fairleigh Dickinson University, Florham-Madison Campus.

In 1908 Henry Ford produced the design for his Model T motor car. It outperformed anything then on the road and at a price affordable to the general public. Automobiles were at first greeted by jeers, jokes, and often angry protest by a horse-drawn society which considered the car unsafe, uncomfortable, unaesthetic, and unpractical. But by 1920 about four million were rattling down American roads, that is, where roads existed. In 1921 the Federal Highway Act began financing a national highway program. Backwoods villages gained access to cities, the East Coast was joined to the West, the North to the South by a mesh of roads and highways. And these highways provided an enormous stimulus to travel and transportation for business and pleasure. People, goods, and ideas traveled and circulated across the land as never before.

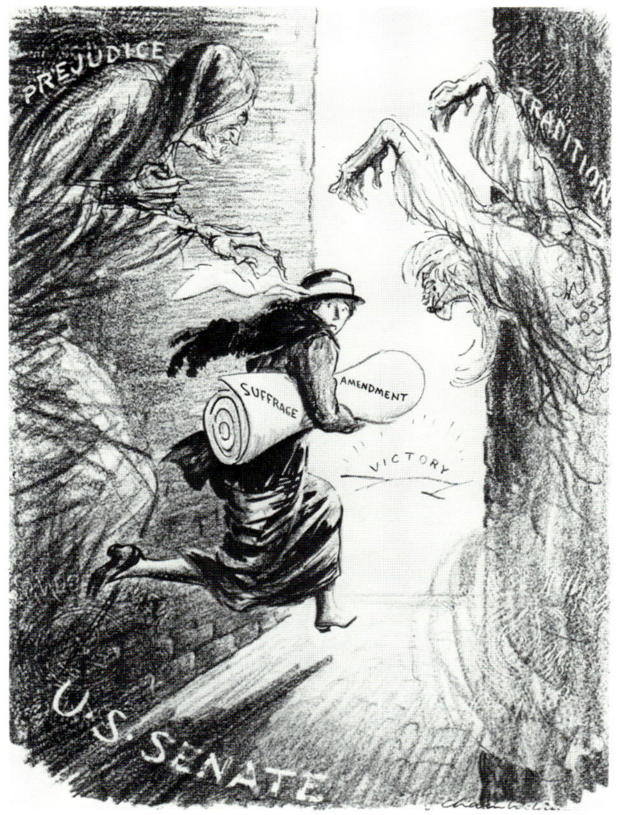

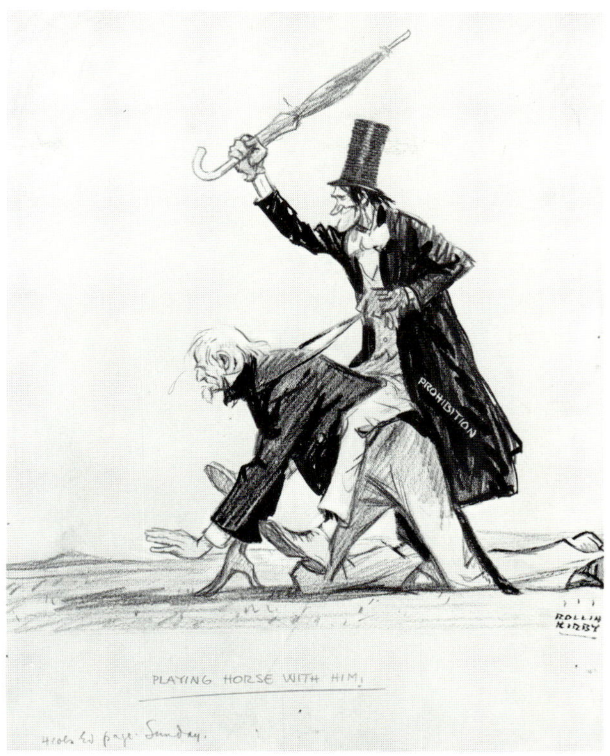

Fig. 126. *Almost Thru the Dark Alley*. Kenneth Chamberlain. 1919. Black crayon, pen, and ink on paper. 22 × 17 in. Courtesy Grunwald Center for the Graphic Arts, University of California, Los Angeles.

Women were finally granted the right to vote on June 4, 1919, when Congress passed the nineteenth amendment to the Constitution stating that no one could be denied their political rights because of sex. It was a long-overdue victory heralded by the Kansas City *Star* as "not just a victory for women alone" but "a victory for democracy and the principle of equality upon which the nation was founded." But "Uncle" Joe Cannon, Speaker of the House, did not see how anything would be different. He pointed out that he had been influenced by five generations of women and that he was the result of their molding. They did not have to have the vote to have influence. Many observers, however, expected that women would be a powerful force for honest government.

Fig. 127. *Playing Horse with Him*. Rollin Kirby. 1921. Lithographic pencil washed with touche on cardboard. 19 7/8 × 14 7/8 in. Courtesy The Metropolitan Museum of Art, Gift of Rollin Kirby, 1944.

After the eighteenth amendment went into effect, Congress passed the National Prohibition Enforcement, or the Volstead, Act to enforce the amendment. President Wilson, in one of his last acts as President, vetoed the act on October 27, 1919, but Congress passed the law over his veto. A multi-million dollar business was immediately declared illegal and went underground. "Bootleggers" supplied forbidden liquor to rural and urban areas alike, and "speakeasies" became as numerous and as popular as saloons had been. Uncle Sam was saddled with prohibition, a sentiment given classic expression by Kirby's "Mr. Prohibition."

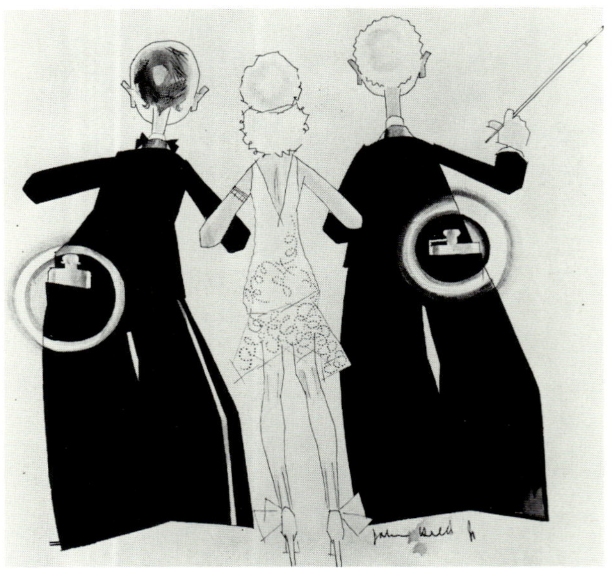

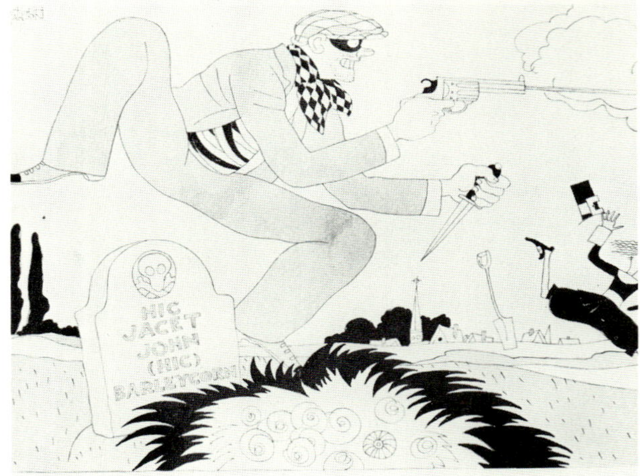

Fig. 128. *"So long as the dry farce lasts, a girl who sips ice-water is looked upon as 'freezing the party.'"* John Held, Jr. June, 1928, in *Harper's Bazaar*. Ink on paper. 7 3/4 × 8 1/16 in. Courtesy the Library of Congress.

Born in Salt Lake City in 1889, John Held, Jr., the "Mormon Kid," was the artist who gave the 1920s one of their most memorable images—the flapper. The flapper seemed to capture the spirit of "The Era of Wonderful Nonsense." In this drawing, which accompanied Emily Post's article entitled "How to Behave," Held has combined two of his images, the flapper and the college kids, all of whom are enjoying the forbidden delights of prohibition.

Fig. 129. *Hic Jacet John (Hic) Barleycorn*. Ralph Barton. 1920s. Ink and blue wash on paper. 8 × 10 in. Courtesy The Swann Collection of Caricature and Cartoon.

Shortly after the enactment of the eighteenth amendment, Rev. Billy Sunday held a mock funeral for "John Barleycorn," complete with a twenty-foot coffin and horse-drawn hearse. In his eulogy he denounced John Barleycorn as "God's worst enemy" and "Hell's best friend," but now with the advent of Prohibition, "The slums soon will be only a memory. We will turn our prisons into factories and our jails into storehouses and corncribs." But crime and corruption did not cease. On the contrary, Ralph Barton shows it rising from Barleycorn's grave as a gangster who drives the Puritans away to gain profit and power from the sale of illegal spirits.

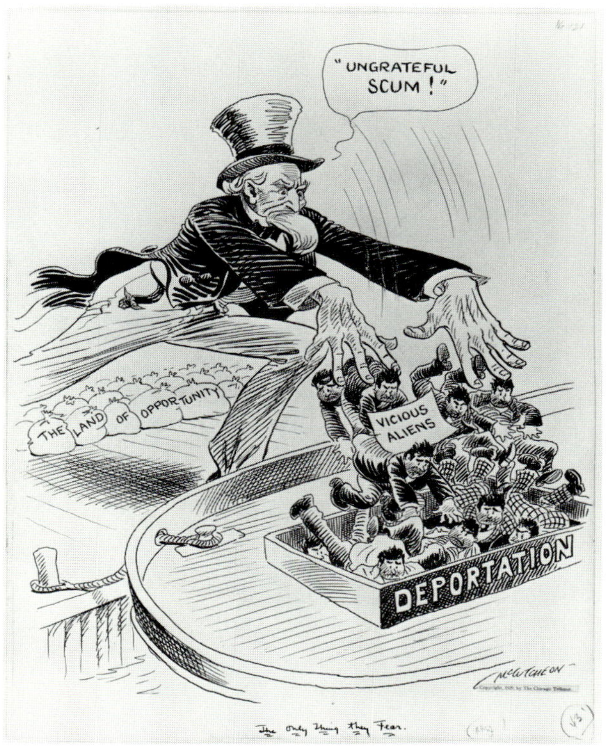

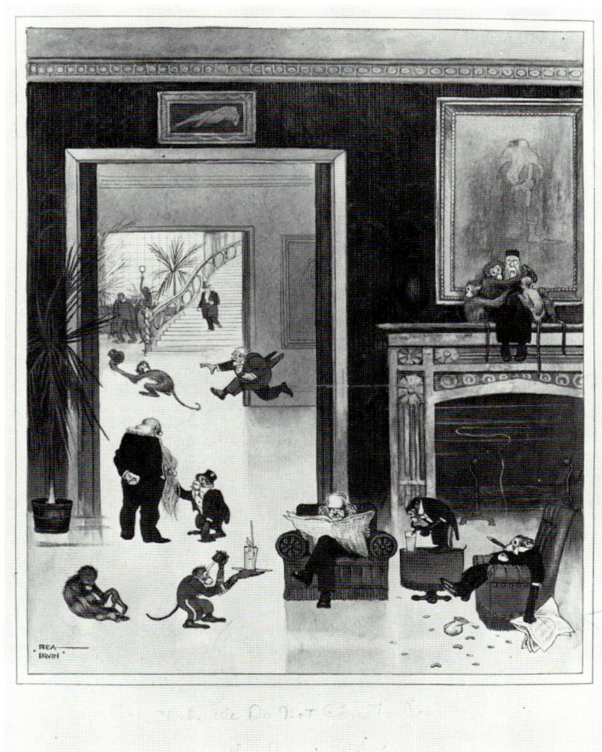

Fig. 130. *The Only Thing They Fear*. John Tinney McCutcheon. 1929. Pen and ink on paper. 18 3/4 × 14 5/8 in. Courtesy The Chicago Historical Society.

On January 1, 1920 Attorney General A. Mitchell Palmer began a crackdown on "foreign subversives." The Great Red Raid resulted in two thousand arrests in thirty-three cities across the U.S.A. Fears aroused by Russia's Bolshevik Revolution and the general xenophobia and super-patriotism engendered during the First World War culminated in this attack on aliens, socialists, and other political and social non-conformists. Answering charges that the United States was behaving autocratically in deporting these "trouble-makers," Attorney General Palmer replied, "that in our determination to maintain our government we are treating our alien enemies with extreme consideration. To deny them the privilege of remaining in a country which they have openly deplored as an unenlightened community, unfit for those who prefer the privileges of Bolshevism, should be no hardship."

Fig. 131. *The Darwin Club*. Rea Irvin. 1914 in *Life*. Ink and wash on paper. 15 1/2 × 13 in. Courtesy The Swann Collection of Caricature and Cartoon.

As Darwin's concept of evolution spread, it had great impact on the intellectuals, many of whom tried to adapt it to society in general. They reasoned that if natural selection worked among the animals, the same sort of procedure was working in human society at a more refined level. Herbert Spencer coined the term that seemed to sum up Darwin's ideas for many people: the survival of the fittest. Rea Irvin seems in this drawing to be asking who the fittest really are, or at least what kind of behavior would characterize a member of the fittest.

119

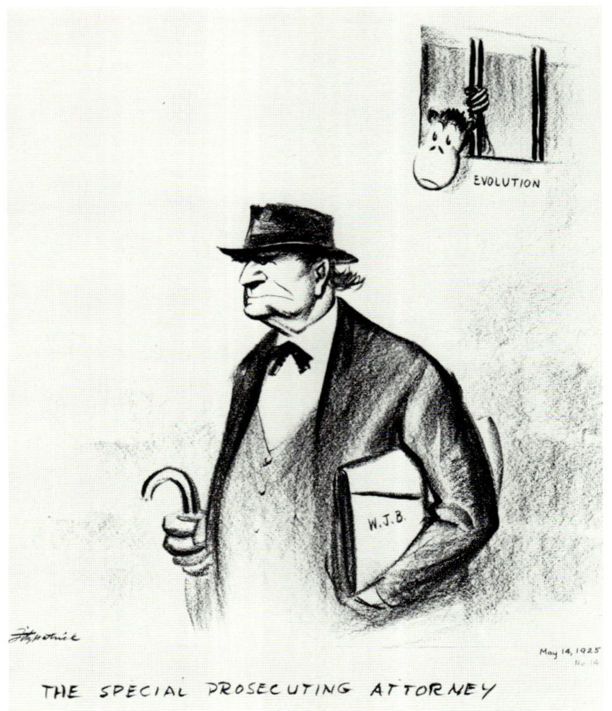

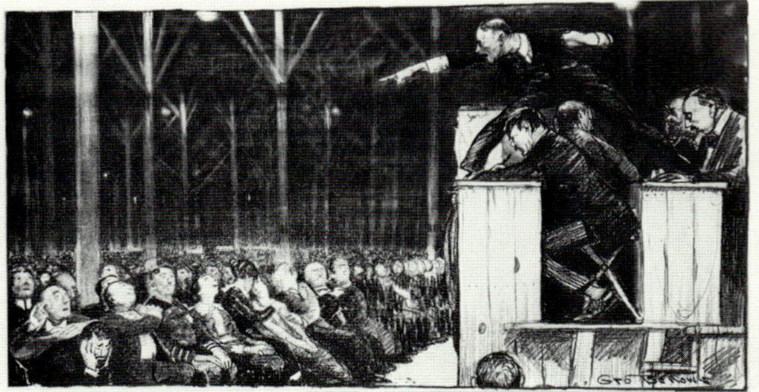

Fig. 132. *The Special Prosecuting Attorney*. Daniel Robert Fitz-patrick. May 14, 1925. Crayon on paper. 26 × 21 7/16 in. Courtesy The State Historical Society of Missouri, Columbia.

Fig. 133. *Billy Sunday*. George Bellows. 1923. Lithograph. 9 × 16 1/2 in. Courtesy Boston Public Library, Print Department.

A Tennessee state statute of 1925 forbade any public educational institution from teaching the "theory that denies the story of the divine creation of man as taught in the Bible." Thinking this law unconstitutional, John T. Scopes purposely taught the theory of evolution and was tried the following July for violation of the act. His case attracted nation-wide attention, and William Jennings Bryan and Clarence Darrow came to Tennessee to represent the prosecution and the defense. "Civilization is on trial," said Darrow as the trial began. The trial climaxed when Darrow called Bryan to the stand to testify as an expert on the Bible. Scopes was convicted, but the fine was set aside because the trial court had authorized a fine larger than the law permitted.

William Ashley Sunday, better known as Billy, was a professional baseball player from Chicago before he was ordained as a Presbyterian minister in 1903. Then he became one of the most famous revivalists of the 1920s, holding meetings across the nation as Americans were returning to "that Old Time Religion," enforcing prohibition, and denouncing evolution. According to one historian, Billy Sunday was one of the "big time operators" with "hard-sell showmanship, mass soul-saving, and massive profits."

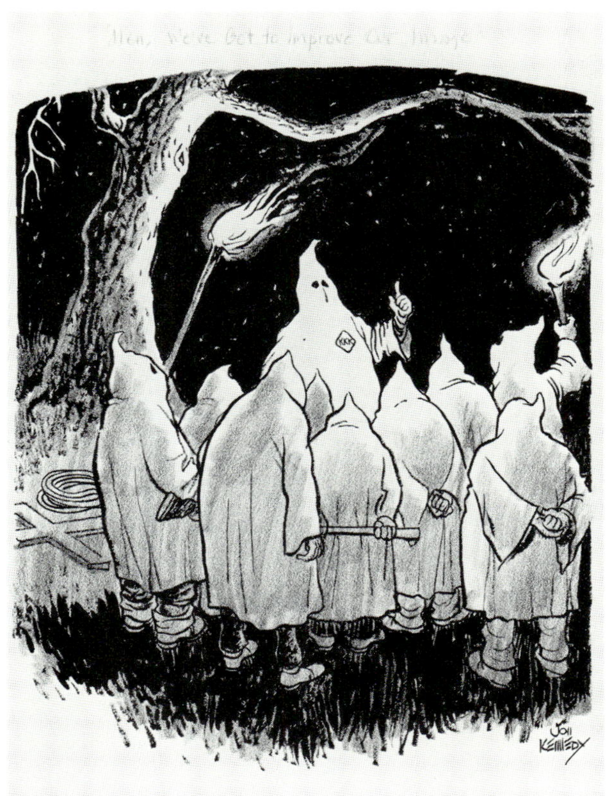

Fig. 134. *Men, We've Got to Improve Our Image*. Jon Kennedy. 1960s. Crayon on paper. 13 3/4 × 10 11/16 in. Courtesy The State Historical Society of Missouri, Columbia.

The Ku Klux Klan, an organization founded in the South during Reconstruction, returned to power during the 1920s, organizing around anti-Catholic, anti-Semitic, anti-immigration, anti-Negro, and enforcement of prohibition stands. So strong in 1924 that it split the Democratic Party, the Klan was soon discredited and lost most of its members. It was virtually destroyed when the Baltimore *Sun* ran a series of stories on its illegal activities, and the Indiana Grand Dragon was convicted of murder.

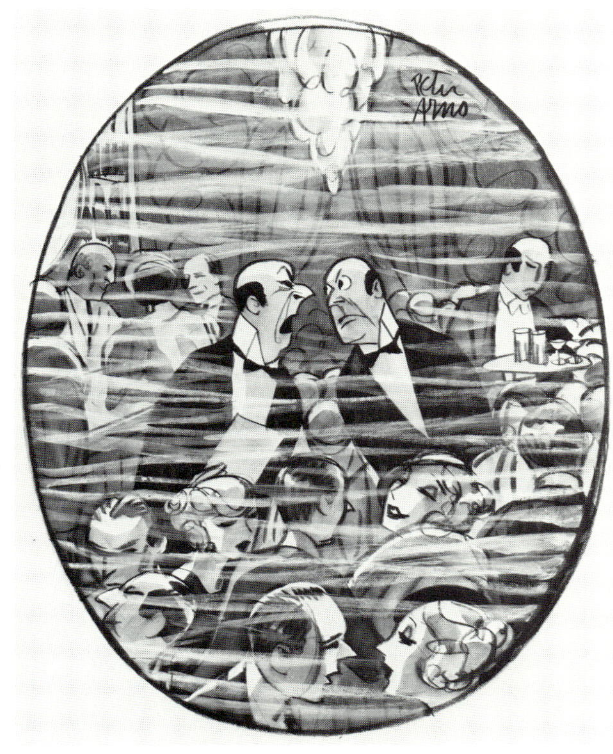

Fig. 135. *Michael! Where's That Air Coming From?* Peter Arno. Nov. 26, 1932, in *The New Yorker*. Ink and wash on paper. 21 × 14 in. Courtesy The Swann Collection of Caricature and Cartoon.

A dropout from Yale in 1923, Peter Arno understood New York City's café society as well as anyone. A member of a respected New York family who changed his name so as not to embarrass them, he was also a member of the world of flappers and speakeasies and bandleader in a nightclub called The Rendezvous. When Harold Ross started *The New Yorker* magazine, Arno, with pictures like this, helped him create a magazine definitely not intended for Ross' imaginary "old lady in Dubuque."

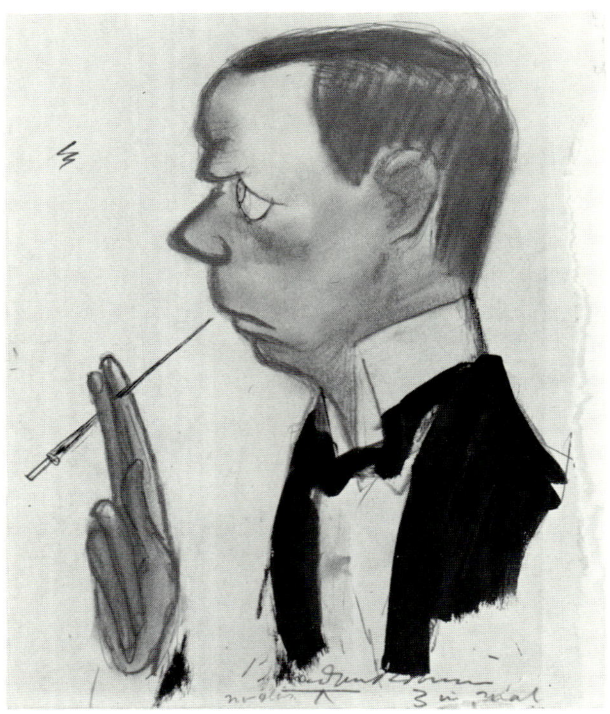

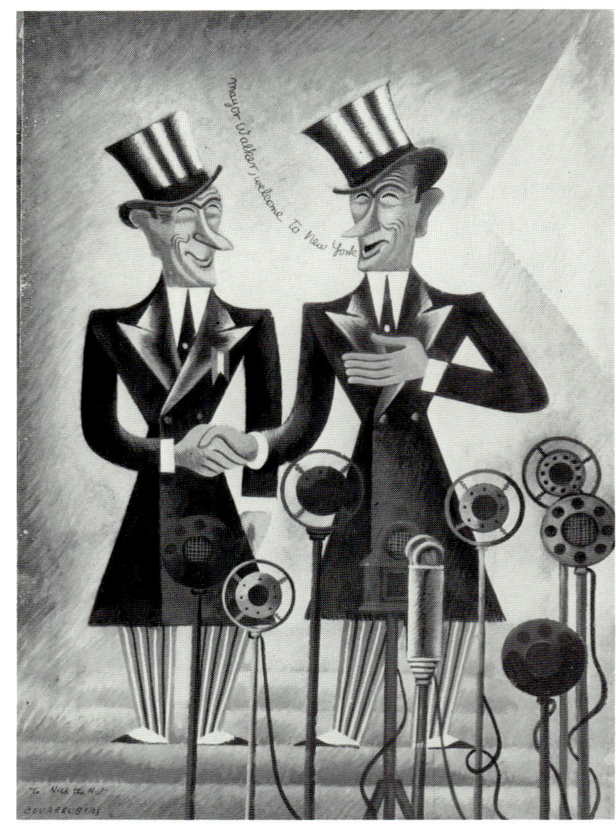

Fig. 137. *Mayor Walker, and Himself*. Miguel Covarrubias. 1920s. Tempera and watercolor on paper. 16 × 11 in. Courtesy The Nikolas Murray Collection, The Iconography Collection, Humanities Research Center, University of Texas, Austin.

Fig. 136. *Head of Sinclair Lewis*. Boardman Robinson. 1923. Ink and red crayon on paper. 8 7/8 × 7 in. Courtesy The Minneapolis Institute of Arts, Gift of David M. Daniels.

In the twenties and thirties many young American writers and artists fled the puritanical structures of American society for the freedom of the Bohemian life in European cities. But Sinclair Lewis remained in America to write about Americans. His great novels, *Babbitt*, *Arrowsmith*, *Elmer Gantry* and *Dodsworth* laid bare the hypocrisy and shallowness of American middle-class values and culture. In 1930 he was awarded the Nobel Prize for Literature, the first American author to be so honored.

The man who seemed to lead New York City in the ways of the 1920s was Mayor Jimmy Walker, a rather average fellow but one who could translate the increasingly complex problems of the nation's largest city into terms the common man could understand. Mayor Walker also fitted in. His racy, big-city ways attracted many votes. He kept show girls on the side, although he was married. He took seven vacations during his first two years in office, although New York City was beset with problems. And he hastily resigned in 1932 after several charges of corruption were leveled against his administration. He lived in Europe for several years, then returned to New York to live out his years as president of a record company.

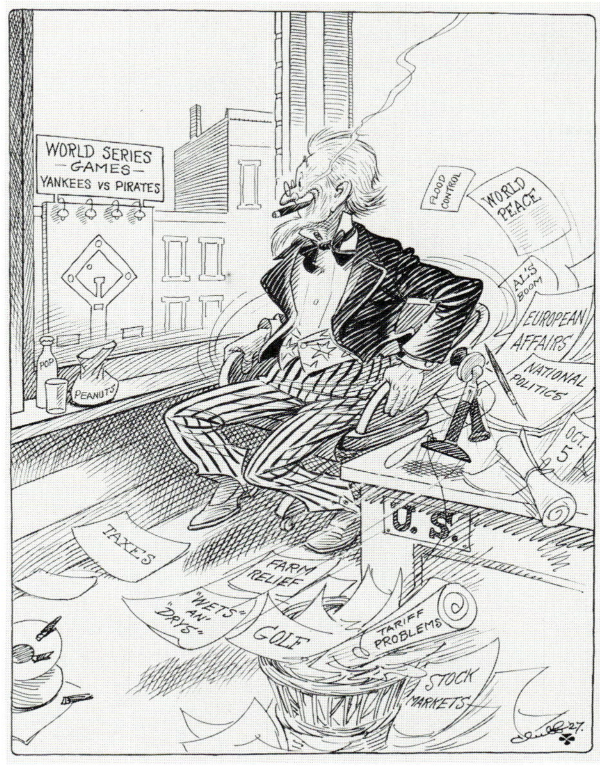

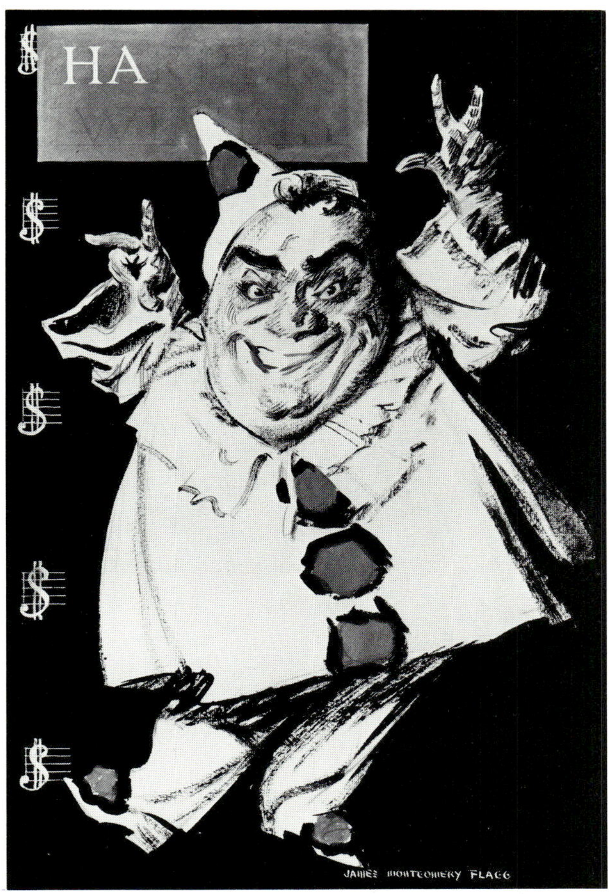

Fig. 138. *Let the ''Swatting'' Begin*. John Clubb. 1927. Ink and brush on paper. 19 × 14 7/8 in. Courtesy The Murray A. Harris Collection of Graphic Art, North Hollywood, Calif.

In the twenties sports, particularly spectator sports, captured the American public interest as never before, and baseball became the ''national pastime.'' This interest was fanned by a new breed of journalist, the sportswriter, and the radio as well as the newspaper spread the sports news. This new breed included such notables as Damon Runyon, Grantland Rice, and Ring Lardner. Other writers had their comments too. George Bernard Shaw described baseball as a combination of ''cricket . . . , puss-in-the-corner, and Handel's *Messiah*.'' In 1927, the date of this cartoon, the World Series pitted the New York Yankees against the Pittsburgh Pirates. That year Babe Ruth hit his peak, knocking a record sixty home runs. Uncle Sam is shown turning his attention away from a desk full of urgent national matters to enjoy instead America's national sport.

Fig. 139. *Enrico Caruso*. James Montgomery Flagg. Apr. 25, 1914, in *Harper's Weekly*. Dry brush, ink, tempera, wash on paper. 24 × 17 1/4 in. (sight). Courtesy Mr. and Mrs. Draper Hill, Memphis, Tenn.

Born in Naples, Italy, in February, 1873, Enrico Caruso swept into New York City to perform in the Metropolitan Opera in 1903, which he called ''the goal of every opera singer's desire.'' Here he is pictured as Pagliacci in the fifth of a series called ''Captains of Industry'' done for the cover of *Harper's*. Widely loved for his sense of humor, his generosity, and his beautiful voice, Caruso became a popular performer with an international reputation. Flagg himself was proud of this caricature.

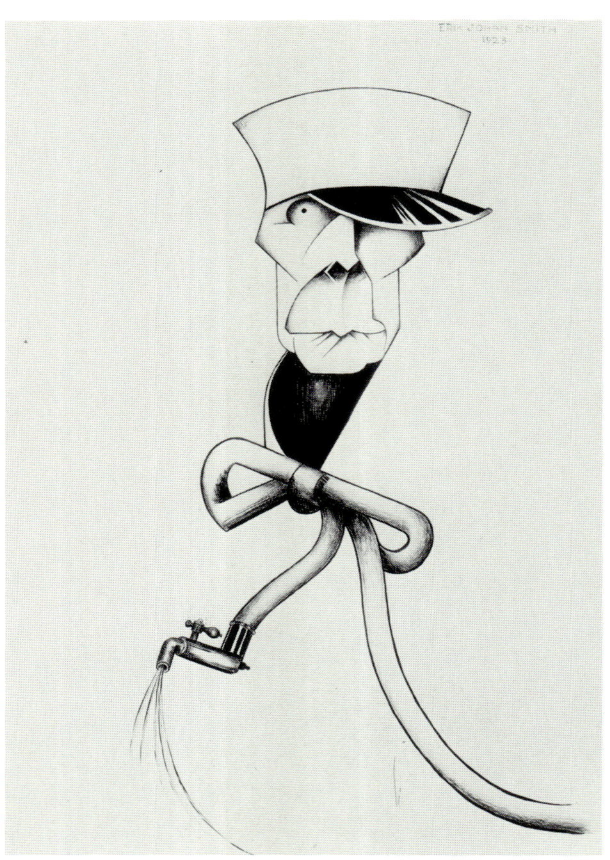

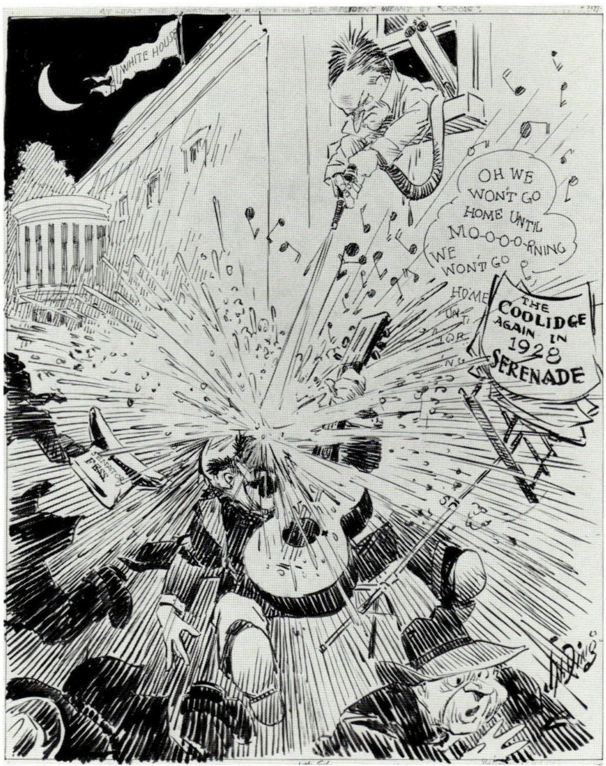

Fig. 140. *John D. Rockefeller, Sr., a caricature*. Erik Johan Smith. 1923. Pencil and ink on paper. 23 1/2 × 13 1/2 in. Courtesy Jonson Collection, University of New Mexico, Albuquerque, Gift of Mrs. Jerome Frank.

John D. Rockefeller was one of the first great, wealthy men of the United States. A deeply religious man who began his career by becoming a partner in a produce commission business in 1859, Rockefeller soon got into oil refining. In 1870 he and his associates organized Standard Oil Company of Ohio, which he developed into a company that dominated the oil refining industry. In 1892 he was forced to break up his holdings because of an adverse Supreme Court decision, but he continued to manage his vast empire through the holding company, Standard Oil of New Jersey, which the Supreme Court dissolved in 1911. Late in life Rockefeller developed a passionate interest in philanthropy and gave away over one-half billion dollars through the world-famous Rockefeller Foundation before his death in 1937.

Fig. 141. *At Least One Senator Now Knows What the President Meant by Choose*. Jay Norwood Darling. October 22, 1927, in the Des Moines *Register*. Pen and ink on paper. 28 1/2 × 22 1/2 in. Courtesy The University of Iowa Libraries, Iowa City.

When President Calvin Coolidge announced in 1927 that "I do not choose to run for President in 1928," he left many observers wondering if that meant that he would accept a draft. Ohio Senator Simeon Davison Fess, who was temporary chairman of the Republican National Convention and made the keynote address, apparently thought so and intended to nominate Coolidge at the end of his speech. But his hopes were "doused" by Coolidge's adamant refusal to accept.

124

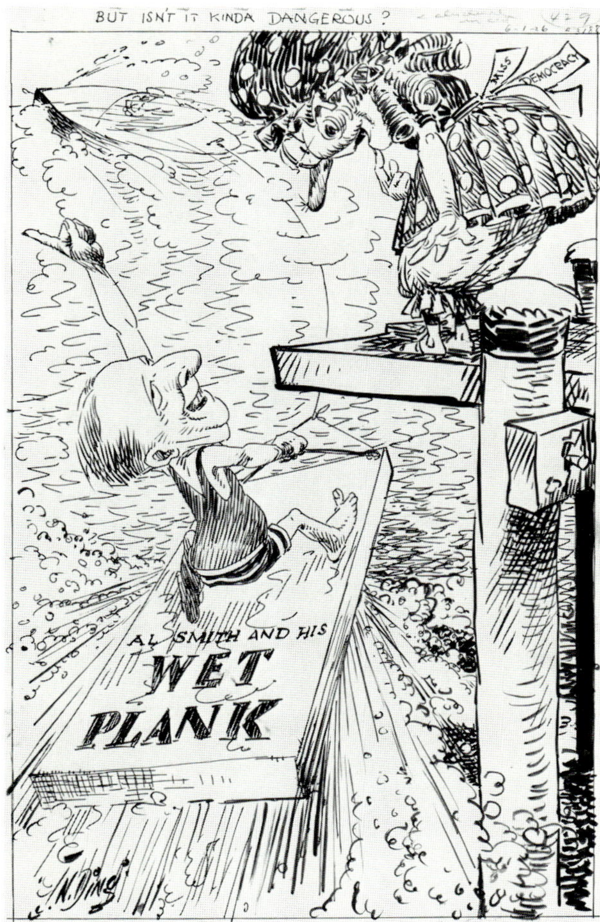

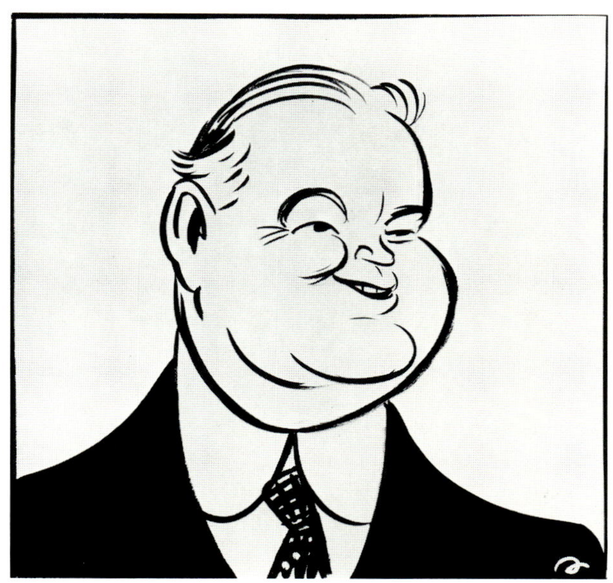

Fig. 142. *But Isn't It Kind of Dangerous?* Jay Norwood Darling. June 1, 1926. Pen and ink on paper. 22 1/2 × 14 1/2 in. Courtesy The University of Iowa Libraries, Iowa City.

A veteran of the New York State legislature and Tammany Hall, Alfred E. Smith ran for President in 1928 on a platform featuring repeal of prohibition. "Ding" Darling realizes that Smith is on dangerous ground, as did H. L. Mencken: "Those who fear the Pope outnumber those who are tired of the Anti-Saloon League." Despite his charm and poise, Smith embarrassed the Democrats by clinging to his Lower East Side pronunciation of words like "raddio."

Fig. 143. [Caricature of Herbert Hoover.] Emilio Angelo. 1940 in the Philadelphia *Inquirer*. Ink on paper. 13 × 13 in. Courtesy Herbert Hoover Presidential Library, West Branch, Iowa.

Herbert Hoover carried the aura of "Coolidge prosperity" to the Presidency in 1928, but the Great Depression marked him indelibly as a Depression President. Known as an able engineer, businessman, and administrator, Hoover thought the Depression to be only temporary and never expended the creative energy he had lavished on the Belgian relief effort and U. S. Food Administration during World War I. He oversaw the Reconstruction Finance Corporation, but his conservative faith in individual initiative prevented him from forcefully using it.

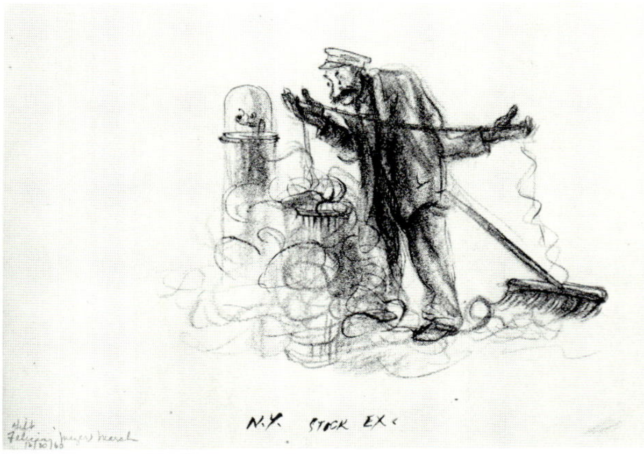

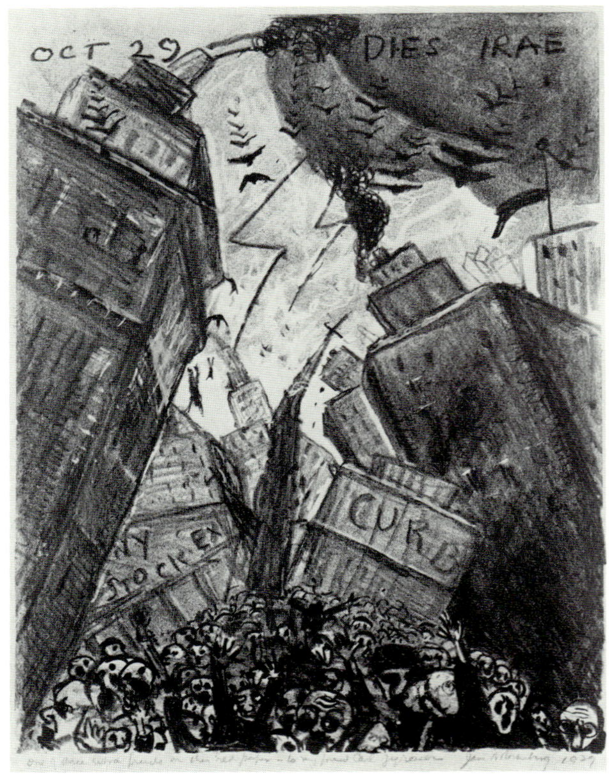

Fig. 145. *Oct. 29. Dies Irae*. James Rosenberg. Lithograph on colored paper. 13 3/4 × 10 1/2 in. Courtesy Philadelphia Museum of Art, Carl and Laura Zigrosser Collection.

In September, 1929, the stock market began to ease downward, then it dropped sharply—and did not surge back. Foreign investors began to withdraw their money; prudent Americans began to wonder. Thursday, October 24, sent them into panic as millions of shares of stocks changed hands, and prices fell uniformly. But the following Tuesday was disastrous. No one knows how many shares really were sold, although the official total is in excess of sixteen millions. By the end of 1929 more than $30 billions, a sum equal to twice the national debt, had disappeared. It would be years before the country realize the magnitude of the disaster.

Fig. 144. *N. Y. Stock Ex*. Reginald Marsh. 1929. Crayon and ink on paper. 6 1/2 × 7 1/2 in. Courtesy the Library of Congress.

The 1920s were a zany, get-rich-quick era in which millions of Americans "played" or watched the Stock Market. The vice-president of General Motors summed it up well: "Everybody ought to be rich." Others saw the Stock Market as the national passion. Some play the horses, some gamble, some play Wall Street.

126

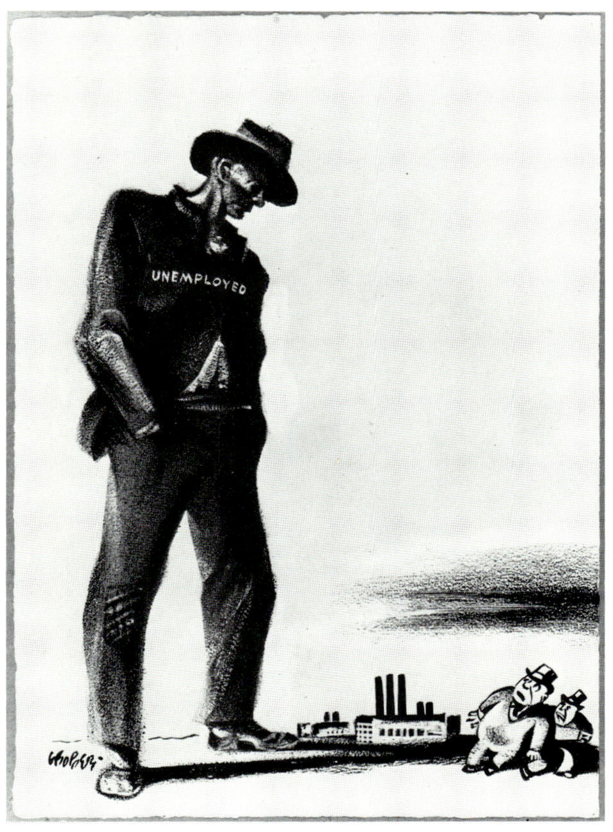

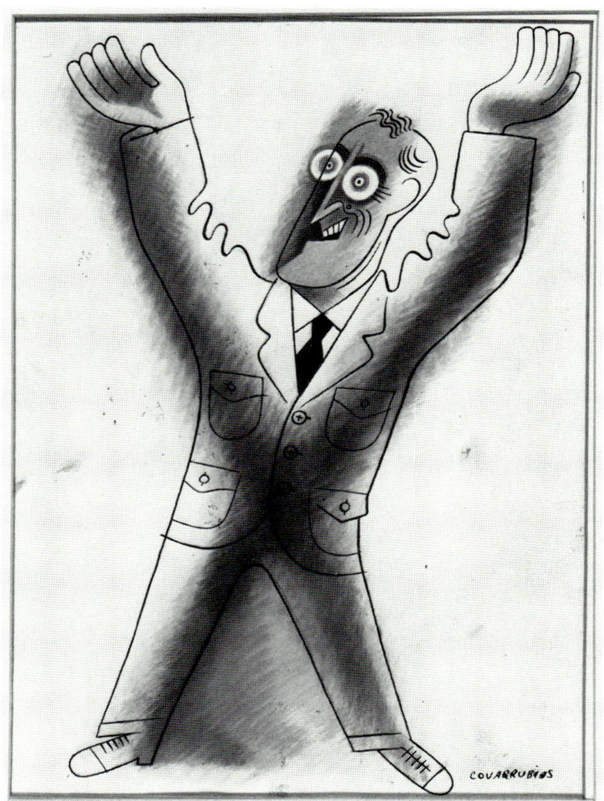

Fig. 147. *Franklin D. Roosevelt*. Miguel Covarrubias. 1930s. Pen and ink wash on paper. 13 3/4 × 9 1/2 in. Courtesy The Nikolas Murray Collection, The Iconography Collection, Humanities Research Center, University of Texas, Austin.

Franklin Delano Roosevelt was not an economist, but he was a political genius. Realizing that the country needed at least the semblance of action, he began his administration with a dramatic speech, then moved into a legislative program the likes of which the country had not seen. "First of all, let me assert my firm belief that the only thing we have to fear is fear itself—nameless, unreasoning, unjustified terror . . . . We are stricken by no plague of locusts. . . . Plenty is at our doorstep, but a generous use of it languishes in the very sight of the supply." The government and the people would now have an opportunity to remedy the ills of the nation because "the money changers have fled from their high seats in the temple of our civilization." With that he moved into the famous 100 days, which saw enactment of most of the New Deal legislative program.

Fig. 146. *Unemployed*. William Gropper. 1930. Mixed media on paper. 18 × 13 in. Courtesy William Gropper.

As the Great Depression was felt throughout the nation, millions lost their jobs. The United States had seen depression before, but never one that continued year after year and spread worldwide. No one really knew how many Americans were out of work—between twelve million and sixteen million. Perhaps the most damage, however, was done to the psyche. "'Depression' shows man as a senseless cog in a senselessly whirling machine which is beyond human understanding and has ceased to serve any purpose but its own," said Peter F. Drucker.

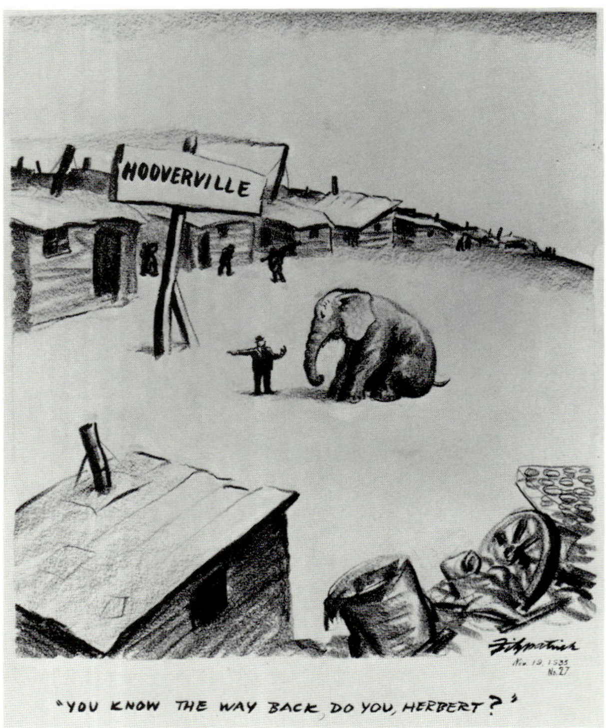

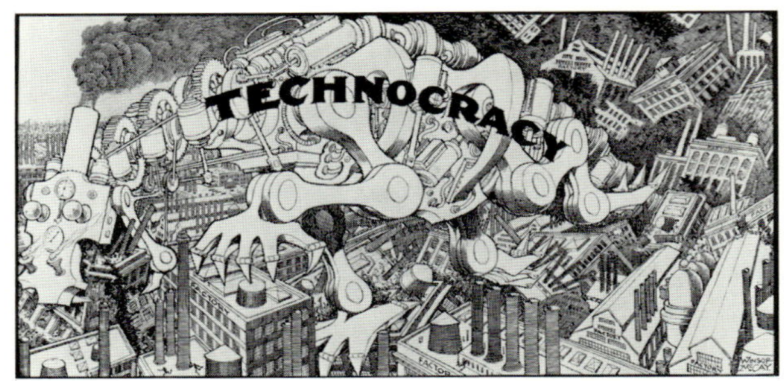

Fig. 148. *"You Know the Way Back Do You, Herbert?"* Daniel Robert Fitzpatrick. Nov. 19, 1935. Crayon on paper. 23 1/2 × 20 in. Courtesy The State Historical Society of Missouri, Columbia.

Among the most graphic reminders of the depression and its havoc were the "Hoovervilles," shanty-towns where the unemployed and poor lived in slum conditions. "I had not the stomach to stay long at the Hoovervilles I came upon here and there," wrote Matthew Josephson; "they were sores on the body politic, and they stank. Here was the unsanitary by-product of our free-wheeling economy, with its haphazard institutions of private charity and its limited local relief." As the Hoovervilles spread, former President Hoover's promise of two chickens in every pot and a car in every garage sounded hollow. "Hoover blankets" were newspapers, broken down mule-drawn wagons were "Hoover wagons," and pockets turned inside-out were "Hoover flags." Fitzpatrick suggests in this cartoon that the Republican elephant will have to find his way back to the White House through the Hoovervilles.

Fig. 149. *Technocracy Devouring the City*. Winsor McCay. n. d. Pen, ink, colored pencil on paper. 11 × 22 in. Courtesy The Chesler Collection, Library, Fairleigh Dickinson University, Florham-Madison Campus.

Although there were few workable ideas that President Roosevelt could employ in combating the Depression, one that gained overnight popularity, except with skeptics like McCay, was "Technocracy," an idea unveiled in an article by Howard Scott of New York in December, 1932. His idea was that national affairs would be regulated by experts rather than by elected officials. His plan was novel but broke down when applied to something as vague as the price system. Technocracy fitted the mood of the early thirties and many grasped at it as the solution to the country's problems, but practical men only smiled. "Nobody could really make anything out of technocracy and Howard Scott," commented the New York *World Telegram*, "but they find it's a great thing to think about."

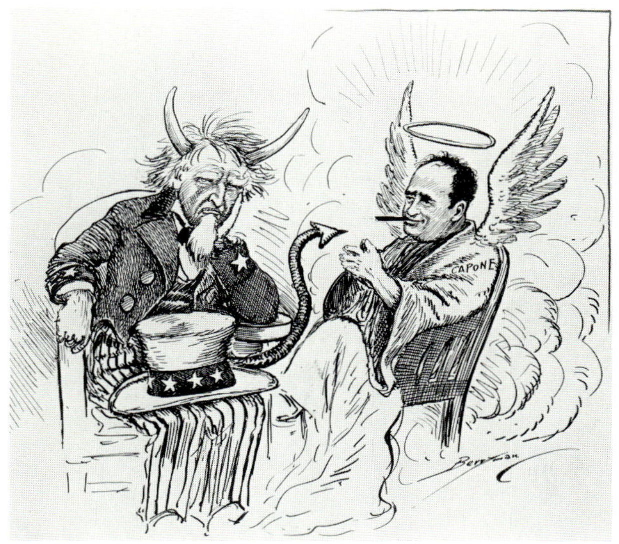

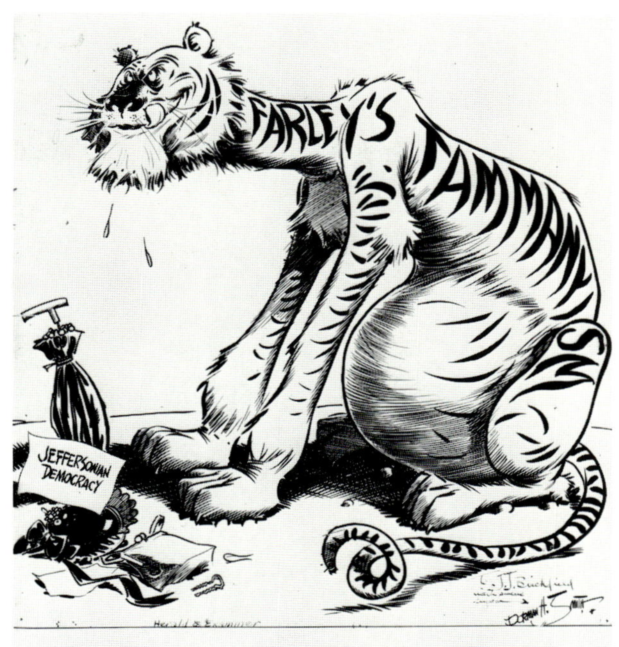

Fig. 150. *When Al Capone's Attorney Finished His Address to the Jury*.
C. K. Berryman. 1931. Ink on paper. 12 9/16 × 14 1/8 in. Courtesy
the Library of Congress.

The Big Guy of all the organized mobsters was Al Capone of
Chicago, who had fought his way up through the organization
from a New York slum. Devoting his time to organizing the
gangsters, Capone soon had the largest mob in Chicago, and
operated primarily by guaranteeing the illegal establishments in
his district "protection" from police raids or raids by rival gangs.
Capone collected an income from each of them and kept himself
"clean." By 1929 he was worth probably $20 millions. But the
gangster who was too big for local and state government was not
too big for the federal government. In 1931 he was tried for income tax evasion, then was indicted for 5,000 separate charges
of bootlegging. He was sentenced to eleven years in prison. He
got out in eight, with time off for good behavior, but he was a
broken man. He died in 1947 at age 48.

Fig. 151. *Another of Those Feasts of Love*. Dorman H. Smith. June
29, 1940 (?). Ink on paper. 21 11/16 × 20 3/16 in. Courtesy Mr. and
Mrs. Draper Hill, Memphis, Tenn.

As manipulator of Franklin D. Roosevelt's political fortunes,
James Farley impressed many people as the Tammany tiger run
amuck—trampling over Jeffersonian democracy in the form of
the lady who has just been devoured. Farley was credited with
being an astute supporter whose skillful politics led to Roosevelt's presidential nomination in 1932.

129

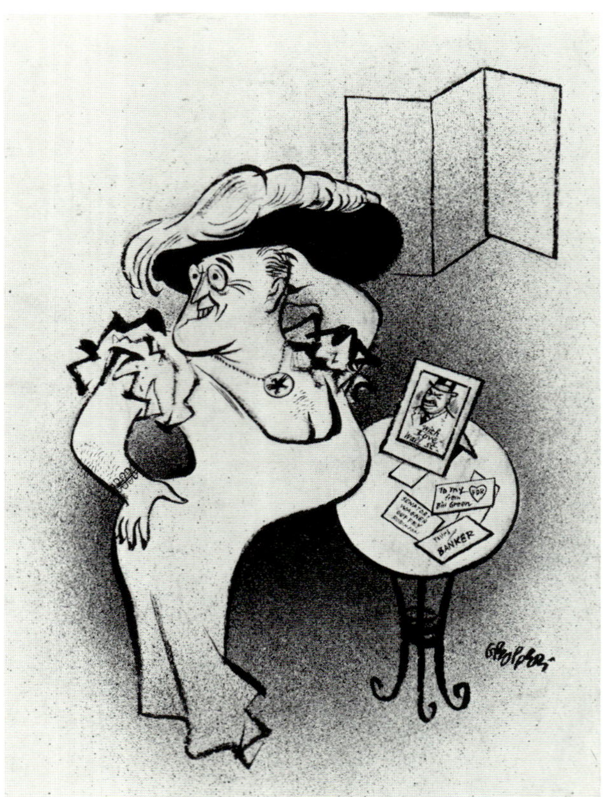

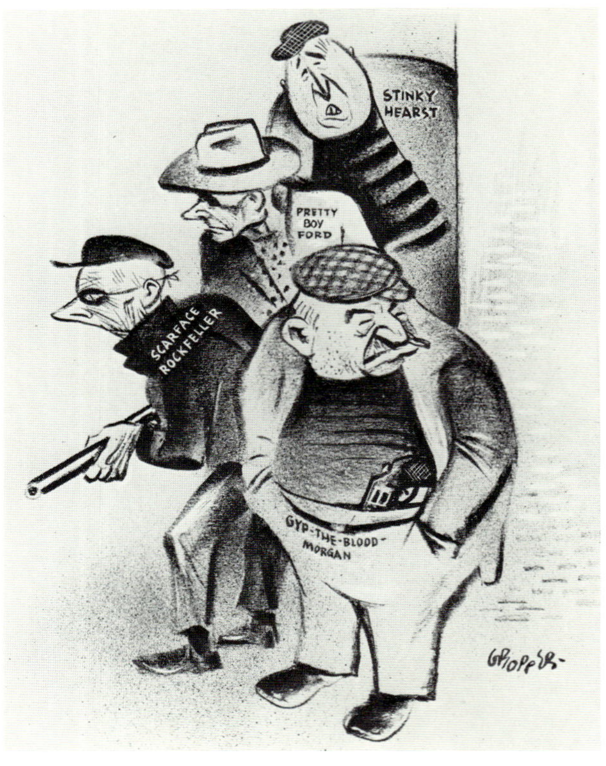

Fig. 153. [Caricature of J. P. Morgan, John D. Rockefeller, Henry Ford, and William R. Hearst as thugs.] William Gropper. Ink and crayon on paper. 14 1/4 × 11 1/8 in. Courtesy Collection of Morris George Hecht.

The so-called Robber Barons ruled the age of industrialism but came face to face with economic disaster and a growing federal government during the Depression. Able to have their way so long as the government did not intervene, the "captains of industry" had to yield to the force applied by the countervailing power of government regulation. "I do not believe that in the name of that sacred word, individualism, a few powerful interests should be permitted to make industrial cannon fodder of the lives of half the population of the United States," President Roosevelt announced as he noted the collapse of "equality of opportunity" and the control of the economic system by some 600 corporations. He called for a more equal distribution of the wealth as well as a change in the nature of the economic institutions that permitted such inequality.

Fig. 152. *"Come Up and See Me Sometime."* William Gropper. 1934. Ink on paper. 17 × 12 1/2 in. Courtesy William Gropper.

This anti-Roosevelt cartoon by Gropper pictures the President as temptress Mae West wearing the NRA eagle as a bauble and receiving love letters from supporters of labor interests such as William Green (president of the American Federation of Labor) and Senators Robert Wagner (sponsor of the Wagner Bill, which established the National Labor Relations Board) and Joe Robinson (who literally died trying to support Roosevelt in his later battles with the Supreme Court). At the same time he is receiving tokens from the bankers of Wall Street.

130

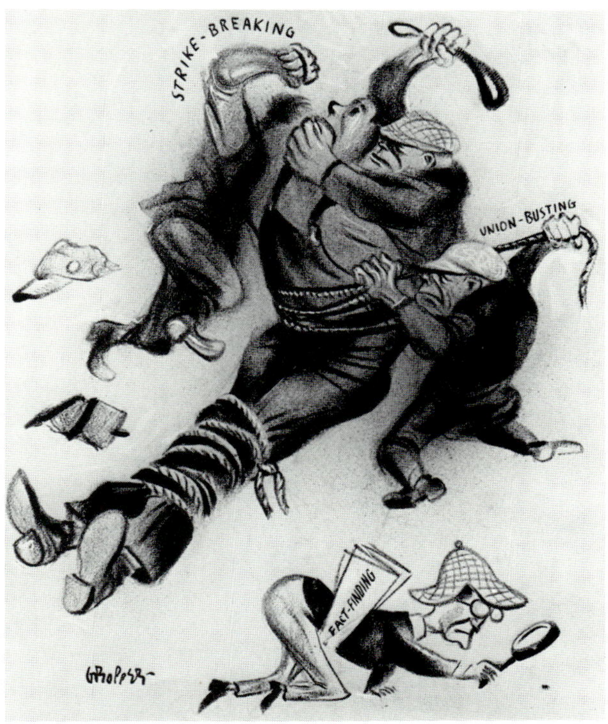

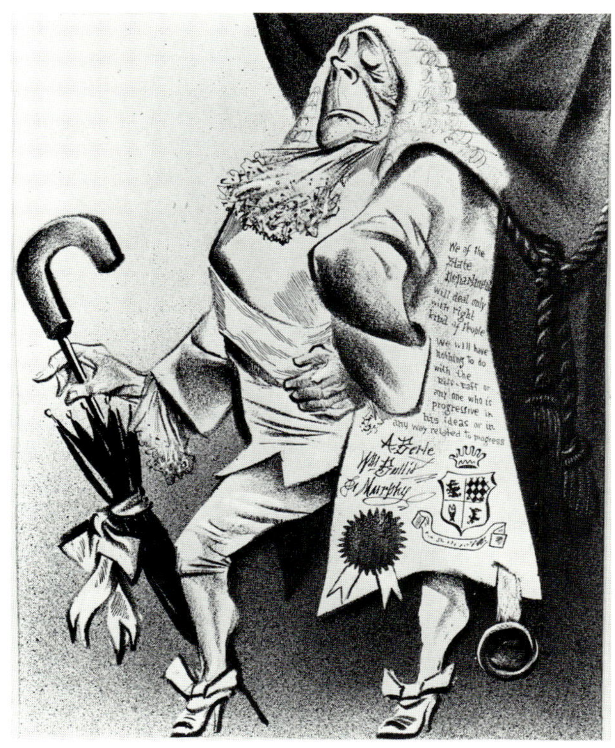

Fig. 154. *Strike-breaking*. William Gropper. 1930s. Brush and ink on paper. 14 × 11 in. Courtesy William Gropper.

Due largely to the tireless efforts of John L. Lewis, American labor made large legal gains that permitted men to join unions and use the unions to bargain with their bosses. Putting these rights into practice, however, was more difficult. Some employers still hired strike-breaking crews or hired guns. A strike might get a union man injured or killed. In this cartoon Gropper belittles the government enforcement agencies who go looking for insects while major crimes are being committed. "Labor, like Israel, has many sorrows," said Lewis in an eloquent summary. "Its women weep their fallen and they lament for the future of the children of the race."

Fig. 155. *The State Department*. William Gropper. c. 1937. Crayon, ink, and white highlights on paper. 14 1/16 × 11 in. (sight). Courtesy William Gropper.

As it became more evident that Europe was headed for war and that America was entrenching in isolationism, President Roosevelt, in the words of King George VI, "led public opinion [toward involvement] by allowing it to get ahead of [him]." In this cartoon Gropper personifies the attitude of the State Department in leading the public. Die-hard isolationists, which before 1940 counted many progressives among their ranks, saw Roosevelt and his advisors, especially the "Brain-Trusters," as disregarding the will of the people in most matters.

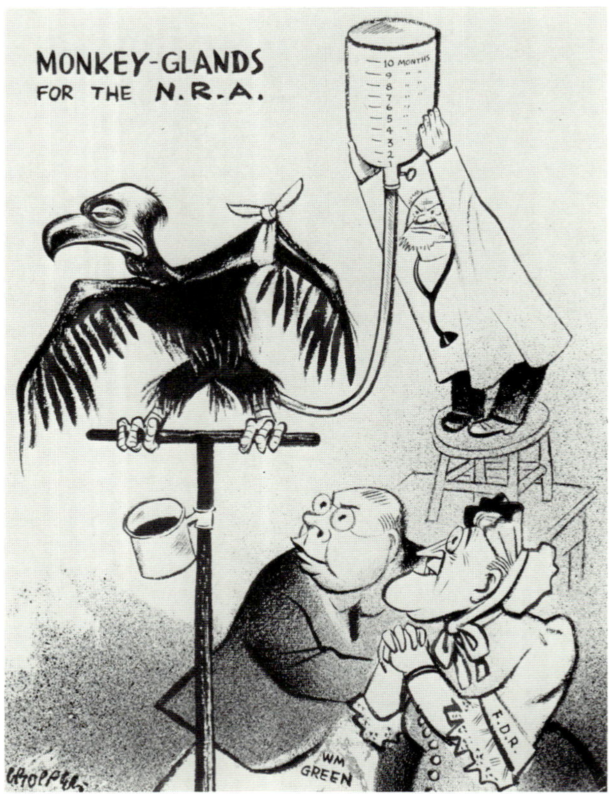

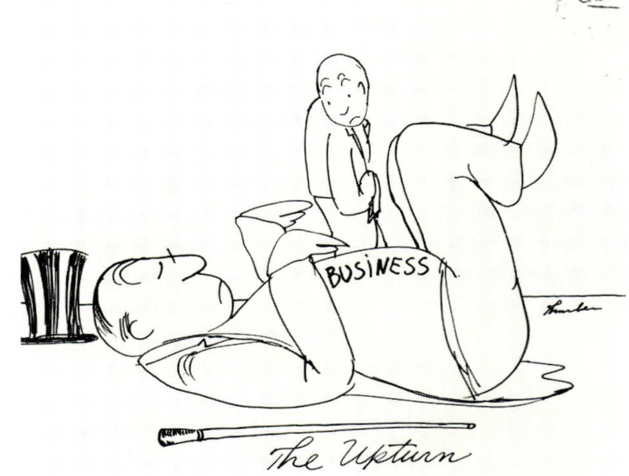

Fig. 156. *Monkey-Glands for the N. R. A.* William Gropper. 1930s. Ink on paper. 14 3/4 × 10 3/4 in. Courtesy Collection of Morris George Hecht.

The National Recovery Administration (NRA) was created in 1933 by executive decision, approved by Congress. It was intended to regulate wages, working hours, and, indirectly, prices. Director Hugh Johnson energetically applied himself to his task, but businessmen damned it as "creeping socialism," and labor leaders called it "business fascism." The Hearst newspapers claimed that NRA really stood for "No Recovery Allowed." This cartoon by Gropper was probably done before the Supreme Court invalidated it in May, 1935, during an era in which William Green, president of the A. F. of L., and Roosevelt were still hopeful that the agency would perform the economic miracles they had hoped.

Fig. 157. *The Upturn*. James Thurber. 1934. Pen and ink on paper, glued to portion of wastebasket. 9 × 12 in. Courtesy Ohio State University Libraries, Columbus.

In the summer, 1933, most everyone agreed that the worst of the depression was over. Business confidence had returned, and people assured each other that prosperity was on its way. The Stock Exchange showed some life as the Dow-Jones index turned upward and the volume of trading topped any month's performance since October, 1929. But the situation had not really changed. "The Upturn" was as dead as Thurber depicts here. Factories still stood idle. Purchases were not up. The poor did not have jobs. There was more to conquer than the fear that President Roosevelt had warned about.

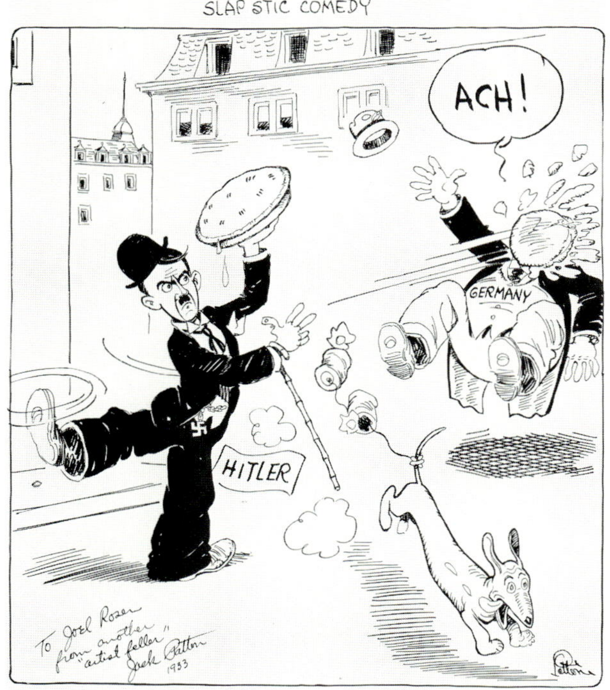

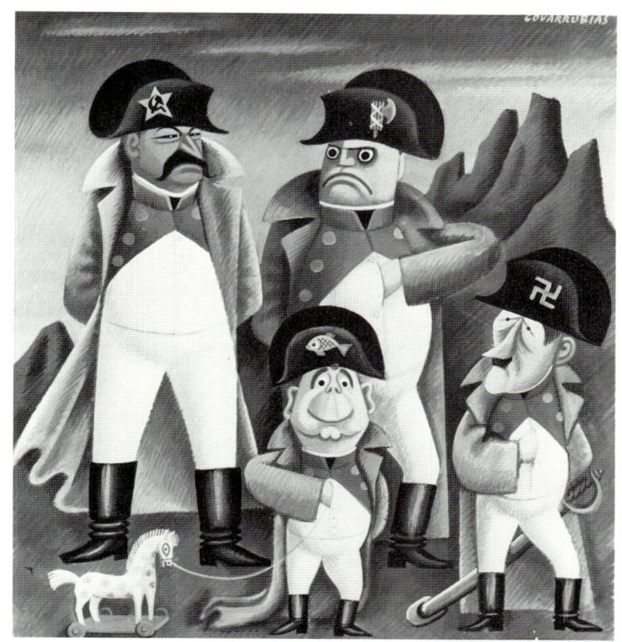

Fig. 158. *Slap Stic Comedy*. Jack Patton. 1933. Ink with white highlights on paper. 12 3/4 × 11 1/8 in. Courtesy Collection of Joel Rosen, Fort Worth.

Capitalizing on the confusion, despair, and frustration following defeat in World War I, Adolf Hitler gained political power in Germany and quickly abolished the Republic and established the Third Reich. Cartoonist Jack Patton shows Hitler in the guise of Charlie Chaplin, the master clown of American slapstick comedies, tossing a pie in the face of the Weimar Republic. In 1933 the world could still regard Hitler as something of a joke, as Chaplin often did in his routine. By 1939, however, Hitler had proved his diabolical characteristics were real.

Fig. 159. *The Four Dictators*. Miguel Covarrubias. 1930s. Watercolor on cardboard. 17 1/2 × 15 in. Courtesy The Swann Collection of Caricature and Cartoon.

The 1930s is often referred to as the decade of the dictators. Here Miguel Covarrubias has depicted three well-known ones with one aspirant. Joseph Stalin, Benito Mussolini, and Adolf Hitler are shown with Huey P. ("Kingfish") Long of Louisiana, who, until his assassination in the State Capitol building of Louisiana, was a radical threat to President Franklin D. Roosevelt.

133

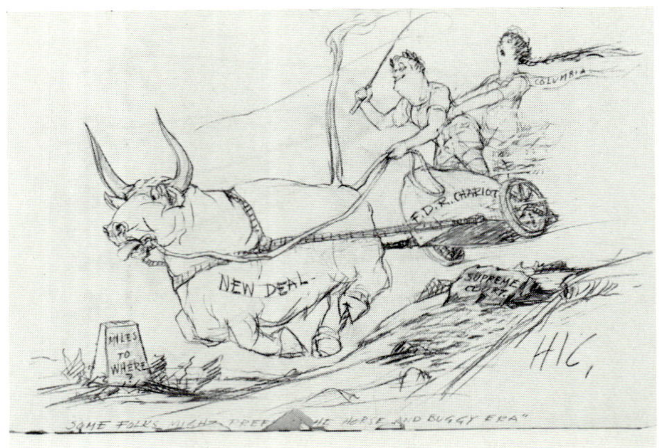

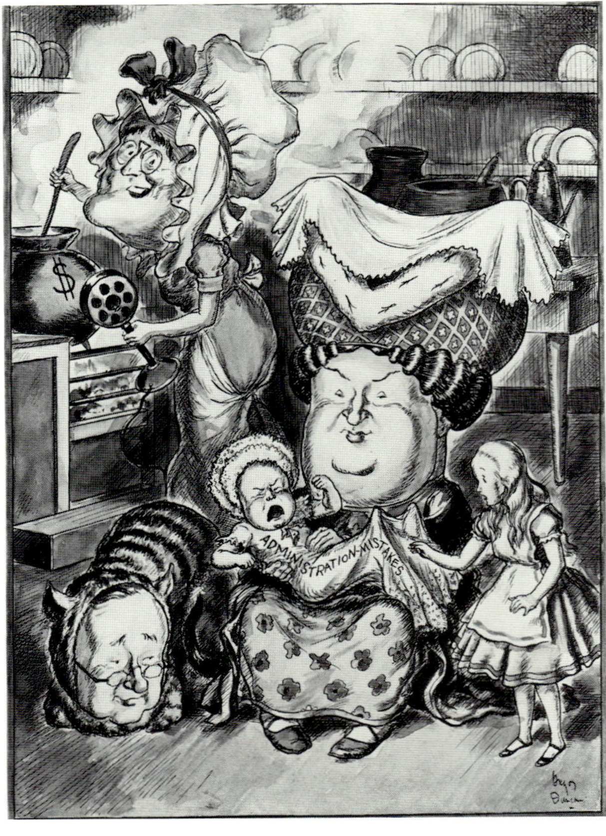

Fig. 160. *"Some Folks Might Prefer the Horse & Buggy Era."* Henry I. Cobb. 1935–1936. Ink on paper. 20 × 29 7/8 in. (irregular). Courtesy Collection of Paulette Greene, Rockville Centre, New York.

The New Deal, a dramatically different approach to government, shocked American society with its introduction of scores of novel social legislative measures, including the Social Security Act, minimum wage and hour principles, and the Federal Deposit Insurance Corporation. People acknowledged that the New Deal started the country moving again, but the foremost question in everyone's mind, including FDR's, was "to where?"

Fig. 161. [Roosevelt in *Alice in Wonderland.*] Gregory Duncan. 1930s. Watercolor on paper. 11 1/2 × 11 1/2 in. Courtesy The Swann Collection of Caricature and Cartoon.

In Duncan's parody of one of John Tenniel's famous *Alice in Wonderland* illustrations, Franklin Roosevelt, as the cook, stirs a pot of money which he hopes will quiet the squalling "Administration Mistakes." Jim Farley, a Democratic politico and one of Roosevelt's presidential advisers, is portrayed as the irascible Duchess. The ever-changeable Cheshire Cat is Secretary of the Interior, Harold Ickes, a former Republican who abruptly switched his support to Roosevelt and the Democrats in 1932.

134

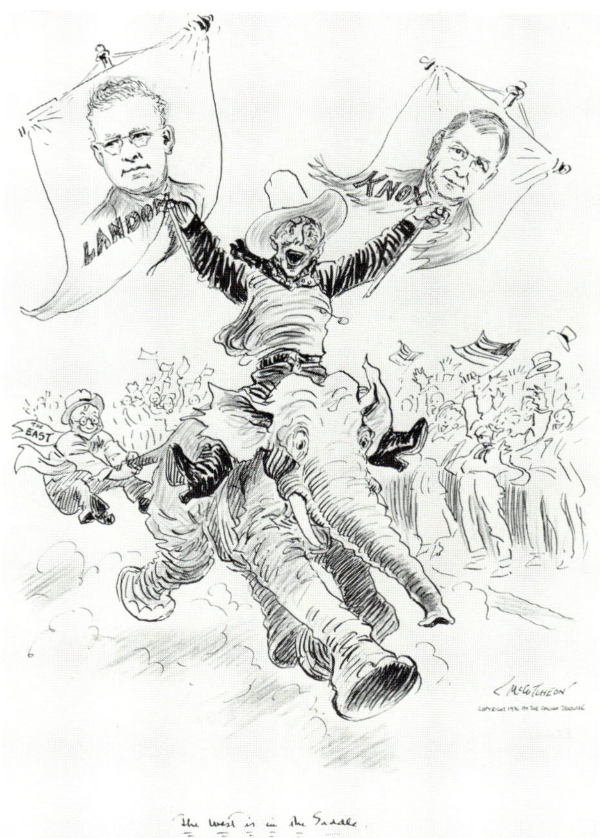

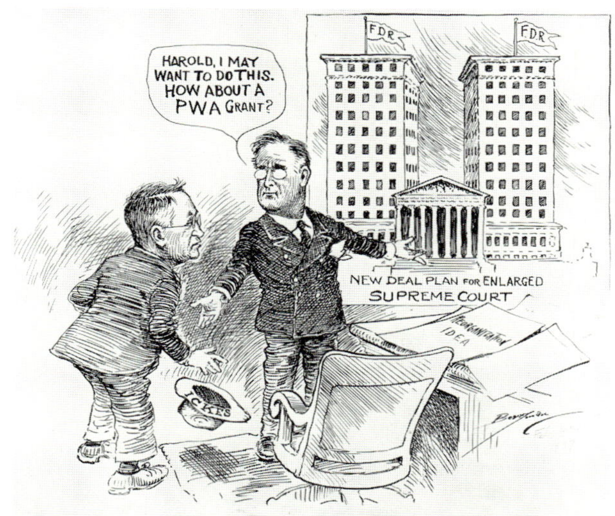

Fig. 163. *New Deal Plan for Enlarged Supreme Court*. C. K. Berryman. Feb. 10, 1937. Ink on paper. 12 1/4 × 14 1/8 in. Courtesy the Library of Congress.

Fig. 162. *The West is in the Saddle*. John Tinney McCutcheon. 1936 in the Chicago *Tribune*. Ink on paper. 21 × 14 in. (sight). Courtesy The Newberry Library, Chicago.

In 1936 the Republicans selected Alfred Landon and Frank Knox to challenge the incumbent Roosevelt. Both were Mid-Westerners, which was unusual since a sectional mix is usually sought for a presidential ticket, but the G. O. P. had great hopes for Governor Landon of Kansas. Landon had an appealing, down-to-earth personality and had implemented the state's recovery programs without incurring debt. He had no chance, however, as he was overwhelmed by Roosevelt's New Deal programs.

In 1935 and 1936 the Supreme Court declared several New Deal programs unconstitutional and the Administration was furious at what it considered impediments to national progress and recovery from the Depression. On February 5, 1937, Roosevelt sent a bill to Congress to replace six Supreme Court Justices and forty-four federal judges with younger, more able men. Roosevelt's "Court Packing" plan caused great contention among congressional Democrats and caused many people to question Roosevelt's motives and political integrity. In Berryman's cartoon Harold Ickes, Administrator of Public Works, is shocked by Roosevelt's judicial building plans.

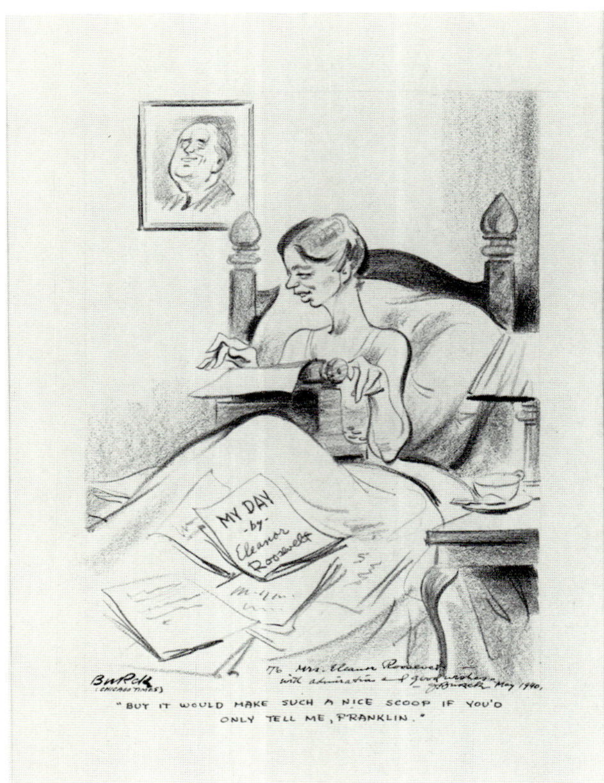

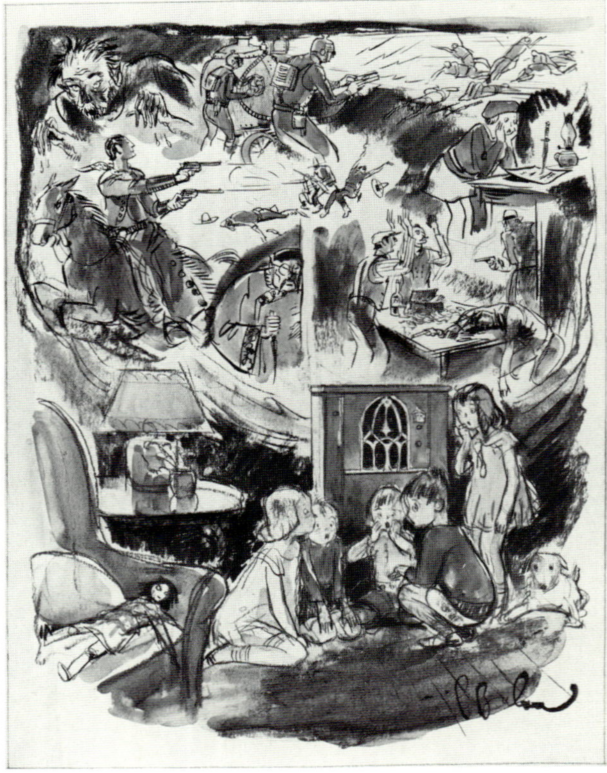

Fig. 164. *"But It Would Make Such a Nice Scoop if You'd only Tell Me, Franklin."* Jacob Burck. May, 1940, in the Chicago *Times*. Ink and crayon on paper. 22 1/2 × 15 1/4 in. Courtesy Franklin D. Roosevelt Presidential Library, Hyde Park, New York, Gift of the Armand Hammer Foundation.

Eleanor Roosevelt was one of America's most active First Ladies. Her intense concern for social welfare took her from city slums to the wastes of the Dust Bowl. And she wrote a syndicated column, "My Day," which reported her observations and concern for what she saw. This cartoon, which was one of her personal favorites, shows her wishing that her husband would reveal to her his intention regarding a third term in 1940.

Fig. 165. *Listening to the Radio*. Perry Barlow. 1930s. Ink and wash on paper. 20 × 17 in. Courtesy The Swann Collection of Caricature and Cartoon.

The radio, like the automobile, was a sweeping technological advance of the twentieth century and had enormous social implications. The radio industry began with the tinkering of a few hobbyists on homemade sets after the First World War. In 1920 Westinghouse built the first broadcasting station in Pittsburgh. By 1927 there were seven hundred stations in the United States, and the radio was standard furniture in the American home. It provided news, information, culture, and entertainment instantaneously, at all hours, to all sectors of the population.

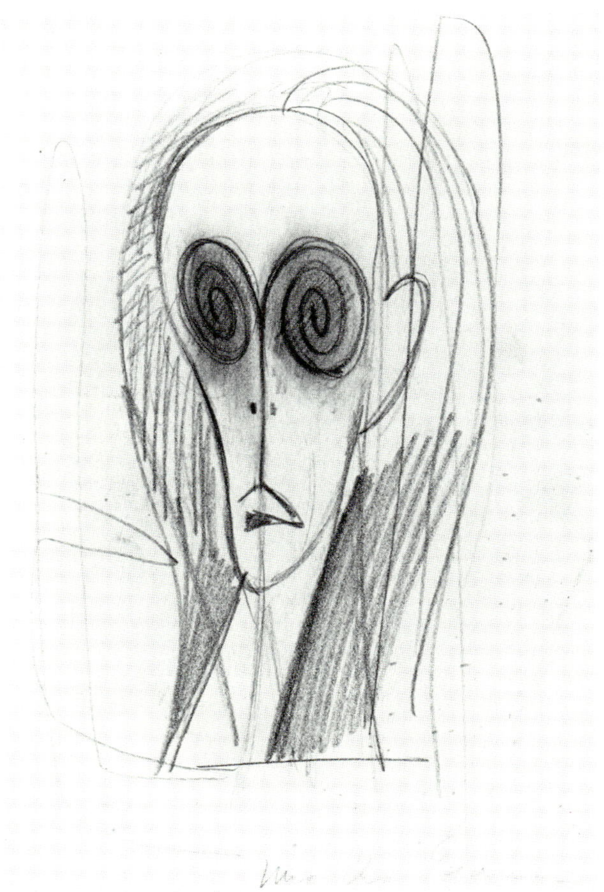

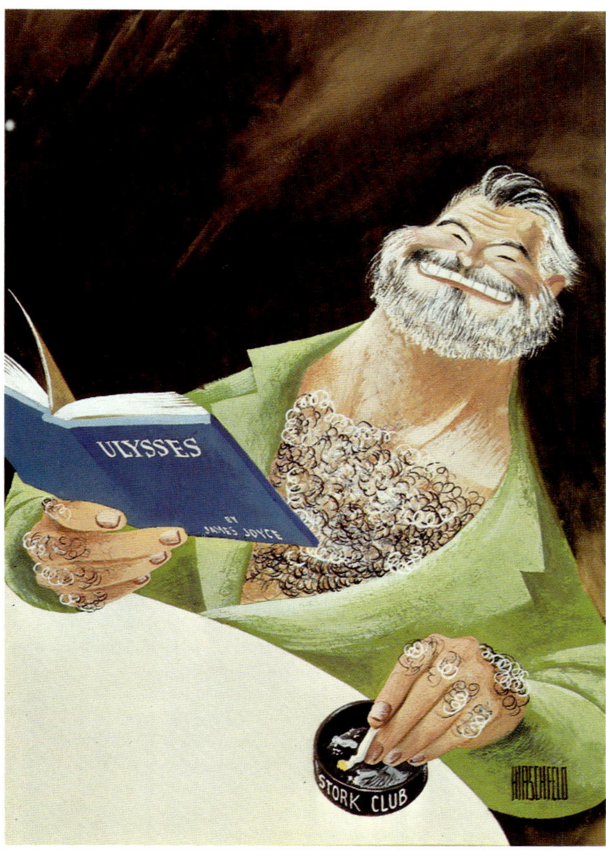

Fig. 167. *Ernest Hemingway*. Albert Hirschfeld. 1930s. Gouache on paper. 12 1/4 × 8 1/4 in. Courtesy The Iconography Collection, Humanities Research Center, University of Texas, Austin.

Fig. 166. *Martha Graham*. Miguel Covarrubias. 1930s. Pencil on paper. 8 × 5 in. Courtesy The Swann Collection of Caricature and Cartoon.

One of America's greatest contributions to the arts of the twentieth century has been the development of modern or interpretive dance. Early in the century American dancers such as Isadora Duncan, Ruth St. Denis, and Ted Shawn eschewed the strictures of classic ballet, seeking a freer expression of emotion and ideas by movement. Martha Graham, a student of St. Denis and Shawn, developed a new technique of dance based on sudden and subtle contraction and release which gave the dancing of her company and students from 1929 to the present a distinctive power of movement and expression.

Ernest Hemingway, one of America's greatest authors, spent much of his life as an expatriate, and most of his writings deal with disaffected Americans adrift among other cultures and peoples. Hemingway eschewed intellectual or social pretensions and, though in the vanguard of twentieth century literary developments, cultivated a rugged anti-intellectual image. Hirschfeld depicts him reading James Joyce's *Ulysses* in the Stork Club, a book that had been banned in the United States as obscene until 1934. It was this kind of narrowminded prudishness that had driven the young Hemingway abroad. After achieving international fame, however, he returned home to be lionized by New York nightclub society. Here we see the burly Hemingway enjoying success, social prominence, and a masterpiece of modern literature.

137

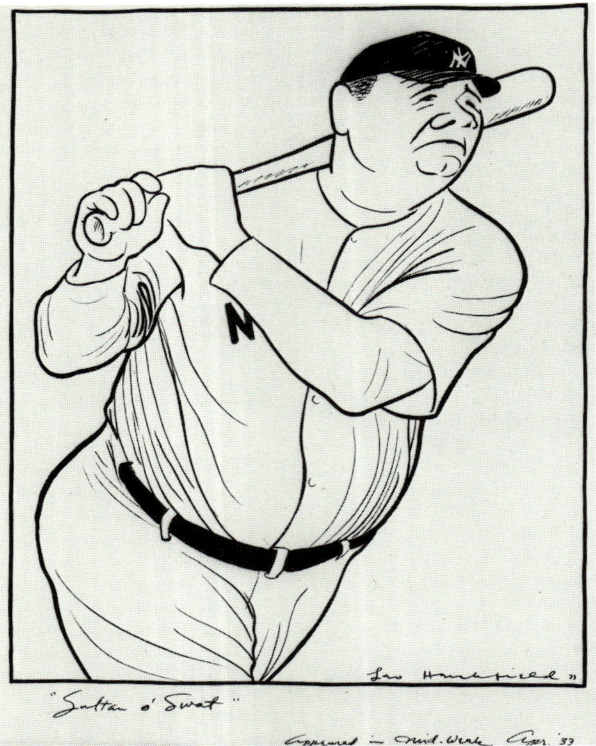

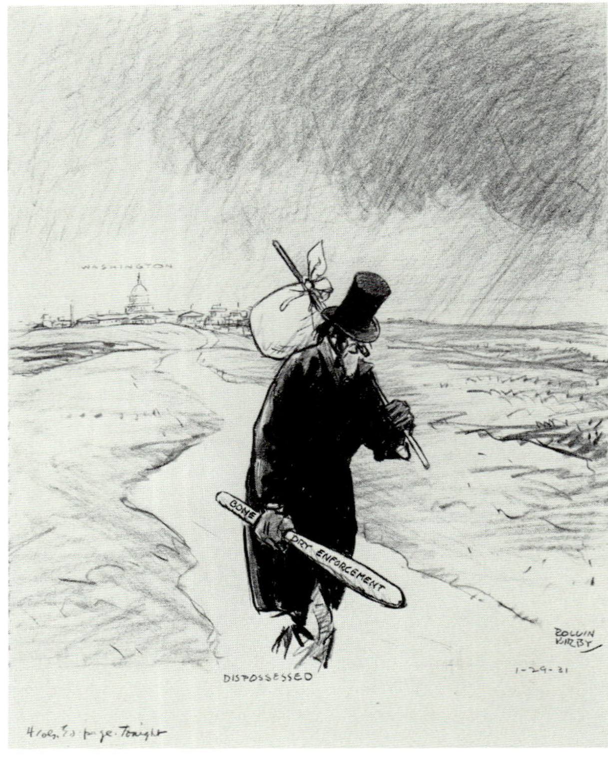

Fig. 168. *Sultan o' Swat*. Leo Hershfield. Apr., 1933. Pen and ink on paper. 12 3/4 × 9 3/4 in. Courtesy National Baseball Hall of Fame and Museum, Inc., Cooperstown, New York.

George Herman (''Babe'') Ruth was one of America's greatest and most beloved sports heroes. After beginning as a pitcher with the Boston Red Sox, Ruth batted his way to fame with the New York Yankees. As a member of one of the most formidable Yankee teams of all time, Ruth helped bring seven pennants to New York between 1921 and 1932. When Yankee Stadium was built in 1923, it was dubbed ''the house that Ruth built.'' It was built for him, too, with a specially-designed short right field fence that helped him on his way to a record sixty home runs in 1927. Babe was the second player voted into the Baseball Hall of Fame in 1936.

Fig. 169. *Dispossessed*. Rollin Kirby. Jan. 29, 1931. Pencil, black ink, blue crayon on paper. 16 1/4 × 12 1/4 in. Courtesy Dartmouth University, Hanover, N. H.

When *Literary Digest* polled almost five million people in 1930 it found more than fifty percent either against prohibition or in favor of some kind of modification. The Wickersham Commission, assigned to study prohibition, soon reported the same ambivalent conclusions in January, 1931. Of the eleven members, two favored repeal, four modification, and five further experiment. The commission concluded that prohibition was not working, but that it should be continued. Here Kirby shows that ''bone dry enforcement'' is a thing of the past although the country is still ''saddled'' with Mr. Prohibition. That too was removed in December, 1933.

138

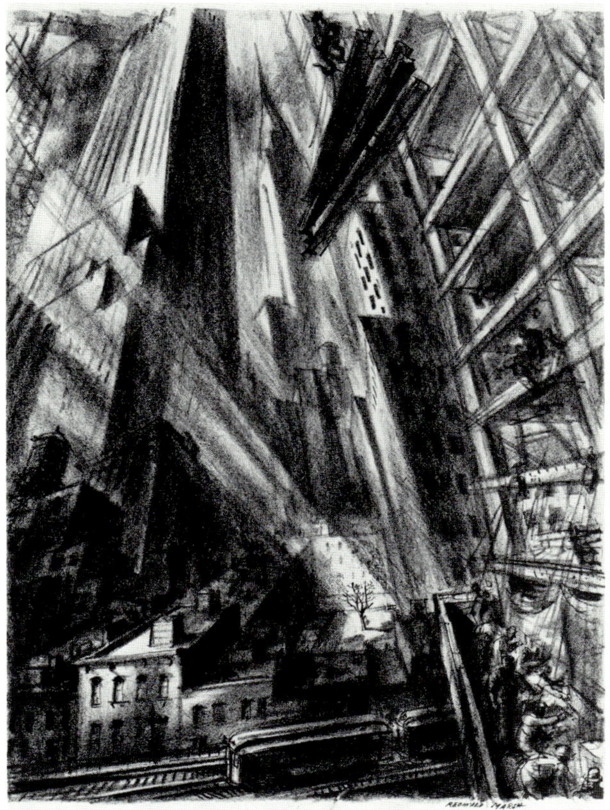

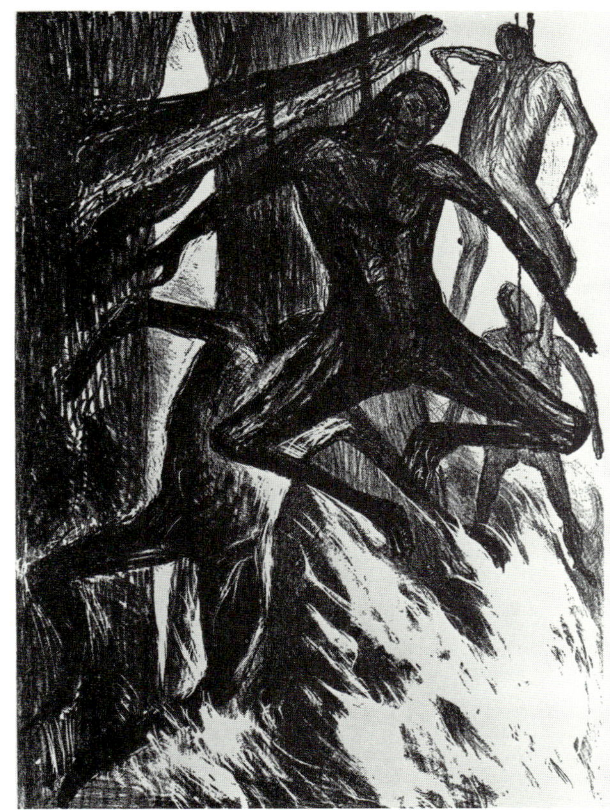

Fig. 171. *The Hanged Man* (from the portfolio *The American Scene*, No. 1). José Clemente Orozco. 1933–1934. Lithograph. 12 3/4 × 8 15/16 in. Courtesy The Museum of Modern Art, New York City, Gift of Abby Aldrich Rockefeller.

The great Mexican muralist Orozco here has turned his attention to the American landscape, attempting to graphically illustrate the staggering statistics on lynching in the United States. Between 1885 and 1950 more than 4,000 persons were lynched, more than 3,300 of them Negroes. In 1935 alone it has been estimated that lynchings were occurring at the rate of one every three weeks. The Great Depression drove millions of people out of work and pushed their families below the poverty line. Under such circumstances Negroes especially suffered, because the racial hatred only increased. Amid such conflicting values, Orozco has made an eloquent comment on the "land of the free" where "liberty and justice for all" prevails.

Fig. 170. *But Only God Can Make a Tree*. Reginald Marsh. 1930s. Lithograph. 20 1/2 × 13 5/8 in. Courtesy the Library of Congress.

In the fall of 1937 the stock market took another nose-dive, wiping out gains made during the first five years of the Roosevelt administration. The New Deal had not cured all the nation's ills, or even most of them. Lewis Mumford concluded that, "Our metropolitan civilization is not a success. It is a different kind of wilderness from that which we have deflowered." Naturalist Joseph Wood Krutch commented that it was a "gloomy vision of a dehumanized world."

139

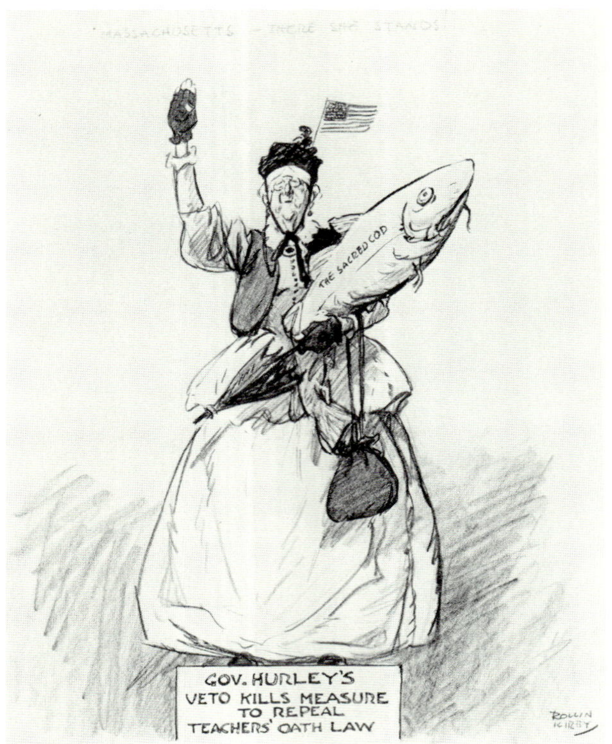

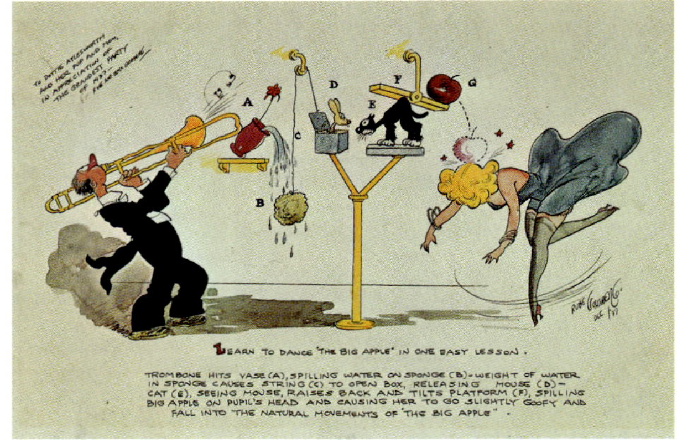

Fig. 172. *Massachusetts—There She Stands!* Rollin Kirby. Apr., 1937. Black crayon, black ink, blue pencil heightened with white wash on paper. 17 7/8 × 11 3/4 in. Courtesy Fogg Art Museum, Harvard University, Cambridge, Mass., Gift of Mrs. Frederic T. Lewis in memory of Dr. Frederic T. Lewis.

In 1935 widespread legislation supported by the Daughters of the American Revolution, the American Legion, the Hearst newspapers, and the Elks was introduced requiring teachers and professors (in many states those in private and parochial as well as public schools) to take oaths of loyalty to their state and the national constitutions. Opposition to these teacher's oath laws was equally widespread; in Massachusetts it was led by Harvard President J. B. Conant. Conant and his supporters fought for a repeal of the measure for two years, until such was passed by the Massachusetts legislature on April 1, 1937. The next day, contrary to expectations, Governor Hurley surprised everyone by vetoing the measure.

Fig. 173. *Learn to Dance "The Big Apple" in One Easy Lesson.* Reuben ("Rube") Goldberg. Dec., 1937. Pen, ink, and watercolor on paper. 14 1/2 × 21 in. Courtesy The Swann Collection of Caricature and Cartoon.

As *Time* magazine explained in 1937, "the Big Apple" is "danced in a circle by a group." As in a Virginia reel, one dancer calls the steps, which produces a lot of "floating power and fannying." "The Big Apple invariably ends upon a somewhat reverent note, with everybody leaning back and raising his arms heavenward," the "Praise Allah" movement. Goldberg, famous for his crazy inventions, devised a foolproof method of Big Apple instruction.

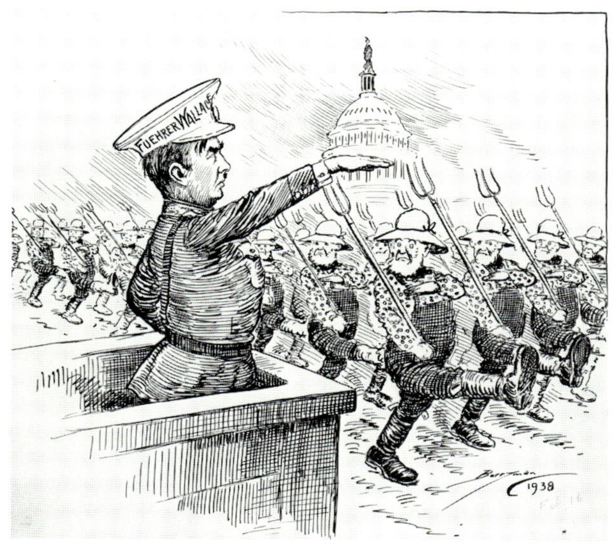

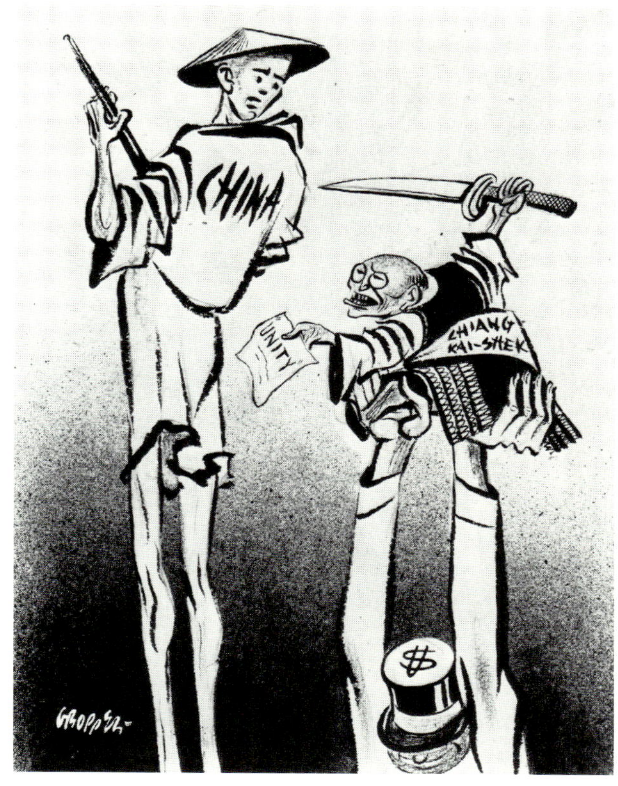

Fig. 175. *U. S. Supporting Chiang Kai-Shek against China*. William Gropper. 1938. Ink on paper. 14 × 10 in. Courtesy William Gropper.

Fig. 174. *The Fuehrer Wallace*. C. K. Berryman. Feb. 16, 1938. Ink on paper. 12 1/4 × 14 1/16 in. Courtesy the Library of Congress.

For his Secretary of Agriculture, President Roosevelt picked Henry A. Wallace, a man who had successfully edited *Wallace's Farmer* and had built a respectable business producing and selling hybrid seed corn. As head of the Agricultural Adjustment Administration, Wallace went through a political metamorphosis and became an ardent socialist. He ran against Truman and Dewey for President in 1948, then reversed himself and published *"Why I Was Wrong"* late in life.

One of President Truman's great problems immediately following World War II was the Chinese situation. For years Nationalist President Chiang Kai-Shek had been waging a losing battle against Mao Tse-Tung and the Communist rebels. Three times the pair met under American auspices to try to work out an agreement, but Mao knew he could win, and Chiang would sacrifice nothing to gain a settlement. Even General George C. Marshall gave up in disgust. Secretary of State Dean Acheson issued a Truman administration "white paper" in 1949 acknowledging that China had been "lost."

141

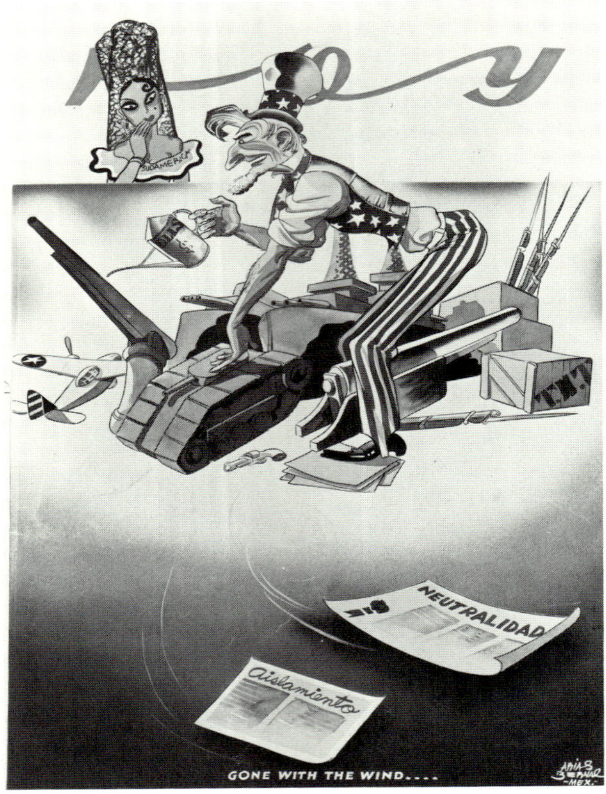

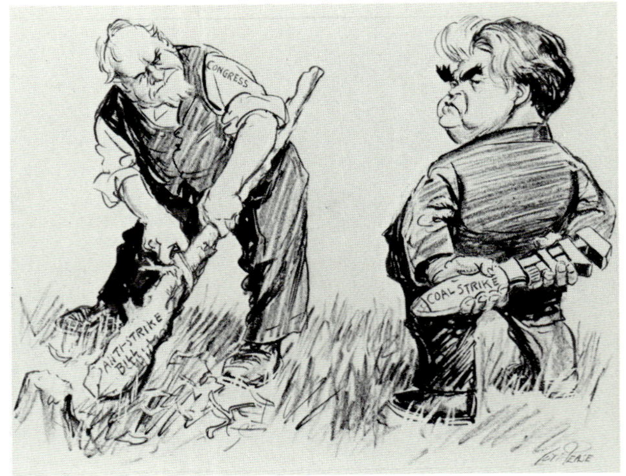

Fig. 176. *Gone With the Wind . . . .* Antonio Arias Bernal. 1940. Watercolor on paper. 20 1/2 × 15 1/2 in. Courtesy The Swann Collection of Caricature and Cartoon.

By the summer of 1940 the Fascists controlled all of Europe except hard-pressed Great Britain. Still professing neutrality, President Roosevelt took steps to aid the Allies. In spite of vocal isolationist opposition, he urged an unprecedented arms production build-up and supported the Act of Havana (July, 1940), a defense agreement which provided that America would defend Latin America in case of Fascist aggression there. In September he instituted the first compulsory peacetime draft in American history. In Argentinean Arias' cartoon, South America, which enjoyed cordial relations with both the United States and Germany, watches Uncle Sam's pledges of neutrality and isolationism blow away as he pours funds and energy into armaments.

Fig. 177. *John L. Lewis vs. Congress*. Lute Pease. 1944 (?) in Newark *Evening News*. Charcoal, pencil, and ink on paper. 15 1/4 × 19 1/4 in. Courtesy Rutgers University Library, New Brunswick, N.J.

During the Second World War American labor honored a "no-strike" pledge. An exception occurred in 1943 when John L. Lewis, leader of the United Mine Workers, called for a walk-out. An angry Congress passed the Smith-Connally Act, overriding a presidential veto. The Act authorized the president to seize strike-bound factories, compelled "cool off" periods before walk-outs, and prohibited union contributions to political campaigns. The cartoon by Lute Pease depicts the head-on confrontation of John L. Lewis and the Congress, which was in no mood for reformist or social legislation. In 1944, as President Roosevelt put it, "Dr. New Deal" had to give way to "Dr. Win-the-War."

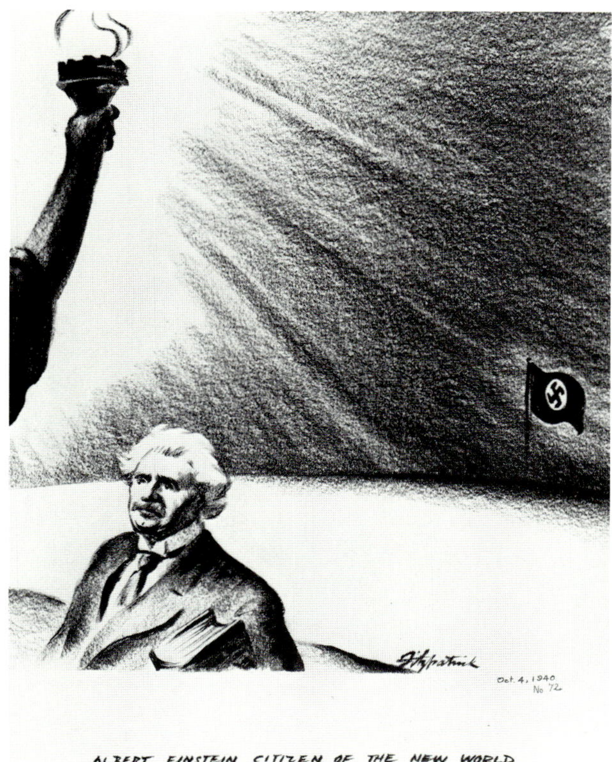

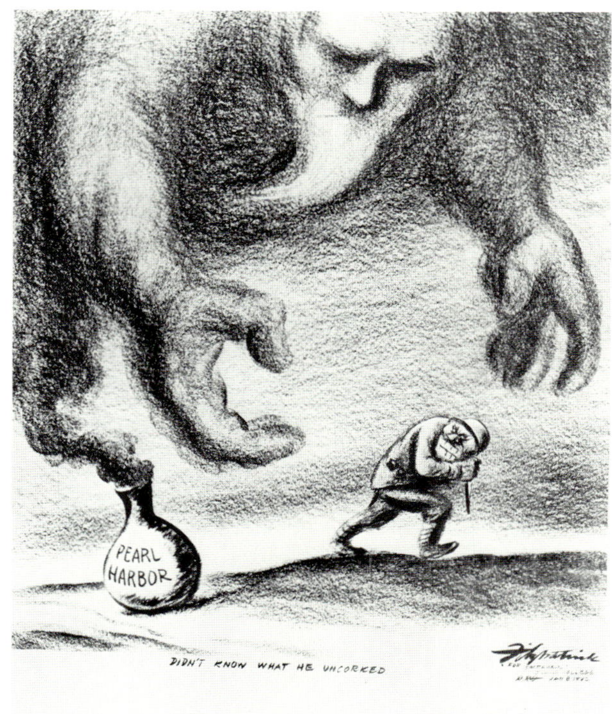

Fig. 178. *Albert Einstein, Citizen of the New World*. Daniel Robert Fitzpatrick. Oct. 4, 1940. Crayon on paper. 23 15/16 × 19 15/16 in. Courtesy The State Historical Society of Missouri, Columbia.

Albert Einstein was the director of theoretical physics at the Kaiser Wilhelm Institute in Berlin and had received the Nobel Prize for Physics in 1921 for his Theory of Relativity. However, the Nazis were more interested in his Jewish parentage than his accomplishments and reputation. They confiscated his property and revoked his German citizenship in 1934. He subsequently immigrated to the United States, assuming a post at the Institute for Advanced Study at Princeton, where he continued to pursue his research until his death in 1955.

Fig. 179. *Didn't Know What He Uncorked*. Daniel Robert Fitzpatrick. 1942. Watercolor, crayon, and ink on paper. 20 × 17 5/8 in. Courtesy The Murray A. Harris Collection of Graphic Art.

The United States watched the European war and prepared for ultimate involvement, but still clung to neutrality as late as December, 1941. Noting the strong isolationist tendencies and believing that America would be drawn into the war anyway, Japanese strategists decided that a surprise attack might keep America out of the war altogether by strengthening the isolationists, and at the very least would give Japan the advantage of choosing the point at which to begin the war in the Pacific. Although the attack on Pearl Harbor was more successful than the Japanese had even hoped, it served to unify the divided Americans and permitted them to enter the conflict determined to win, to gain revenge for the "sneak attack."

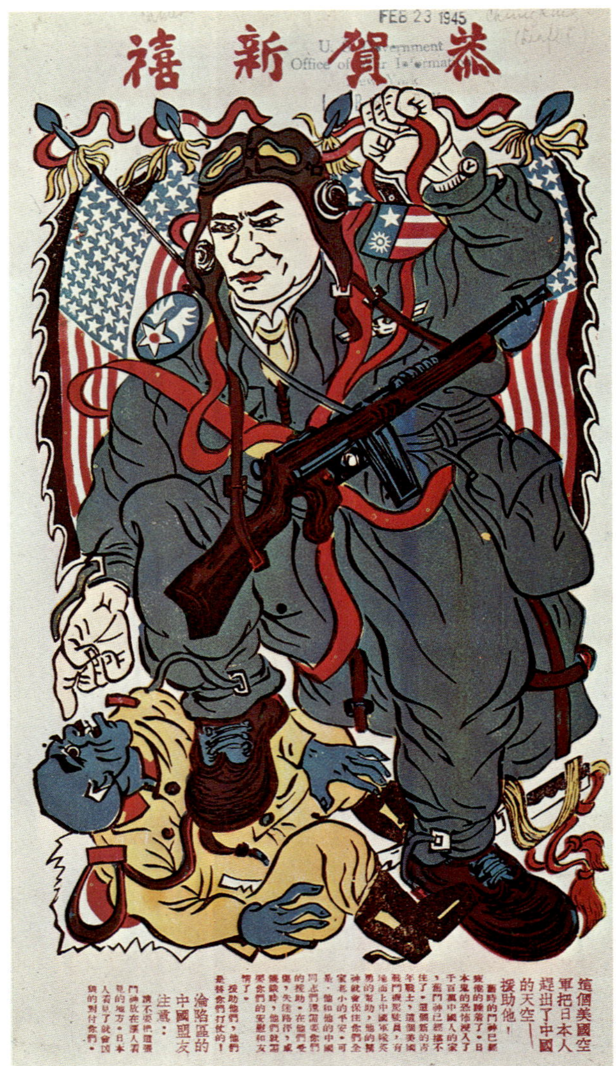

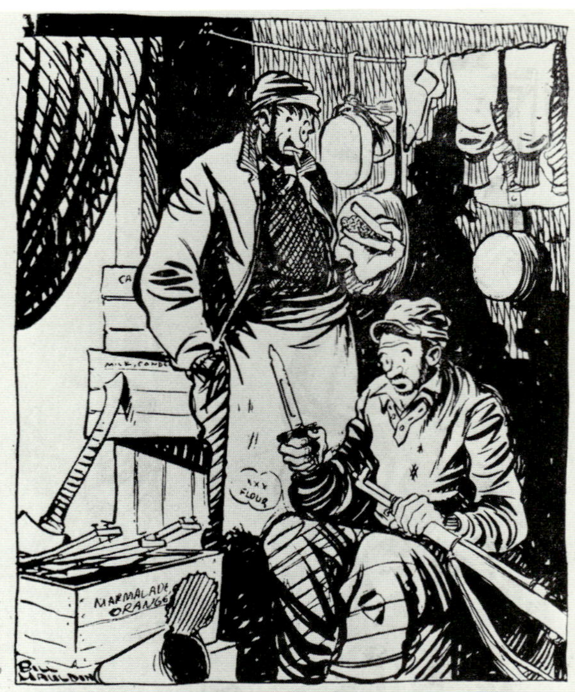

Fig. 180. [Chinese leaflet of an American pilot.] Anonymous. Early 1940s. Original cannot be found. Photographic copy courtesy American Heritage Publishing Company. Courtesy the Library of Congress.

This Chinese likeness of an American pilot was passed out during World War II in an effort to help Americans shot down by Japanese planes over Mainland China. The script at the bottom asks the Chinese should help any American pilot looking like the caricature, and that they should not let the Japanese occupation forces see the leaflet or they would be tortured.

Fig. 181. *"I'll be damned. Did you know this can opener fits on the end of a rifle?"* Bill Mauldin. 1940s. 4 13/16 × 3 7/8 in. Book page. Courtesy Fred White, Jr., Bryan, Tex.

Too often the history of World War II merges into a glorious battle waged by America after being deceitfully attacked by the Japanese at Pearl Harbor. Historians emphasize the tremendous war effort, the unprecedented production, the success of American arms. Bill Mauldin, the "G. I. cartoonist," effectively presents the common soldier's view of the war. The individual had not changed, although war had been taken over by engineers. Willie and Joe became the symbol of every American G. I. in the war.

144

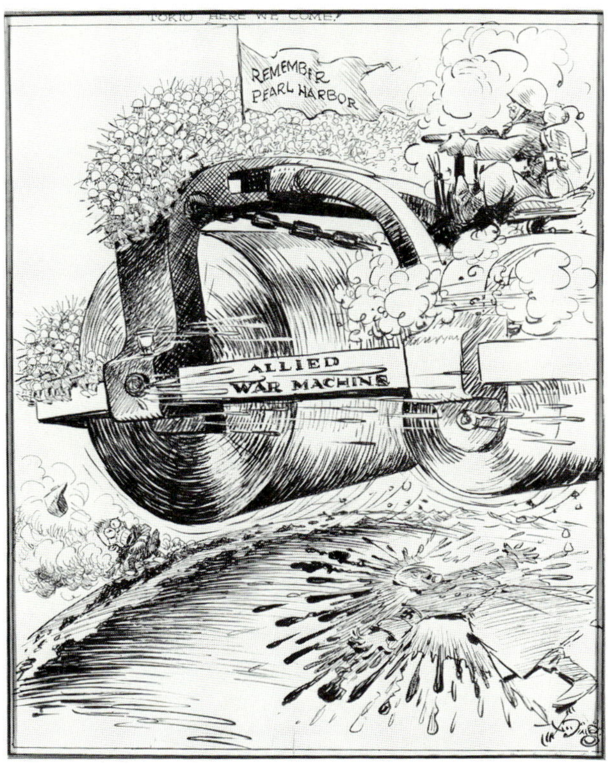

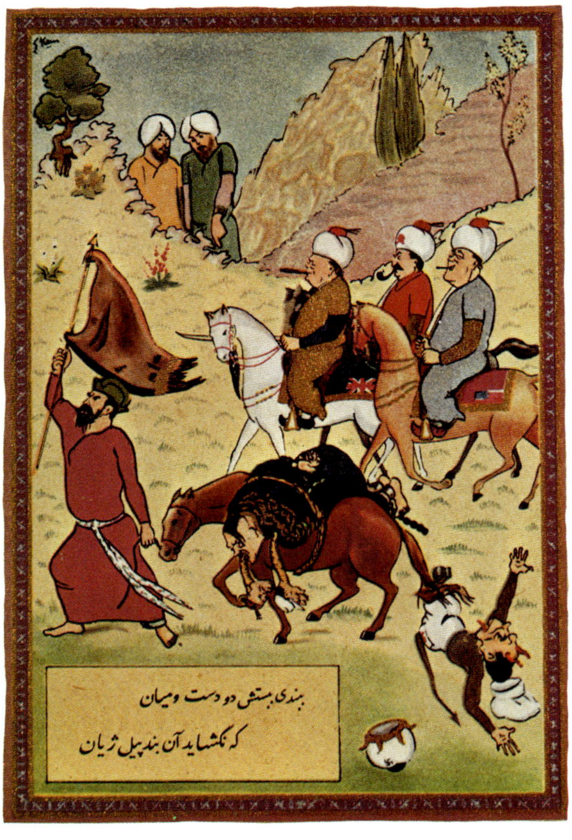

Fig. 182. *Tokio Here We Come*. Jay Norwood Darling. c. 1944. Pen and brush on paper. 28 5/8 × 22 3/4 in. Courtesy William A. Farnsworth Library and Art Museum, Rockland, Me.

The Japanese attack on Pearl Harbor inspired an immediate change in the American opinion toward the war. The country immediately mobilized, both public opinion and military forces. By 1943 American factories were producing 40% of the world's total arms supply with fifteen million citizens in the armed forces. Until the defeat of Germany, however, the brunt of this effort was focused on Europe. With the situation in hand there, Americans turned their fury toward the Pacific, and headed for the Japanese home islands.

Fig. 183. [Teheran Conference.] Anonymous. 1943. Colored postcard. 4 × 5 in. Courtesy Franklin D. Roosevelt Presidential Library, Hyde Park, N. Y.

In November and December, 1943, Prime Minister Churchill, President Roosevelt, and Premier Joseph Stalin met in the Iranian capital for the first of several three-power conferences. The main topic of conversation was the projected British-American invasion of Western Europe, supported by a flanking invasion in southern France and a Soviet counter-offensive against Germany from the east. Stalin reaffirmed his promise to enter the war, and the three leaders laid plans for an international peace-keeping organization to be established after the war.

145

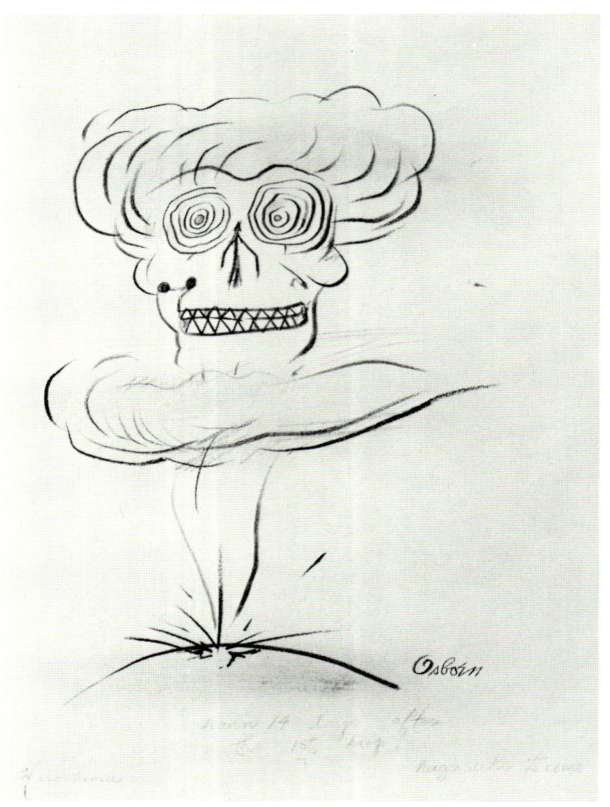

Fig. 184. *Hiroshima*. Robert Osborn. 1945. Crayon and pencil on paper. 13 1/4 × 10 in. (with text). Courtesy the Library of Congress.

The climax of the war against Japan was the dropping of the first atomic bomb on the Japanese city of Hiroshima in August, 1945. With an explosive force of more than 20,000 tons of TNT, the bomb destroyed over four square miles of the city and killed or injured more than 160,000 persons. Osborn did the drawing fourteen days after the devastation of Hiroshima.

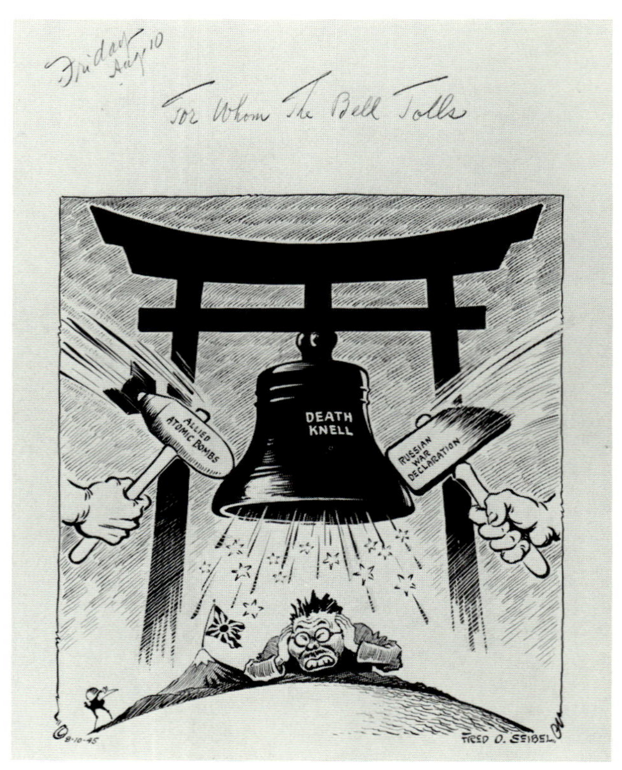

Fig. 185. *For Whom the Bell Tolls*. Fred O. Seibel. Aug. 10, 1945, in Richmond *Times–Dispatch*. Pen and ink on paper; caption in pencil. 23 1/8 × 14 7/16 in. Courtesy University of Virginia Library, Charlottesville.

With the dropping of the second atomic bomb on Nagasaki, Fred O. Seibel produced this cartoon pointing out that the bell was tolling for the Japanese even if they did not know it. There was some doubt in the United States that the Japanese would surrender when they did not immediately give up after the first bomb was dropped, but it was a difficult decision for a split government to reach. The Japanese had sent a team of physicists to Hiroshima to determine whether it was really an atomic bomb. By the time the scientists had returned to Tokyo, made their report, and the government considered its decision, the Americans had already dropped the second bomb, which brought complete surrender.

146

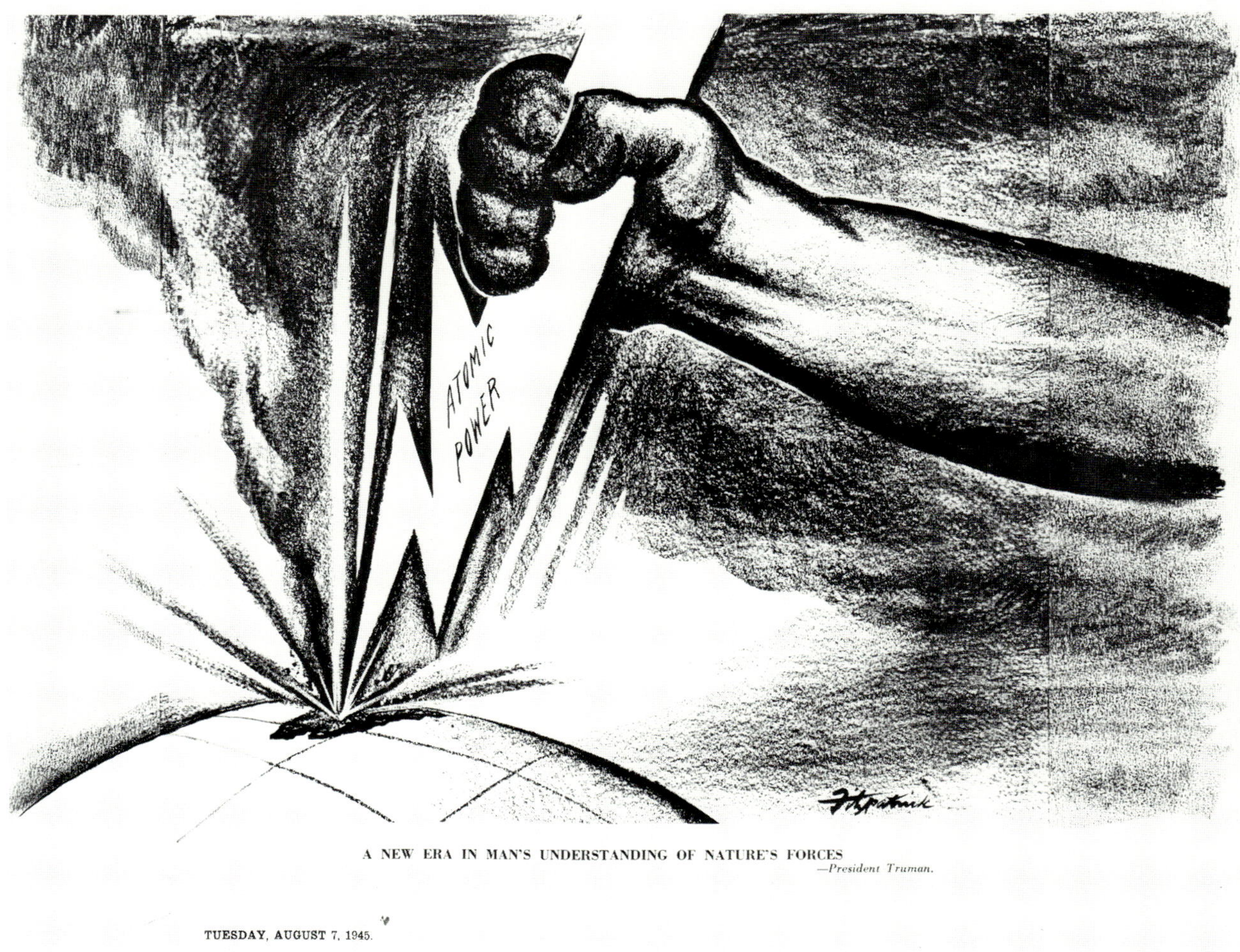

Fig. 186. *A New Era in Man's Understanding of Nature's Forces*. Daniel Robert Fitzpatrick. Aug. 7, 1945, in the St. Louis *Post-Dispatch*. Crayon on paper. 14 1/8 × 11 in. Courtesy The State Historical Society of Missouri, Columbia.

With the dropping of the atomic bomb on the Japanese city of Hiroshima, the world entered the atomic age, and Fitzpatrick saluted this new power the following day with this cartoon. Albert Einstein had urged that the bomb be developed only because he feared that Germany was developing it. Now he was concerned that the bomb would be misused. Although there were immediate questions concerning the welfare of a Europe devastated by warfare, the greater question that is still not satisfactorily solved is how the nations will handle atomic power.

147

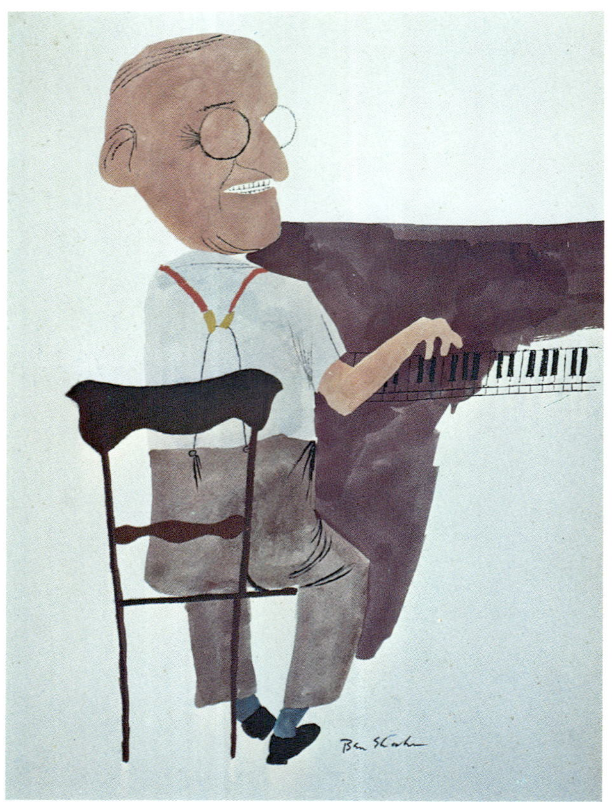

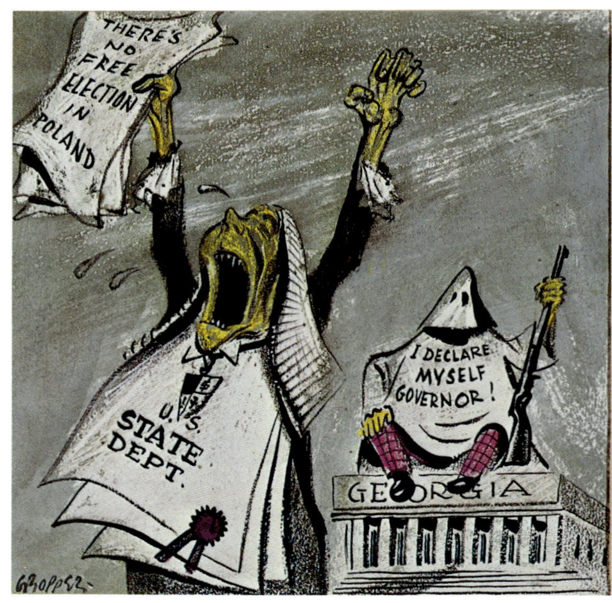

Fig. 187. [Harry Truman at the piano.] Ben Shahn. 1948. Water-color on paper. 23 1/2 × 15 1/2 in. Courtesy Harry S. Truman Library and Museum, Independence, Mo.

President Harry S Truman guided the United States during the first faltering steps of the atomic age with unusual decisiveness. He was rudely introduced to the atomic age with President Roosevelt's sudden death, but quickly absorbed the necessary information to make required decisions. He became well-liked through his first term in office because of his directness, his "down to earth" personality, and his affinity with the common people. His performances at the piano became his trademark, and his familiar rendering of *The Missouri Waltz* became his campaign song. Ben Shahn did this watercolor in preparation for a larger study of Truman and Thomas Dewey, the Democratic and Republican candidates in the election of 1948.

Fig. 188. *There's No Free Election in Poland*. William Gropper. 1948. Mixed media. 9 1/2 × 9 3/4 in. Courtesy William Gropper.

Churchill and Franklin Roosevelt agreed to permit the Soviet Union to occupy and dominate Poland after World War II, with the Soviet promise that they would allow free elections in Poland so the Polish government-in-exile could be properly represented. When the naïve Allies realized that Poland was now a Soviet satellite, they grew bitter. Gropper points out in this cartoon that while Russia was crushing political liberty in Poland, Eugene Talmadge was being elected governor of Georgia after a recount in which enough votes to give him the victory had been "found." He might well have added Texas, for it was in 1948 that Lyndon B. Johnson won his disputed race for the U. S. Senate.

148

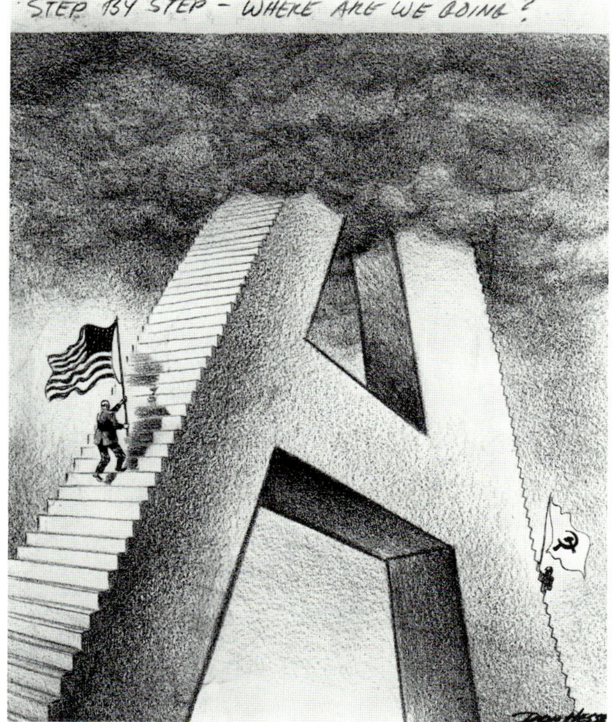

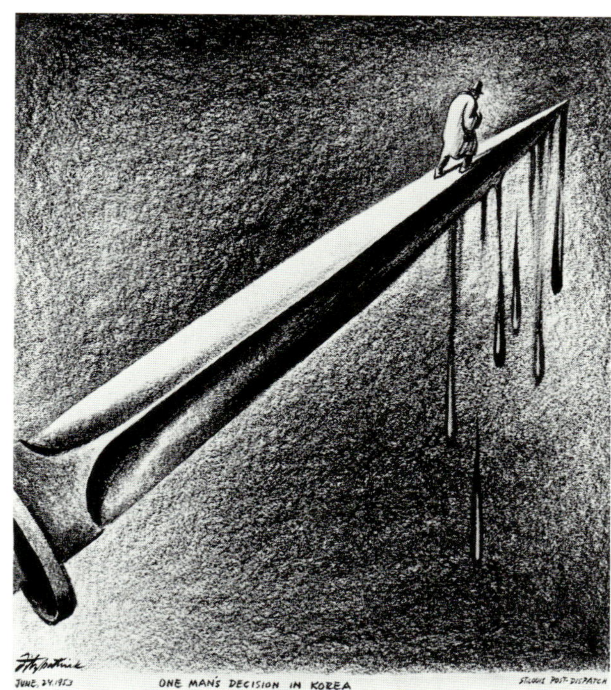

Fig. 189. *Step by Step—Where Are We Going?* Don Hesse. 1950s. Ink, crayon, and pencil on paper. 11 1/4 × 9 in. Courtesy the Library of Congress.

When Secretary of State John Foster Dulles announced that the United States would depend less on traditional arms and more on the ''deterrent of massive retaliatory power,'' the United States and the Soviet Union, both of whom possessed the super-bomb, or hydrogen bomb, were locked in an unending arms race. Both countries experimented with larger and more powerful bombs, invested more in ''defense,'' and entered every confrontation with the threat of nuclear disaster prominent. Both countries were trying for, in the words of the day, a ''bigger bang for the buck.''

Fig. 190. *One Man's Decision in Korea*. Daniel Robert Fitzpatrick. June 24, 1953, in the St. Louis *Post-Dispatch*. Ink, crayon, and gouache on paper. 15 3/8 × 13 1/8 in. Courtesy the Library of Congress.

On June 25, 1950, the North Korean Communists attacked South Korea, and President Truman committed U. S. forces with the sanction of the United Nations but without congressional authorization. Truman organized a wartime cabinet, placed the United States on a semi-wartime status, and declared a national emergency. He later sought and received congressional support for his actions, but he had involved the United States in the Korean War by virtually a one-man decision.

149

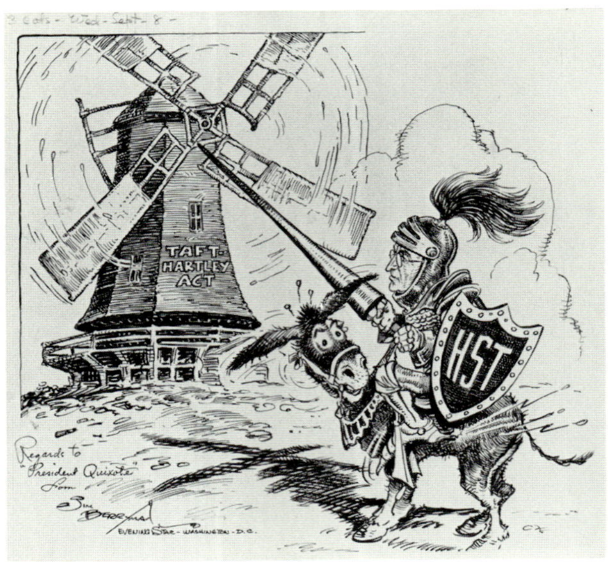

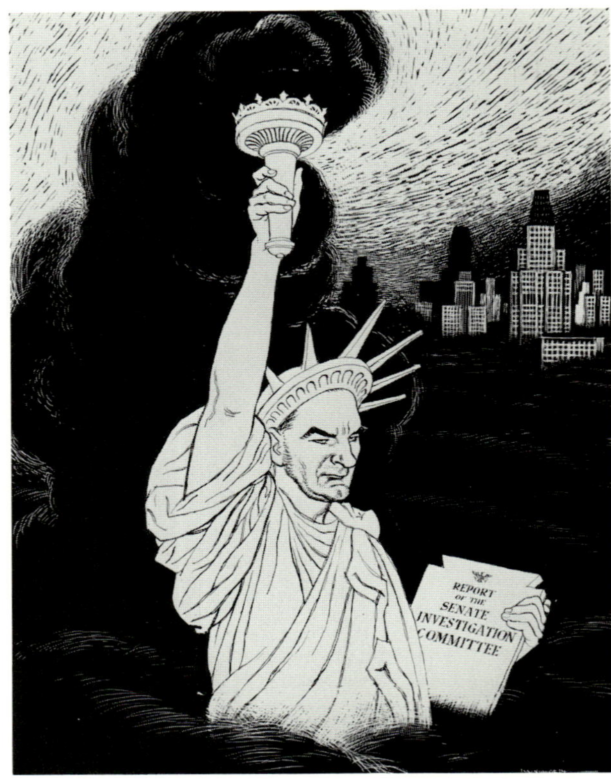

Fig. 191. *Taft-Hartley Act*. Jim Berryman. 1948 in the Washington *Evening Star*. Pen and ink on paper. 12 5/8 × 13 5/8 in. Courtesy Harry S. Truman Library and Museum, Independence, Mo.

Returning the nation to peacetime economic conditions following the war was difficult at best. Truman's unwillingness to abandon price controls was blamed for a wave of strikes that swept the country in 1945–1946 and led to sweeping Republican victories in the 1946 congressional elections. Using the votes as a mandate, Congress moved toward more conservative measures including the Taft-Hartley Act in 1947. Called the ''slave labor law'' because it forced men to work against their will (during the sixty-day ''cooling-off'' period before a strike is permitted), the Act probably unified and strengthened unions because of their unanimous opposition to it and assured President Truman's surprising victory in 1948.

Fig. 192. '' . . . *that we here highly resolve that this nation, under God, shall have a new birth of freedom . . .'' A. Lincoln, Gettysburg Address*. Leslie Illingworth. Mar. 17, 1954, in *Punch*. Scratchboard and pen. 14 1/4 × 11 in. Courtesy Mr. and Mrs. Draper Hill, Memphis, Tenn.

Another shock of the post-war era was the Cold War that the United States and the Soviet Union slipped into almost unnoticed until the lines were clearly drawn across Europe and Asia. The confrontation included an atomic arms race (punctuated by spies, investigations, and executions), the ''loss'' of China, and active intervention in Korea. Crediting virtually all the country's problems to Communist infiltration in the State Department and other branches of government, Senator Joseph McCarthy of Wisconsin began a one-man campaign to ''clean out'' the government. Thrashing about aimlessly—not one of his charges resulted in a conviction—McCarthy attracted widespread attention among countrymen who also were groping for answers in the increasingly complex world.

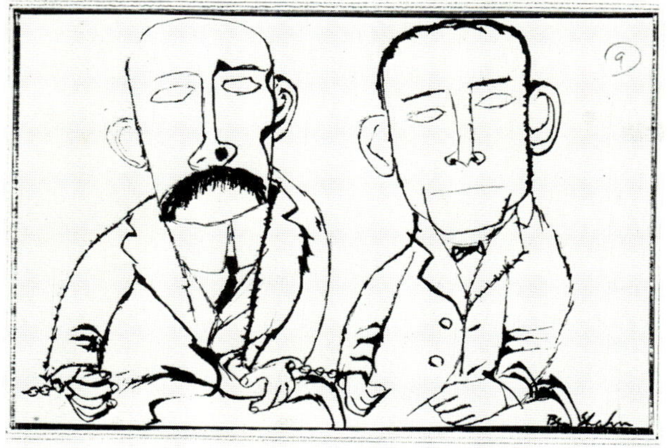

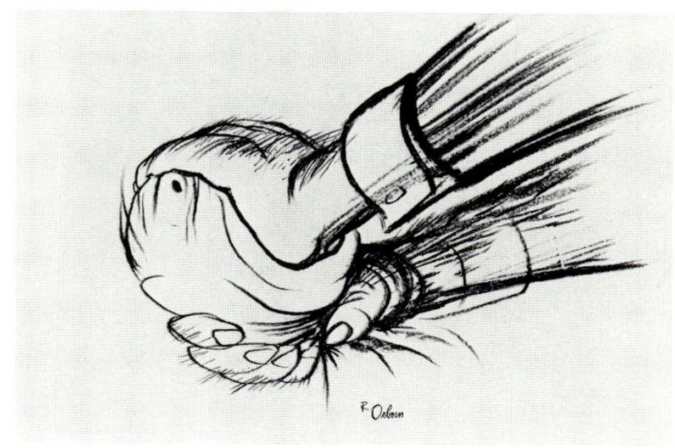

Fig. 193. *Sacco and Vanzetti*. Ben Shahn. 1952. Ink on paper. 5 3/4 × 8 3/8 in. (sight). Courtesy Fogg Art Museum, Harvard University, Cambridge, Mass.

Although anarchists Sacco and Vanzetti were convicted and executed for murder in 1927, Ben Shahn, who was convinced of their innocence, continued to draw and paint them and scenes from their trial. As the McCarthy mania gripped the country, Shahn and other artists like William Gropper looked to our history to find examples that became articulate reminders of other miscarriages of justice, a comment that they could make with a historical figure without fear of reprisal from McCarthy.

Fig. 194. *If You Differ With Me We Will Silence You*. Robert Osborn. 1954. Ink and crayon on paper. 14 15/16 × 21 in. Courtesy The Swann Collection of Caricature and Cartoon.

Robert Osborn was more direct, depicting the fear and lack of freedom of speech that prevailed during McCarthy's reign. After a televised appearance in which McCarthy accused an army dentist of being "pink," the public began to see him as dictatorial and cruel, and he lost influence. In September, 1954, the Senate censured him, and he vanished from the national scene almost as quickly as he had arrived. He died in 1957.

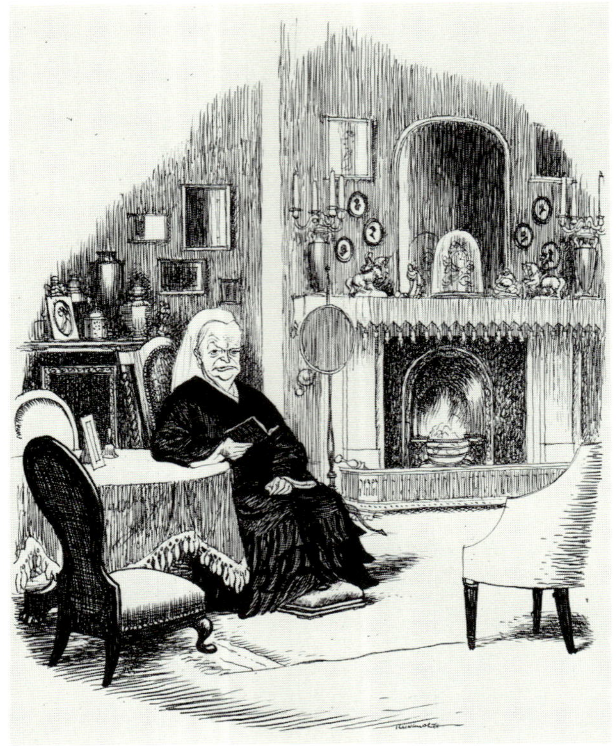

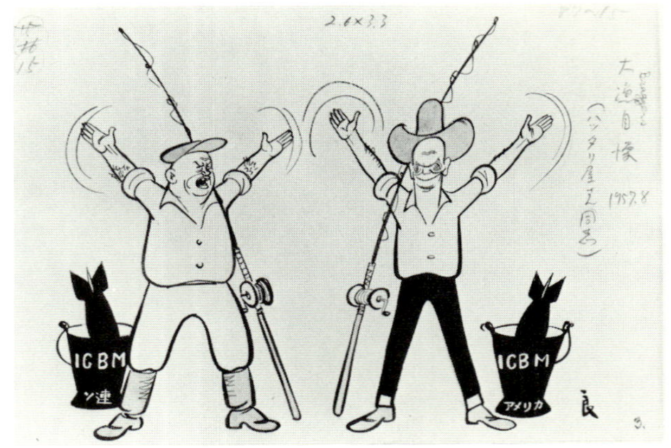

Fig. 195. *"Please understand there is no depression in this house, and we are not interested in the possibilities of defeat. They do not exist."* (Queen Victoria). Leslie Illingworth. Mar. 19, 1958, in *Punch*. Pen and brush on paper. 13 9/16 × 10 3/4 in. Courtesy Mr. and Mrs. Draper Hill, Memphis, Tenn.

When the economy plunged and unemployment soared (ending the post-war prosperity) in 1957, President Eisenhower fore-stalled tax cuts and refused substantial federal subsidies to stimulate economic recovery. The situation was first called a "recession," Eisenhower's administration preferring not to use the dreaded term "depression." Illingworth here comments on the President's apparent belief that the economic threat will vanish if he does not recognize it.

Fig. 196. *Braggers*. Nasu. 1957. Ink on paper. 7 9/16 × 10 11/16 in. Courtesy The State Historical Society of Missouri, Columbia.

As the United States and the Soviet Union continued their arms race, developing increasingly larger bombs and more powerful carriers, the disarmed Japanese grew more discontent. In this cartoon the Japanese artist Nasu shows President Eisenhower and Soviet Premier Nikita Khrushchev bragging about their missiles. The Japanese are particularly sensitive to nuclear con-frontations as a result of their being the only nation in the world to have felt the devastation of an atomic bomb.

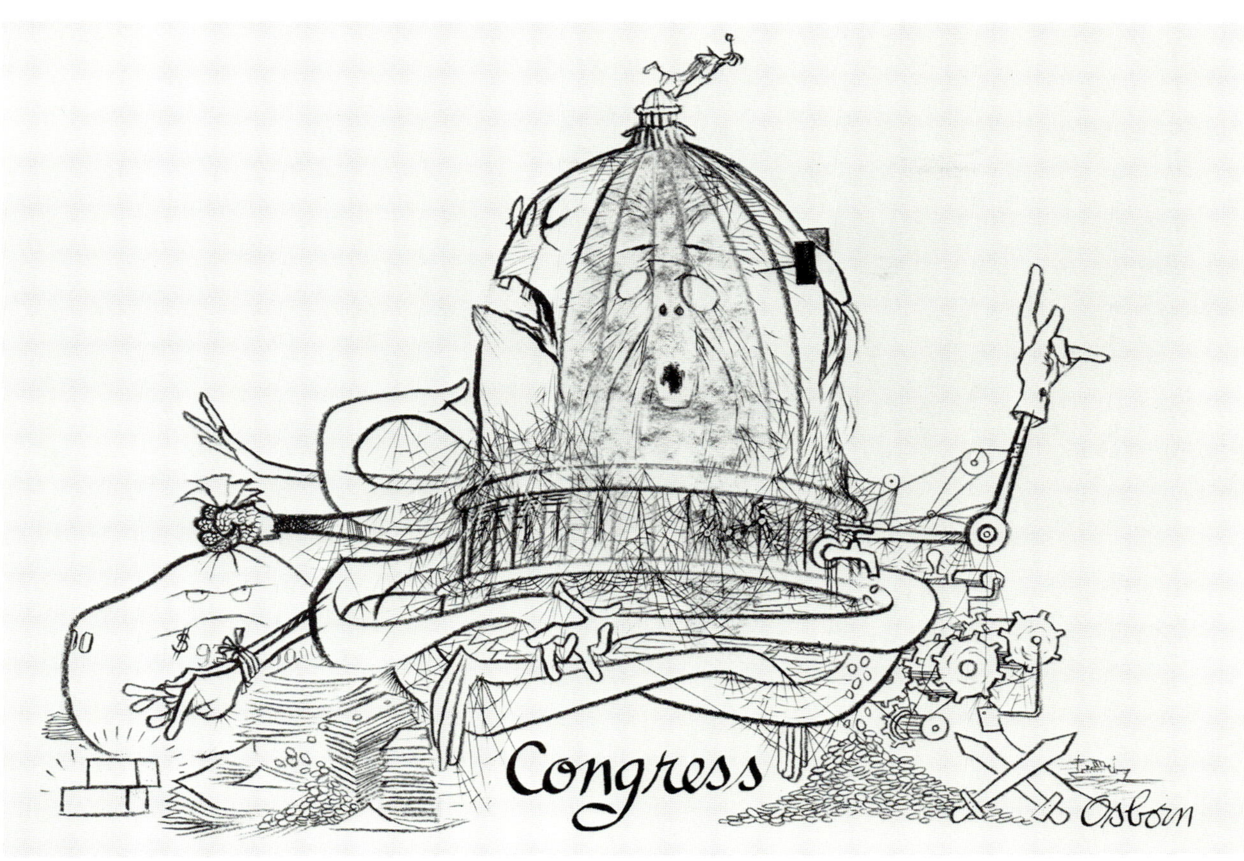

Fig. 197. *Congress*. Robert Osborn. 1950s. Ink and crayon on paper. 14 13/16 × 20 9/16 in. Courtesy The Swann Collection of Caricature and Cartoon.

Congress developed a bad reputation during the late 1940s and 1950s. President Truman had a Republican Congress and blamed virtually all the failures of his administration on the "do nothing 80th Congress." Eisenhower had Democratic Congresses, so he also had a convenient excuse for any administration shortcomings.

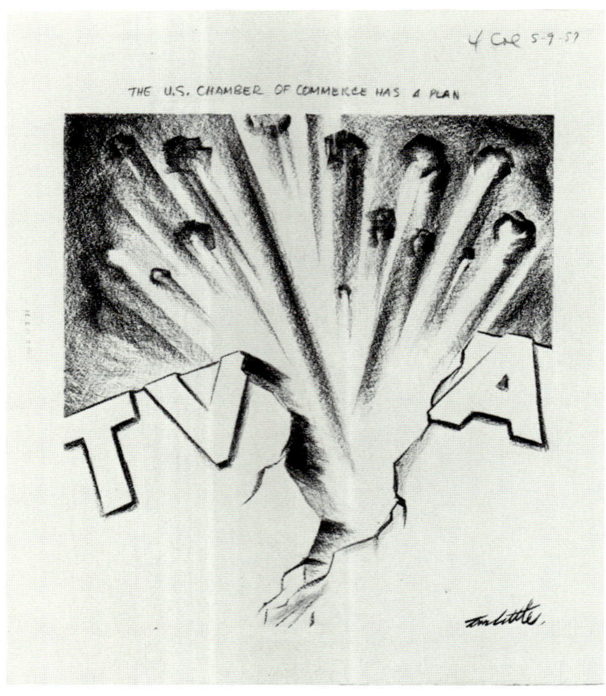

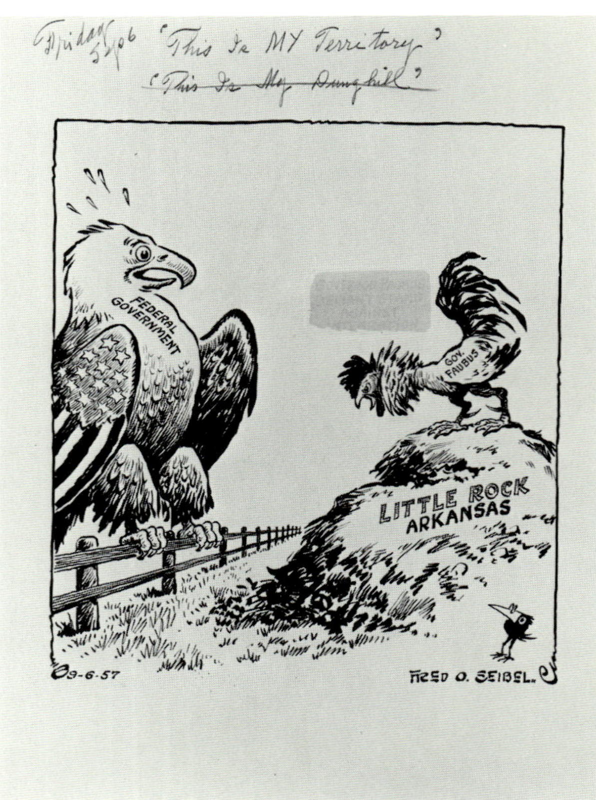

Fig. 198. *The U. S. Chamber of Commerce Has a Plan*. Tom Little. May 9, 1957, in the Nashville *Tennessean*. Charcoal on paper. 20 × 23 in. Courtesy Tom Little Cartoon Collection in Special Collections, Joint University Libraries, Nashville, Tenn.

The Tennessee Valley Authority was a giant undertaking designed to harness the powerful Tennessee River to provide power for the more than 4.5 million people living in its valley. A success under President Roosevelt's New Deal, the TVA found disfavor under Republican President Eisenhower, who favored private development of power and attempted to circumvent the TVA by allowing private businesses to develop plants on the Mississippi River. Eisenhower referred to TVA as "creeping socialism," but quickly rescinded the words as many supporters of TVA protested. The U. S. Chamber of Commerce, of course, sided with private businessmen in the development of power.

Fig. 199. *This Is My Territory*. Fred O. Seibel. Sept. 6, 1957, in the Richmond *Times-Dispatch*. Pen and ink on paper; caption in pencil. 20 × 15 1/16 in. Courtesy University of Virginia Library, Charlottesville.

In the wake of the 1954 Supreme Court decision declaring that "separate but equal" school facilities were unconstitutional, the Little Rock, Arkansas, school system was preparing to desegregate Central High School. The incident probably would have passed unnoticed had not Governor Orval Faubus, needing an issue for his third campaign, decided to send in National Guardsmen to "grease the way." Although the Guardsmen were sent largely for a political end, the incident was widely regarded as being in opposition to the Supreme Court's ruling when it occurred, as Seibel shows in this cartoon.

154

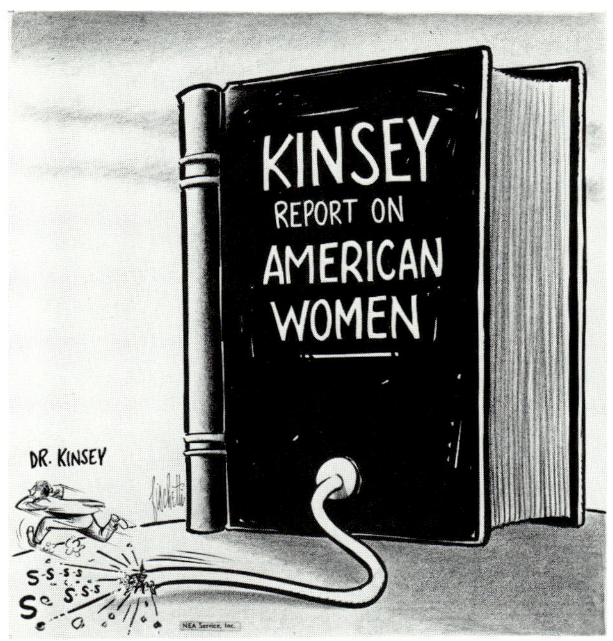

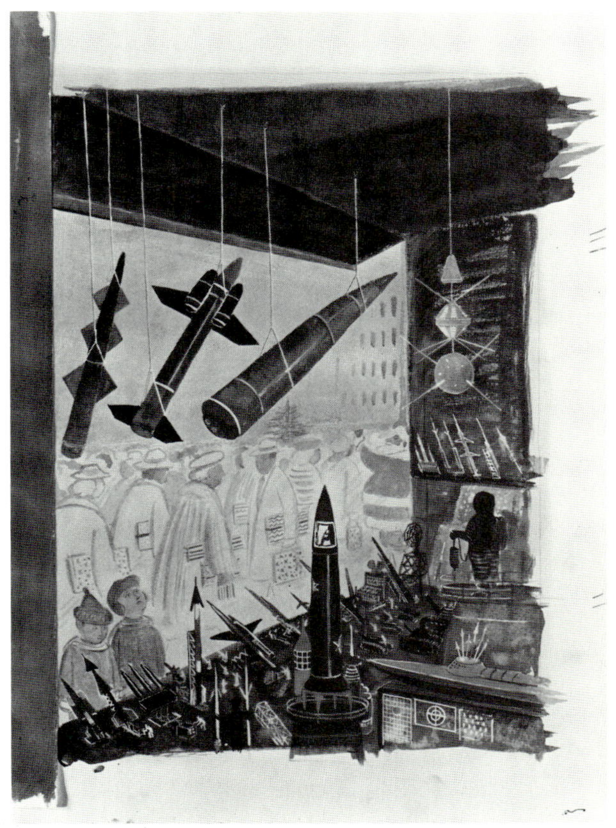

Fig. 200. *And Now the K-Bomb*. John Fischetti. 1953. Ink, crayon, and gouache on paper. 14 1/2 × 11 9/16 in. Courtesy the Library of Congress.

Alfred Charles Kinsey, renowned American biologist, in 1948 published *Sexual Behavior of the Human Male* and in 1953 *Sexual Behavior of the Human Female*. These were the culmination of thousands of personal interviews across the country regarding sexual attitudes and practices among men and women. It was a pioneer effort in the scientific study and investigation of human sexuality. The discussion of sexuality was still a taboo for a wide segment of the American public in the 1950s, and the findings of Kinsey's study were shocking to many.

Fig. 201. *The Space-Age Toy Shop*. A. Kovarsky. 1950s. Watercolor on paper. 23 3/4 × 17 3/4 in. Courtesy The Swann Collection of Caricature and Cartoon.

Kovarsky's cartoon reflects modern society's fascination with the technology of destruction and violence as the children gaze at a fantastic array of destructive gadgetry available for their Christmas selection. The toys, of course, merely reflect the time, money, and energy adults pour into the proliferation of space-age engines of war.

155

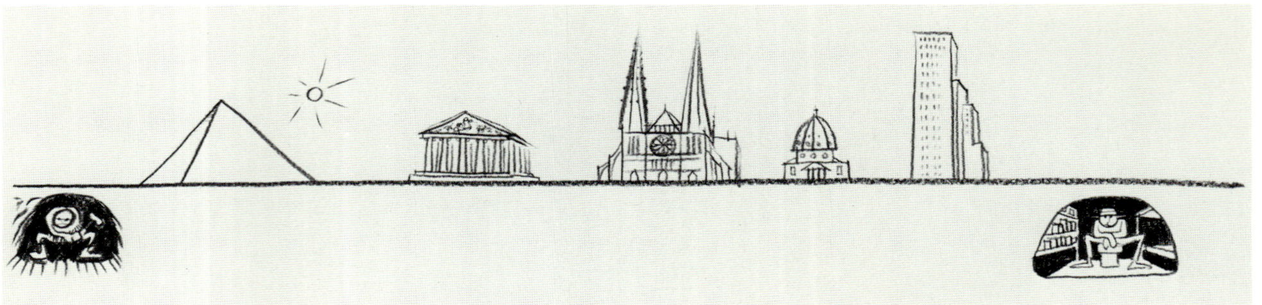

Fig. 202. *History of Man*. Robert Osborn. 1950s. Crayon on paper. 11 1/2 × 15 1/16 in. Courtesy The Swann Collection of Caricature and Cartoon.

The Cold War, the arms race, and constant confrontation convinced many Americans that World War III was just around the corner. Urged by various government agencies to prepare, thousands of citizens constructed their own bomb shelters to protect them from the "ultimate blast." To cartoonist Osborn this was the ultimate state of man, as he has traced civilization in this drawing from cave-dwellers, through classical Egypt, through Classical Antiquity, the Middle Ages, and the Modern Age, to the present century. Apparent is his question as to whether this civilized age is any better than the age of the cave-dwellers.

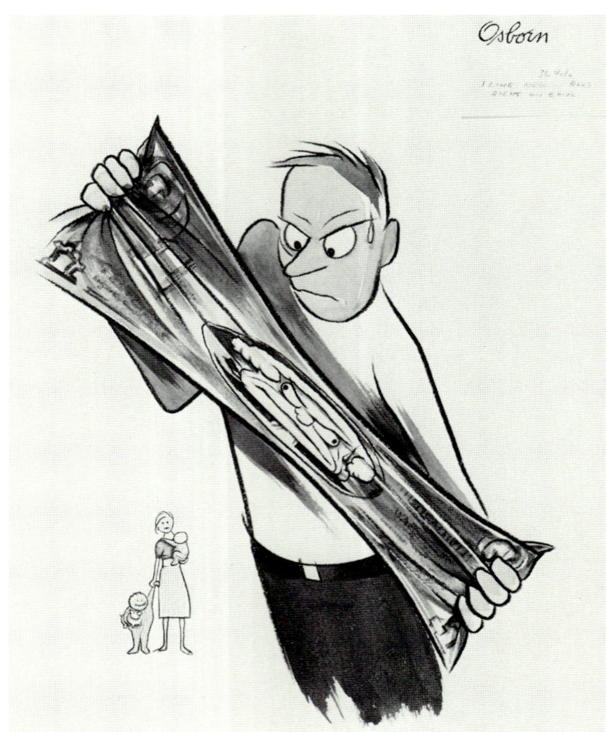

Fig. 203. *Inflation*. Robert Osborn. 1950s. Crayon and watercolor on paper. 17 5/16 × 13 3/16 in. Courtesy The Swann Collection of Caricature and Cartoon.

Making earnings stretch to meet expenditures in a time of inflation seems a perennial problem in American society, and Robert Osborn captured graphically the situation that existed for many families in the 1950s.

156

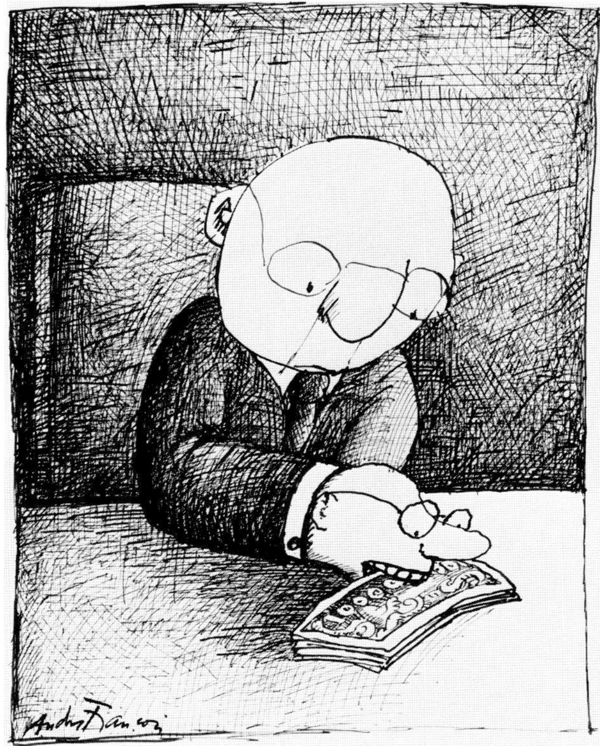

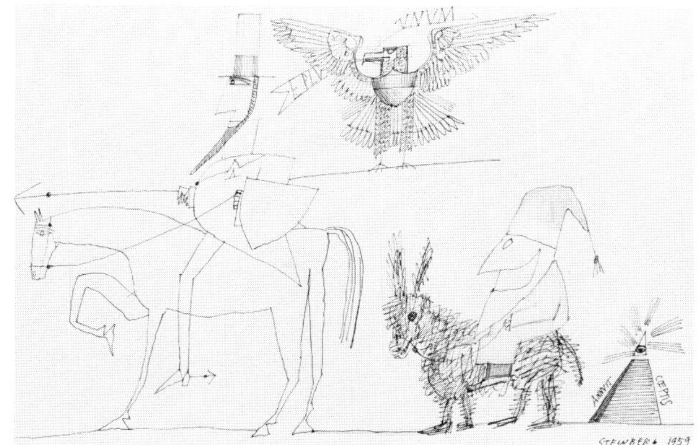

Fig. 204. *Smaller Does Not Mean Better*. André François. 1970s. Ink on paper. 11 3/4 × 9 1/2 in. (sight). © André François in the New York *Times*.

Inflation did not disappear with the 1950s, as André François shows in this cartoon first reproduced on the Op-Ed page of the New York *Times*. It increased to double-digit proportions and became one of the leading domestic problems in the 1970s.

Fig. 205. *Uncle Sam and Santa Claus as Don Quixote and Sancho Panza*. Saul Steinberg. 1959. Ink on prepared paper. 14 1/2 × 23 1/4 in. Courtesy Fogg Art Museum, Harvard University, Cambridge, Mass., Purchase—Gifts for Special Uses Fund through Mrs. Ernest Angell.

In this cartoon Steinberg mixes Abraham Lincoln with Uncle Sam in the figure of Don Quixote, and Santa Claus is Sancho Panza. Perhaps he is suggesting that the United States is ready to defend (or dominate) the world with force and dollars.

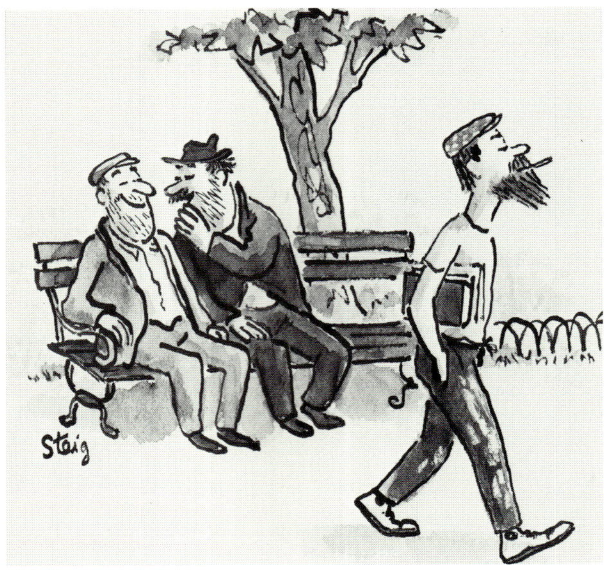

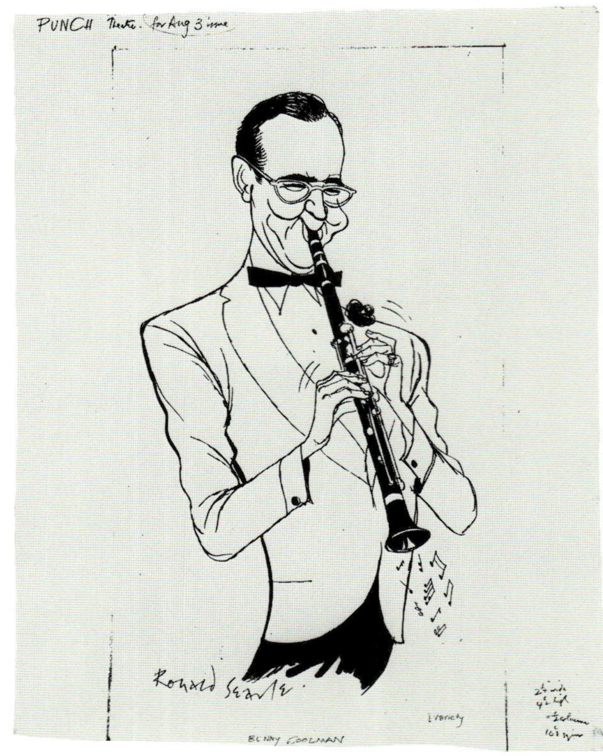

Fig. 207. *Benny Goodman*. Ronald Searle. 1950s. Ink on paper. 13 1/4 × 7 in. Courtesy The Iconography Collection, Humanities Research Center, University of Texas, Austin.

Fig. 206. *Beatniks*. William Steig. 1950s. Ink and wash on paper. 10 × 8 in. Courtesy The Swann Collection of Caricature and Cartoon.

After the disillusioning experience of Korea, some young Americans rebelled against the pervasive conformity of the fifties. The "Beat Generation," or "beatniks" (a play on the word, Sputnik), emerged in San Francisco and Los Angeles in beards, berets, and black leotards and studying Zen Buddhism. In their special jargon, borrowed primarily from jazz musicians, they espoused a cynical, but passive philosophy which sought to establish a subculture, rather than exert change on society at large.

In the 1930s the popular jazz style began to acquire a "new" sound. It coupled a unique syncopated energy with a full orchestration requiring a "big band." This was "swing" and it was to make the music industry big business. The radio, records, and movies blared its catchy rhythms across the nation, and American troops took it with them in World War II. Benny Goodman formed his first band in 1934 and two years later had already acquired Gene Kruppa, Teddy Wilson, and Lionel Hampton, the great swing musicians who formed the core of his orchestra. Goodman's ability to spot and hold talent, along with his showmanship, managerial ability, as well as his musical virtuosity, earned him the well deserved title, "King of Swing."

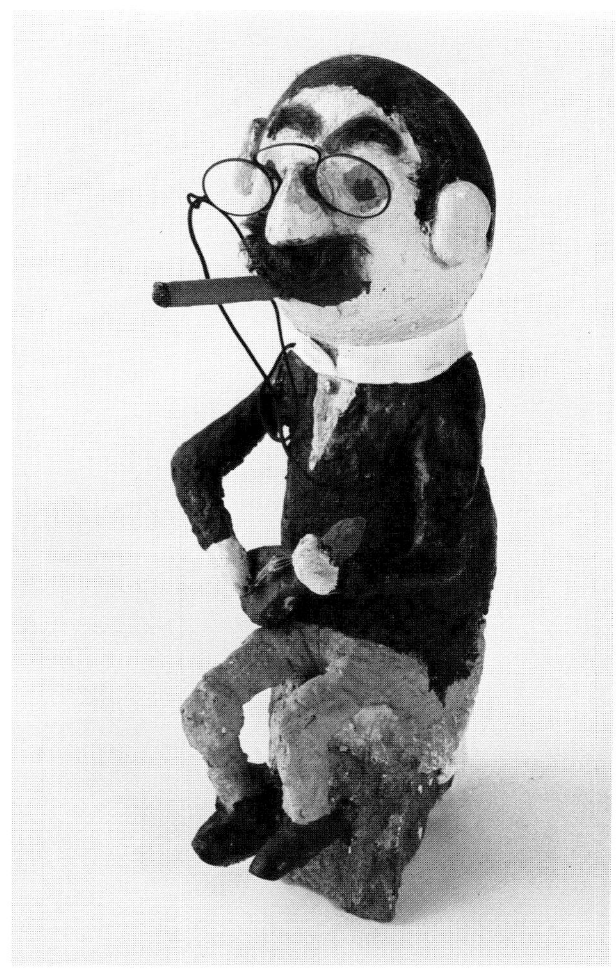

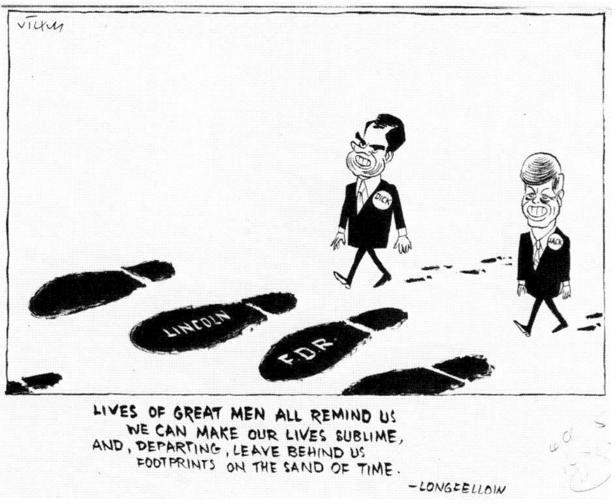

Fig. 209. *The Lives of Great Men*. Victor Weisz (''Vicky''). Sept. 29, 1960, in the London *Evening Standard*. Pen, brush, opaque white, blue pencil on paper. 15 1/8 × 18 1/2 in. Courtesy Mr. and Mrs. Draper Hill, Memphis, Tenn.

Fig. 208. *Groucho Marx*. Anonymous. c. 1955. Hair, wire, glass, painted stones and plaster. 16 in. high. Courtesy Bert Hemphill, New York City.

As television became an increasingly popular American pastime during the 1950s, certain personalities developed as the old *Amos 'n' Andy* radio show had developed during the 1930s. Groucho Marx, a member of the famous Marx brothers comedy team that had made several movies during the 1930s, became one of the best known quiz show hosts, conducting *You Bet Your Life* with a combination of jokes, ad libs, and zany questions, the most famous of which is ''Who is buried in Grant's Tomb?''

The presidential candidates in the 1960 campaign were both much younger than their recent predecessors in that office. Many voters also felt that both Kennedy and Nixon were motivated by personal ambition rather than ideological conviction and that neither was really adequate for the job. In their televised debates Kennedy was prone to invoke the memory of Franklin Roosevelt while Nixon recalled Abraham Lincoln to dignify and sanction their respective political philosophies and attitudes towards issues of the day. This cartoon contrasts the insignificant figures and footprints of the two presidential hopefuls with the enormous historical impressions of the former leaders they sought to follow.

159

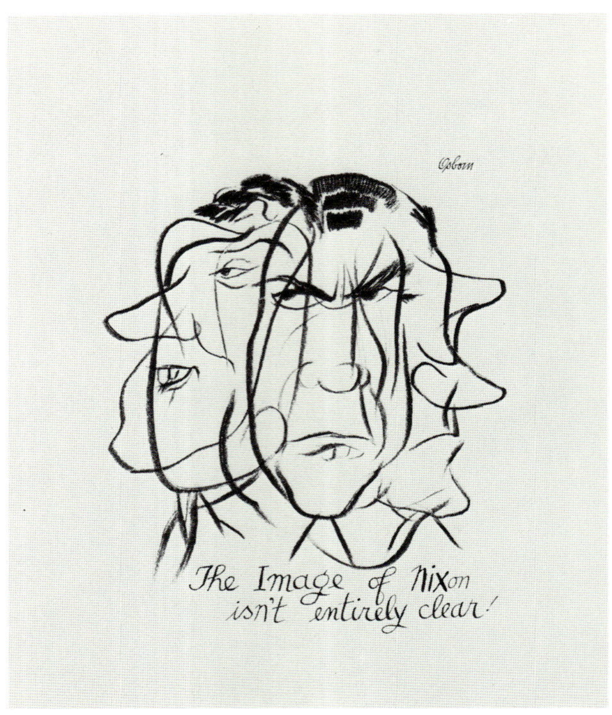

Fig. 210. *The Image of Nixon Isn't Entirely Clear*. Robert Osborn. 1960 (?). Crayon and ink on paper. 14 15/16 × 11 7/8 in. Courtesy The Swann Collection of Caricature and Cartoon.

President Nixon was the target of many critical remarks during his unsuccessful 1960 campaign against John Kennedy. Perhaps the most famous question posed to the electorate is, "Would you buy a used car from this man?" But the most prophetic, in hindsight, is probably this caricature by Osborn showing that Nixon was not being as straightforward even then as he claimed to be.

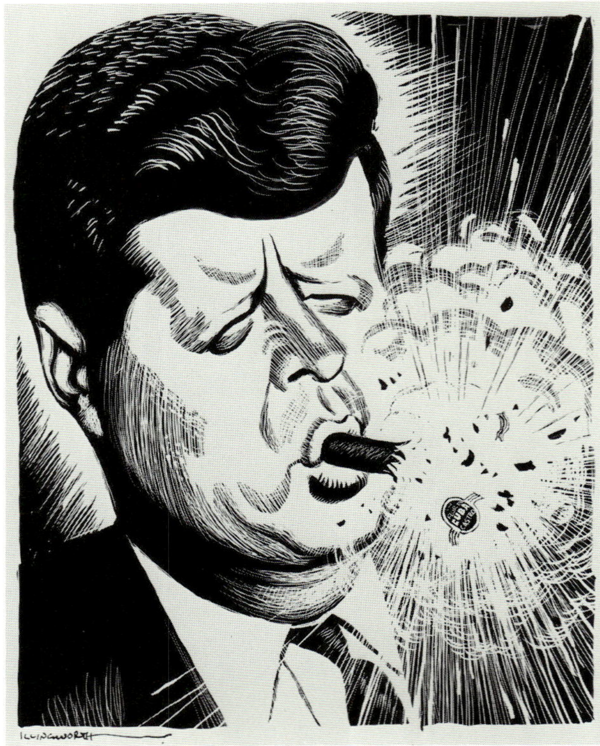

Fig. 211. [Kennedy and exploding Cuban cigar.] Leslie Illingworth. Apr. 21, 1961. Scratchboard. 11 3/16 × 8 13/16 in. Courtesy The National Library of Wales.

Castro had seized power in Cuba during Eisenhower's term, and shortly before he left office, Eisenhower broke diplomatic relations with the Cuban government because of Castro's Communist leanings. When President Kennedy learned of the plans to invade Cuba from Central Intelligence Agency officials, he thought it unwise to change them since he had taken such a hard line on Cuba during the campaign. In April, 1961, some 1,500 Cuban exiles and Americans landed at the Bay of Pigs. The badly-planned assault immediately collapsed and 1,200 of the invaders were taken prisoner. The United States had denied having anything to do with the invasion, but when it miscarried so badly, Kennedy shouldered the blame.

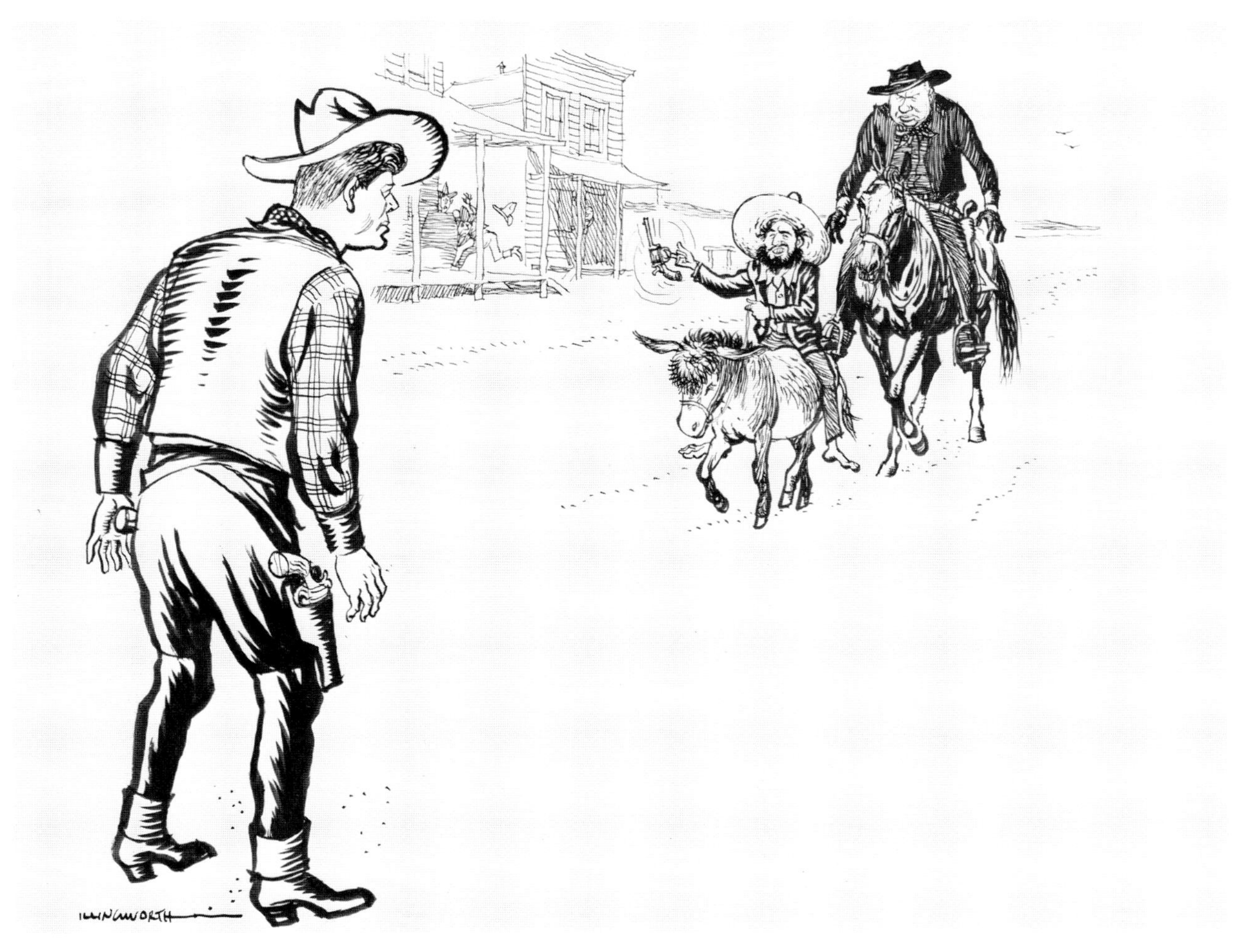

Fig. 212. *Cuban Missile Showdown*. Leslie Illingworth. Oct. 24, 1962, in the London *Daily Mail*. Brush and pen on paper. 12 1/2 × 14 1/8 in. Courtesy The Swann Collection of Caricature and Cartoon.

Perhaps President Kennedy's most famous personal confrontation with another foreign leader was his Vienna meeting with Soviet Premier Nikita Khrushchev. Khrushchev tested the young President, hoping to uncover a weak spot or lack of character, which he would soon try under international pressure. The Soviet leader thought Kennedy would not oppose the installation of Soviet missiles in Cuba after the embarrassment of the Bay of Pigs, but he was mistaken. Upon receiving word that missiles were being installed, Kennedy placed a naval blockade around Cuba on October 22, 1962.

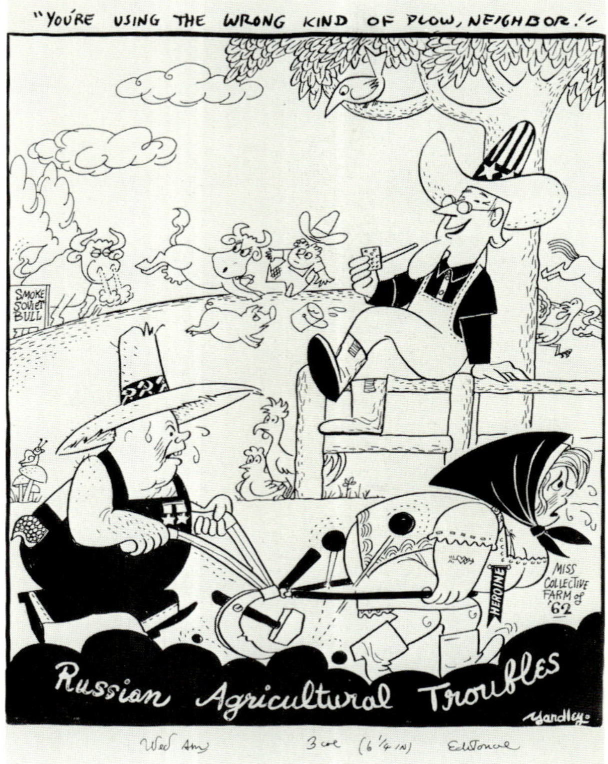

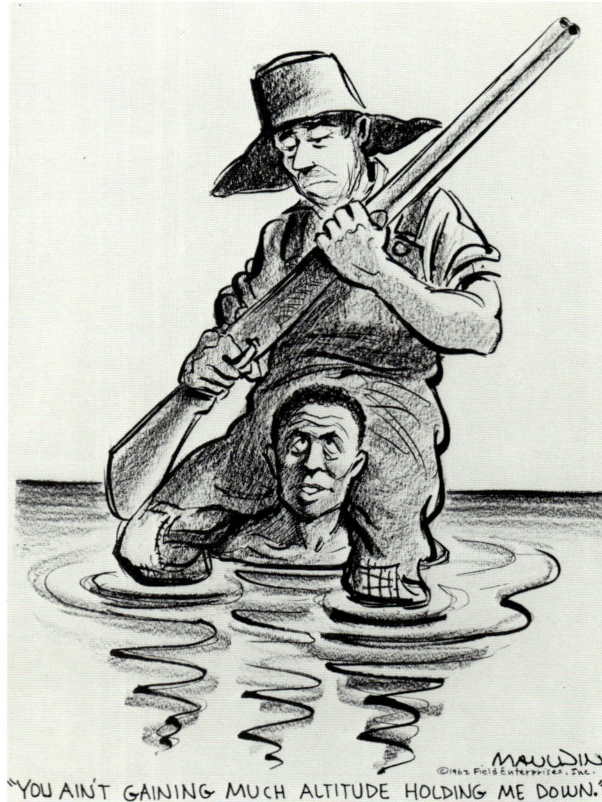

Fig. 213. *"You're using the wrong kind of plow, neighbor!"* Richard Yardley. 1962 in the Baltimore *Sun*. Ink with white highlights on paper. 18 15/16 × 14 7/8 in. Courtesy Amon Carter Museum, Fort Worth.

Competition in the Cold War reached new proportions when Premier Khrushchev visited the United States in 1959. During the course of his tour he made his now-famous "we will bury you" remark, which the American propaganda machine turned into one of the most effective anti-Soviet campaigns of the Cold War. Khrushchev claimed that he meant that Communists would "bury" Capitalists economically, but most Americans felt certain that he meant militarily. Khrushchev's boast looked particularly hollow after Soviet agriculture performed so disastrously during the 1960s. This Yardley cartoon comments on the competition between farmer Uncle Sam and the Communists.

Fig. 214. *"You ain't gaining much altitude holding me down."* Bill Mauldin. Oct. 10, 1962. Ink and crayon on paper. 13 × 9 1/2 in. Courtesy Collection of Bill Mauldin.

The public reaction to the 1954 Supreme Court decision which outlawed the segregation of public education (*Brown vs. Board of Education Topeka*) resurrected the specter of racial prejudice which has haunted American society since its beginnings. The Court's recognition of the advantages enjoyed by whites under the "separate but equal" doctrine seemed to signal a major breakthrough in the civil rights struggle, but many areas in the deep South openly resisted the order. The *de facto* segregation of the North also became apparent. Progress has been made slowly, and Mauldin's cartoon is as pertinent today as it was in 1962.

162

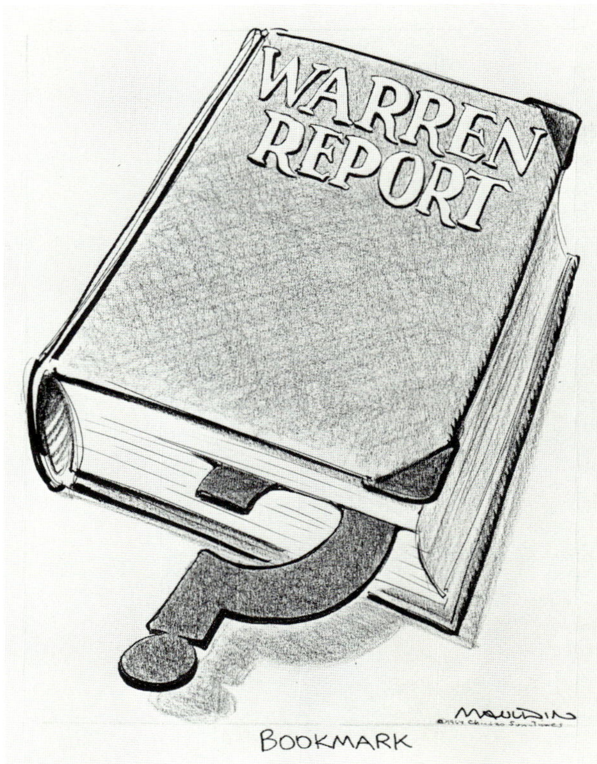

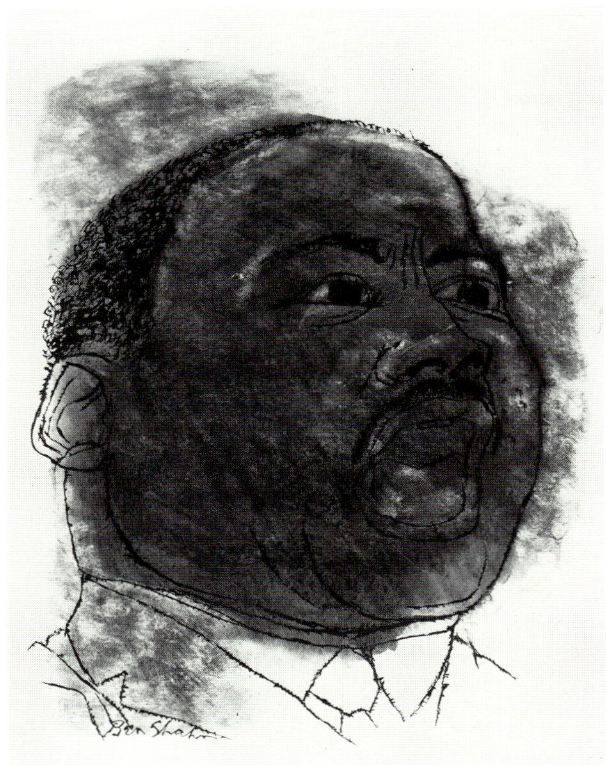

Fig. 215. *Bookmark*. Bill Mauldin. 1967. Ink on paper. 18 × 14 in. (sight). Courtesy Collection of Joel Rosen, Fort Worth, Tex.

Fig. 216. *Martin Luther King*. Ben Shahn. 1965. Pen and ink wash on paper. 26 1/4 × 20 1/4 in. Courtesy Amon Carter Museum, Fort Worth.

As President Kennedy was preparing for the 1964 presidential campaign by making a political ''fence-mending'' trip to Texas, he was tragically assassinated by Lee Harvey Oswald. The special investigating committee, headed by Chief Justice Earl Warren, concluded that Oswald was acting alone in killing the President and wounding Texas Governor John Connally, but after the commission report was made public numerous critics have claimed that the investigation was not thorough enough, and that there are complicating factors that point to conclusions other than those the panel reached.

Martin Luther King was the most outstanding civil rights advocate of the 1960s. Using mass demonstrations of passive resistance, he attracted international attention and sympathy for the battle against the political, economic, and social inequality of the Negro in America. For his effective yet nonviolent efforts he was awarded the Nobel Peace Prize in 1964. In 1968 he was gunned down in a Memphis motel, setting off a chain of riots in the black ghettos of cities across the nation. When King saw this drawing on the cover of *Time* magazine, he reportedly remarked, ''There is a little racism in all of us.''

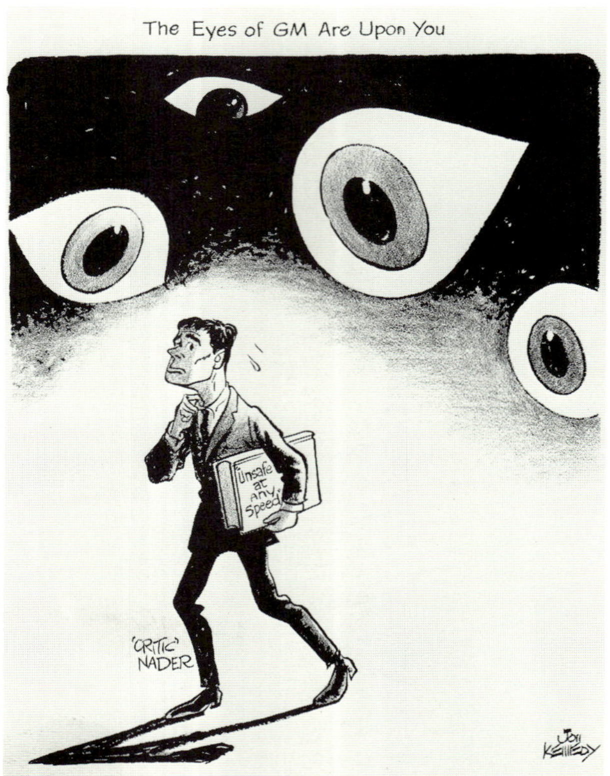

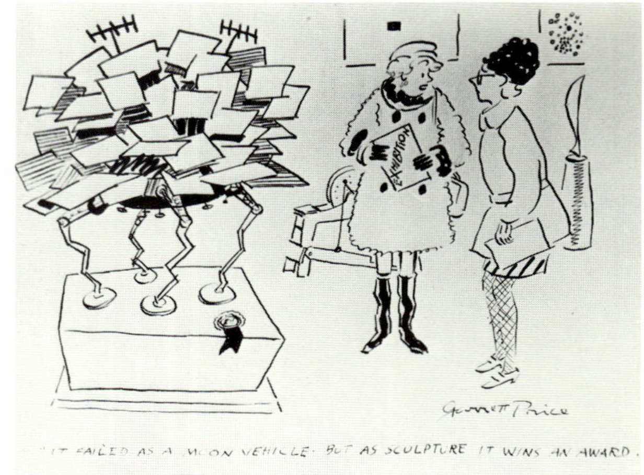

Fig. 217. *The Eyes of GM Are Upon You*. Jon Kennedy. c. 1966–1967. Ink and crayon on paper. 13 11/16 × 11 1/8 in. Courtesy The State Historical Society of Missouri, Columbia.

In 1959 General Motors began to market a new automobile, the Corvair, which won awards and enjoyed phenomenal sales in the early sixties. Then auto industry critic Ralph Nader wrote a book, *Unsafe At Any Speed*, attacking the Corvair as dangerous. In an effort to discredit him and prove him untrustworthy, General Motors harassed Nader with their "gumshoes," according to Nader. But their efforts failed to save the Corvair. In 1969, with economic pressures slowing the sales, GM announced that the Corvair would be discontinued. Nader, meanwhile, had become the country's leading consumer watchdog.

Fig. 218. *It failed as a moon vehicle but as sculpture it wins an award*. Garrett Price. 1960s. Ink on paper. 9 × 11 1/2 in. Courtesy Nelson-Atkins Museum, Kansas City, Mo., Gift of the artist.

After the Soviet Union launched "Sputnik" and initiated the American-Soviet space race, the American public was deluged with a barrage of extraterrestrial equipment as bizarre and baffling to them as the new trends in the arts, which had by the 1960s left many traditionalists wondering what had become of the fundamental values and standards. Artists turned "found objects" into imaginative creations, giving many of their works a "common touch" that some viewers could not understand, for they had always thought of art in terms of the "uncommon." Mechanical art also was popular among the artists. Such a state of affairs obviously confused many, including the two ladies at this art show.

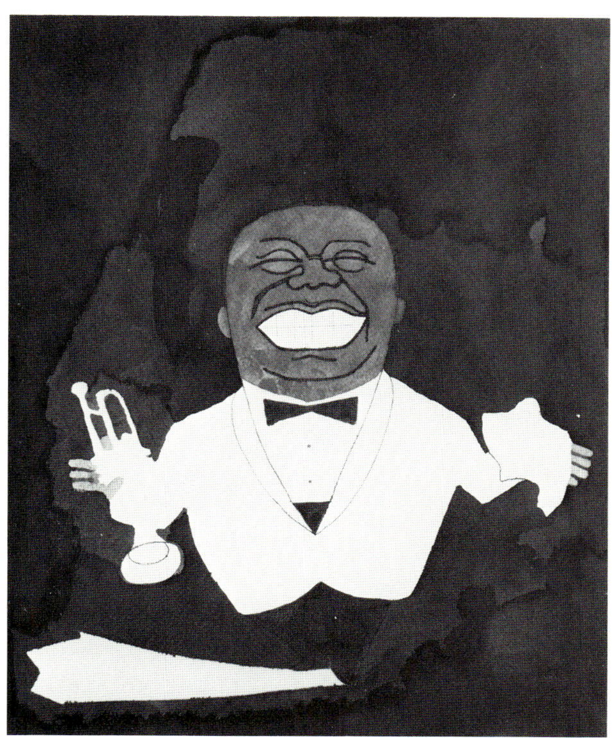

Fig. 219. *Caricature of Louis Armstrong*. Makota Wada. 1968. Watercolor on paper. 13 1/2 × 11 in. Courtesy The Swann Collection of Caricature and Cartoon.

Louis "Satchmo" Armstrong was born on the Fourth of July in the slums of New Orleans. He learned to play the cornet in the Negro Waifs' Home there, and music, jazz, became his career. In 1924 he switched to the trumpet and became an internationally acclaimed master of the horn. Whether improvising in the style of pure jazz or performing a popular tune, "Satchmo" stamped his music with his personal mark, as distinctive as the clenched-tooth grin, white handkerchief, and expansive gesture by which the Japanese cartoonist Makota Wada identifies him.

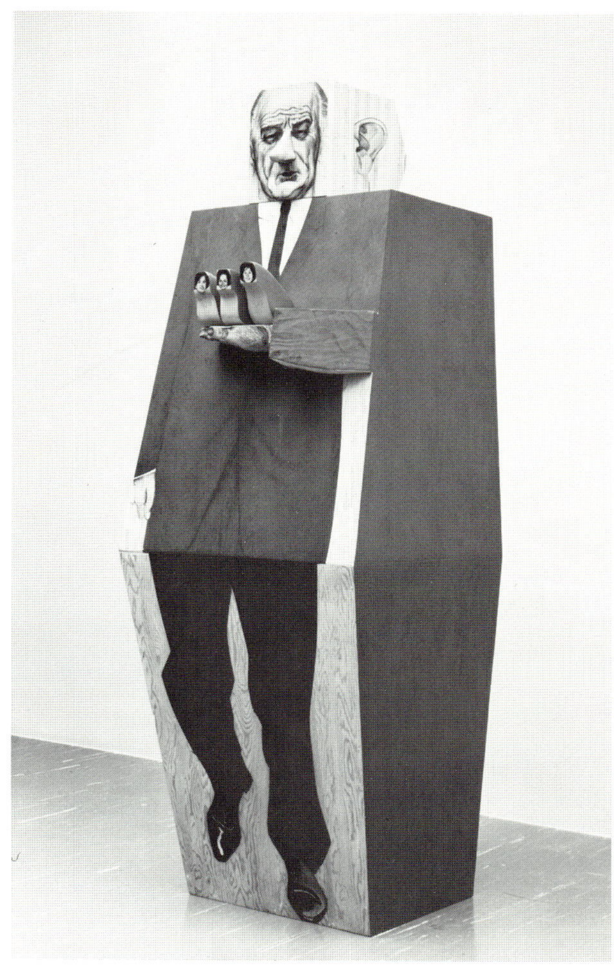

Fig. 220. *LBJ*. Marisol [Escobar]. 1967. Painted wood construction. 80 × 27 7/8 × 24 5/8 in. Courtesy The Museum of Modern Art, New York City, Fractional gift and extended loan from Mr. and Mrs. Lester Avnet, 1968.

Marisol, the pop artist, is known for her life-size three-dimensional representations of both the known and the anonymous people of society and her portrayal of them, via carving, casting, assemblage, and painting, in their characteristic if often ridiculous situations. Here she depicts President Lyndon B. Johnson with his family in his hand: wife Lady Bird and daughters Luci Baines and Lynda Bird. The sheer size of the LBJ statue in comparison with the depictions of the women captures the massiveness, domination, and overpowering qualities that he continually exhibited.

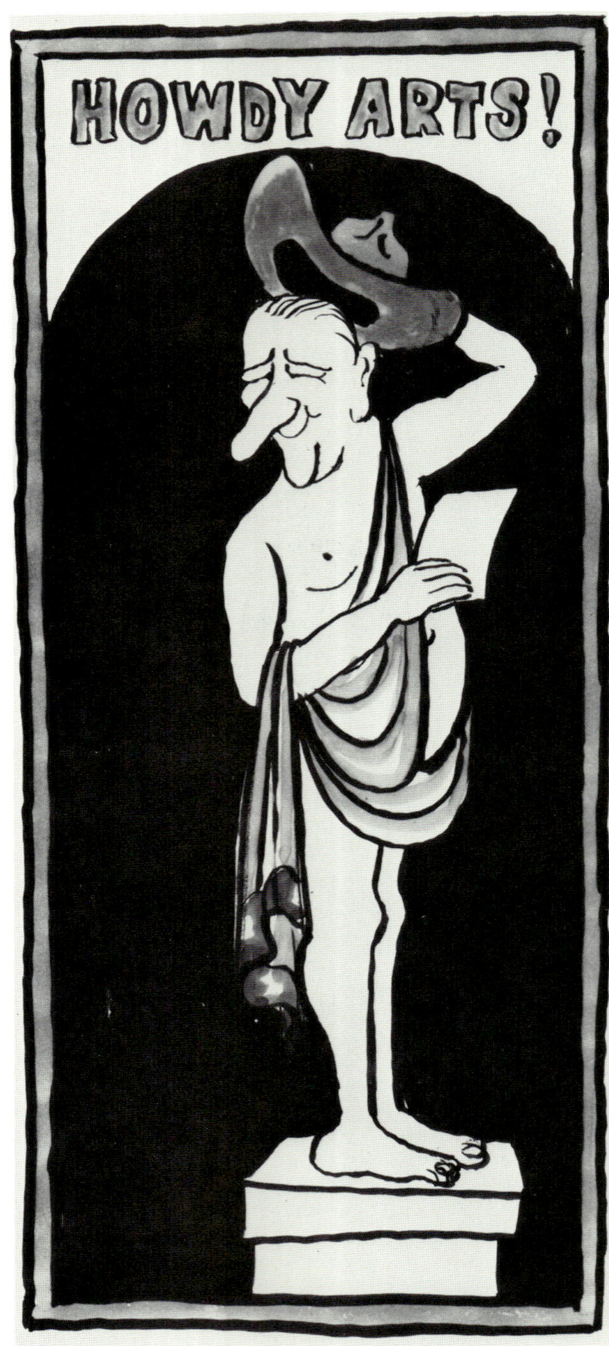

Fig. 221. *Howdy Arts*. Tomi Ungerer. c. 1965. Watercolor on paper. 13 1/2 × 11 11/16 in. Courtesy Galerie Daniel Keel, Zurich, Switzerland.

On June 14, 1965 President Johnson sponsored the White House Festival of the Arts which included the exhibition of American painting and sculpture, performances by American singers, dancers, musicians and actors, and readings by American dramatists and authors from their works. The press hailed it as ''a salute to the creative people of the nation.'' Tomi Ungerer conveys the same message in his cartoon as he contrasts Johnson's Western background with the cultural sophistication that he was trying to bring to the White House.

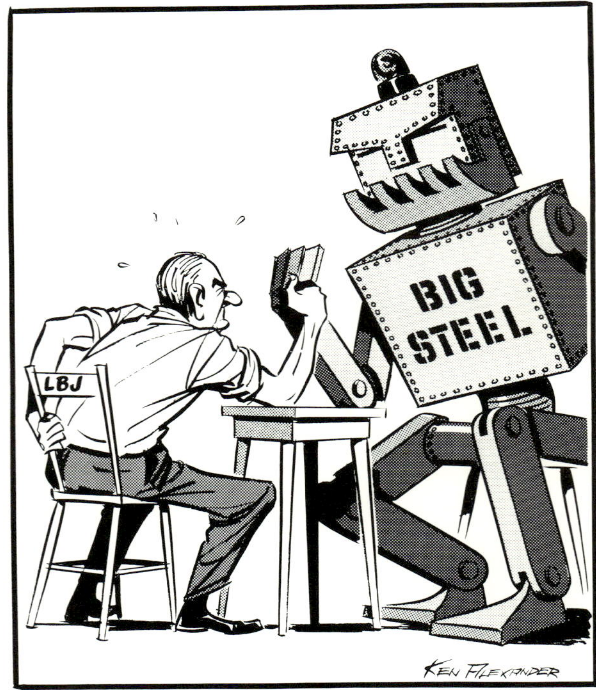

Fig. 222. *LBJ Armwrestling Big Steel*. Ken Alexander. c. 1965. Ink on paper. 14 3/8 × 11 in. Courtesy The Lyndon Baines Johnson Library Collection, Austin, Tex.

In the summer of 1965 President Johnson intervened in a deadlocked struggle between the steel workers' union and the steel industry. The union was to strike on September 1 and implications for the national economy were dismal if the issues could not be settled. ''Come let us reason together,'' pleaded Johnson in his invitation to the chief negotiators. He first got the union to push back the strike date, then managed by using the powers of persuasion at the command of the President to get a settlement before Labor Day.

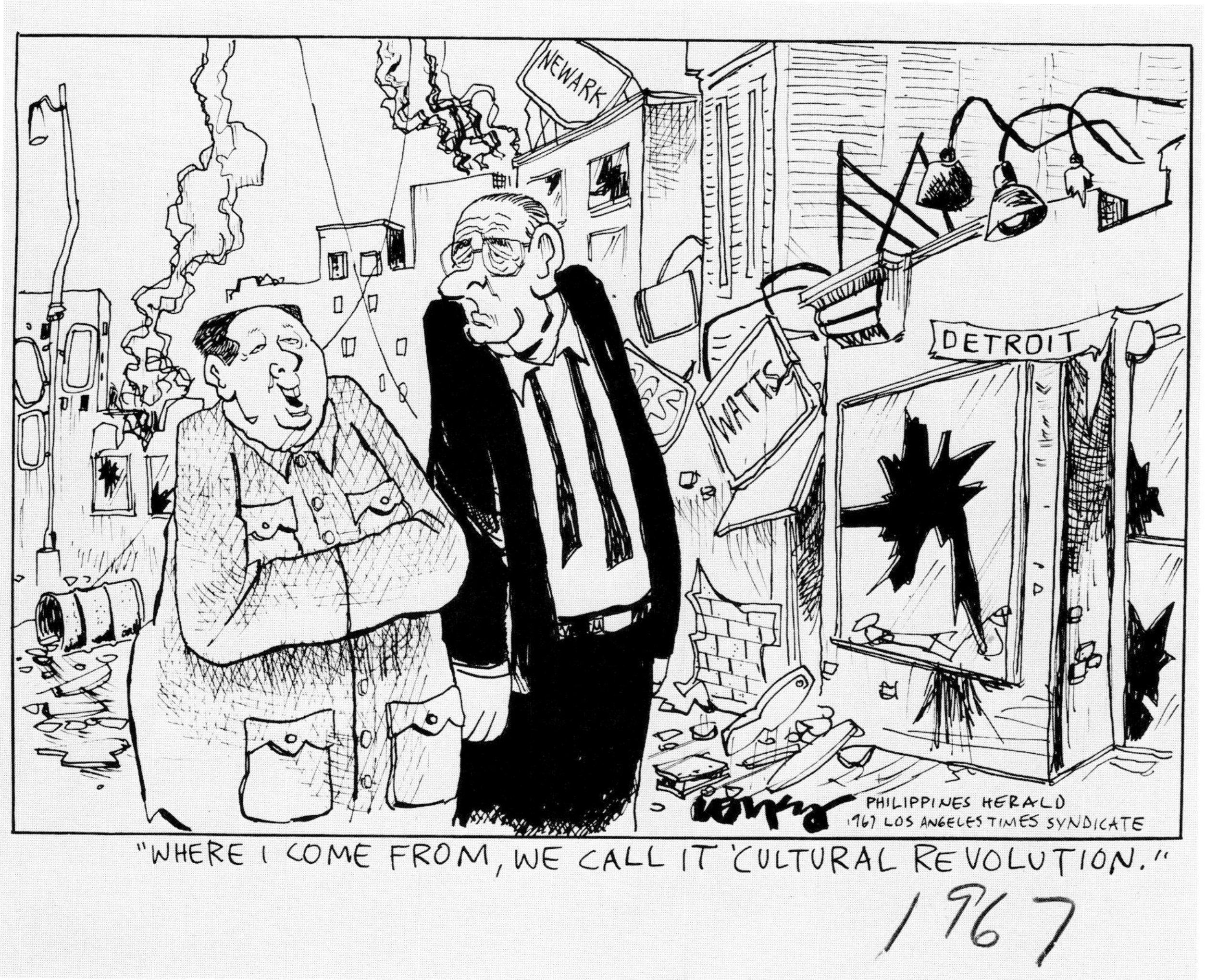

Fig. 223. *"Where I come from, we call it 'Cultural Revolution.'"* Corky Trinidad. 1967. Ink on paper. 10 1/2 × 14 3/8 in. Courtesy The Lyndon Baines Johnson Library Collection, Austin, Tex.

The decade of the sixties witnessed an important tactical shift in the civil rights movement. Along with the rise of new leaders and ideologies in the black community, a series of spontaneous riots shook many metropolitan areas: Watts, a Negro suburb of Los Angeles, was the scene of the first riot in 1965, followed by outbreaks in Newark and Detroit in 1967. Riots also convulsed many cities in Communist China during the sixties, but they resembled the American phenomena only in that they were chiefly instigated by militant young activists against the established power. Trinidad contrasts the reactions of the shaken Johnson, who watched the riots demolish his dreams of a "Great Society," and the inscrutable Chairman Mao, who simply placed himself at the ideological head of the movement and declared that society should be "renewed" so it will not depart from its founding principles.

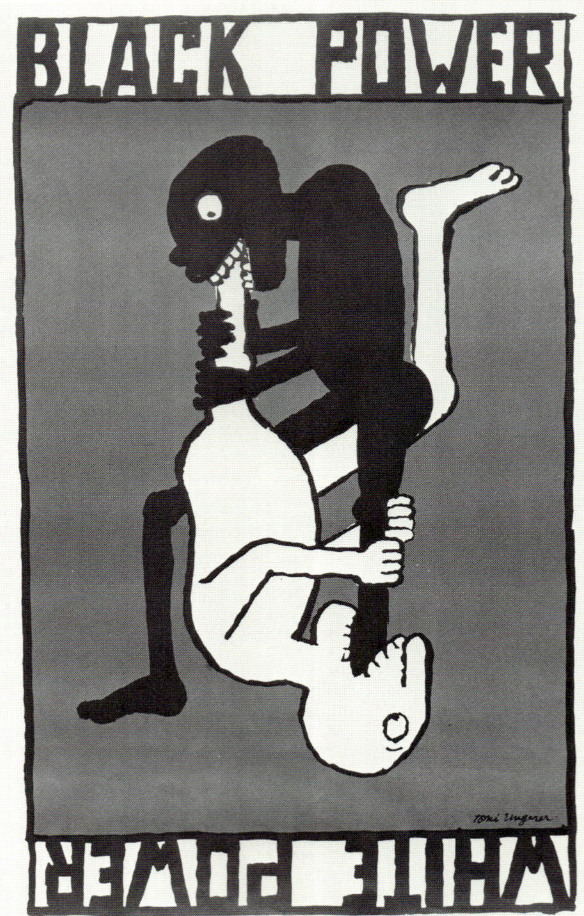

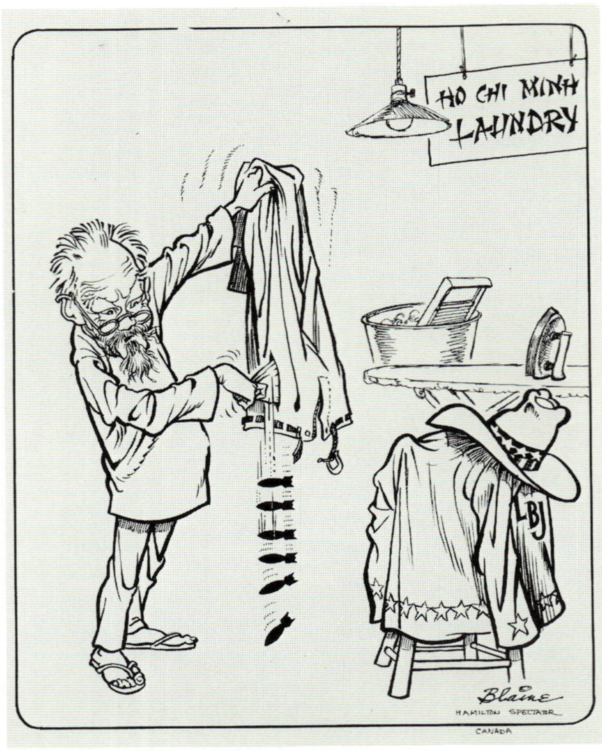

Fig. 224. *Black Power/White Power*. Tomi Ungerer. 1967. Colored poster. 28 × 20 in. Courtesy The International Poster Museum; collection of Mr. Jack Rennert.

"Black Power"—a catch-phrase of the mid-sixties—was a subtle concept with far-reaching implications because it signaled a fundamental change in the attitude of the black man toward himself, his race, and American society. In the popular mind, Black Power acted as an umbrella under which many different philosophies were combined. It included everything from the "Black is beautiful" concept to the manifestos of the militants. Here Ungerer reflects upon the recent violent urban riots and the growing "white backlash" in reaction to them and depicts the black and white separatist movements as destructive of each other and society.

Fig. 225. [LBJ suit at the Chinese laundry.] MacDonald Blaine. c. 1967. Ink on paper. 14 1/2 × 11 3/4 in. Courtesy The Lyndon Baines Johnson Library Collection, Austin, Tex.

On August 5, 1964, the Vietnamese conflict was escalated by President Johnson's retaliation against North Vietnam for attacks on American P. T. boats in the Bay of Tonkin. Johnson pursued a punitive policy toward North Vietnam for the next four years, incorporating routine saturation bombing of Hanoi and other major cities in an attempt to break down the morale and resistance and the ability to prosecute the war in South Vietnam. Canadian cartoonist MacDonald Blaine depicts Ho Chi Minh as a laundryman who, instead of finding loose change, finds bombs in LBJ's trouser pockets.

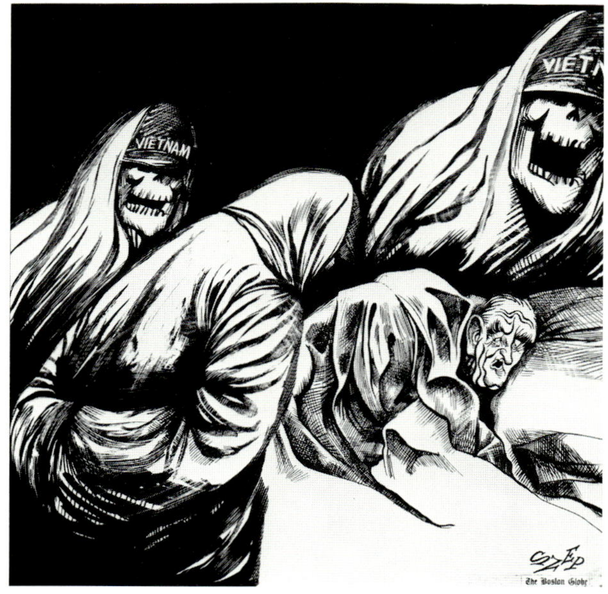

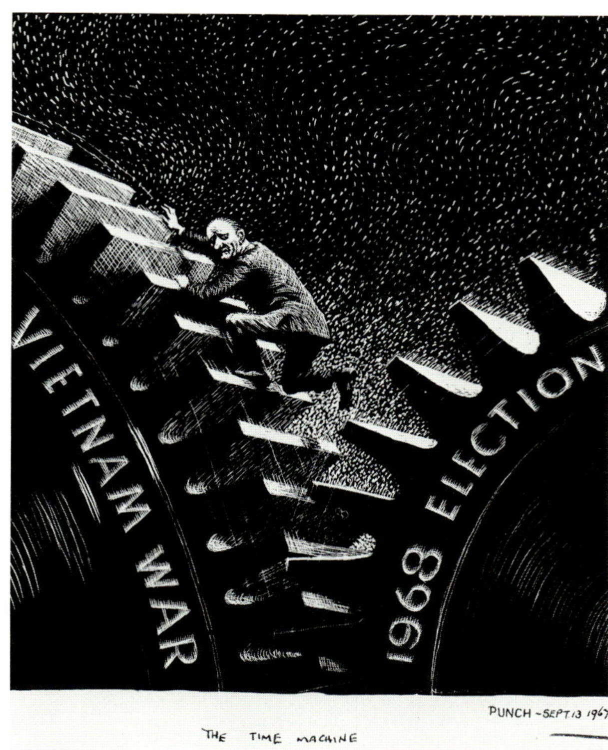

Fig. 227. *The Time Machine*. Leslie Illingworth. Sept. 13, 1967, in *Punch*. Scratchboard. 15 1/4 × 12 1/2 in. Courtesy The Lyndon Baines Johnson Library Collection, Austin, Tex.

Fig. 226. [LBJ and Vietnam Specters.] Paul Szep. 1960s in the Boston *Globe*. Scratchboard. 15 × 14 7/8 in. Courtesy The Swann Collection of Caricature and Cartoon.

President Johnson's main interest while in office was his domestic program. Johnson yearned to do something for the nation's poor and to equalize educational opportunities. However, most of his attention was devoted to foreign issues, with the Vietnam policy leading them all. He inherited his commitment from President Kennedy but increased it, hoping to end the war quickly. The South Vietnamese rebels and North Viet Nam supporters were much stronger than American military advisors had thought, however, and the war outlasted Johnson's terms in office. Thus Szep has caricatured him haunted by the ghosts of Vietnam.

As the 1968 presidential election approached, it became evident that unless President Johnson could dramatically end or downgrade the Vietnam war, his chances of being reelected would be greatly hampered. The public clamored for an end to the war, either by victory or withdrawal. Senator Eugene McCarthy served as a unifying factor for the anti-war forces, drawing an embarrassingly large percentage of the vote in the first presidential primary, considering that he was not really a serious candidate. Johnson pressed the Vietnamese to negotiate, saying that American diplomats would go anywhere in the world to meet. Still there was no positive reaction from Hanoi. As the election primaries drew near, Johnson announced that he would not run, that he would devote the remainder of his term to trying to settle the war issues.

169

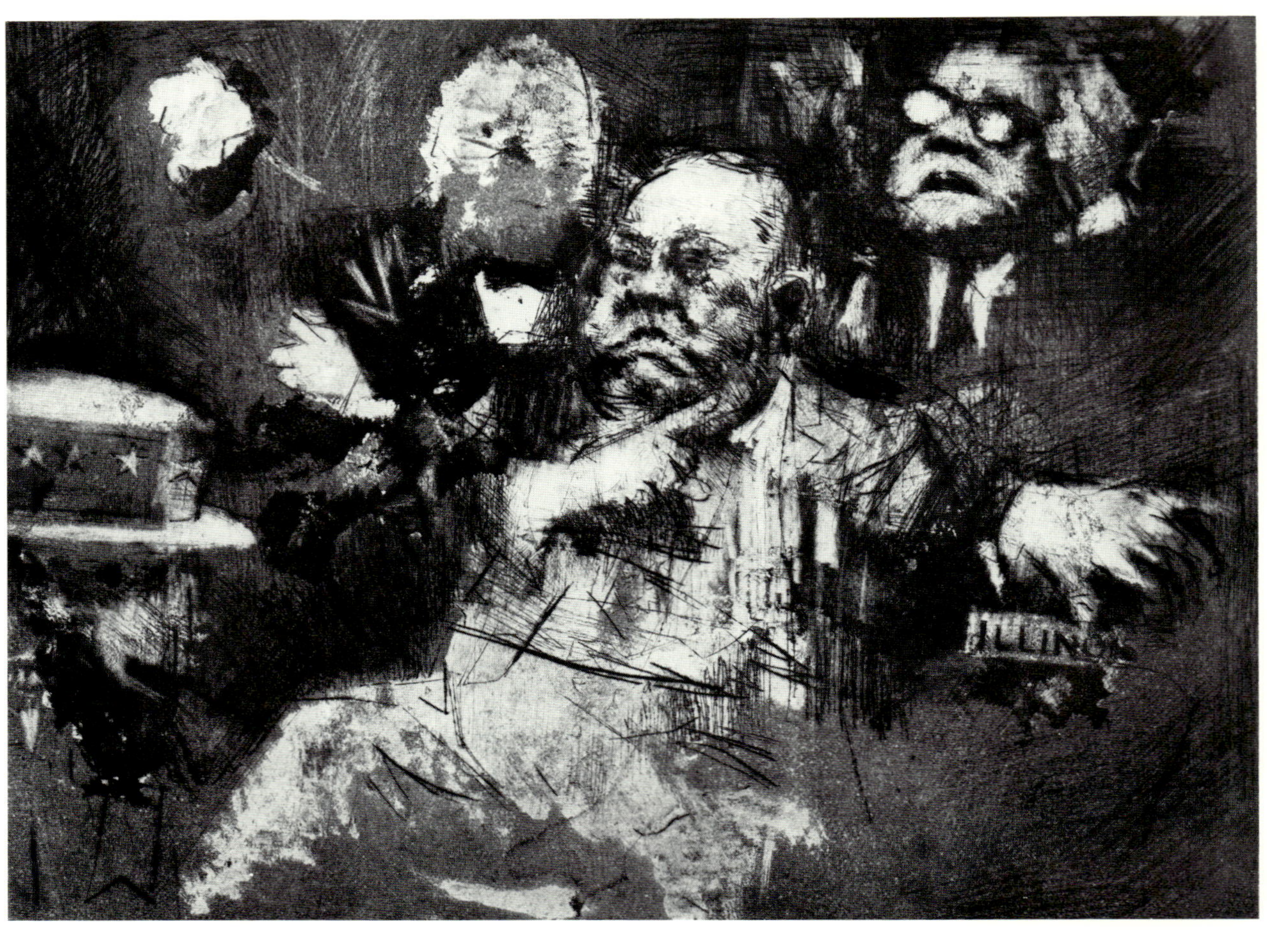

Fig. 228. *Mayor Daley's Gesture*. Jack Levine. 1969. Drypoint and aquatint. 14 7/8 × 23 1/2 in. Courtesy New Jersey State Museum Collection, Trenton, Gift of Mr. and Mrs. David Deitz, 1969.

In some ways Mayor Richard Daley of Chicago overshadowed all other figures at the 1968 Democratic convention, held in his city. In an attempt to prevent the nomination of Hubert Humphrey, thought to be aligned with Johnson's Vietnamese policies, tens of thousands of protesters demonstrated in the streets. Daley directed his 12,000 policemen and 5,000 National Guardsmen in brutal suppression of the demonstrators. Prominent politicians and delegates expressed disgust at the mayor's "police state" tactics, and Chicago became a symbol during the election. Richard Nixon so narrowly defeated Humphrey that many observers commented that Daley's action probably cost the Democrats the presidency.

170

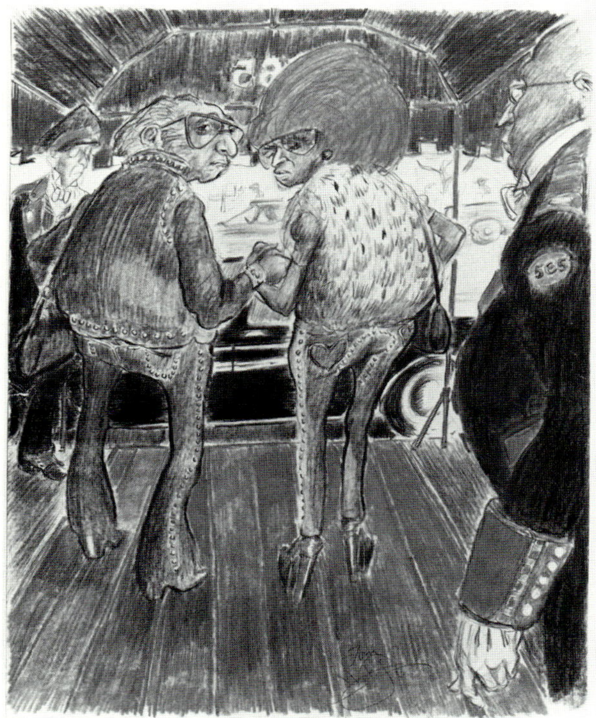

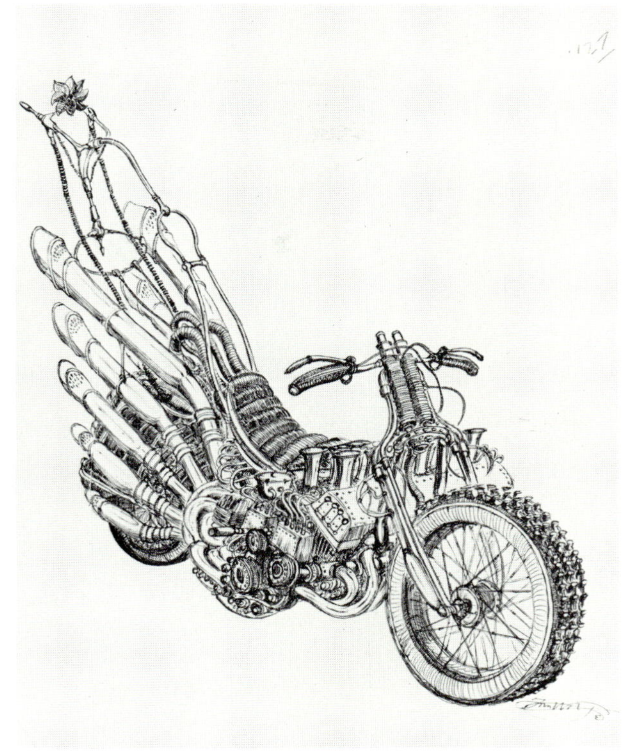

Fig. 229. *The Hilton Hotel*. Tom Wolfe. 1968 in *The Pump House Gang*. Colored crayon on paper. 14 × 11 1/8 in. Courtesy The Tunnell Gallery at Karl Mann Associates, New York City.

This comment by Wolfe points out how much our society is a youth-oriented culture. Even obviously richer and older men and women feel obligated to dress, and presumably to act, in the mode of the ''younger generation'' in order to maintain their ''Beautiful People'' status. Wolfe could also be commenting on the commercialism rampant in our society; assuming that this pair could afford designer clothes, their studded, faded denim jeans are probably *haute couture* products that cost thousands, yet poorer, younger kids around the country make the same products out of ragged, naturally faded products for a few dollars. Because some people need to have their taste certified by both the mark of a designer and youth, however, the designers are able to market such items.

Fig. 230. *Motorcycle*. Tom Wolfe. 1968 in *The Pump House Gang*. Ink on paper mounted on cardboard. 20 × 15 1/4 in. Courtesy The Tunnell Gallery at Karl Mann Associates, New York City.

The anti-hero and the counter-culture emerged as products of American life during the 1960s. Expressions of uniqueness and alternative life-styles gained currency. The motorcycle became an ideal symbol for the new non-conformists; it could be mechanically and visually altered to display personal taste, and it carried ready-made associations with radicalism. Best of all, when its owner could no longer cope, he could (in the tradition of that Great American Individual, the Cowboy) simply take to the open road and ride off into the sunset.

171

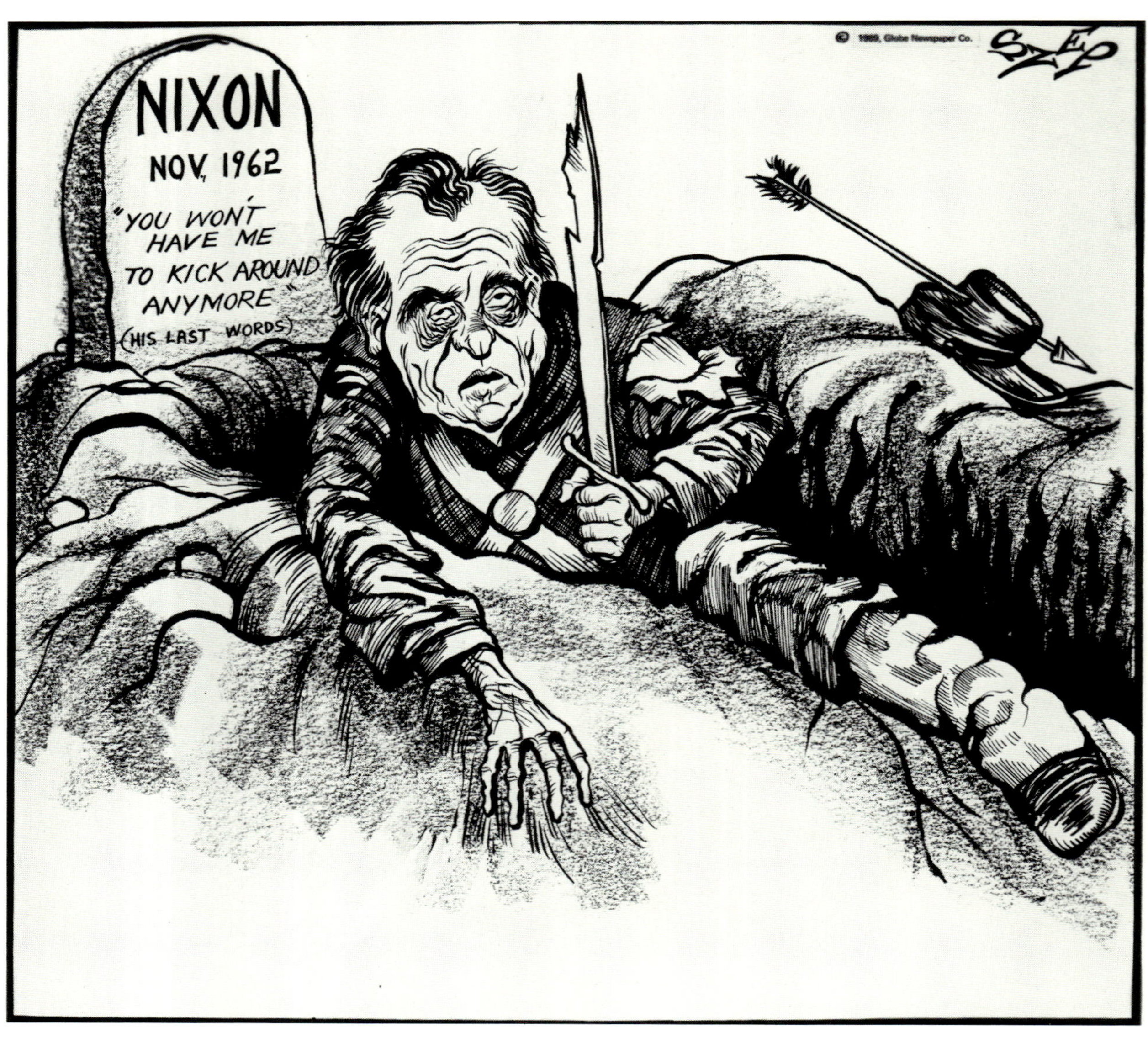

Fig. 231. *Nixon. Nov., 1962. "You won't have me to kick around anymore." (His Last Words).* Paul Szep. 1969 in the Boston *Globe.* Pen, dry brush, charcoal on paper. 14 × 15 1/2 in. Courtesy Boston Public Library, Print Department.

As Eisenhower's Vice-President, Richard Nixon enjoyed the benefits and power of high office, and was deeply hurt and humiliated when he lost the 1960 Presidential race to John Kennedy. Realizing that he had to keep politically active, he returned to his home state of California and challenged incumbent Edmund Brown for the governorship. When he lost that contest, he sank to the depths of despair and embarrassment, and his bitterness manifested itself in his famous "last press conference," in which he lashed out at the reporters for causing his defeat: "you won't have me to kick around anymore." When Nixon reappeared to run for the presidency in 1968, cartoonist Szep showed him emerging from his self-dug grave.

172

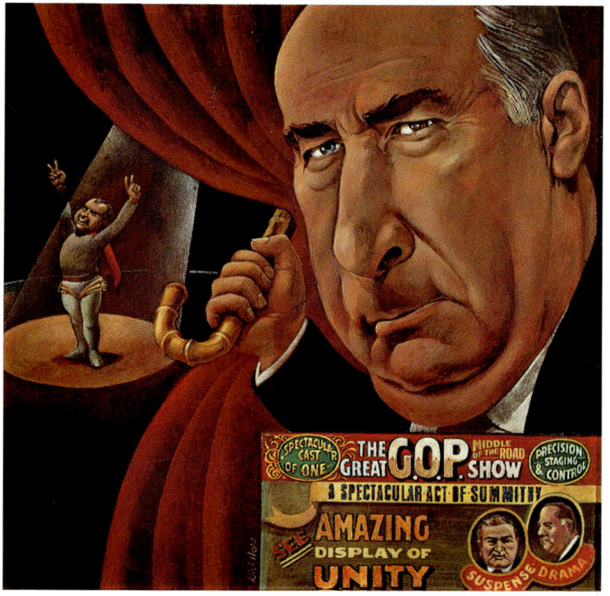

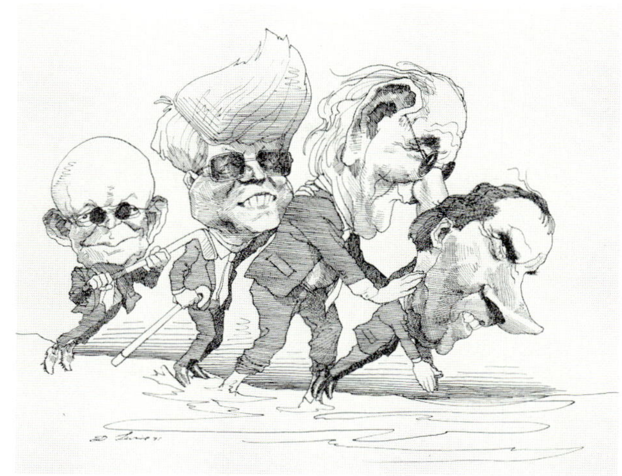

Fig. 232. *The Great G. O. P. Middle of the Road Show*. Richard Hess. 1972. Oil on canvas. 12 × 12 in. Courtesy The Swann Collection of Caricature and Cartoon.

Hoping to capitalize on public sentiment for order and leadership in a tumultuous period, the Republican Party staged an amazing show of order and unity at its 1968 convention. Potential Nixon opponents agreed to serve as chairmen, Governor Nelson Rockefeller agreed to nominate Nixon, and the emphasis was placed on getting most of the party's business handled during prime-time television hours. Nixon's ensuing campaign was managed by John Mitchell, who had a good Wall Street reputation. Recalling the television debates, which turned the 1960 election in favor of John Kennedy, Mitchell allowed Nixon to be seen in only the most favorable situations—before favorable audiences or in carefully managed television appearances. Several critics remarked that Nixon was "packaged" just like a commercial product and sold to the voters.

Fig. 233. *The Blind Leading the Blind*. David Levine. 1971. Ink on paper. 11 × 14 in. Courtesy Forum Gallery, New York City. © by NYREV, Inc., 1971.

As the true nature of the conflict in Vietnam became known, and as more Americans poured into that small Southeast Asian country, many Americans began looking for answers to such perplexing questions as how and why America got involved in the beginning. The search led to an equivocal commitment made by President Eisenhower before he left office. The commitment was increased by President Kennedy and enlarged into a major conflict by President Johnson. President Nixon finally brought most of the American troops home, but not until he had widened the target of bombings to include neutral Cambodia. Thus Levine pictures four American Presidents as being blind on the same issue.

173

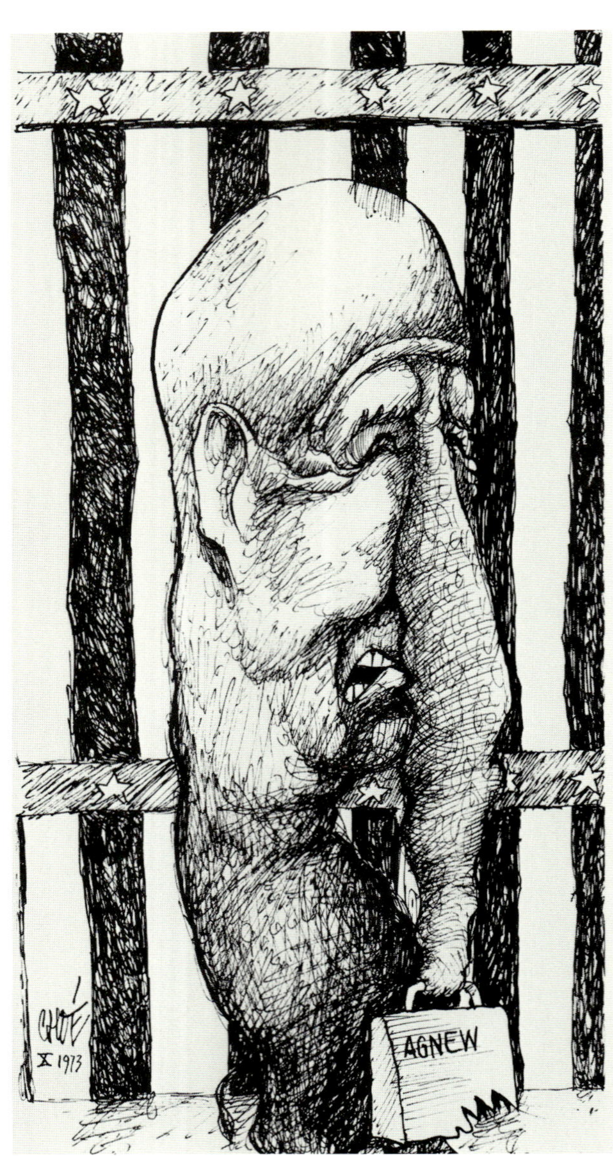

Fig. 234. [Spiro Agnew]. Nguyen Hai Chi ("Choé"). 1973. Ink on paper. 11 1/4 × 5 5/8 in. Courtesy The Swann Collection of Caricature and Cartoon.

Vice-President Spiro Agnew was the leading spokesman in the Nixon administration in favor of "law and order." Disgusted with Nixon's stalling tactics in the Watergate case, most Americans greeted Agnew's full-face confrontation of the charges brought against him—bribery, income tax evasion, and others—with relief, thinking that that was the way an innocent man should react. Agnew then surprised them when, overwhelmed by the evidence produced by the Justice Department pertaining to corruption in his governorship of Maryland as well as during his Vice-Presidency (he apparently received at least $50,000 illegally from one firm alone in a six year period), he pleaded *nolo contendere* to a single charge of income tax evasion and resigned his office. He was fined $10,000, but never served a jail term, as indicated by the South Vietnamese cartoonist "Choé," as his three year sentence was suspended. He had, however, removed himself from the line of Presidential succession, an important fact to Attorney General Elliot Richardson, who oversaw the prosecution of the case.

174

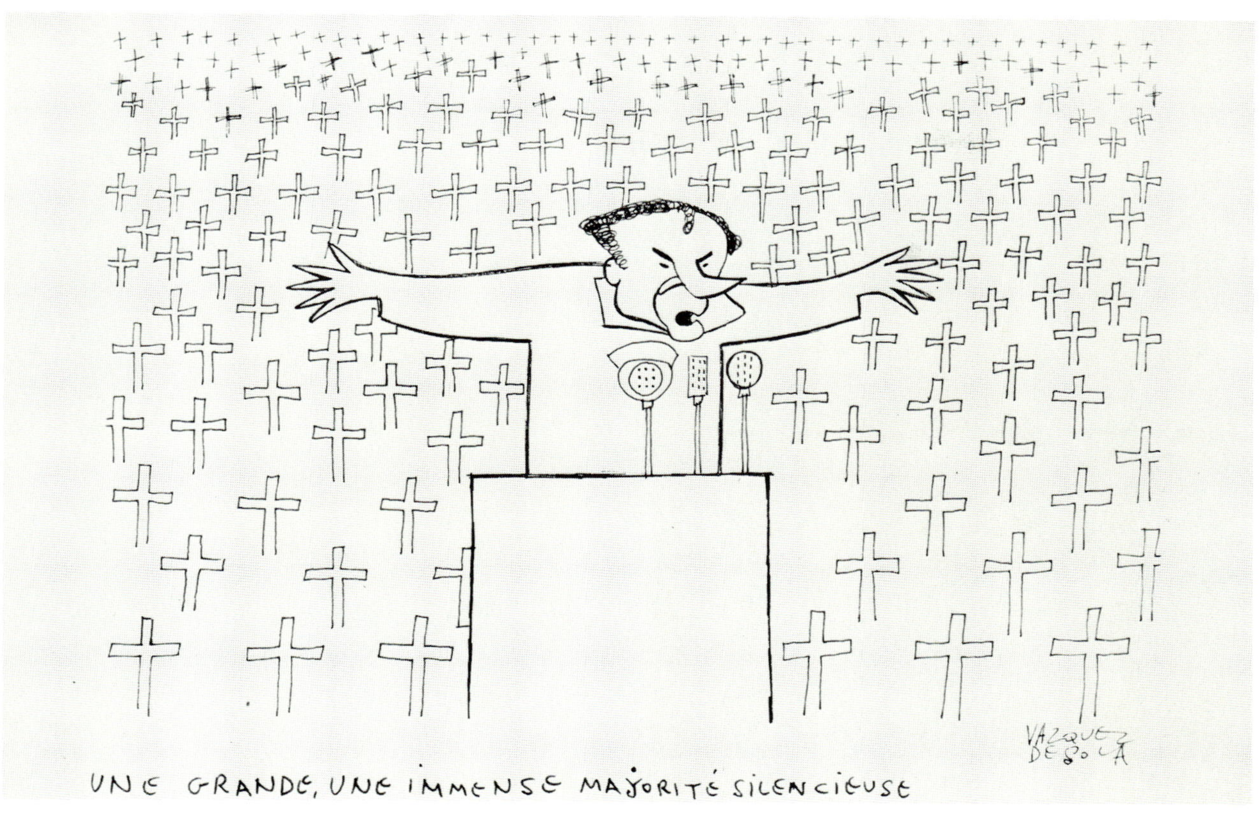

Fig. 235. *Une Grande, Une Immense Mayorité Silencieuse*. Vázquez de Sola. 1970s. Ink on paper. 6 1/4 × 8 5/8 in. Courtesy The Swann Collection of Caricature and Cartoon.

Nixon liked to claim early in his presidency that he had the support of America's "silent majority," which he interpreted to mean the mass of middle-America as opposed to the vocal leftists who marched and staged demonstrations. Vázquez de Sola, an Argentine artist, has interpreted the phrase a bit differently, indicating the thousands of Americans who had died, presumably in Vietnam, since Nixon had taken office. "A large, a huge silent majority," Nixon proclaims to his listeners.

175

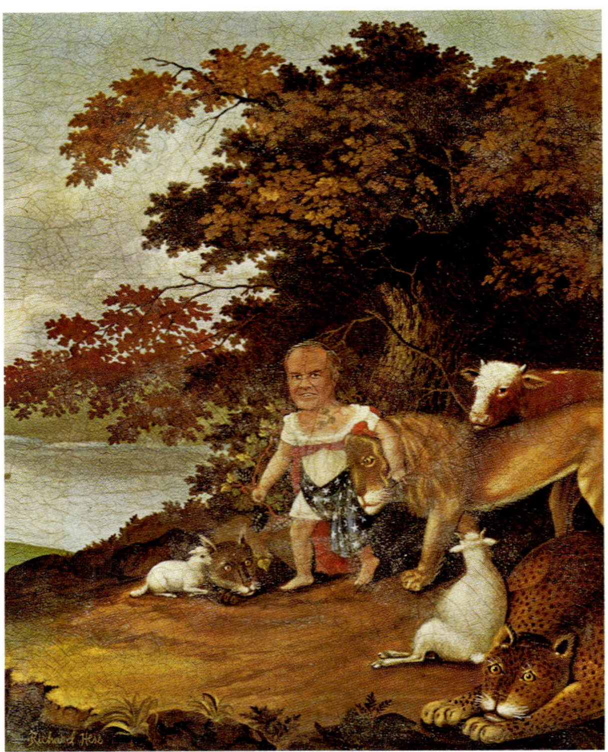

Fig. 236. *The Peaceable Kingdom*. Richard Hess. 1972. Oil on canvas. 15 × 11 in. Courtesy The Swann Collection of Caricature and Cartoon.

The 1972 Presidential election saw a different kind of campaign by Senator George McGovern, the minister's son from South Dakota. Calling for tax reform, an end to corporate privilege, for breaking up monopolies, for a quick end to the Vietnam war, McGovern gathered liberals and young people around himself for an almost evangelical campaign. Parodied here as an innocent child in the style of one of Early American painter Edward Hicks' allegorical renderings of *The Peaceable Kingdom*, McGovern was often accused of naïveté and unrealistic idealism because of his pacifistic attitude toward the war and his proposed social and economic reforms. Nixon won easy reelection.

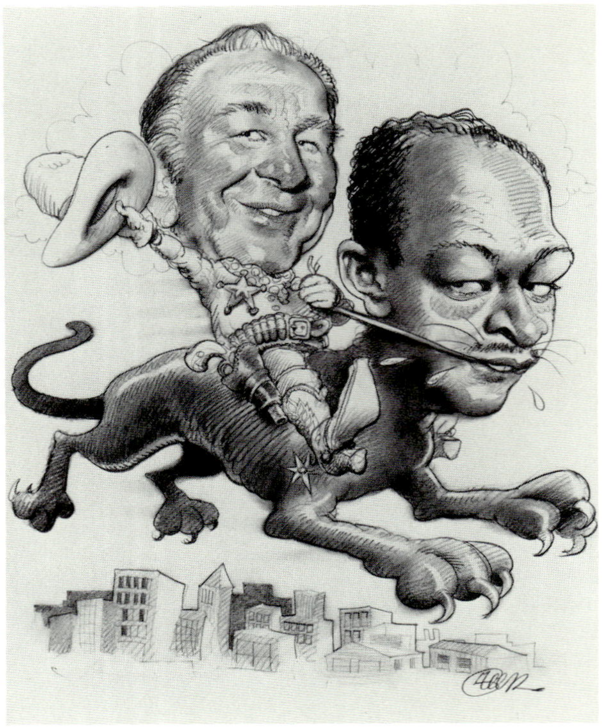

Fig. 237. [Sam Yorty and Tom Bradley.] Peter Green. 1972. Crayon on paper. 23 9/16 × 18 11/16 in. Courtesy The Swann Collection of Caricature and Cartoon.

In 1969 city councilmember and former policeman Thomas Bradley decided to challenge incumbent Sam Yorty in the Los Angeles mayoral race. In a fourteen-candidate primary Bradley emerged with forty-two percent of the vote from an electorate only seventeen percent Negro, but Yorty, with twenty-six percent, qualified for the run-off. After waging a particularly ugly contest, Yorty won, but in a 1973 rematch, Bradley became Los Angeles' first black mayor.

176

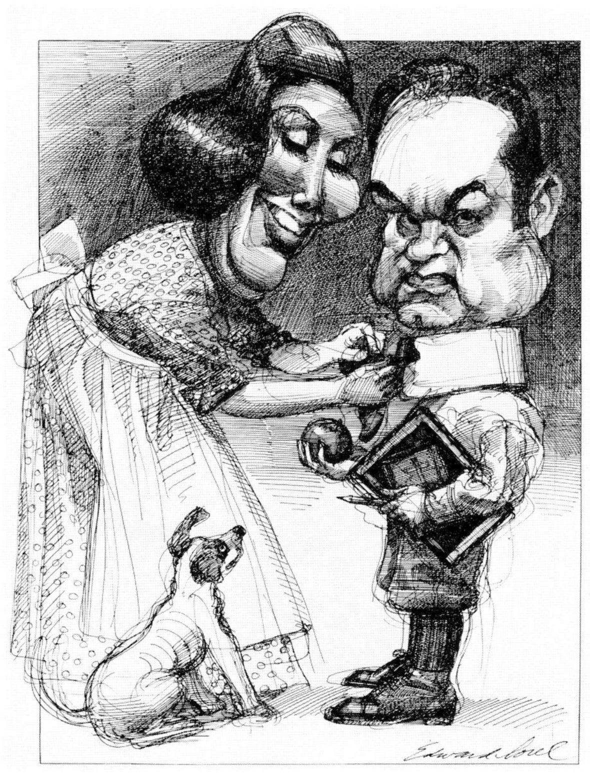

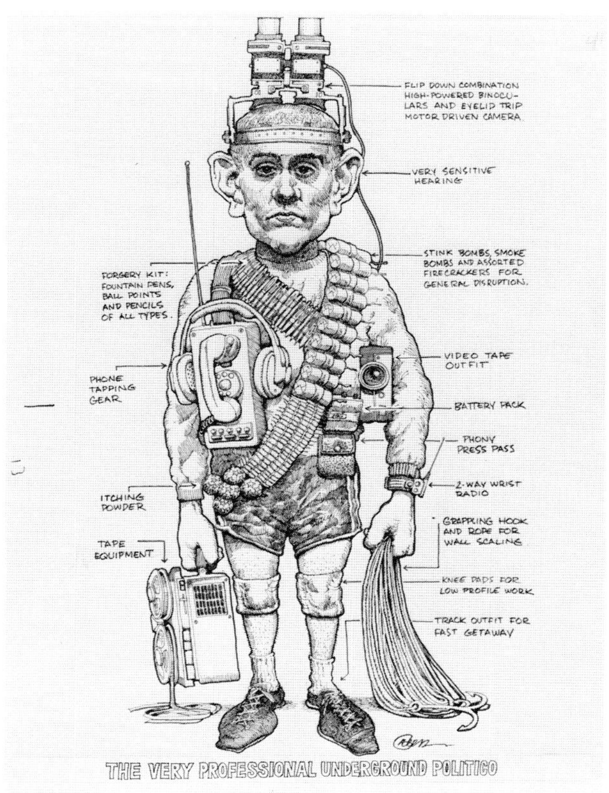

Fig. 238. *Caricature of George and Cornelia Wallace*. Edward Sorel. 1973. Ink on paper. 25 × 19 in. Courtesy The Swann Collection of Caricature and Cartoon.

"I thank God for George Wallace of Alabama," said former Mississippi Governor Ross Barnett as he introduced Wallace to a meeting. "He is a true son of the South." Despite his identification with the South and his strong Southern accent, Wallace managed to become a national candidate by appealing to racism and issues that affected the common man: law and order, tax reform, and the spreading bureaucracy. Wallace almost threw the presidential election of 1968 into the House of Representatives. In 1972 he appeared to be an even better candidate, moving more gracefully before crowds with his beautiful new wife, Cornelia. But an intended-assassin forced him from the race with an almost-fatal wound while he was speaking in Baltimore. Now paralyzed from the waist down, Wallace is still a strong political force in the nation.

Fig. 239. *The Very Professional Underground Politico*. Peter Green. 1973. Ink and gouache on paper. 23 7/16 × 8 13/16 in. Courtesy The Swann Collection of Caricature and Cartoon.

With exposure of the Watergate burglary, public attention was focused on the intelligence-gathering activities of political parties, businesses, and finally of governments. Peter Green here spoofs the spy activities of politicians such as the "White House plumbers," who broke into several private offices and files in search of politically damaging evidence that Nixon could use to harm his political enemies.

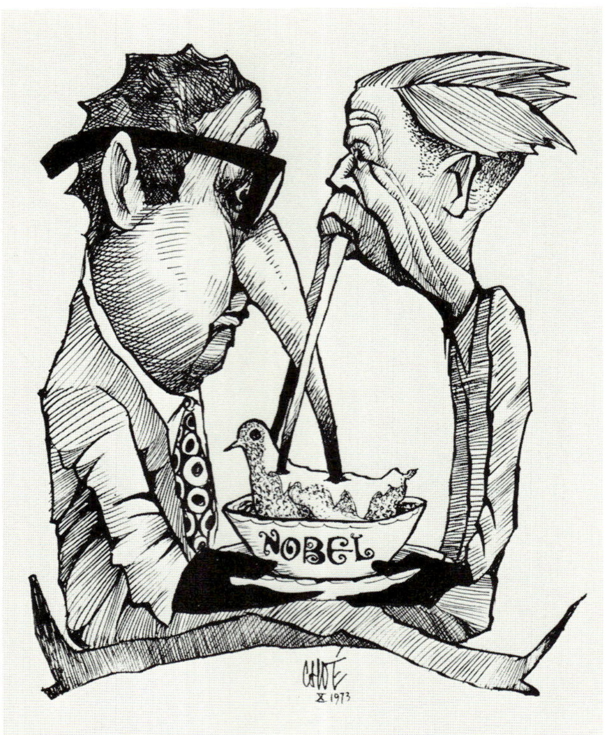

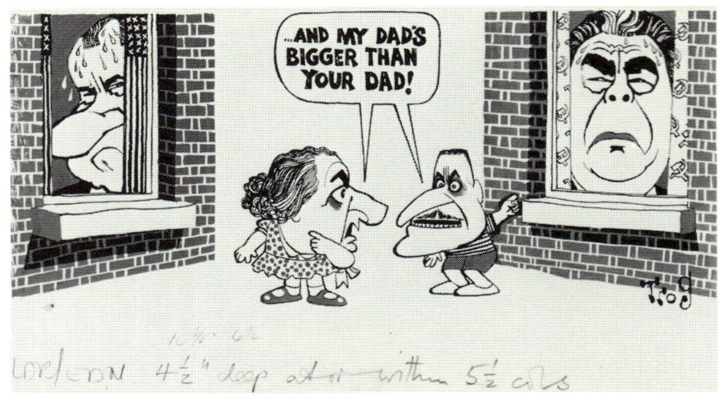

Fig. 240. [Kissinger and Le Duc Tho.] Nguyen Hai Chi ("Choé.") 1973. Ink on paper. 8 3/8 × 7 5/8 in. Courtesy The Swann Collection of Caricature and Cartoon.

Americans began withdrawing from South Vietnam after Secretary of State Henry Kissinger and North Vietnamese Chief Negotiator Le Duc Tho began discussions in 1972. But the fighting did not stop. Both sides violated the cease-fire, and the Communists eventually moved in for a final victory with the fall of Saigon in 1975. The award of the 1973 Nobel Peace Prize to Kissinger and Tho had aroused an unprecedented storm of protest. Even the Nobel committee, which officially awards its prizes by unanimous consent, split, with three out of the five members voting for Kissinger and Tho. "Choé" captures that sentiment here, showing Kissinger and Tho feeding uncomfortably off the dove of peace.

Fig. 241. *My Dad's Bigger Than Your Dad*. Wally Fawkes ("Trog"). Sept. 4, 1970, in the London *Daily Mail*. Ink, gray tempera, with opaque white on paper. 6 5/8 × 15 1/2 in. Courtesy Mr. and Mrs. Draper Hill, Memphis, Tenn.

In October, 1956 Israel invaded Egypt's Sinai Peninsula to regain access to the Suez Canal, beginning a series of hostilities which erupted into war on June 5, 1967. Thereafter Egypt's President Gamal Abdel Nasser acquired a substantially increased arsenal of Soviet armaments, military expertise and economic aid. Golda Meir, Israel's premier, received a comparable supply from the United States, and the stage was set for a major power confrontation in the Mid-East.

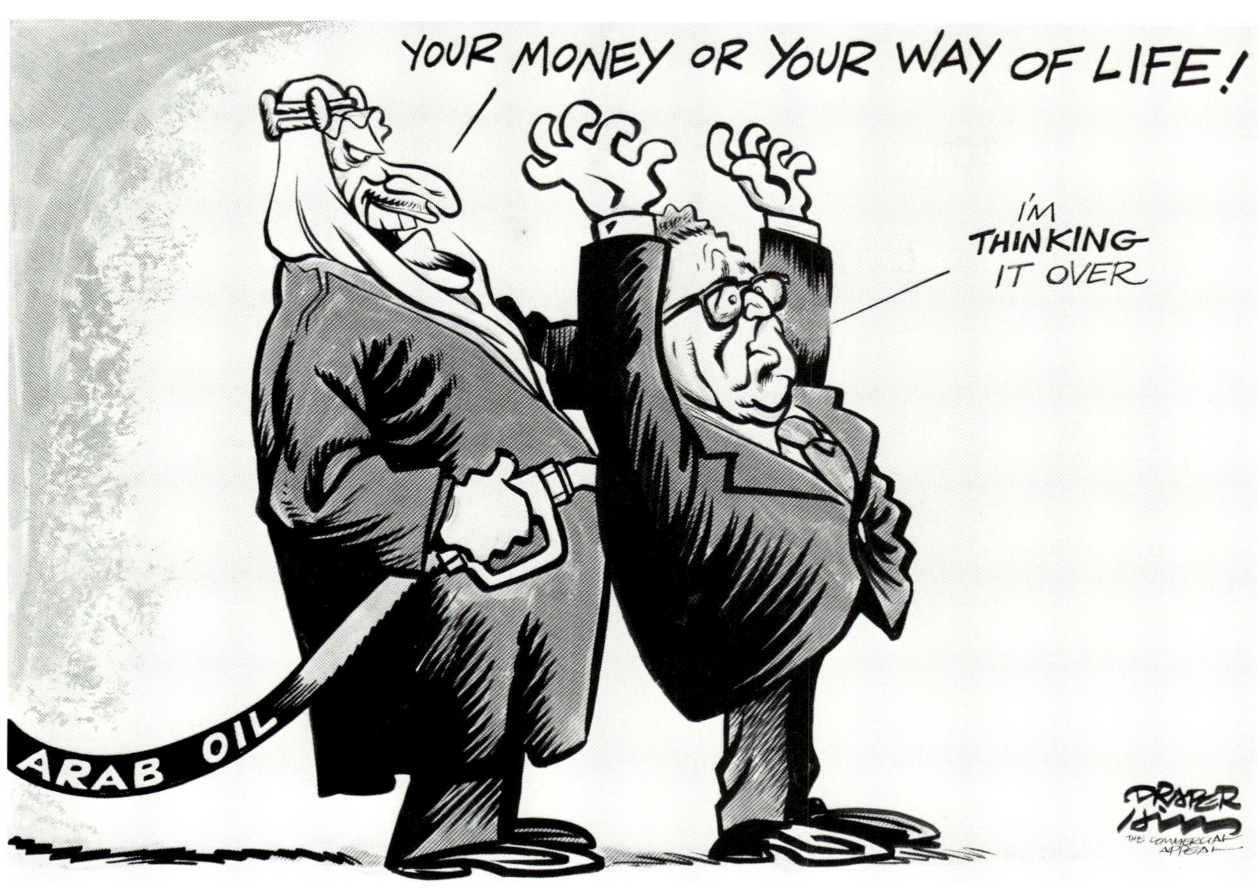

Fig. 242. *"Your Money or Your Way of Life."* Draper Hill. Jan. 5, 1975, in the Memphis *Commercial Appeal*. Brush, pen and ink on toneboard. 15 5/8 × 11 3/16 in. Courtesy Draper Hill, Memphis, Tenn. © *The Commercial Appeal*, Memphis.

Draper Hill has captured the reluctance with which the American public has faced the oil crisis, as Henry Kissinger thinks it over, Jack Benny fashion, before announcing his decision.

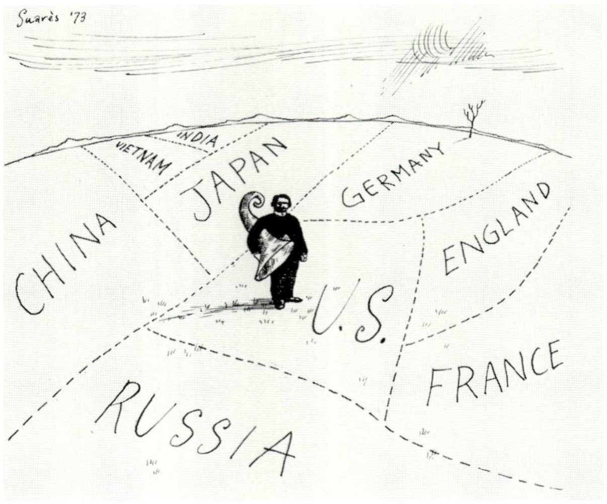

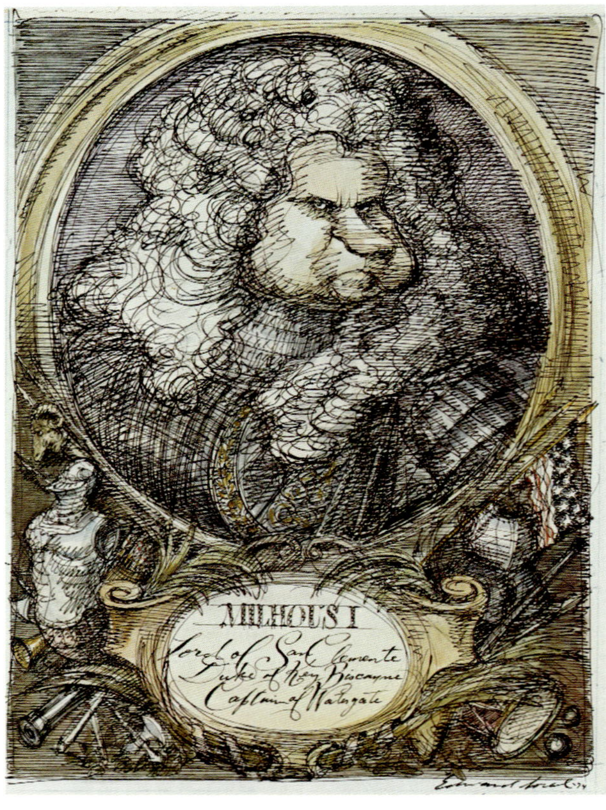

Fig. 243. *Horn of Plenty*. Jean-Claude Suarès. April 14, 1973, in the New York *Times*. Ink on paper. 7 1/2 × 8 in. Courtesy The Swann Collection of Caricature and Cartoon.

This cartoon of a nineteenth century gentleman standing on an international patchwork map accompanied a group of letters to the editor of the New York *Times* concerning capitalism. Some debated that U. S. capitalism had fed the world, others that it had bled it. Suarès cartoon is an equivocal statement taking neither side. The cornucopia could be empty because it has nothing to offer the world or because it has already poured forth its contents to it.

Fig. 244. *Milhous I*. Edward Sorel. 1974. Ink, watercolor, paste-up on paper. 18 1/2 × 14 in. Courtesy The Swann Collection of Caricature and Cartoon.

When President Nixon first took office, reporters began to notice several touches which they compared to the trappings of monarchy: the change in the uniform of the White House guards, the atmosphere in the White House, the aloofness surrounding the President and his aides. When Nixon reacted in the Watergate affair as if he were above the fray, Edward Sorel was inspired to draw him as "Milhous I," a comparison to the autocrat Louis XIV of France and an eloquent comment on a situation that reporters were having difficulty explaining to their listeners and readers without sounding personally offended.

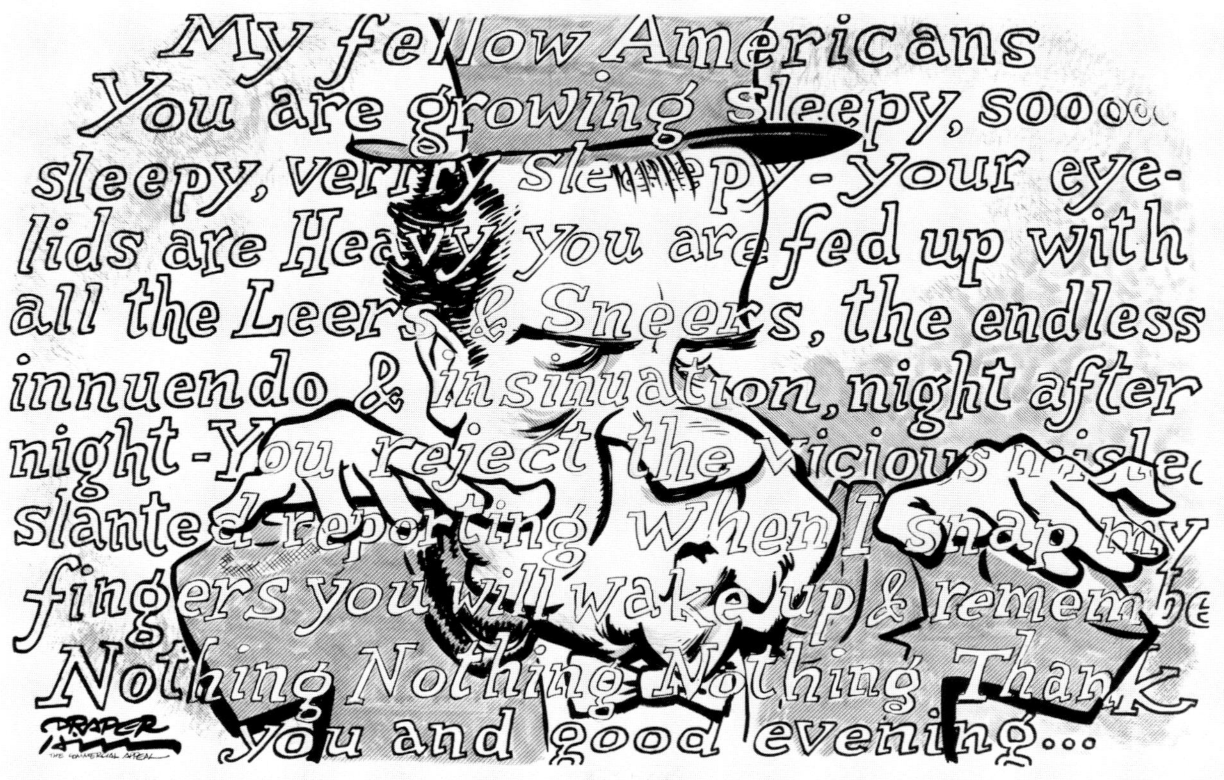

Fig. 245. *Mandate the Magician*. Draper Hill. Jan. 16, 1974. Brush, pen and ink on chemical toneboard. 11 × 16 1/16 in. Courtesy Draper Hill, Memphis, Tenn. © *The Commercial Appeal*, Memphis.

At several points during the Watergate affair, President Nixon went on national television to "clear the air." Each time he seemed to make new revelations while insisting that the Water- gate scandal had been solved, that no other administration of- ficials were involved, and that he had not known about it. Draper Hill has combined this television image of Nixon with the "mandate" from the people that he continually talked of to produce "Mandate the Magician," a caption inspired by the well-known *Mandrake the Magician* comic strip.

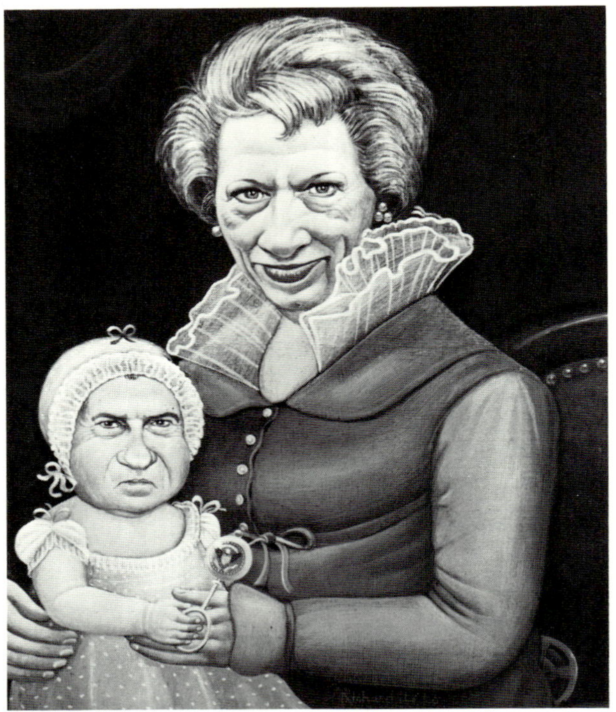

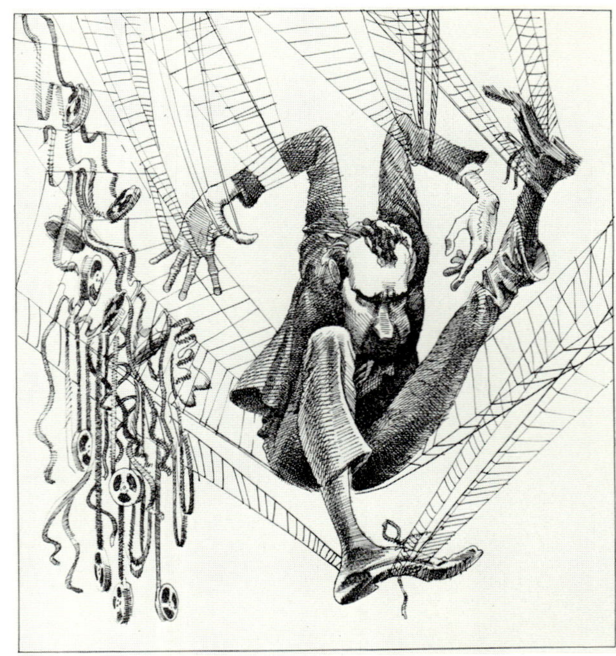

Fig. 247. *Nixon in a Tape Web*. Robert Pryor. 1974. Ink on paper. 12 × 11 in. Courtesy The Swann Collection of Caricature and Cartoon.

Fig. 246. *Rose Mary's Baby*. Richard Hess. 1974. Acrylic on board. 14 × 12 in. Courtesy Richard Hess, New York City.

This picture, which has already become a political classic, suggests that Nixon's personal secretary and loyal staff member Rose Mary Woods, who gave a very suspect explanation of how she accidentally erased a crucial and probably incriminating passage from one of the Watergate tapes that the investigating Grand Jury had subpoenaed, is in fact taking care of Nixon as would the mother of a bungling child. The title is adapted from the film *Rosemary's Baby*.

Nixon fought hard to keep the White House tape recordings from being turned over to the Watergate Grand Jury, but once the Supreme Court had rejected his contention that the tapes could be kept secret because of "national security" and executive privilege, he yielded first the White House Transcripts (type-written transcripts of the recordings), then the tapes themselves. The House Judiciary Committee investigating impeachment then listened to the tapes and was able to understand some damaging passages that the White House Transcripts had listed as inaudible, etc. Thus Nixon really was caught in a web of tape, as Robert Pryor illustrates here.

182

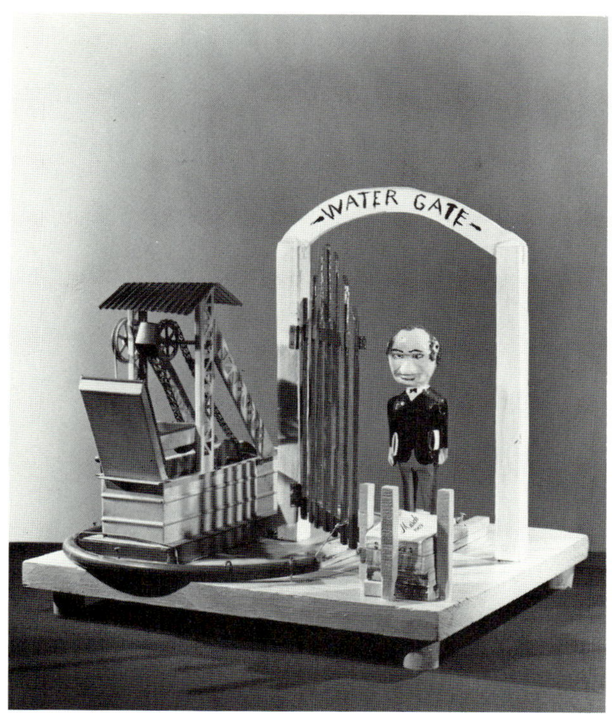

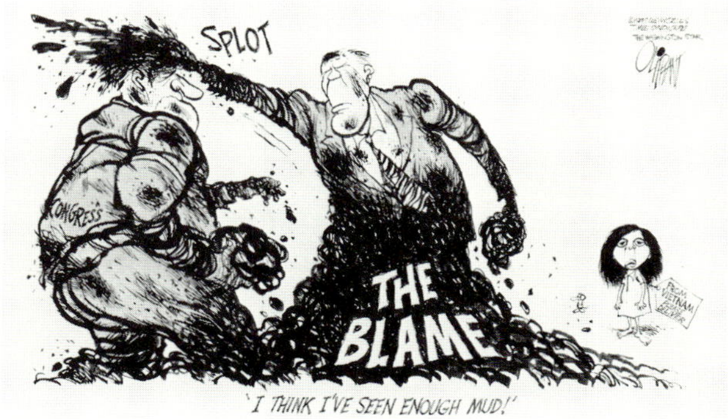

Fig. 248. [Watergate sculpture.] Miles B. Carpenter. 1974. Wood, metal and paper. 13 in. high. Courtesy Bert Hemphill, New York City.

Fig. 249. *I think I've seen enough mud.* Pat Oliphant. 1975. Ink on paper. 11 5/8 × 17 5/8 in. Courtesy Pat Oliphant, Washington *Star*, Los Angeles *Times* Syndicate.

With the pervasiveness of the ''Watergate affair,'' the term ''Watergate'' came into the American dialect as an expression meaning ''dirty tricks.'' Its widespread acceptance is illustrated in the ease with which the entire affair was connected with other bits of American folklore: Every Milhous [millhouse] has a watergate, went one joke. The sculptor has worked other bits of the Nixon scandal into this carving: the income tax evasion, the questionable funding for his San Clemente house.

Here cartoonist Oliphant comments on President Ford's criticism of Congress for ''mudslinging.'' Originally cautious of criticizing the Congress because of his connections and sympathies there, Ford rapidly concluded that Congress was not cooperating with his administration as best it could.

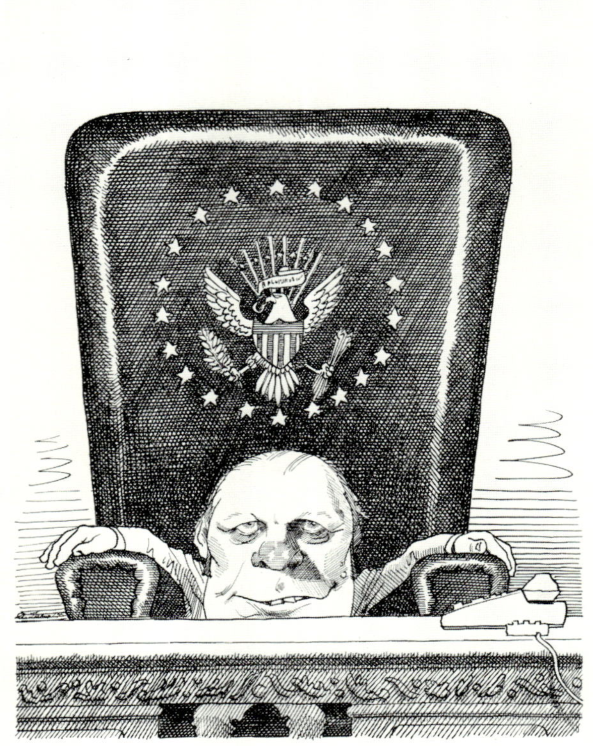

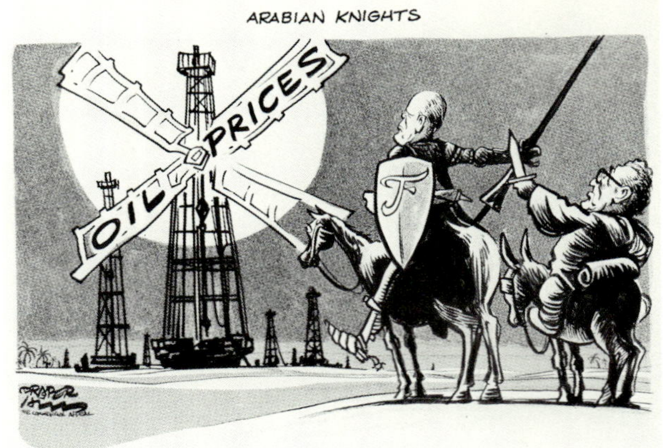

Fig. 250. *Gerald Ford*. David Levine. 1974. Ink on paper. 14 × 11 in. Courtesy Forum Gallery, New York City. © by NYREV, Inc., 1974.

David Levine characterized Gerald Ford as the man who had never aspired to an office higher than the Speaker of the House and the man who had seriously thought of retiring after completing over two decades as congressman. Ford was selected by Nixon to replace Spiro Agnew and elevated to the presidency when Nixon resigned. Levine is suggesting that the presidency (represented by the chair) is probably too big an office for Ford, and Ford himself admitted that the job was more difficult than he had anticipated.

Fig. 251. *Arabian Knights*. Draper Hill. Sept. 29, 1974, in Memphis *Commercial Appeal*. Brush, pen and ink on chemical toneboard. 12 7/16 × 17 9/16 in. Courtesy Draper Hill, Memphis, Tenn. © *The Commercial Appeal*, Memphis.

When the Arab nations increased the price for crude oil, the Western nations were thrown into an economic crisis, complicated by the oil boycott that the Arabs then imposed. Secretary of State Kissinger darkly hinted that in bygone years such a monopolistic action would have been adequate to start a war. Here Draper Hill suggests that Ford and Kissinger are tilting windmills in the tradition of Don Quixote and Sancho Panza in battling the increasing prices.

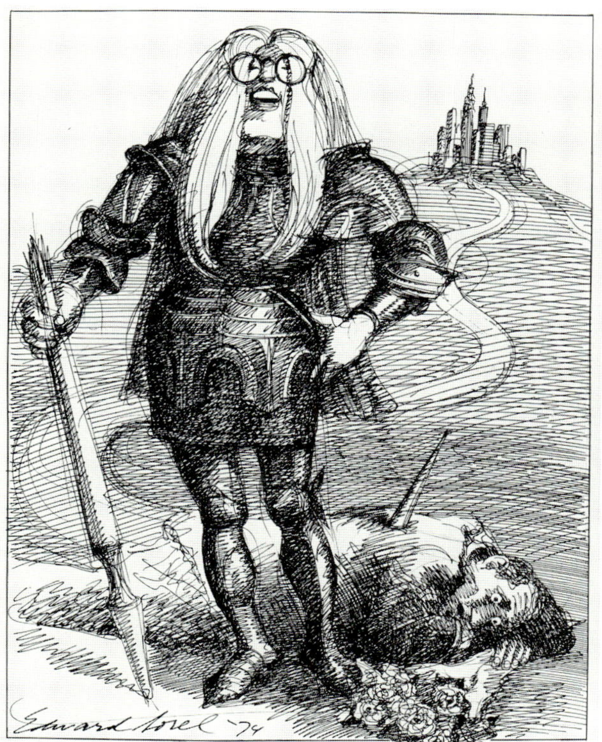

Fig. 252. *Sic Transit Gloria*. Edward Sorel. 1974. Ink on paper. 17 7/8 × 13 1/8 in. Courtesy Edward Sorel.

Woman's liberation leader and feminist writer Gloria Steinem helped raise the consciousness of women in all walks of life to some of the discrimination experienced by women as a class. *Life* magazine revealed, for example, that a woman must have a college degree to earn as much as a man with an eighth grade education. Some of the more militant feminists, like Ti-Grace Atkinson, were anti-men, but Steinem, contrary to the viewpoint in this Sorel caricature, was not among them. She much more opposed unequal pay for equal work and other rational complaints popularized because of the woman's movement.

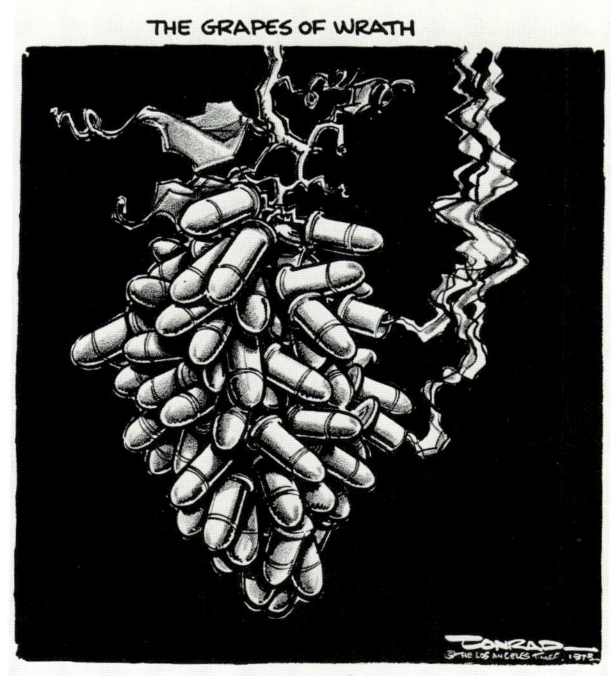

Fig. 253. *Grapes of Wrath*. Paul Conrad. 1974 in the Los Angeles *Times*. Ink wash on paper. 13 1/2 × 11 in. Courtesy The Swann Collection of Caricature and Cartoon.

Employing a title historically connected with migrant labor en route to California during the Dust Bowl years of the 1930s, Paul Conrad has adapted the analogy to the bitter confrontation between Mexican-American laborers and farmers and ranchers today in California.

185

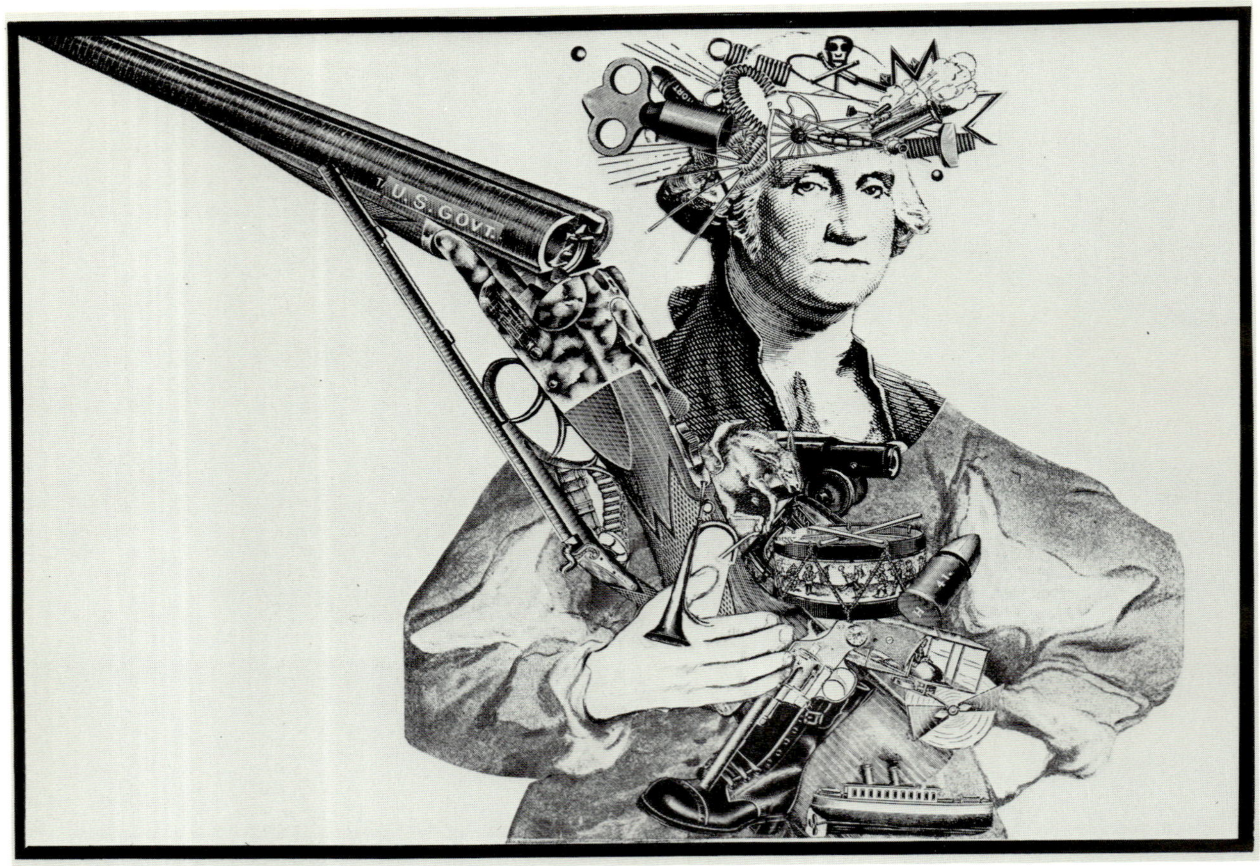

Fig. 254. *"When Johnny Comes Marching Home."* Anita Seigel. 1974 in the New York *Times*. Ink and collage on paper. 8 1/4 × 11 in. Courtesy The Swann Collection of Caricature and Cartoon.

This cartoon uses the picture of Washington from the dollar bill surrounded with a collage of weapons, military paraphernalia, death images, gears and springs, and the title of a popular Civil War marching song to comment on the militaristic character of American political policies in the past and the present.

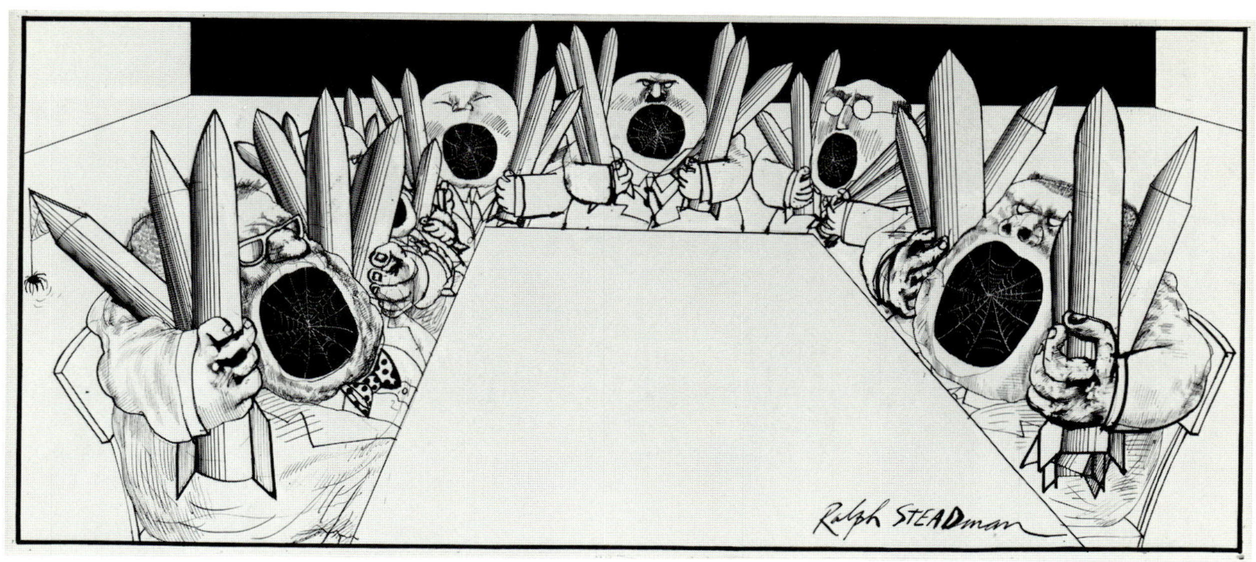

Fig. 255. *Disarmament Talks*. Ralph Steadman. 1971 in the New York *Times*. Pen and ink on paper. Approx. 12 × 18 in. Courtesy Ralph Steadman.

When both the United States and the Soviet Union developed nuclear weapons, each possessed the capacity to destroy the world. With that realization, both nations began a series of dis-armament talks aimed at reducing the tensions and the dangers of the arms race. The SALT (Strategic Arms Limitations Talks) Talks began in 1963 and offered hope that both nations would add to their initial nuclear test ban agreements, but Ralph Steadman sees such conference participants as ever willing to negotiate but refusing to relinquish any power.

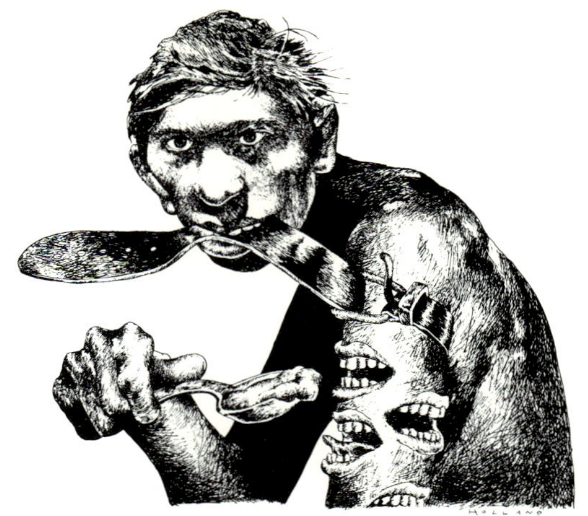

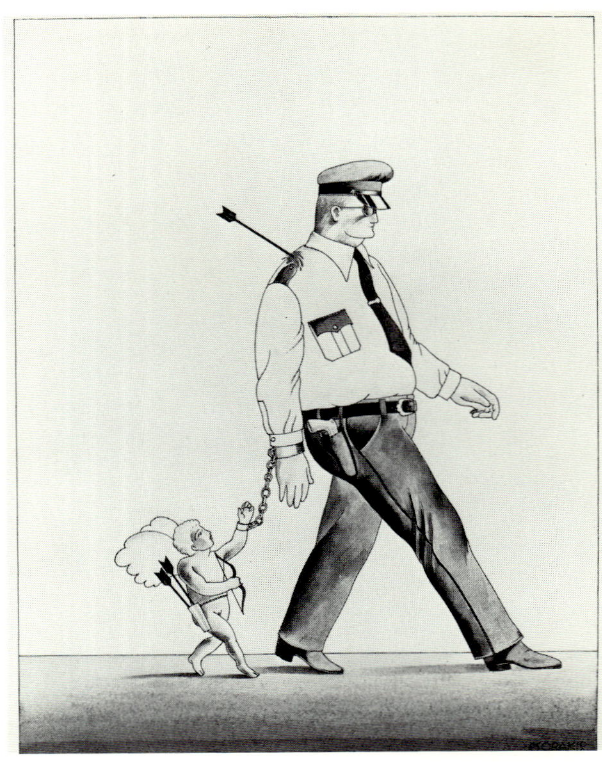

Fig. 256. *The Junkie*. Brad Holland. 1970s. Ink on paper. 14 1/4 × 16 1/2 in. Courtesy Brad Holland, New York City.

Here Brad Holland depicts the plight of the junkie, the heroin addict who is the slave of a drug that he must inject into his veins in ever increasing amounts in order to prevent the violent physical and psychological withdrawal. The size of the drug problem in New York City can be seen in the fact that more than 32,000 addicts were put on the relief rolls as "disabled" to keep them from robbing and stealing to support their habit. Law enforcement officers estimate that heroin addiction is the major cause of increased crime in the cities, where addicts concentrate because of the availability of the drug. This drawing is a caricature of one of the artist's friends, who died of an overdose a few days after the picture was finished.

Fig. 257. *Cupid and the Cop*. Paul Psorakis. 1970s. Watercolor on paper. 14 1/2 × 11 1/2 in. Courtesy The Swann Collection of Caricature and Cartoon.

Perhaps the antagonism between authority and the youth culture of the sixties and seventies was most dramatically illustrated by events at the 1968 Democratic convention in Chicago, when Yippie leader Jerry Rubin exhorted thousands of youth to wreak havoc on the city, aiming especially at the Chicago police, in the name of establishing a new culture based on "freedom." Consequently the young people engaged in numerous confrontations leading to the further polarization of the Yippies and the police. Psorakis' cartoon suggests that the rift was so great that the police would have arrested the mythological love-god Cupid for shooting one of his love-darts.

188

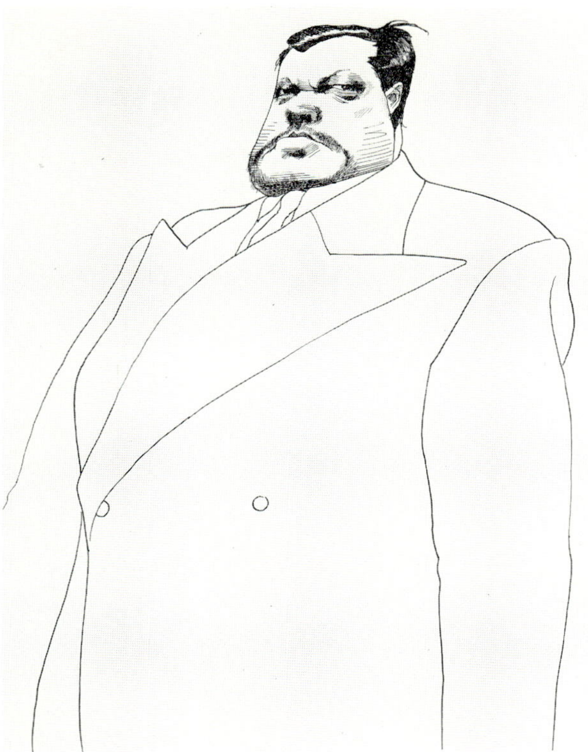

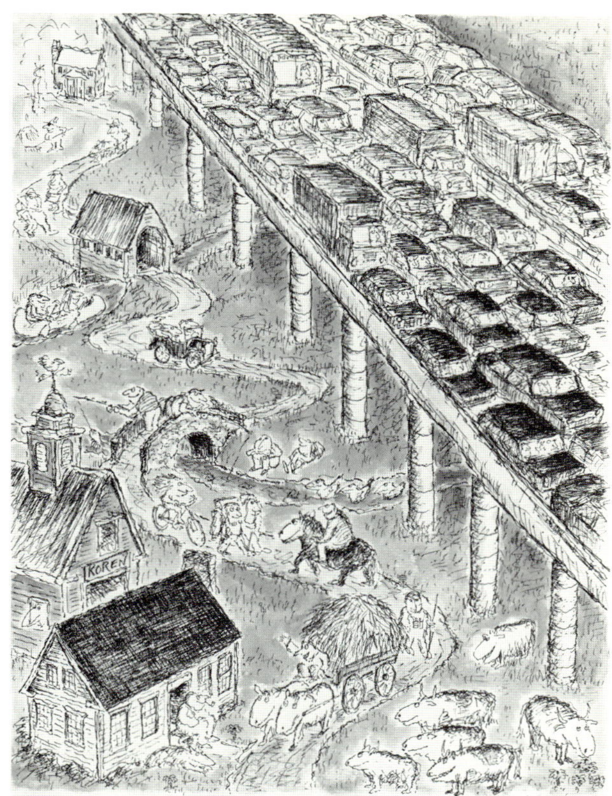

Fig. 258. *Orson Welles*. David Levine. 1970s. Ink on paper. 14 × 11 in. Courtesy Forum Gallery, New York City. © by NYREV, Inc.

As David Levine's cartoon implies, Orson Welles is a giant of American dramatic arts. He first gained national attention in 1938 through his realistic radio adaptation of H. G. Wells' *War of the Worlds*, which many people accepted in horror as the report of a Martian invasion of Earth. He has continued to stun the American public with his brilliant theatrical productions and films such as *Citizen Kane, MacBeth* and *Compulsion*. These Hollywood films are not just movies, they are art. His talent, like his physique, is enormous as an actor, director, writer and producer. And he functions in any of these roles separately or in various combinations.

Fig. 259. *Pollution*. Edward B. Koren. 1971. Watercolor on paper. 26 7/8 × 21 3/8 in. Courtesy The Swann Collection of Caricature and Cartoon.

One of the major domestic issues of the 1970s is air pollution, primarily by factories and automobiles. The air over Hammond, East Chicago, and Gary, Indiana, was so polluted with sulphur-dioxide in 1970—ten times the legal limit—that when it rained the mixture resulted in something akin to sulphuric acid that turned lawns brown, pitted leaves with ulerous holes, and de-feathered birds. Several ecologists have predicted that freak weather combined with air pollution will begin causing waves of mass deaths in urban areas.

189

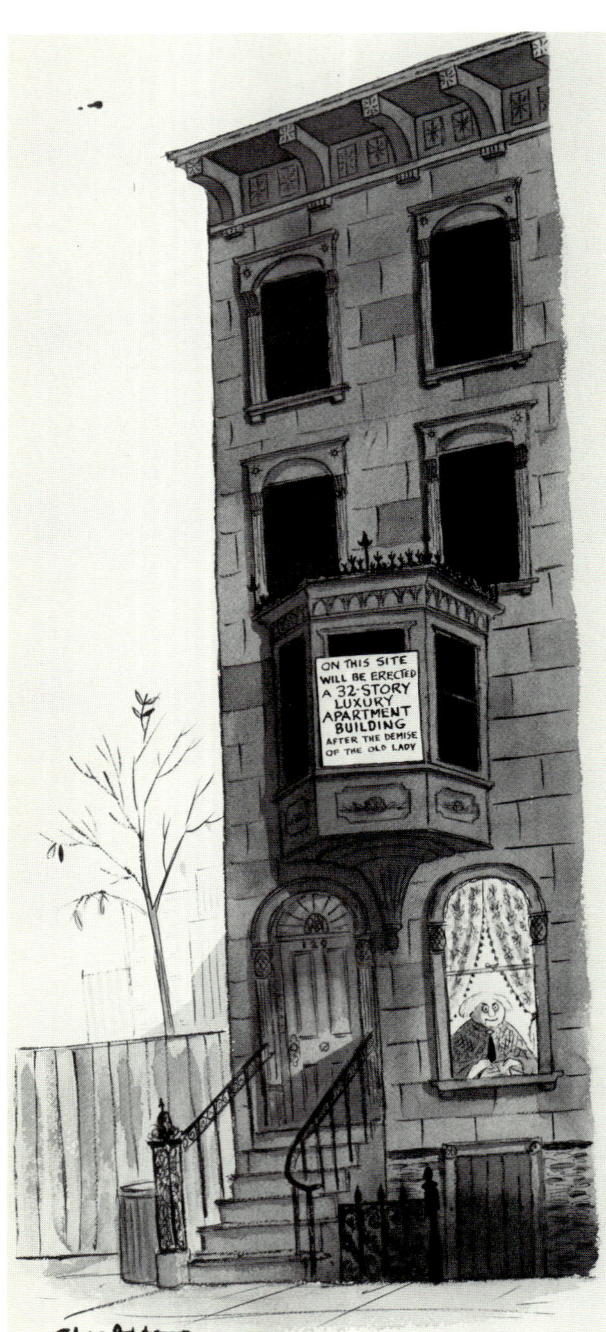

Fig. 260. *"On This Site Will Be Erected a 32-Story Luxury Apartment Building After the Demise of the Old Lady."* Charles Addams. 1970s, in *The New Yorker*. Ink, ink wash, and collage on paper. 27 3/4 × 19 3/4 in. (sight). Courtesy Collection of Mrs. Edgar Tobin.

By 1970 eighty-five percent of the American population lived in urban centers. The consequent need for business and housing space rose dramatically as real estate agents and developers speculated on land acquisition. The skyscraper, the most efficient means of utilizing limited space, became the symbol of the twentieth century, and cities became the scene of constant construction, demolition, and reconstruction. Critics—perhaps Addams' mischievous little old lady among them—complained that "engineering mentality" had taken over, bulldozing historic and aesthetic considerations in its path of "progress."

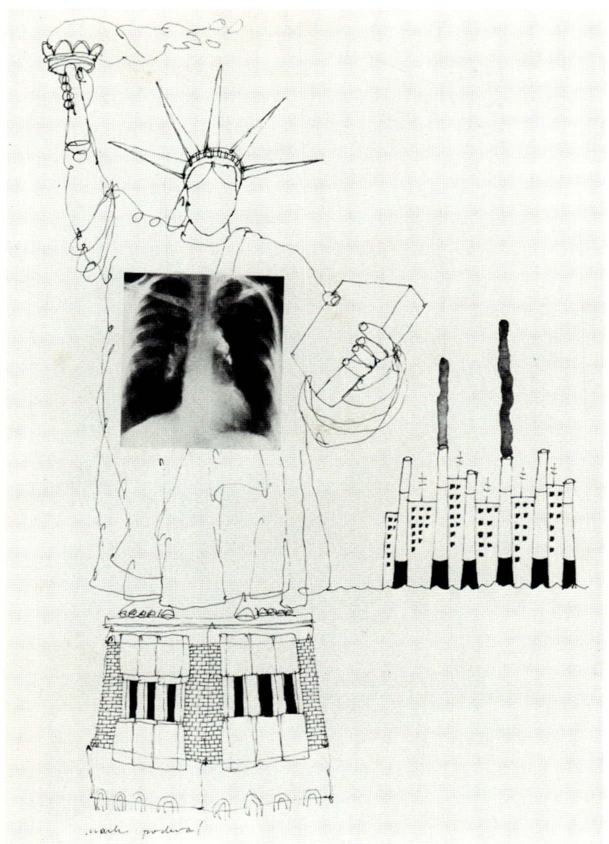

Fig. 261. *"Fun City."* Mark Podwall. 1970. Ink and collage on paper. 16 7/8 × 12 in. Courtesy The Swann Collection of Caricature and Cartoon.

Using the Statue of Liberty symbol, which several cartoonists have employed to represent America and its culture gone awry (see figs. 79, 192, and 262) Mark Podwall has graphically illustrated the fact that air pollution has reached critical proportions. Some doctors have estimated that breathing air on New York City streets can result in the same lung damage attributed to smoking nearly two packages of cigarettes each day.

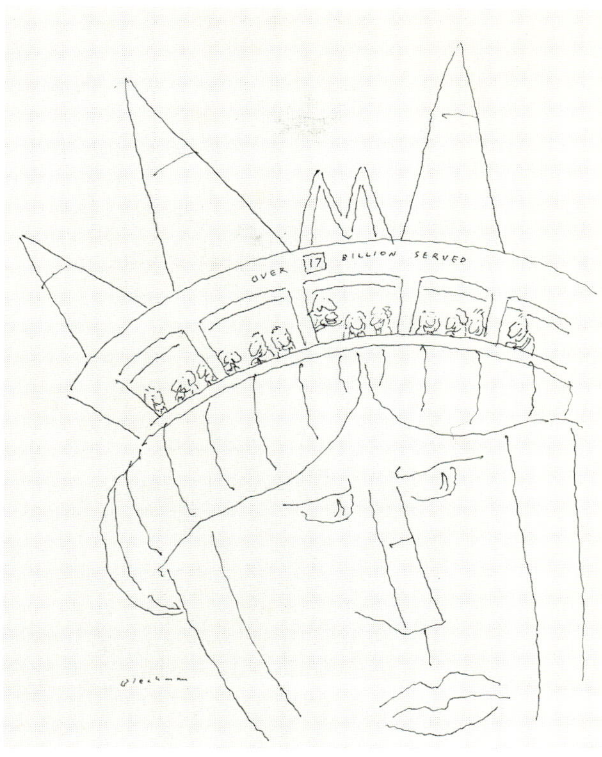

Fig. 262. *Over 17 Billion Served*. R. O. Blechman. Mar., 1974 in *Architecture Plus*. Ink on paper. 14 3/4 × 11 in. Courtesy The Swann Collection of Caricature and Cartoon.

It is often surmised that Manhattanites will endure almost any urban inconvenience, but in 1974, when popular fast-food chains began to locate hamburger stores in some of New York's nicest neighborhoods, residents raised a surprising hail of protest. Blechman indicates that even a worried Statue of Liberty might not be immune from such encroachments.

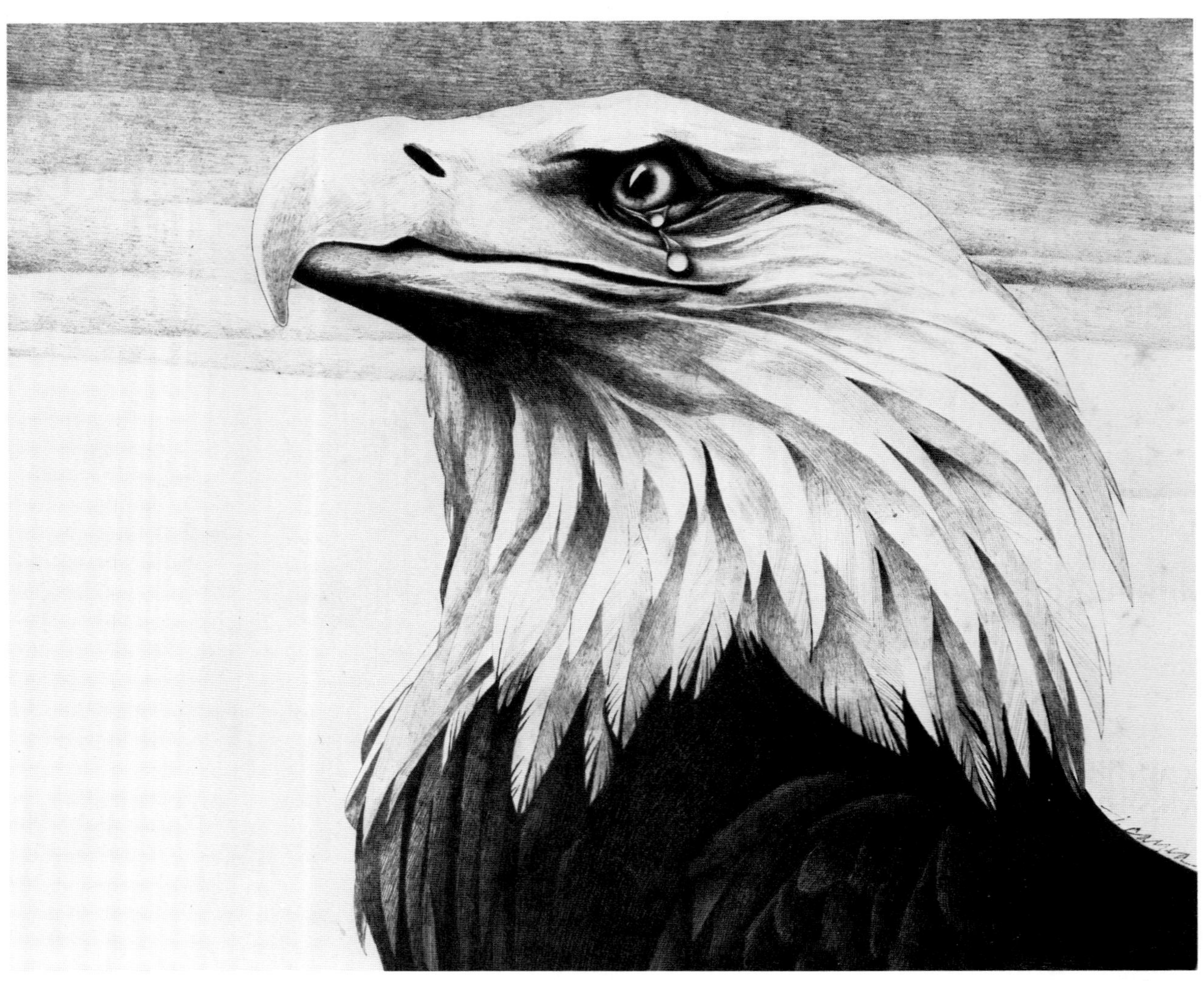

Fig. 263. *The American Eagle*. John Cayea. 1974 in the New York *Times*. Pencil on paper. 9 × 11 in. Courtesy John Cayea.

While various devices have represented the United States in cartoon and caricature over 200 years, the American Eagle probably best captures the spirit as Americans themselves see their country. The Eagle was selected as the emblem on the Great Seal of the United States, was used to illustrate the condition of the country at the time of the Civil War, and is employed here by John Cayea to symbolize America after Watergate, after Vietnam, after the domestic turmoil of the past two decades—a proud nation, humbled by recent events yet still the same powerful country in spirit and substance that began the great experiment two centuries ago.